The media's watching Vault.
Here's a sampling of our coverage.

"With admirable directness, the [Vault 100] tries to measure prestige by prestige."
— *National Law Journal*

"With reviews and profiles of firms that one associate calls 'spot on,' [Vault's] guide has become a key reference for those who want to know what it takes to get hired by a law firm and what to expect once they get there."
— *New York Law Journal*

"The well-written profiles make Vault.com the next best thing to camping out in a company rest room."
— *Yahoo! Internet Life*

"For those hoping to climb the ladder of success, [Vault's] insights are priceless."
— *Money Magazine*

"Vault.com is indispensible for locating insider information."
— *Metropolitan Corporate Counsel*

"The granddaddy of worker sites."
— *US News and World Report*

"Vault.com is another killer app for the Internet."
— *New York Times*

VAULT GUIDE TO
ADVANCED FINANCE AND QUANTITATIVE INTERVIEWS

VAULT GUIDE TO
ADVANCED FINANCE AND QUANTITATIVE INTERVIEWS

BY JENNIFER VOITLE
AND THE STAFF OF VAULT

For information about permission to reproduce selections from this book, contact Vault Inc., 150 West 22nd Street,
New York, New York 10011-1772, (212) 366-4212.

Library of Congress CIP Data is available.

ISBN 1-58131-172-9

Printed in the United States of America

ACKNOWLEDGEMENTS

This book is dedicated to all of my wonderful friends who were always there for me.

Many, many thanks to the outstanding editing talent of Ali Burak Guner and the extraordinary support, enthusiasm and patience of Marcy Lerner. The tireless efforts of Derek Loosvelt to finalize and improve the text is gratefully acknowledged as well. Finally, thanks to Ed Shen, Kelly Shore and the entire Vault staff for their support and help.

Vault would like to acknowledge the assistance and support of Matt Doull, Ahmad Al-Khaled, Lee Black, Eric Ober, Hollinger Ventures, Tekbanc, New York City Investment Fund, American Lawyer Media, Globix, Hoover's, Glenn Fischer, Mark Hernandez, Ravi Mhatre, Carter Weiss, Ken Cron, Ed Somekh, Isidore Mayrock, Zahi Khouri, Sana Sabbagh and other Vault investors. Many thanks to our loving families and friends.

Jefferies = **results**

JEFFERIES

Entrepreneurial Spirit at Work

JEFFERIES & COMPANY, INC.   1-888-JEFFERIES   WWW.JEFCO.COM

Get on the
front line faster.

TD Securities offers excellent opportunities for growth and career development.

Are you a self-starter willing to take on challenges right from the outset? Are you a strong team player interested in becoming a member of a dynamic organization? If so, consider a career at TD Securities - a leading investment dealer with offices in over 20 cities around the globe.

To find out more about us, visit Careers at www.tdsecurities.com.

Where Deals Get Done.

who benefits most
from your hard work?

That's the question that makes many people consider working for themselves. The freedoms of self-employment offer great choices that affect the quality of your life and the lives of others. You choose with whom you want to work and the level of success to which you aspire. With hard work, your income can be a reflection of your energy, commitment and drive—not someone else's expectations.

With 145 years of industry experience, Northwestern Mutual understands the importance of its Financial Representatives making the right self-employment choices—because success begins with choosing the path that's right for you.

Take the online Self-Employment Screen and explore the opportunities that are most suitable to your personality. Log on to http://careers.nmfn.com and explore "Begin Now."

Send resume to:
resume@northwesternmutual.com

Northwestern Mutual
FINANCIAL NETWORK®

Are you there yet?®

www.nmfn.com

Table of Contents

INTRODUCTION

Your First Step

Congratulations on taking your first step to succeeding in your advanced finance interviews. This book was written to give you the technical background needed to master that interview – compiled into one convenient volume. Quantitative and Wall Street interviews are notoriously tough, and with good reason. These types of jobs pay very well – and a lot of people want them.

This book will give you the edge you need to succeed. This is the book the writers and editors wish they had when they were interviewing. It is the distillation of years of experience in the finance field, in teaching finance and in numerous interviews. Vault editors have even taken interviews just to find out what kinds of questions interviewers are currently asking, in order to bring you the latest in this book.

In quantitative interviews, mastery of the subject matter is assumed – it is your starting point. You will also have to convince your interviewer(s) you are the right fit for the firm and have the experience and background that they are looking for. Of course, no book can give you that – though the *Vault Guide to Finance Interviews* gives you helpful pointers in that direction.

What this book *can* do is help you review and master the required subject matter, without which no amount of charm will get you by. (Although charm is always good.)

Also unique to this book are strategies to help you succeed on those tough interview questions that you may not be prepared for. Some questions you may get are deliberately designed to be impossible to answer. The interviewer just wants to see how you think and how you approach problems. Remember, all of the easy problems have already been solved. The problems you will see on the job will likely be things that no one has quite seen before.

Still, you will find some interviewers who will ask questions straight out of textbooks (one insider reports receiving the following question in a recent interview with Bloomberg: "What is an equivalence statement in FORTRAN and why would it be used?") It is simply the style of certain companies and interviewers to ask questions from textbooks, so you should be prepared for this if you want to land a job. For inside information on interviewer style, you may want to check out the Vault message boards. For everything else, let this book be your guide. Wherever possible, we've used questions from actual interview experience, including the interviewer's comments on what they were looking for (when we could get it).

It is our hope that you will find the problem solving strategies and the material in this book indispensable to you even after you land your job. Good luck!

Problem Solving Strategies

What do you do when confronted with an interview question you have absolutely no idea how to solve? We recommend the following strategies – it should help you handle most anything thrown at you.

Strategy #1	Cite from memory
Strategy #2	Draw a figure
Strategy #3	Work backwards
Strategy #4	Formulate an equivalent problem
Strategy #5	Enumerate all cases
Strategy #6	Search for a pattern
Strategy #7	Bracket the answer – solve the extreme cases
Strategy #8	Relate to something you know
Strategy #9	Take advantage of symmetry

Remember to RELAX. Try to see these interviews simply as conversations. It is a chance for interviewers to evaluate you, but remember, you are also deciding if you want to work there as well. The more relaxed and calm you are, the easier it will be for you to think creatively, which is often what is required in finance interviews. Also, try to think of the tough interview questions as amusing little problems (the interviewer probably does). One recent interviewee reports having an interviewer grill her relentlessly on currency forwards, interest rate parity and so on. When the job seeker finally reported being unsure of the approach to one question, "The interviewer laughed and said, 'Don't worry. If you had known the answer to this problem, I would have found something else that you don't know. That's my job.'"

Remember, sometimes you will be able to use one strategy by itself to answer a question, but imagine what a powerful approach it is when you can combine two or more. Those tough interview questions won't have a chance. You will see the above strategies used throughout this book, and identified to help you remember them. Often, problems can be approached from more than one angle, so don't feel that you must use the approach we show.

Sample Questions

1. You have a sheet of paper and an infinite supply of tokens. I also have an infinite supply of tokens. We take turns placing tokens on the paper, one token at a time. We cannot place tokens on top of other tokens (no overlapping), and the tokens cannot extend over the edges of the paper. The last player to place a token on the paper wins. What is your winning strategy? (This is called a "strategy game" question, and is an actual question recently asked on a hedge fund interview.)

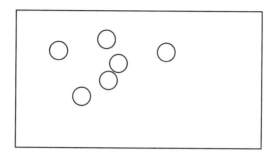

Solution: Don't freak out if you see something like this. The interviewer is just trying to get a sense of how you attack a new problem. Let's go through our list of tactics. Tactic #1 will not work here. Tactic #2 has promise: Try breaking it down into smaller sub-problems. What if the paper were so small that only a single coin could fit on it?

In this case your strategy would be to go first. After you place your coin, your opponent has no place to place his, and you win. Next, what if the paper were big enough for two coins? Here, you place your coin in the dead center of the sheet so your opponent can't place his coin. Again, your strategy would be to go first.

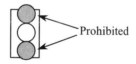

This tactic can be repeated until you have derived the correct answer: You always move first, and if you play the game properly, you will always win.

2. What do you think is the major factor impacting the profitability of an airline? (This was an actual question asked in a Goldman Sachs equity quantitative research interview.)

Solution: This is another question that the interviewer doesn't expect you to have memorized, but expects you to go through a reasoning process enumerating possible factors affecting airline profitability to come up with the most important one. You could say, "passenger meals, labor costs, weather delays, leasing costs, marketing, maintenance, price wars," but the major cost driver is probably "fuel."

3. Would the volatility of an enterprise be higher or lower than the volatility of its equity? (Actually asked by a Goldman Sachs interviewer who kept coming back to this in one form or another during the interview.)

Solution: This is a straightforward Statistics or Corp Finance 101 question. Even if you have never seen this exact question before, it can be reasoned out. In the following response we employ a combination of tactics #1 and #5.

Corporations usually have both debt and equity (we reason.) So, suppose you have a portfolio consisting of w percent equity and (1-w) percent debt. We calculate volatility as the square of the standard deviation of stock returns. Then

$$\sigma_p^2 = w\sigma_E^2 + (1-w)\sigma_D^2 + 2w(1-w)Cov_{D,E}\sigma_E\sigma_D$$

Assume that the covariance is zero. Then $\sigma_p^2 = w\sigma_E^2 + (1-w)\sigma_D^2$

Now, consider three cases.

Case one: There is no debt.
Then the variance of the enterprise (σ_p above) is equal to the variance of the equity.

Case two: There is no equity.
Then the variance of the enterprise (σ_p above) is equal to the variance of the debt.

Case three: There is a combination of the two.
We have bracketed the answer already in cases one and two: the result must lie in between these. Now a judgment must be made. Assume that the volatility of the debt is lower than the volatility of the equity. Then the volatility of the enterprise with both debt and equity will be lower than the volatility of the equity alone, since the volatility of the enterprise is somewhat of a weighted average of both debt and equity. Also, note that we multiply the volatility of the equity by w, a fraction assumed to be less than one. The only way that we could have volatility of the enterprise higher than that of equity alone would be if $\sigma_D > \sigma_E$ and if w were negative (impossible). To see this, rearrange the equation to $\sigma_p^2 = w(\sigma_E^2 - \sigma_D^2) + \sigma_D^2$. If the vol of debt equals vol of equity, vol of the enterprise still equals vol of the equity.

BOND
FUNDAMENTALS

This is the chapter that you will need to know if an interviewer or headhunter asks, "Do you know bond math?" – and you want to answer, "Yes."

Bond Basics

A bond is a contract to provide payments according to a specific schedule. Bonds are long-term securities with maturities exceeding one year, in contrast to bills, or other short-term debt such as commercial paper, which have maturities of less than one year. The bond universe is huge. There are treasury bonds, agency bonds, junk bonds, corporate bonds, zero coupon bonds, municipal bonds, sovereign bonds, tax-free bonds and so forth. In addition to all of these, there are options on bonds, options on options on bonds, and so on. (These will be covered in detail in later sections.) Finally, most bonds are highly sensitive to interest rates, so we will have to study the yield curve in some detail. For now, we will cover the fundamental financial concepts required in valuation of bonds.

Bonds are different from equity

In the contractual agreement of a bond, there is a stated **maturity** and a stated **par value**. This is unlike an equity, which has no maturity and no guaranteed price at maturity. To express this definite price at maturity, we say that *bonds converge to par value at maturity*. This defined par value makes the volatility of a bond generally lower than a share of stock (equity), especially as maturity draws close.

However, don't get the idea that bonds are without risk or uninteresting. Quite the contrary. According to a February 28, 2000, *BusinessWeek Online* article ("Is the Bond Market Ready for Day Traders?"), "Bonds are no longer the stodgy investments they once were… What most people don't know is that the 30-year Treasury bond has the same volatility as an Internet stock." Constructing models for bond valuation is one of the tougher challenges out there. Bonds have many inherent risks, including default risk, basis risk, credit risk, interest rate risk and yield curve risk, all of which may not apply to equity or equity-like securities.

Bond ratings

Bonds are generally considered to be less risky than equity (except for junk bonds), so they can generally be expected to have lower rates of return. In the world of bonds, we are concerned with the credit rating of the company or municipality that issued the bond. Credit ratings are provided by major ratings agencies, including Moody's, Standard & Poor's, and Fitch. You may wish to familiarize yourself with these ratings (http://www.standardandpoors.com/, http://www.moodys.com/, http://www.fitch.com. Recently, a Goldman Sachs interviewer quizzed one of this book's editors on ratings of corporate bonds and subsidiary liability in case of default. Of course, you may not have to worry about this if you do not have this type of experience listed on your resume, but remember, *anything* on your resume, no matter how long ago or obscure, is fair game.)

Bond ratings affect the ease and cost of obtaining credit for the corporation issuing the bonds. The higher the rating – AAA is the highest S&P rating, for example – the lower the cost of credit. As the corporation's credit rating declines, it gets more and more expensive for the corporation to raise new funds. Most corporate treasuries are concerned with possible ratings downgrades and check frequently with ratings agencies before undertaking something that could potentially result in a downgrade. Downgrades can also affect investors, as many fixed income managers in asset management firms have mandates to hold only corporate-grade bonds and better. If a corporation's bonds fall to the "junk" category (see, for example, Xerox, May 2002), the institutional investors in the company may have to sell their holdings to comply with client requirements. This dumping – which could be large holdings of the bonds – makes the price of the bonds drop.

Before pushing forward with valuation of bonds under scenarios such as the above, we have to review the time value of money, which is possibly the most important concept in finance. You will see this over and over again in various forms, so there's no time like the present.

Time Value of Money

Discounting, present and future value

If you deposit $1,000 in a bank or money market account today, you expect to earn some interest on your investment so that, as time passes, the value of your investment grows. (If it did not, you would probably not put your money in the bank.) If you are earning a rate of 10% a year, at the end of the year you will have your original $1,000 plus the interest earned, 10% of the principal invested ($1,000) or $100. The total value of your investment is then $1,000 + $100 = $1,100 = $1,000(1 + r)$, where r is the interest rate in percent for the period. In general, the future value of an initial investment P_0 over n compounding periods is given by the formula

$$P_N = P_0\left(1+\frac{r}{n}\right)^{nt}$$

where:
n = number of compounding periods in time interval t
t = time interval
r = the interest rate earned per compounding period (assumed constant)
P_0 = the initial value (principal)
P_N = the final value

The above formula then gives **the future value of money**. This type of formula is called **simple compounding**. Many important results in finance are based on this very simple principal of the time value of money.
NOTE: The value P_N is often called "the future value" and P_0 "the present value". So we could also write

$$FV = PV\left(1+\frac{r}{n}\right)^{nt}$$

Example (Annual Compounding) What is the value of $1,000 after one year if interest is only compounded once per year? Here n = 1, t = 1 year, r = 10%/year, P_0 = $1,000.

$$P_1 = \$1,000\left(1+\frac{0.10}{1}\right)^1 = \$1,100$$

Example (Semi-Annual Compounding): What is the value of $1,000 after one year if interest is compounded twice per year? Here n = 2 and:

$$P_1 = \$1,000\left(1+\frac{0.10}{2}\right)^2 = \$1,102.5$$

*Example **(Quarterly Compounding)*** What is the value of $1,000 after one year if interest is compounded four times per year? Here n = 4 and:

$$P_1 = \$1,000\left(1+\frac{0.10}{4}\right)^4 = \$1,103.81$$

Example (Daily Compounding) What is the value of $1,000 after one year if interest is compounded each trading day? Here n = 250 and:

$$P_1 = \$1,000\left(1+\frac{0.10}{250}\right)^{250} = \$1,105.15$$

The value of the investment increases as we compound more and more frequently since interest is being compounded on interest. In the limit as n approaches infinity, we have continuous compounding, which gives the future value of money as:

$$P_t = P_0 e^{rt}$$

Example (Continuous Compounding) What is the value of $1,000 after one year if interest is compounded continuously?

$P_1 = \$1,000 e^{0.1*1} = \$1,105.17.$ It should not surprise you that this answer is very close to the result that we obtained with daily compounding.

What if you will be investing over a period of time in, say a savings account for retirement? To develop the formula, suppose you invest $1,000 for the next five years at a constant 10%/year. How much will you have at the end of the year? Assume you invest at the beginning of each year and interest is paid once per year.

Year Zero: Initial $1,000 invested, will stay in account for five years.
Year One: Another $1,000 invested, will stay in account for four years.
Year Two: Another $1,000 invested, will stay in account for three years.
Year Three: Another $1,000 invested, will stay in account for two years.
Year Four: Another $1,000 invested, will stay in account for one year.

So our account will contain an amount of
$1,000(1+0.1)^5+$1,000(1+0.1)^4+$1,000(1+0.1)^3+$1,000(1+0.1)^2+$1,000(1+0.1)^1=$6,715.6 after five years.
In terms of a formula,

$$P_t = \sum_{i=1}^{n} CF_i\left(1+r\right)^i = CF\sum_{i=1}^{n}\left(1+r\right)^i$$

since the investments at each year (CF_i) are the same each year.

This is an interesting application for retirement saving: If a 20-year old could earn 10%/year on average, how much would they have at age 65?

Solve the problem by figuring how much there would be after 20 years, then use the simple compounding formula to take it forward another 25 years.

What if a person waits until age 40 to start saving for retirement? How much would they have to save per year to end up with the same amount as the saver who began at age 20?

Solving this, you'll understand why so many people are planning to work past age 65 these days.

Present value of a future dollar The same formulas can be used to solve for the present value of a future payment. We just have to solve for P_0. For *n* compounding intervals per year,

$$P_0 = P_N\left(1 + \frac{r}{n}\right)^{-nt}$$

and for continuous compounding, $P_0 = P_t e^{-rt}$.

NOTE: In this case, the rate r is called the discount rate since $P_0 < P_t$ *always*.

Example You are promised a payout of $1,000,000 ten years from now. (Financial application: this is used to value a zero coupon bond.) If the discount rate is 10%, what is this payout worth today?

Use the continuously compounded formula. $P_0 = \$1,000,000e^{-0.1*10} = \$367,879$. You should be indifferent between a payout today of this amount and a future payment of $1,000,000 in ten years.

Now, what if you have a series of cash payments? (Either these terminate at some future time or go on to infinity -- such types of payments are called *perpetuities*.)

In the first case, suppose you buy a bond paying 8% per year for the next 10 years. At the end of 10 years, you will receive your last interest payment plus return of your principal. Assume that the principal is $1,000. What is this bond worth today? (Later we will see that there are three scenarios that can occur depending on what the investment rate r is. For now, assume that you can earn 10% by placing money in a savings bank.) All we do is take each payment and discount it back to the present. We are paid 0.08*$1,000 each year or $80 (the "**coupon payment**".) We discount the first payment over a one-year period, the second payment over a two-year period and so on. At the end of 10 years, we have $80 plus the return of our principal for a total of $1,080 to be discounted back ten years. It is really like working ten independent problems and summing together.

$$PV = \frac{\$80}{(1+r)^1} + \frac{\$80}{(1+r)^2} + \frac{\$80}{(1+r)^3} + \frac{\$80}{(1+r)^4} + \frac{\$80}{(1+r)^5} + \frac{\$80}{(1+r)^6} + \frac{\$80}{(1+r)^7} + \frac{\$80}{(1+r)^8} + \frac{\$80}{(1+r)^9} + \frac{\$1,080}{(1+r)^{10}}$$

PV = $877. In terms of a formula, we have

$$PV = \sum_{i=1}^{n} \frac{CF_i}{(1+r)^i}$$

where the values of CF_i for i = 1 to n-1 are the coupon payments, and the last cash flow, CF_n, is that year's coupon payment plus the return of par. Observe that this formula reduces to the one we had earlier when n =1. Also we have assumed that the discount rate r is constant over the life of the investment.

Technical Note: To be more general, we should actually discount each year by the prevailing discount rate, r_i, at year i. Then we have:

$$PV = \sum_{i=1}^{n} \frac{CF_i}{(1+r_i)^i}$$

The preceding formula is very important and will be used over and over.

Annuity: If the payments CF are constant over a period, this is called an annuity. Common examples include mortgage and car loan payments.

Perpetuity: Now, what if we receive a payment of CF forever? We take the limit as n approaches infinity and use this result instead. To use this approach, r has to be constant. It turns out that

$$\lim_{n \longrightarrow \infty} \sum_{i=1}^{n} \frac{CF}{(1+r)^i} = \frac{CF}{r} \text{ so } PV_{Perpetuity} = \frac{CF}{r}$$

Want to check without using any calculus? Just use a spreadsheet with any i and r you want. Let n increase until the answer stops changing (in Excel, the function PV is used as "**=PV(r,n,pmt)**" or "=PV(0.1,10,80)" for r = 0.1, n = 10 and PMT = 80). You will find that you approach the value of 800, or CF/r = $80/0.1. Remember the above formula because you will see it again.

This formula can be used to value **perpetual debt** that a corporation may have. The corporation may have fixed income liabilities on its books that have a finite expiration period, but if it can keep "rolling over" the debt, it can be valued as a perpetuity. Here, the rate r is the average coupon payment on the corporation's debt. This formula can also be used to value a company in the mature stage where it is stable and paying out a constant dividend. Then, r plays the role of the risk of the company, or **hurdle rate**. This model can be used if it is assumed that the company is a **going concern**, i.e. it will operate into perpetuity.

As an example, what if a company is paying out dividends of $1.35/share at a hurdle rate of 20%? What is the company worth on the basis of this model?

Value = $1.35/0.20 =$6.75/share.

Gordon growth model

This is used for valuing cash flows such as debt or stock dividends that are projected to grow at a constant rate g. Then,

$$PV = \frac{CF_0(1+g)}{(1+r)^1} + \frac{CF_0(1+g)^2}{(1+r)^2} + \frac{CF_0(1+g)^3}{(1+r)^3} + \cdots = CF_0 \sum_{i=1}^{n} \frac{(1+g)^n}{(1+r)^n}$$

In the limit as n approaches infinity, we get

$$PV = \frac{CF_0}{r-g}$$

For example, in the above, suppose that the company's dividend policy is to grow the dividend 10%/year for perpetuity. The value of the company should be calculated using the Gordon Growth Model. We need to know the current dividend, CF_0 = $1.65. Then, $PV = \dfrac{\$1.65}{0.2-0.1}$ =$16.5/share. This *should* be higher than the value with no growth, and it is.

Slick Trick: Now that we know the formulas for annuities and perpetuities, we can come up with a shortcut for calculating the value of an annuity that pays from i = 1 to n. This means we won't have to sum that long series again. First, look at the cash flow diagram of a perpetuity paying cash flow C at discount rate r:

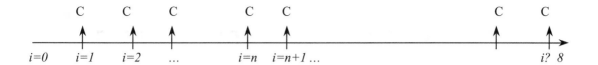

The present value of this perpetuity (call it PV_1) has already been shown to be

$$PV_1 = \frac{C}{r}$$

Next, consider a perpetuity paying C that doesn't start until time i = n+1. The value of this perpetuity at time n is $\frac{C}{r}$, and to get the present value at i=0, just discount back by dividing by $(1+r)^n$. So the value of the perpetuity at i=0 (call it PV_2) is

$$PV_2 = \frac{1}{(1+r)^n} \frac{C}{r}$$

Now we can find the value of the annuity running from i = 0 to i=n. We just take the infinite perpetuity running from time i=0 to infinity, PV_1, and chop off the part we don't want: the value of the perpetuity running from i = n+1 to infinity. Hence,

$$PV = \frac{C}{r} - \frac{1}{(1+r)^n} \frac{C}{r} = \frac{C}{r}\left(1 - \frac{1}{(1+r)^n}\right)$$

This can be used to value a stream of coupons from a bond. The formula can be easily modified to handle the full coupon bond by just adding on a term representing the PV of the principal repayment, so we would have:

$$PV_{coupbond} = \frac{C}{r}\left(1 - \frac{1}{(1+r)^n}\right) + \frac{P}{(1+r)^n}$$

Example: Let's go back to that 10-year, 8% coupon bond at a discount rate of 10%. Tedious calculations gave its value as $877. Using the above formula gives:

$$PV_{coupbond} = \frac{80}{0.1}\left(1 - \frac{1}{(1+0.1)^{10}}\right) + \frac{1,000}{(1+0.1)^{10}}$$

=$491.56+$385.54 = $877.1

Bond Prices and Relationships to Yields

We have laid all of the necessary foundation for pricing bonds. In fact, we have already started pricing bonds. It is now time to talk about three types of bonds: discount bonds, par bonds and premium bonds. There is only one thing that differentiates these three types of bonds: the spread between the discount rate r and the coupon rate i.

Discount bond

In the previous example, our bond sold at less than the face value of $1,000. This is an example of a discount bond. The reason it sold for less than its face value ("less than par") is because the coupon interest rate, 8%, is lower than the discount rate r. Think about it: The discount rate r is the expected interest rate an investor could earn by investing in a vehicle such as high-yield treasuries. If the investor could earn 10% elsewhere, but this bond is only paying 8%, shouldn't the investor be compensated for taking a lower interest rate? The bond is said to be *selling at a discount to par*.

Par bond

If the bond is *selling for par*, that is, the present value is equal to the face value, here $1,000, the bond is said to be selling at par or a par bond. We look at the general formula

$$PV = \frac{C}{r} - \frac{1}{(1+r)^n}\frac{C}{r} + \frac{1}{(1+r)^n} = 1 \text{ if } C = r \text{ where C is the coupon rate and r is the discount rate.}$$

Since we know that the PV of a payment P at time n is just $\frac{P}{(1+r)^n}$, the last term above, the only way that this can be is if i = r. If this occurs, the bond is paying interest at the rate r and we have a par bond.

Premium bond

On the other hand, if the bond pays a rate that is higher than the prevailing rate r, it will be priced higher than par and is called a premium bond.

We also have to now interject reality into the story. Unless the yield curve is flat, interest rates do change with time to maturity ("tenor"). Let's take a look at a yield curve from May 3, 2002. The following data is from Bloomberg.com (but you can see yield curves in many places).

Tenor, months	Yield, %
3	1.75
6	1.89
24	3.21
60	4.4
120	5.09
360	5.59

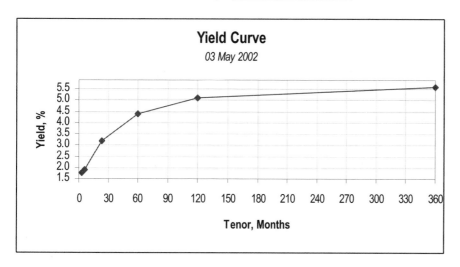

The fact that the yield curve is not flat means that we have to use different discount rates to value each cash flow. For example, if we had a cash flow at two years, we would use the rate of 3.21% from the table above; a cash flow ten years out would be discounted at a rate of 5.09% and so on. "Missing" data in between the given points (such as three years, four years and so forth) must be calculated. We will have much more to say about these topics in the Fixed Income Section. For now, to make things easy, assume that the following has been calculated:

Tenor, months	Yield, %
12	2.33
24	3.21
36	3.61
48	4.00
60	4.4

Let's value a five-year bond paying a coupon of 3.5%. On a bond with face value of $1,000 we will then receive $35 each year (assuming for simplicity that we have annual compounding.) Here is a table of our cash flows, discount rate and present value of each cash flow.

Tenor, months	Yield, %	Cash Flow	PV Cash Flow
12	2.33	35	34.20
24	3.21	35	32.86
36	3.61	35	31.47
48	4.00	35	29.91
60	4.4	1035	834.52
PV Bond			$ 962.97

Why is the bond priced below par? We have different discount rates. In some sense, the "average" rate used must be lower than the coupon rate. We can determine this average rate by setting the present value

Thus, since $PV = \sum_{i=1}^{n} \frac{C}{(1+y)^i} + \frac{Par}{(1+y)^n}$, for our example,

of the price of our bond equal to the present value of a bond with the same cash flows but a uniform rate r.

$$\$962.97 = \frac{\$35}{(1.0233)} + \frac{\$35}{(1.0321)^2} + \frac{\$35}{(1.0361)^3} + \frac{\$35}{(1.04)^4} + \frac{\$1,035}{(1.044)^5} = \frac{\$35}{(1+y)} + \frac{\$35}{(1+y)^2} + \frac{\$35}{(1+y)^3} + \frac{\$35}{(1+y)^4} + \frac{\$1,035}{(1+y)^5}$$

We solve *by y* by trial and error, using a spreadsheet and the Solver function, or with our formula for an annuity. We find that the value of *y* that satisfies the above equality is 4.34%. This special *y* is called **the yield of the bond**. That's all yield is: just a mathematical concept that is used to allow us to compare different bonds on a level playing field. Otherwise, how would we rank bonds? Is it correct to say that a bond with a higher coupon is a better investment? You can't just rank by coupon since different bonds have different maturities. Note that on Bloomberg's page, they show the current yield as 4.35%, very close to ours, but we assume that they use slightly different interpolation methods.

Now we are in a position to explore the very critical relationship of price to yield.

Price and yield are inversely proportional: as yield increases, price decreases. As yield decreases, price increases.

(We repeat this statement because it is so important. You can think of it as the "first law of bond dynamics" if you want.)

You can see from the equation above that if yield is higher than 4.34% required to maintain the equality, we will be dividing by a larger number so the PV (price of bond) should decrease. And if we decrease the yield we are dividing by a smaller number, so the price will increase. Practically, this makes sense.

Bonds must converge to par at maturity

Yield is the mathematical mechanism by which we get from the present to the future. So, if a price is low, we have to have a whopping large yield to climb to par. If price is already high, say, close to par, we don't need very much growth to get to par. This is such a crucial fact that you may want to build your own bond model on a spreadsheet and explore the effects of varying yield.

Taylor Series Expansion

Suppose you have information about a function at one point and want information about that function at some other point. For a simple example, suppose Gordon is now located 200 miles east of Chicago. He is traveling due west at 60 miles/hour and is very anxious to make his class. How would he be from Chicago after one hour of driving if he decides to accelerate his speed at a steady 10 miles per hour over that hour (so that his speed after one hour is 70 mph)? Or, consider another example: suppose you have the price of a bond at a certain yield. What would the price of that bond be if the yield changes by one percent? You may not realize it, but to solve these and similar problems you use the principles of **Taylor Series expansions**. Taylor Series are even used to derive the Black-Scholes equation and Ito's Lemma, which we will come to later. In fact, if you have taken physics and are familiar with the equation of time position of a particle $x(t) = x_0 + v_0 t + 1/2\ a_0\ t^2$, you have are already used Taylor Series.

So, here is the theory that you need to know:
A continuous, differentiable function f may be expanded in a Taylor Series about a point k as follows:

$$f(x) = \sum_{n=0}^{\infty} \frac{f^{(n)}(k)}{n!}(x-k)^n = f(k) + f'(k)(x-k) + \frac{f''(k)}{2!}(x-k)^2 + \frac{f'''(k)}{3!}(x-k)^3 + \cdots$$

The distance *x-k* must be small and the derivatives must exist at k. Note that the Taylor Series includes an infinite number of terms. In practice, we can only take a finite number of terms, and there will be truncation error due to the contribution of the terms that are dropped. So, f(x) is approximated by a finite-number-of-terms Taylor Series, plus a truncation error. For example, the second-order Taylor Series expanded about the point k is given as:

$$f(x) = \sum_{n=0}^{\infty} \frac{f^{(n)}(k)}{n!}(x-k)^n + R_3 = f(k) + f'(k)(x-k) + \frac{1}{2!}f''(k)(x-k)^2 + R_3$$

where R_3 is the truncation error, consisting of the sum of terms n = 3 to infinity. Also note that if we are just approximating polynomials of degree n, the Taylor Series of order n will give an exact result. (The Taylor Series of order n *is* a polynomial of order n.) Graphically, what we are trying to do is this:

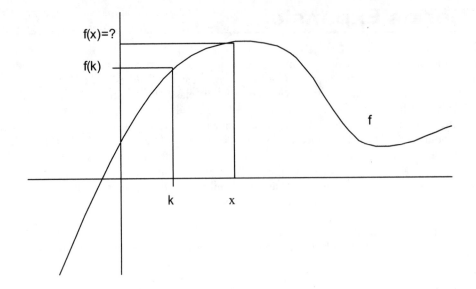

The assumptions are that the function exists over the range of interest of expansion (that is, it is continuous between k, the known point, and x, the point you are trying to forecast), and that the derivatives above exist. Note that the right hand side is completely known so you can just add it up to get your forecast for f at the desired point. So, a Taylor Series expansion is simply a technique to make an *approximation* of the behavior of the function f(x) over the interval (k,x). If you knew the actual function f(x), you could simply evaluate it at the desired value x. The assumption is that you do not know what f will be at x, and need some way to estimate it.

Actual practice tip: You don't even really need to know the actual function f(x) as long as you know, or can estimate, the values of f and its derivatives at the point k. You'll see this in pricing bonds using duration and convexity.

Let's try an example. (We'll do a math problem first, for confidence, and then we'll move on to finance.)

Example   Let the function be $f(x) = x^3 - x - 1$. We already know that $f(2) = 2^3 - 2 - 1 = 8 - 3 = 5$. To check Taylor Series, assume that you only have information about f and its derivatives at the point $x = 1$ (this will be the "k" in the Taylor Series equation, the known point), and we seek the value of the function f at 2, the unknown point.) We need to have all of the values of f and derivatives at the known point to forecast what f will be at 2. How many derivatives is enough? The more you use, the better the approximation, and there are formulas that tell how far you must go to fall within an acceptable error. In this case, we will compare approximations with using the first derivative only, the first and second derivatives, and the first three derivatives (which will give the exact solution for this cubic function).

$f(x) = x^3 - x - 1$	$f(1) = 1^3 - 1 - 1 = -1$
$f'(x) = 3x^2 - 1$	$f'(1) = 3(1)^2 - 1 = 2$
$f''(x) = 6x$	$f''(x) = 6(1) = 6$
$f'''(x) = 6$	$f'''(1) = 6$

Using first derivative only: $f(2) \sim f(1) + f'(1)(2\text{-}1) = -1 + 2(2\text{-}1) = 1$. Error $= 5 - 1 = 4$

Using first two derivatives: $f(2) \sim f(1) + f'(1)(2\text{-}1) + f''(1)(2\text{-}1)^2/2 = 1 + 6/2 = 4$. Error $= 5 - 4 = 1$.

Using first three derivatives: $f(2) \sim f(1) + f'(1)(2\text{-}1) + f''(1)(2\text{-}1)^2/2 + f'''(1)(2\text{-}1)^3/6 = 4 + 6/6 = 5$.

Error $= 5 - 5 = 0$.

Note how the error between the true (known) value and our approximation decreases as we increase the number of derivatives used. What we are doing is providing more and more information in order to more closely approximate the unknown value.

Also, note that it really isn't necessary to know the definition of the function. In the real world, we might just know the derivative values. We could have just as easily solved this just knowing the values f(1), f'(1), f''(1) and so on, but the values would have to be known to us in some way.

Note: If the function f depends on two variables, such as x and y, we just differentiate with respect to each. We have

$$df = f(x+dx, y+dy) - f(x,y) = \frac{\partial f}{\partial x}dx + \frac{\partial f}{\partial y}dy + \frac{1}{2!}\left(\frac{\partial^2 f}{\partial x^2}dx^2 + 2\frac{\partial^2 f}{\partial x \partial y}dxdy + \frac{\partial^2 f}{\partial y^2}dy^2\right) + \cdots$$

This is called the **Multivariate Taylor Series**. It can be used to estimate to the value of f at a point (dx, dy) away from a point (x,y) at which f is known. It requires knowledge of the above derivatives at (x,y).

Example Let f(x,y) = x²y. Suppose we only know the value of f for x = 1 and y = 3, so that f(1,3) = 3. Let's say f represents the price of an option, x the price of a stock and 1 represents the time parameter. We are interested in estimating the value of f if x and y change a small amount, say by 1 each. (Of course, we could just plug in the x and y values to get f(2,4) = 16, but we want to try out our Taylor Series approximation here. Later we will use just such a method to derive the Black-Scholes equation for pricing options.) To estimate using Taylor Series, we need the derivatives.

$$\frac{\partial f}{\partial x} = 2xy, \frac{\partial f}{\partial y} = x^2, \frac{\partial^2 f}{\partial x^2} = \frac{\partial}{\partial x}\left(\frac{\partial f}{\partial x}\right) = 2y, \frac{\partial^2 f}{\partial x \partial y} = \frac{\partial}{\partial x}\left(\frac{\partial f}{\partial y}\right) = \frac{\partial}{\partial y}\left(\frac{\partial f}{\partial x}\right) = 2x, \frac{\partial^2 f}{\partial y^2} = \frac{\partial}{\partial y}\left(\frac{\partial f}{\partial y}\right) = 0$$

Then, df = $2xydx + x^2dy + \frac{1}{2}2ydx^2 + 2xdxdy + \frac{1}{2}0dy^2 + \cdots$

= $2(1)(3)(1) + (1)^2(1) + \frac{1}{2}2(3)(1)^2 + 2(1)(1)(1) + \frac{1}{2}0(1)^2 + \cdots$

=6+1+3+2 = 12. This is the change in f caused by moving from (1,3) to (2,4), so the new value of f is the sum of the old value of f plus the change, f(2,4) = f(1,3) + df = 3 +12 = 15. Note that since we truncated the series after the second order terms, we still have truncation error to account for. But it will do for a first approximation.

Example The price change of a bond caused by the change in yield can be estimated by expanding P as a function of y in a Taylor Series. Using just the first two terms, we have:

$$dP = \frac{dP}{dy}\Delta y + \frac{1}{2}\frac{d^2P}{dy^2}\Delta y^2 + ...$$

What is the price change if Δy = 1%, the first derivative of P with respect to y is equal to –6,721 and the second derivative of P with respect to y is 60,600? Just plug into the formula to get dP = -$64.18.

In following sections, we will see more Taylor Series, including finding out where the above derivatives came from and what they mean, and in deriving the Black-Scholes equation and numerical approximations for its solution.

Why do you need to know the Taylor Series? It is often the case that we have information about something at a certain point, say, in time, for example, and want to know what it might be another other point in time (this is called forecasting.) If you know the rate at which the function is changing, and have reasonable expectations that this rate will remain constant over the time interval of interest, you can use Taylor Series to project the future value. Also, notice how adding more terms improves our estimate of the unknown value. (Of course, the more information we have, the better). This is the theory underlying the convexity of a bond idea, coming up in the next sections.

Bond Price Derivatives

Let's delve deeper to see more precisely how price changes with yield. To do so, we have to take a derivative. To make it easy on ourselves we will just use the constant cash flow C as from a coupon-paying bond. Then,

$$\frac{\partial P}{\partial y} = \frac{\partial}{\partial y} \sum_{i=1}^{n} \frac{C}{(1+y)^i} + \frac{Par}{(1+y)^n} = \frac{\partial}{\partial y}\left[\frac{C}{(1+y)} + \frac{C}{(1+y)^2} + \frac{C}{(1+y)^3} + \cdots + \frac{C}{(1+y)^n} + \frac{Par}{(1+y)^n} \right]$$

$$\frac{\partial P}{\partial y} = \frac{-C}{(1+y)^2} + \frac{-2C}{(1+y)^3} + \frac{-3C}{(1+y)^4} + \cdots + \frac{-nC}{(1+y)^{n+1}} + \frac{-nPar}{(1+y)^{n+1}}$$

If we factor out $-\dfrac{1}{1+y}$ then the denominator will look like it did for P:

$$\frac{\partial P}{\partial y} = -\frac{1}{1+y}\left[\frac{C}{(1+y)} + \frac{2C}{(1+y)^2} + \frac{3C}{(1+y)^3} + \cdots + \frac{nC}{(1+y)^n} + \frac{nPar}{(1+y)^n} \right] = -\frac{1}{1+y}\left[\sum_{i=1}^{n} \frac{iC}{(1+y)^i} + \frac{nPar}{(1+y)^n} \right]$$

Now divide both sides by P. We then have

$$\frac{1}{P}\frac{\partial P}{\partial y} \cong \frac{1}{P}\frac{\Delta P}{\Delta y} = -\frac{1}{(1+y)}\frac{1}{P}\left[\sum_{i=1}^{n} \frac{iC}{(1+y)^i} + \frac{nPar}{(1+y)^n} \right] = -\frac{1}{(1+y)}D_{MAC}$$

Where $D_{MAC} = \dfrac{1}{P}\left[\displaystyle\sum_{i=1}^{n} \dfrac{iC}{(1+y)^i} + \dfrac{nPar}{(1+y)^n} \right]$ is defined as *Macauley Duration*.

The *Modified Duration*, D_{MOD}, is defined as $D_{MOD} = \dfrac{1}{(1+y)}D_{MAC}$, so $\dfrac{1}{P}\dfrac{\partial P}{\partial y} = -D_{MOD}$

(The negative sign is used since we define positive duration as occurring when an increase in yield causes a decrease in price, the normal result. We will see later that certain special fixed income instruments can have negative duration.)

Dollar duration

Duration is used to make an estimate of how our bond's price will change in response to a change in yield. Duration measures the bond's first-order sensitivity to a change in yield. It can most easily be thought of as the change in price for a 100bp yield. The units of duration are time and it will have the same units as the coupon payment interval (one year, one-half year, one-quarter year etc.)

Before moving to an example, a definition: "basis point", or "bp" for short, is just an alias for "1/100 of a percent." Basis points are a frequent unit of measure in fixed income. There are 100bp per 1%, so "100bp" is a way of saying "1%".

Example: If the Macauley duration of a bond is known to be 7.25 years when the price is $1,000, yield is 8% and the yield changes by 100 bp, what will be the change in the bond's price? Just use the formula and solve for ΔP:

$$\Delta P = -\frac{P\Delta y}{1+y} D_{MAC}$$

So, $\Delta P = -\dfrac{\$1,000(0.01)}{1+0.08} 7.25 = -\$67.13$. Let's see how good a job this did. We already used this bond before, this is the ten-year, 8% par bond. Since it is a par bond its price is known: $1,000. If the yield changes by 100 bp so that it is now 8% + 1% = 9%, the price of the bond will be

$$P = \sum_{i=1}^{10} \frac{80}{(1+0.09)^i} + \frac{\$1,000}{(1+0.09)^{10}} = \frac{80}{0.09}\left(1 - \frac{1}{(1+0.09)^{10}}\right) + \frac{1000}{(1+0.09)^{10}} = \$935.82.$$

So, the actual change in price is $1,000 – $935.82 = $64.18. (Notice how handy our little shortcut is.) Here's how to do this in Excel: We make a column of coupon payment times (i = 1,…, 10, for this example); a column for cash flows (coupon rate/number of payments/year times par value); a column for present value of each coupon payment (PVCF); and a column with time-weighted values of the cash flows, i*PVCF. Then duration = the sum of i*PVCF over the sum of PV of cash flows.

Duration of a Bond	
Coupon Rate	8%
Par Value of Bond	$1,000
Term (years)	10
Initial Yield	8%
Number of coupons/year	1

Coup Time	Cash Flow	PV of CF	t * PVCF
1	$80	74.074074	74.07407
2	$80	68.587106	137.1742
3	$80	63.506579	190.5197
4	$80	58.802388	235.2096
5	$80	54.446656	272.2333
6	$80	50.41357	302.4814
7	$80	46.679232	326.7546
8	$80	43.221511	345.7721
9	$80	40.019917	360.1793
10	$1,080	500.24897	5002.49
Sum		$ 1,000.00	7246.888

Macauley Duration	7.2469
Modified Duration	6.7101

Duration of zero coupon bond

For a zero coupon bond, the duration will be the same as the tenor of the bond, because we only receive one cash flow and it's at the end of the period. How sensitive are zeros to price changes? Since there are no coupons, we can go back to basics and find that since

$$P_{zero} = \frac{Par}{(1+y)^n}$$

$$\frac{\partial P}{\partial y} = \frac{-nPar}{(1+y)^{n+1}} = -n\frac{1}{1+y}\frac{Par}{(1+y)^n} = -n\frac{1}{1+y}P, \frac{1}{P}\frac{\partial P}{\partial y} = \left(-\frac{1}{1+y}\right)n \Rightarrow D_{MAC} = n$$

For a zero at par and yield of 8%, a 100 bp change in yield would cause a price change of

$$\Delta P = -n\frac{P\Delta y}{1+y} = -10\frac{\$1,000(0.01)}{1+0.08}$$

=\$92.59. Because this is the same formula we had for the coupon-paying bond (except D_{MAC} is replaced by n, which is larger than D_{MAC} for a coupon bond), the prices of zero coupon bonds are extremely sensitive to changes in yield.

These durations are called **dollar durations** because they are expressed in terms of currency.

Dollar convexity

Now we need to talk about why there is an error between the change in price calculated using duration and the actual change in price that would occur. If we plot bond price as a function of yield (again using our 10-year 8% bond) we get a graph like the following.

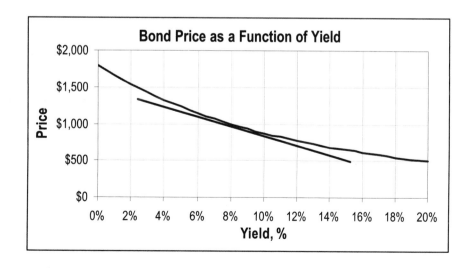

Note that the graph is not linear, but has a slight curve to it. This curve is known as **convexity**. This means that as yields increase, the curve flattens: the bond price becomes less sensitive to changes in yield. When yields are low, the price of the bond is extremely sensitive to changes in yield. Just using duration alone assumes that the bond is equally sensitive to yield changes at any yield. So, we see that using duration alone to estimate price sensitivity is not such a problem at high yields, but can lead to large errors when yields are low. *Using Duration alone to estimate price changes is reasonable only for small changes in yield, where the price-yield curve can be assumed to be approximately linear.*

Computing the price approximation

How do we include the effects of convexity in our price calculations? Recall the Taylor Series expansion. We can expand price in terms of y in order to solve for ΔP. The expansion of P in terms of y is:

$P(y+\Delta y) \cong P(y) + \dfrac{\partial P}{\partial y}\Delta y + \dfrac{1}{2}\dfrac{\partial^2 P}{\partial y^2}\Delta y^2$. Solving for ΔP and substituting our definition of duration gives:

$$P(y+\Delta y) - P(y) = \Delta P = \dfrac{\partial P}{\partial y}\Delta y + \dfrac{1}{2}\dfrac{\partial^2 P}{\partial y^2}\Delta y^2 = -PD_{MOD}\Delta y + \dfrac{1}{2}\dfrac{\partial^2 P}{\partial y^2}\Delta y^2 + \textit{Truncation Error}$$

The second term is the adjustment that needs to be added to our price to account for the effects of

convexity. Defining *dollar convexity* as $C = \dfrac{\partial^2 P}{\partial y^2}$ then $\Delta P = -PD_{MOD}\Delta y + \dfrac{1}{2}C\Delta y^2 + \textit{Truncation Error}$

Because here the convexity is positive, convexity has value: it increases the price of the bond. Units of convexity are in the unit of time, squared. A formula for use in a spreadsheet can be determined by taking the second derivative of the P(y) equation with respect to y; the result is:

$$\frac{\partial^2 P}{\partial y^2} = \sum_{i=1}^{n} \frac{i(i+1)C}{(1+y)^{i+2}} + \frac{n(n+1)Par}{(1+y)^{n+2}}$$

For example, re-computing the price change of our 10-year bond including the convexity of 60,531 gives the total price change due to a change of 100bp in the yield as change due to duration + change due to convexity:

$\Delta P = -\$1,000(6.7101)0.01 + \dfrac{1}{2}60.531(0.01)^2 = -67.101 + 3.027 = -\$64.074$. This is much closer to the actual price change of $P(0.09) - P(0.08) = 935.82 - \$1,000 = -\$64.18$.

Price value of a basis point (PVBP)

A common measure of duration is the **price value of a basis point**. You may sometimes see this referred to as the **dollar value of a basis point**. This is a measure of bond price volatility. As the name implies, this has to do with the price change resulting from a one-basis point, or 0.01%, change in yield. (We calculated the price impact on our 10-year 8% bond resulting from a 100 bp change. This is the same calculation but with a change of 1bp.)

Price of Bond at 8%	Price of Bond at 8.01%	Difference (PVBP)
$1,000	$999.33	0.67

Note that it does not matter if we increase or decrease the yield by 1bp; it is such a small amount that it makes no difference. You should get the same answer either way. Sometimes this may be quoted "per $100 of par value" so be aware of the conventions being used.

Estimating effective duration and effective convexity

If we divide the formula for ΔP by P, we get an expression for the percentage price change of the bond. Then

$$\frac{\Delta P}{P} = -D_E \Delta y + \frac{1}{2} C_E \Delta y^2$$

where D_E and C_E are known as the **effective duration** and **effective convexity** of the bond, respectively. (This duration is the same duration we have been using, except the convexity is now divided by P.)

If we have prices, we can estimate duration and convexity using finite-difference approximations of the

derivatives $\frac{\partial P}{\partial y}, \frac{\partial^2 P}{\partial y^2}$. From Taylor Series Approximations these are derived as:

$$\frac{\partial P}{\partial y} \cong \frac{P(y + \Delta y) - P(y - \Delta y)}{2\Delta y}, \text{ so } D_{MOD} \cong -\frac{P(y + \Delta y) - P(y - \Delta y)}{2P\Delta y}$$

$$C = \frac{\partial^2 P}{\partial y^2} \cong \frac{P(y + \Delta y) - 2P(y) + P(y - \Delta y)}{\Delta y^2}, \quad C_E = \frac{1}{P}\frac{\partial^2 P}{\partial y^2} \cong \frac{P(y + \Delta y) - 2P(y) + P(y - \Delta y)}{P\Delta y^2}$$

Example: A summary of three bond prices is summarized below.

Yield, %	Price
7	1,070.24
8	1,000
9	935.82

The estimate of duration for a 100bp change in yield for our $1,000 bond at a yield of 8% is

$$D_{MOD} \cong -\frac{P(8\% + 1\%) - P(8\% - 1\%)}{2(1000)(0.01)} = \frac{935.82 - 1070.24}{2(1000)(0.01)} = 6.72$$

which is a pretty good approximation. Now, the convexity is calculated as:

$$C \cong \frac{P(y+\Delta y)-2P(y)+P(y-\Delta y)}{\Delta y^2} = \frac{P(9\%)-2P(8\%)+P(7\%)}{0.01^2} = \frac{935.82-2(1,000)+1070.24}{0.01^2} = 60,600$$

This is also reasonably close to the 60,531 we calculated in Excel. The effective convexity is C/P = 60.6.

The percentage price change is then

$$\frac{\Delta P}{P} = -D_E \Delta y + \frac{1}{2} C_E \Delta y^2 = -6.72(0.01) + 0.5(60.6)(0.01)^2 = -0.0642$$

so $\Delta P = -0.0642(\$1,000) = -\$64.17$ as before.

Portfolio duration and convexity

Suppose a fixed income manager is trying to decide between two portfolios. Portfolio A is a bullet portfolio (one made up of bonds with maturities clustered at a single point on the yield curve) consisting of our 10-year, 8% coupon bond. Portfolio B is a barbell portfolio (one made up of bonds with maturities concentrated at both the short and long ends of the yield curve) consisting of a 2-year, 5% bond and a 20-year, 12% bond. The manager is concerned with the effect of yield curve shifts on the performance of the portfolios and wants to choose the best one. Since the duration of a portfolio of bonds is just the sum of weighted durations of each bond (where the weights are the percentage held of each bond), it is easy to choose the weights of portfolio B so that the duration matches the duration of Portfolio A. This is called a duration-matched portfolio. We have the following durations:

Bond	Mod Duration, years
2 Year	1.86
10 Year	6.71
20 Year	7.47

For the barbell portfolio "B" we have $D_B = w_2 D_2 + w_{20} D_{20} = w_2 D_2 + (1-w_2)D_{20} = w_2 1.86 + (1-w_2)7.47$. This should be set equal to the duration of portfolio "A", or 6.71 years. Solving for w_2, we find $w_2 = 0.1355$, so 13.55% is invested in the 2-year bond and 86.45% is invested in the 20-year bond. Now the fixed income manager constructs scenarios of expectations of future yield curve shifts and wishes to know the price change of the portfolios under each scenario.

Yield Curve Shift Scenarios		
Yield Curve Point	Scenario 1 shift, %	Scenario 2 shift, %
2 Year	100	100
10 Year	100	0
20 Year	100	-100

We have that $\frac{\Delta P}{P} = -D_E \Delta y + \frac{1}{2} C_E \Delta y^2$. We will ignore convexity changes in the following, but they could very easily be included.

Scenario 1 For Bond A, we have $\frac{\Delta P}{P} = -D_{EA} \Delta y = -6.71(0.01) = -6.71\%$. For Bond B,

$\frac{\Delta P}{P} = -\sum_{i=1}^{n} w_i D_{Ei} \Delta y = -w_2 D_2 \Delta y - w_{20} D_{20} \Delta y = -0.1355(1.86)(0.01) - 0.8645(7.47)0.01 = -6.71\%$. It

should not come as a surprise that the price change in both cases is the same, since this is why we constructed portfolio B with the weights that we did.

Scenario 2 For Bond A, there is no change in price since the 10 year point on the yield curve does not shift. For Bond B, we have

$\frac{\Delta P}{P} = -w_2 D_2 \Delta y - w_{20} D_{20} \Delta y = -0.1355(1.86)0.01 - 0.8645(7.47)(-0.01) = 6.21\%$.

So portfolio B will outperform Portfolio A if this scenario occurs. Note that portfolios of equal duration will experience the same price change (neglecting convexity effects) only when the yield curve undergoes a parallel shift. If the yield curve shifts in a non-parallel manner, the price change will no longer be the same. This illustrates the fact that duration is just a measure of **interest rate risk** (the risk that the yield curve will shift in a parallel manner), and not **yield curve risk** (the risk that the yield curve will shift in a non-parallel manner.) Including convexity will not solve this problem. A good way to deal with yield curve risk is to construct the portfolio using **key rate durations** (also known as "partial durations"). Key rate duration is portfolio duration calculated using certain so-called "key rates." Key rate duration is a measure of the sensitivity of a bond to a single point on the yield curve. For example, if the sensitivity of a 5-year Treasury to a 100-bp change in the yield curve is desired, you would shift the zero curve by 100 bp and calculate the new price of the bond. The key rate duration is given by the percentage change in the price of the bond. Specific key rates may be found, for example, on Bloomberg.com. Key rate duration is often referred to as partial duration because, in calculating it, you only consider exposure to a section of the yield curve. Key rate durations can be used to assess the effect of any yield curve shifts on the portfolio.

Sample Questions and Answers

Questions

1. What is the duration of a 10-year zero coupon bond?

2. Which is more volatile, a 30-year zero coupon bond or a 30-year 6.5% coupon bond?

3. What's the value of a stock if it currently pays a dividend of $2.50, the hurdle rate is 15% and the dividend is growing at an expected rate of 3%/year?

4. If you saw a 5-year, 10% coupon bond yielding 10% listed for $995, would you buy it? Assume that the coupons are paid annually and use simple compounding.

5. What happens to bond prices when interest rates increase? Why?

6. If you are a trader and have an idea that rates will decrease, what strategy could you adopt to profit from this?

7. Which should be cheaper and why: a 20-year, 7% coupon bond, or a 20-year, 8% coupon bond?

8. If you have a bond and it is $100 at a yield of 6%, $95 at 7%, and $90 at 8%, what is the modified duration? What is the effective convexity?

9. What is the duration of a fixed income ladder portfolio consisting of a 5-year bond with a duration of 4.6, a 10-year bond with duration of 7.2, and a 20-year bond with duration of 14.3? Assume that you hold equal proportions of all bonds.

10. What would be the impact of a 100 bp increase to the yield curve to a par bond with duration of 7.52? Is this the price you would see on a Bloomberg? Why or why not?

11. What is duration? Is it constant for all yields? What is convexity and why is it important?

Answers

1. 10 years. No calculations required. The duration of an n-year zero is just n.
2. The zero coupon bond is the most volatile.
3. Use the Gordon Growth model: $PV = CF_0/(r-g) = \$2.5/(.15-.03) = \$20.83$.
4. Yes, because this is a par bond (coupon equals yield) and should be trading at par ($1,000).
5. Except for rare exceptions (some types of mortgage bonds, for example) bond prices decrease when interest rates increase. If you had a 5-year par bond paying 8% coupons, and suddenly the 5-year treasury went to 9%, your bond would be worth less than before because investors would be getting less than the current rate.
6. If you think rates will drop, this implies that bond prices will increase. You should buy bonds (zero coupon in particular.)
7. You don't really need to do any calculations since the maturities and (we assume) the rest of the variables are the same for each bond, except for the coupon. The 7% coupon bond should be cheaper since, ceteris paribus, $\sum_{i=1}^{n} \frac{\$7}{(1+r)^i} + \frac{100}{(1+r)^N} < \sum_{i=1}^{n} \frac{\$8}{(1+r)^i} + \frac{100}{(1+r)^N}$
8. A straightforward calculation: use the definition (see section "Estimating Effective Duration and Convexity"). Make a table:

Yield, %	Price
6	100
7	95
8	90

$D_{MOD} = -\dfrac{P(y+\Delta y)-P(y-\Delta y)}{P2\Delta y}$. Since we are given data +/- 1% from a center point of 7%, Δy has

to be 1%, there is no other choice. Then $D_{MOD} = -\dfrac{P(7\%+1\%)-P(7\%-1\%)}{P_{7\%}2(0.01)} = -\dfrac{90-100}{95(2)(0.01)} = 5.26$

years. For convexity,

$C_E = \dfrac{1}{P}\dfrac{P(y+\Delta y)-2P(y)+P(y-\Delta y)}{\Delta y^2} = \dfrac{1}{95}\dfrac{P(8\%)-2P(7\%)+P(6\%)}{(0.01)^2} = \dfrac{1}{95}\dfrac{90-2(95)+100}{(0.01)^2} = 0.$

(Is this surprising? The price appears to be linear with yield: each 1% change in yield results in a $5 change in price, at least in this region. Had this been noticed, no calculations would have been necessary.)

9. Straight-forward calculation: $D_P = w_5D_5 + w_{10}D_{10} + w_{20}D_{20} = 1/3(D_5 + D_{10} + D_{20}) = 1/3(4.6+7.2+14.3)=8.7$

10. Interviewer is looking for a straight definition, and interpretation:

$D_{MOD} = -\dfrac{1}{P}\dfrac{dP}{dy} \cong -\dfrac{1}{P}\dfrac{\Delta P}{\Delta y}$ so $\Delta P = -P\Delta y D_{MOD} = -\$1,000(0.01)7.52 = -\$75.2.$

The new price would be calculated as $1,000 - 75.2 = $924.8. But this is not the price that would be shown on Bloomberg because we have neglected convexity and higher-order terms. Duration is just a first-order approximation.

11. Duration is a measure of the bond's sensitivity to yield curve movements. It is defined as:

$$D_{MOD} = -\dfrac{1}{P}\dfrac{dP}{dy}$$

It is steep when yields are low, and flattens as yields get higher, meaning the sensitivity of a bond's price to changes in yields decreases as yields increase. The price-yield curve is convex and the duration gives a good approximation only for small changes in yield where the price-yield curve can be assumed to be close to linear. Large errors occur when Δy increases. To account for the curvature of price with respect to yield, we need to include a second-order term. This is known as convexity, the second derivative of price with respect to yield. Since the second derivative is positive over the curve, convexity increases price. If it is neglected, the price calculated using duration alone would be too low.

Summary of Formulas

Future Value of P_0 $\qquad P_t = P_0\left(1 + \dfrac{r}{n}\right)^{nt}$

using continuous compounding: $\ P_t = P_0 e^{rt}$

Present Value of P_t $\ P_0 = P_t\left(1 + \dfrac{r}{n}\right)^{-nt}$

Using continuous compounding: $\ P_0 = P_t e^{-rt}$

Present Value of Stream of Cash Flows $\ PV = \sum_{i=1}^{n} \dfrac{CF_i}{\left(1 + r_i\right)^i}$

PV of Annuity (short cut) $\ PV = \dfrac{C}{r} - \dfrac{1}{\left(1+r\right)^n}\dfrac{C}{r}$

Present Value of Perpetuity $\ PV_{Perpetuity} = \dfrac{CF}{r}$

Gordon Growth Model (Perpetuity with growth rate g) $\ PV = \dfrac{CF_0}{r - g}$

Price of a Bond $\ P = \dfrac{C}{r}\left(1 - \dfrac{1}{\left(1+r\right)^n}\right) + \dfrac{Par}{\left(1+r\right)^n}$

Price Change of a Bond $\ \dfrac{1}{P}\dfrac{\partial P}{\partial y} = -D_{MOD}$

Macauley Duration $\ D_{MAC} = \dfrac{1}{P}\left[\sum_{i=1}^{n} \dfrac{iC}{\left(1+y\right)^i} + \dfrac{nPar}{\left(1+y\right)^n}\right]$

Modified Duration $\ D_{MOD} = \dfrac{1}{\left(1+y\right)}D_{MAC}$

Dollar Convexity $\ C = \dfrac{\partial^2 P}{\partial y^2}$

Price Change of Bond due to Change in Yield $\Delta P = -P D_{MOD}\Delta y + \dfrac{1}{2}C\Delta y^2 + Truncation\,Error$

Numerical Approximations of Duration and Convexity:

Duration $D_{MOD} \cong -\dfrac{P(y+\Delta y)-P(y-\Delta y)}{2P\Delta y}$

Convexity $C = \dfrac{\partial^2 P}{\partial y^2} \cong \dfrac{P(y+\Delta y)-2P(y)+P(y-\Delta y)}{\Delta y^2}$

Taylor Series Expansion (Single Variable)

$$f(x) = \sum_{n=0}^{\infty}\frac{f^{(n)}(k)}{n!}(x-k)^n = f(k)+f'(k)(x-k)+\frac{1}{2!}f''(k)(x-k)^2+\frac{1}{3!}f'''(k)(x-k)^3+\cdots+\frac{1}{M!}f^{(M)}(k)(x-k)^M + R_M$$

Increase your T/NJ Ratio
(Time to New Job)

Use the Internet's most targeted job search tools for finance professionals.

Vault Finance Job Board

The most comprehensive and convenient job board for finance professionals. Target your search by area of finance, function, and experience level, and find the job openings that you want. No surfing required.

VaultMatch Resume Database

Vault takes match-making to the next level: post your resume and customize your search by area of finance, experience and more. We'll match job listings with your interests and criteria and e-mail them directly to your in-box.

VAULT
> the insider career network™

STATISTICS

Random Variables

Statistics concerns itself with distributions and properties of **random variables**. A random variable ᴠ thought of as a drawing from a distribution whose outcome prior to the draw is uncertain, or stochasᴛ. The outcome of a roll of a pair of dice, the next song that will be played on the radio, what the Fed will do in next Tuesday's Open Market Committee meeting, next month's peso/USD exchange rate, and next year's return on the S&P500 index are all random variables, because the outcome is uncertain prior to the occurrence of the event. Although, of course, we cannot predict the outcome of random variables, we can form expectations of them. And forming expectations of random financial variables is at the very heart of finance. We will be developing the properties of these variables as we move through this chapter. First, we need to distinguish between discrete and continuous random variables.

A **discrete random variable** can take on a countable number of values (that is, finite). Discrete random variables include the roll of dice in a craps game, roulette outcomes and lottery picks and. For a roll of a single die, the ultimate outcome is unknown prior to the event taking place, but we know that there are six possible outcomes: either 1, 2, 3, 4, 5 or 6 will be rolled. There are no other possibilities. We have covered them all. One and only one of these outcomes will ensue. These facts are required in all of the distribution of outcomes. The set of possible outcomes is called the **event space**, or **states of nature**. The set of outcomes must be **mutually exclusive** and **collectively exhaustive**. When we assign a probability to each possible state of nature, we can then form expectations of the random variable.

A **continuous random variable** can take on any value in a given range, which may be $(-\infty, +\infty)$. Examples of continuous outcomes would be those variables that have an uncountable (or infinite) number of possible outcomes. These would include stock returns. You could imagine a return of –10%, -9.9%, -9.99%, -9.999%, …, 1.45%, 46%, … and any value, actually. With leverage you could even go beyond –100%. Tomorrow's temperature is a random variable that will be drawn from a random distribution of possible temperatures. When senior manager Gordon ponders the future value of his Lucent stock options, he might use a continuous distribution.

Rules governing probabilities associated with distributions

$0 < p < 1$

1. All probabilities must be greater or equal to zero and less than or equal to one.
2. The sum of all probabilities (discrete distribution) or integral of probabilities (continuous distribution) must equal one.
3. The set of outcomes must be mutually exclusive and collectively exhaustive.

No matter the form of the random variable, we need to think about what type of distribution the outcomes will have. For the discrete variable, hopefully we can enumerate all outcomes and assign expected probabilities to them. For example, assuming we have a fair die, there is an equal probability of each outcome {1,2,3,4,5,6} occurring. Since there are six possible outcomes, there is a one in six probability of each outcome. It gets a little more complicated when we talk about a continuous random variable. We might do some scenario analysis and estimate that the probability of losing 10% on our portfolio is 23.1%. But it is unlikely that the ultimate return will be *exactly* what we expect. Instead, we can calculate the probability that the return will fall in some *range* about the expected outcome. To do this, we need to have a good idea of the nature of the distribution of returns.

Univariate distribution functions

Each random variable is a draw from some distribution, even if the distribution is unknown. The draws can be "without replacement" or "with replacement." The roll of a die or a return on a stock is sampled with replacement, while a lottery drawing is preformed without replacement. We also expect successive draws to be "independent." The flip of a coin, the roll of a die or a return on a stock should not depend on what happened before. Distributions of outcomes of independent random variables should exhibit no pattern or memory.

There are other distributions where successive outcomes depend on what happened before, such as random walks and Markov chains. In statistics, you often consider processes that have no memory: the value of the next (unforeseeable) observation is independent of past history; it depends only on the current level of the variable. So, if stock prices are Markovian, this means that prior history of the stock's price process does not help predict future values. The best estimator of the next observation is the current observation. Random walks are examples of Markov chains, as are outcomes from roulette wheels, craps and other (fair) games of chance. Some lottery scheme vendors claim that future lottery picks can be guaranteed by studying the past numbers drawn. They look for patterns in the data, in a way similar to technical traders.

Discrete density function

If we let the symbol X represent the random variable "outcome of a roll of dice," then the event set of the random variable X is the set x ={1,2,3,4,5,6}. Each outcome of this set is equally probable. There are six total outcomes, so the probability distribution associated with the outcome set is {1/6,1/6,1/6,1/6,1/6,1/6}. A **univariate distribution function** is a distribution function associated with a single random variable, such as this example of the roll of a die. Another term for this type of probability distribution is **discrete density function**. This particular example is called a **uniform density** since all outcomes are equally probable: if we graphed them, we would just have a horizontal line. Note that the area under this curve is one, as required: area = base*height = 6*1/6 = 1.

Another common example is the tossing of a fair coin. Each toss can have one of two outcomes, either tails (T) or heads (H). Like the roll of a die, a successive toss is independent of the prior result. Each outcome has a probability of 1/2 of occurring.

Multivariable distribution functions

It is very interesting to think about what happens if we combine two (or more) independent random variables. What will the resulting probability distribution and outcome space look like? The resulting distribution of outcomes of such experiments is called a **joint probability distribution**. A familiar example is the game of craps, in which two die are rolled simultaneously. Each die has its own distribution of outcomes and probabilities. We already found that the set of outcomes is a uniform distribution when a single die is rolled. But what happens when we roll two simultaneously? First of all, notice that we can't get a result of "1" anymore. However, we can get a "12," which was impossible before. The possible outcomes in this case are the sum of each individual outcome,

$$x = \sum_{i=1}^{6}\sum_{j=1}^{6} i + j$$

But does the distribution still look uniform? That is, does each outcome {2,3,4,5,6,7,8,9,10,11,12} have equal probability of occurring? The answer to this question is crucial to gambling success.
To begin to figure this out, I make a table of all of the possible outcomes:

Die 1 is ... / Die 2 is ...	1	2	3	4	5	6
1	2	3	4	5	6	7
2	3	4	5	6	7	8

3	4	5	6	7	8	9
4	5	6	7	8	9	10
5	6	7	8	9	10	11
6	7	8	9	10	11	12

Now we tally up the results.

Result	Number of Ways to Occur	Set of Outcomes Leading to Result	Probability of Occurring
2	1	{1,1}	1/36
3	2	(1,2},{2,1}	2/36
4	3	{1,3},{2,2},{3,1}	3/36
5	4	{1,4},{2,3},{3,2},{4,1}	4/36
6	5	{1,5},{2,4},{3,3},{4,2},{5,1}	5/36
7	6	{1,6},{2,5},{3,4},{4,3},{5,2},{6,1}	6/36
8	5	{2,6},{3,5},{4,4},{5,3},{6,2}	5/36
9	4	{3,6},{4,5},{5,4},{6,3}	4/36
10	3	{4,6},{5,5},{6,4}	3/36
11	2	{5,6},{6,5}	2/36
12	1	{6,6}	1/36

(Notice that the strategies "draw a figure," "look for a pattern," "enumerate all cases," and even "exploit symmetry" could have been used to solve this.) What are the probabilities of each outcome? To find out, we first sum up the number of possible outcomes: this is the sum of numbers in the second column, or 36. The probability of each individual result occurring is just the number of ways each can occur, divided by the total number of outcomes -- this is a *general result*. And you will see that if you check this, the probabilities sum to one. The probabilities for our game are shown in the last column above. The probability of "1/36" for rolling a 12, for example, means that there is only one way to roll a 12, out of 36 possible outcomes. So the next time you see someone buying a 12 in Vegas, you will know that this is a low probability bet. The number having the highest frequency (probability of occurring) is 7. You can see that the probability distribution is definitely not uniform. If you graph it, it will look like the following:

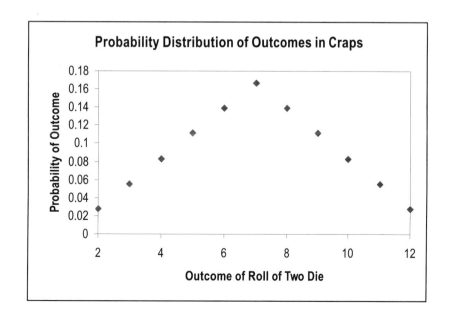

The distribution does not appear to be linear, so we conclude that the outcome of the sum of two uniform distributions is not uniform. Even though this may seem like a simple example, there is a lot that we can learn from it -- just because it is so simple, and we can completely describe and understand it.

Key Statistical Figures

It is often desired to summarize large sets of data so that they may be better understood and compared. To do this, we want some kind of measure of **central tendency** of the data. There are three measures of central tendency that will be of interest: the **mean**, the **median** and the **mode**. These measures are important, because we will use them to help us determine the expected value of a random variable. We will also use simple descriptive statistics, including **range**, **minimum**, **maximum**, **interquartile range**, **variance, standard deviation** and **skewness**.

In the following we consider a time series of the monthly returns of a particular stock over the past nine months {8%,-10%,0%,5% ,-6%,-6%,7%,13%,6.5%}. It's always a good idea to graph the data you are trying to understand to look for tendencies and trends, and to visually identify any outliers.

Dot Plot of Stock Returns (%)

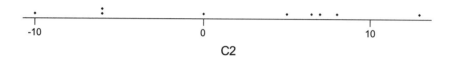

C2

The data appear to be clumped toward the right of the x-axis. The following is a description of the measures of central tendency of the data:

Mean

The mean of a set of numbers is the same as its average. The mathematical definition of mean is

$$\bar{x} = \frac{\sum_{i=1}^{n} x_i}{n}$$

We use an overbar on x to represent the mean of all of the x_i. In statistics, when speaking of distributions, the symbol μ is usually used. The mean of a distribution is very important. In many cases, this is the best estimate we have of an expected future value.

Example *What is the mean of our stock market returns?*
Just sum up all of the values and divide by the number of data points, or 0.175/9=1.94%.

Example *What is the mean of the outcomes of the roll of two simultaneous die?*
Sum up 2,3,4,5,6,7,8,9,10,11 and 12 and divide by 11 to get 7.

(Quick Trick: to add a sequence of numbers increasing by one and running from 1 to n, the formula is $\frac{n(n+1)}{2}$. For example, the sum of integers 1, 2, 3, ..., 99,100 is (100)(101)/2 =5050. To do our problem, we have 2, 3,4, ..., 11,12, which almost matches the required form but is offset by one. Just shift back by 1 to do the sum 1, 2, ... , 11 = 66, average = 6, then add back 1 to get our average, 7.) Is it a coincidence that the mean result is also the most frequent result? If you roll a pair of die, the combination 7 is more likely to occur than any other combination. But this is also the most frequent observation. It turns out that, in this case, the mean is the same as the median and the mode.

Median

To calculate the median, the data must first be sorted in ascending order. The median is the middle value of the sorted series. The median is useful because half of the data will lie below it and half above it. Comparison of the median to the mean gives us an idea of the skewness of the distribution. The sorted data are {-10%,-6%,-6%, 0%, 5%, 6.5%, 7%, 8%, 13%}. We have nine data points, so the median is the fifth number in the sorted series of numbers, or 5%. This means that half of the returns lie below 5% and half lie above 5%. So, if I wanted to know the expected return of the stock next month, which number should I use? The mean of 1.94%? The median of 5%? The most recent return of 6.5%? How about the return occurring most frequently?

Mode

The mode tells us which response occurs with greatest frequency. Distributions can have a single mode, no mode or multiple modes. In the roll of a single die, all responses occur with the same frequency, so there is no mode. In the roll of two dice, the outcome "7" occurs with greatest frequency. In the stock return example, we have a return of –6% occurring as the mode.

Range, maximum and minimum

We would now like an idea of the dispersion of the data. The range provides a simple measure of the dispersion of the data and is defined as

Maximum – Minimum values of data set.

The maximum and minimum of a data set are interesting numbers in themselves. For the return data, the maximum is 13%; the minimum is –10%. This makes the range 23%. The range of the roll of a pair of die is 12-2=10. The range provides an idea of how tightly clustered the data are about the mean, particularly when it is normalized by dividing by the sample standard deviation (which we'll discuss later in this chapter). (There was a question about the range of data on this year's CFA level II exam that tripped up many people who were not expecting to see it.) However, the range will be skewed by excessively large or small data elements. To do a better job we can use the interquartile range.

Interquartile range

The data can be sorted and divided into equally sized groups. If there are outliers, they can be removed if desired, and the remaining data classified. If n sorted data points are to be divided into four groups, the first quartile Q_1 is the data point given by $\frac{n+1}{4}$. The third quartile Q_3 is the $\frac{3(n+1)}{4}$ th point, and the median Q_2 is the $\frac{2(n+1)}{4}$ th point. If the number we calculate for the Q_i isn't an integer, interpolation is used. The first quartile for the stock return data is $10/4^{th}$ point = 2.5^{th} point. This means to go halfway between the second and third point. Since both are equal to –6, $Q_1 = -6$. $Q_3 = 3*2.5 = 7.5$. Again we interpolate midway between the seventh and eighth points to get $Q_3 = (7+8)/2 = 7.5$. The interquartile range is defined as the difference $Q_3 - Q_1$, here $7.5 - (6) = 13.5$. This is often thought of as a better measure of dispersion than the range, because excessive values that may lie on the extremes of the data set (such as may occur in distributions of wealth) will not skew the result as they are excluded from the interquartile range.

Variance

The best measure of dispersion from the mean is the variance (σ^2). This is defined as the sum of squared differences of each data point from the mean. These differences are called **deviations from the mean**. Then

$$\sigma^2 = \frac{\sum_{i=1}^{n}(y_i - \bar{y})^2}{n-1} = \frac{\sum_{i=1}^{n}\delta_i^2}{n-1}$$

Month i	R_i (%)	R_i - μ	$(R_i - \mu)^2$
1	-10	-11.94	142.67
2	-6	-7.94	63.11
3	-6	-7.94	63.11
4	0	-1.94	3.78
5	5	3.06	9.34
6	6.5	4.56	20.75
7	7	5.06	25.56
8	8	6.06	36.67
9	13	11.06	122.23
Sum	17.5		487.22
Mean μ	1.944		
Variance			60.90

Notice that we divide by $n-1$, not n, in computing the variance. There are deep statistical reasons for this (see the following paragraph**), but the main reason is that we really don't know the true population (except in simple, constructed cases such as craps or flips of coins). We are just estimating the variance of the unknown, true population with the variance of our sample. It turns out that this means we have to divide by $n-1$.

**Suppose that we actually have the true population. Then, the variance would be computed as

$$\sigma^2 = \frac{\sum_{i=1}^{x}(x_i - \mu)^2}{n}$$, where μ = population mean and n is the total number of points. However, in practice

we do not know the mean μ, but can only approximate it with the mean of the sample we take, $\bar{x}$. This sample mean may or may not be reflective of the true population mean, so we divide by $n-1$ rather than n to

compensate for this fact. This way, the sample variance $s^2 = \dfrac{\sum_{i=1}^{x}(x_i - \bar{x})^2}{n-1}$ that we compute will hopefully

be, neither larger nor smaller than the true population variance σ^2.

Standard deviation

The standard deviation (σ) is the true measure of dispersion. It is just the square root of the variance, equal to 7.804% in the preceding example. (In Excel: **=STDEV(range of numbers)**). For the roll of a single die, the standard deviation is 1.87. We will find that normal distributions can be uniquely described by the mean and the standard deviation. The standard deviation is used as a measure of risk in finance. If portfolios of assets are normally distributed, they can be ranked according to return and risk. This is the basis of the **efficient markets hypothesis**. In a normal distribution, there is a 68.2% probability that the data will lie within one standard deviation of the mean; a 95.5% probability that the data will lie within two standard deviations of the mean, and a 99.7% change that the data will lie within three standard deviations of the mean. For the roll of a die, $\mu - \sigma = 3.5-1.87 = 1.63$ and $\mu + \sigma = 3.5+1.87 = 5.37$. This means that about two-thirds of the data, or four data points, should lie between 1.63 and 5.37 (or 2 and 5 in integer values), which they do -- even though the data are not normally distributed.

(*Quick trick*: To remember whether variance or standard deviation is equal to σ, just remember that σ starts with one s. So does standard deviation. Variance, then, must be σ^2.)

Correlation

We have talked about simple, independent experiments, but financial data are often correlated. This means that the data move somewhat together, influencing each other. Since the S&P500 is made up of 500 large-cap stocks, factors that influence large caps will also move the index. Bond prices are sensitive to interest rates. Automakers Ford and GM are probably influenced by common macroeconomic factors. Gold and silver may have some association. Sometimes assets move in opposite directions, such as a call on a stock and a put on the same stock, or holding gold in a portfolio that is heavy in risky tech stocks having high market βs. The degree of association or comovement between two variables is called **correlation (r)**. Another term that can express this idea is **covariance**. The degree of covariance between assets within a portfolio must be included when calculating the variance of a portfolio.

The correlation coefficient r can take on values from -1 to $+1$, with -1 meaning perfect negative correlation and $+1$ meaning perfect positive correlation. A value of zero implies no correlation, while low values indicate virtually no association between the variables.

The definition of correlation between two variables x and y is:

$$r = \frac{\sum_{i=1}^{n}(x - \bar{x})(y - \bar{y})}{(n-1)\sigma_x \sigma_y}, -1 \le r \le 1$$

correlation coefficient = r

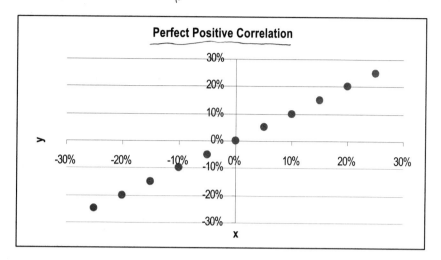

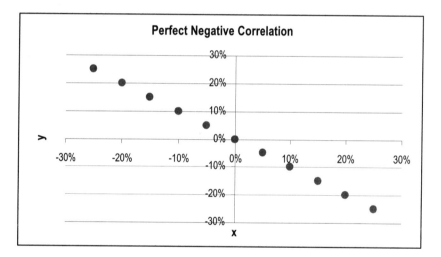

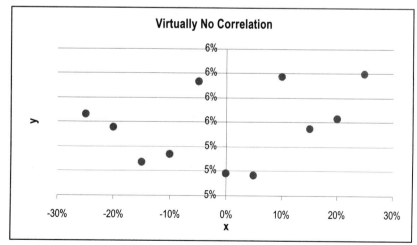

As an example, we calculate the correlation between monthly change in a hypothetical airline's profit as a function of change in fuel prices. The graph of the data is shown below.

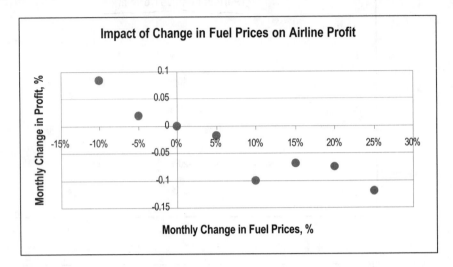

There seems to be a negative correlation, as we would expect. Using the formula will enable us to assign a quantitative value to this association.

$$r = \frac{\sum_{i=1}^{n}(x-\bar{x})(y-\bar{y})}{(n-1)\sigma_x \sigma_y} = \frac{-5.4\%}{(7)(12.25\%)(6.82\%)} = -0.9313$$

Month i	x Change in Price of Airline Fuel $/gal	y Airline Profit Change (%/qr)	x-μ_x	y-μ_y	(x-μ_x)(y-μ_y)
1	-10%	8.3%	-17.5%	11.8%	-2.1%
2	-5%	1.9%	-12.5%	5.4%	-0.7%
3	0%	0.0%	-7.5%	3.5%	-0.3%
4	5%	-1.8%	-2.5%	1.6%	0.0%
5	10%	-10.0%	2.5%	-6.5%	-0.2%
6	15%	-6.9%	7.5%	-3.4%	-0.3%
7	20%	-7.5%	12.5%	-4.0%	-0.5%
8	25%	-11.9%	17.5%	-8.5%	-1.5%
Sum	60.0%	-27.9%			-5.4%
Mean	7.5%	-3.5%			
Stdev σ	12.25%	6.82%			
Correlation					-0.93138588

This can also be done immediately within Excel using the CORREL function, which will give the same answer. Note that the correlation of any asset with itself is one since

$$r = \frac{\sum_{i=1}^{n}(x-\bar{x})(x-\bar{x})}{(n-1)\sigma_x\sigma_x} = \frac{\sum_{i=1}^{n}(x-\bar{x})^2}{(n-1)}\frac{1}{\sigma_x^2} = \frac{\sigma_x^2}{\sigma_x^2} = 1$$

Coefficient of determination

The square of r is known as ρ, the coefficient of determination (ρ), which can run from 0 to 1.

Coefficient of determination $\rho = r^2$ $0 \le \rho \le 1$

Skewness

If data have a reasonably strong tendency to cluster about some value, we can define moments of the distribution. The mean is often referred to as the first moment, variance is the second moment and **skewness** is the third moment of the distribution. If the histogram of a distribution looks like the dice-rolling example, there is no skew – the data are symmetric about the mean, which is equal to the median and the mode. The distribution of effective monthly Federal Funds since 1958 shown below is skewed to the right:

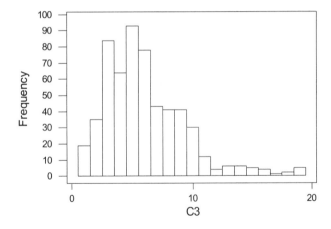

In this histogram there are many more data values to the right than to the left. The mean (6.021) is higher than the median (5.45). Other examples of distributions skewed to the right include histograms of national income. In terms of sheer numbers, there are less people earning higher incomes (or rates above the average rate for this period) than there are people earning incomes below the mean. The very high incomes (rates) skew the mean to the right. To remember, imagine a symmetric distribution that is anchored at its mean. Now slide one tail out far to the right and you would have a graph like the above.

The histogram of the fed funds rate over the period Jan 95-Mar 02 tells a different story: Several months of very low rates skew the curve out to the left. For these data, the mean (5.169) is below the median (5.460).

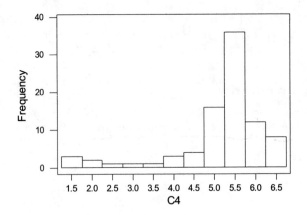

Permutations and Combinations

In statistics, we often draw from samples and are interested in how many different combinations are possible. For example, say you were given a survey in which you were asked to rank ten food/recipe websites in order of your preference. If you had never used any of the sites before, what would be the probability that you would choose a specific ordering? (Note that here you are sampling "without replacement," because you are not allowed to pick the same one more than once.) Your choice for the top website could be any one of the ten sites. Your second choice has to come from the pool of nine remaining candidates. For your third choice there are only eight left to select from, and so forth. So the number of possible choices is 10*9*8*7* ... * 1 = 10 factorial, 10! The probability of choosing one particular combination of websites out of these 10! possibilities is then 1/10!, which equals one in 3,628,800.

Another way to solve such a problem, as long as the number of cases is small, is to draw trees. How many different outcomes can we get by flipping a coin three times? Examination of the first two throws yields the following results: We see that for one flip, the possible outcomes are {T,H}, each with a probability of ½ of occurring. For two flips there are four possible outcomes: two tails, one tail and one head, one head and one tail, and two heads. Each has an equal probability of ¼. Taking it out one further step to flipping a third time, we find eight possible outcomes: {TTT, TTH, THT, THH, HTT, HTH, HHT, HHH}. In general, after n flips there are 2^n possible outcomes and, if we care about order (that is, TH is different from HT), each outcome has a probability of $1/(2^n)$.

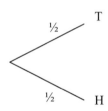

One Flip of A Coin

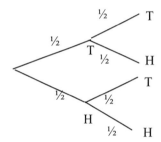

Two Flips of A Coin

Let's extend this further. In the Powerball lottery drawing, five balls are drawn, without replacement, from a container of 49 balls. The balls are numbered from 1 to 49. The player has to choose the five balls that will be drawn. What is the probability of choosing the right numbers? Well, the first number has a 1 in 49 chance of being drawn; the second a 1 in 48 chance of being drawn; the third, 1 in 47; the fourth, 1 in 46; and the fifth, 1 in 45. So the odds of correctly selecting the five Powerball numbers are 1/(49*48*47*46*45) = 1/228,826,080 or one in over 228 million.

We can generalize this result, too. If you are making *x* selections from a set of *n* objects, where *n>x*, you can choose from *n* objects for your first choice, *(n-1)* objects for your second choice, *(n-2)* for your third and so on. When you get to your last choice, you will have (n-x+1) objects available to choose from. The number of possible arrangements of *n* objects chosen *x* at a time is called the permutation $_nP_x$.

Thus, $_nP_x = n(n-1)(n-2) ... (n-x+1)$.

This can be simplified by multiplying by *(n-x)!/(n-x)! = (n-x)(n-x-1)(n-x-2) ...(2)(1)/((n-x)(n-x-1)(n-x-2) ...(2)(1))*. Why on earth would we do this? Because it simplifies the numerator to *n!* and the denominator to *(n-x)!* Thus,

$$_nP_x = \frac{n!}{(n-x)!}$$

Remember this one. It is a popular interview question. Re-solving our Powerball problem using this formula gives the number of ways to choose 5 objects from a set of 49 as

$$_{49}P_5 = \frac{49!}{(49-5)!} = \frac{49*48*47*46*45*44!}{44!} = 49*48*47*46*45 = 228,826,080$$

But is this the right answer? No, because we don't care about order. Choosing the numbers 1,9,14,27,46 gives the same result as choosing 46,27,14,1,9 and so on. For cases where we are not concerned with the order of the result, we use a *combination*. When we threw a coin twice, if we want to know the probability of throwing one head and one tail, we would accept either state of nature {H,T} or {T,H}. The probability is then equal to Pr(H) + Pr(T) = ½. If the question were, "what is the probability of first throwing a head and then throwing a tail?" the answer would be Pr(H) times Pr(T), since the probability of success is conditional on first throwing a head. The number of combinations of x objects chosen from $_nP_x$ is then

$$_{n}C_x = \frac{n!}{x!(n-x)!} = \frac{1}{x!}\,_{n}P_x$$

We just divide the number of permutations by $x!$ which is the number of possible arrangements of x objects. So, the odds of hitting five Powerball numbers are 228,826,080 divided by 5!(or 120), or 1,906,884. To win the Powerball jackpot, you must also correctly choose one red ball from a container of 42. This is known as the Powerball number. The probability of hitting this one is easy: just 1 in 42. But you must also get the first five balls correct. In this case, the total probability of winning is (1/42)*(1/1,906,884) = 1/80,089,128. Remember, when an outcome depends on the realization of a prior outcome, you have to multiply the probabilities. If it does not (independence), you add the probabilities. So, what is the probability of next week's Powerball pick being the same as a combination that has already occurred?

Functions of Random Variables

Of interest here are the expectations of random variables such as future returns on stocks and interest rate movements: What will the means and standard deviations be?

Linear Functions

First things first: constants. The expected value of a constant is the constant: $E(\alpha) = \alpha$. The bank tells you that your savings account will earn 2.5%/year. There can be no variation in this amount. Your expectation of interest earned is 2.5% for the year. The expected variance of the constant is zero – a constant is to remain constant.

$$\sigma^2(\alpha) = 0$$

Given a discrete random variable X, the expected value E(X) is given by

$$E(X) = \sum_{i=1}^{x} xP(x)$$

for a discrete random variable and

$$E(X) = \int xP(x)dx$$

for a continuous random variable.

If we multiply the random variable X by a constant α, what will be the expectation? It is the constant times the expectation of the random variable: $E(\alpha X) = \alpha E(X)$.

This can be proven by carrying out the integration $E(\alpha X) = \int \alpha xP(x)dx = \alpha \int xP(x)dx = \alpha E(X)$.

If we have a random variable Z that is a linear combination, $\alpha + \beta X$, $E(Z) = E(\alpha + \beta X)$, which is just $E(\alpha) + E(\beta X) = \alpha + \beta E(X)$.

For variance we have:
$var(\alpha R) = \alpha^2 var(R)$

What is the expected variance of the random variable $Z = \alpha + \beta X$? $\sigma_Z^2 = var(\alpha + \beta X)$.

Then
$\sigma_Z^2 = var(\alpha + \beta X) = var(\alpha) + var(\beta X) = \beta^2 \sigma_X^2$.

The standard deviation is the square root of the variance, but we have to take absolute values of α in the expectation because we want positive standard deviation.
$\sigma_{\alpha R} = |\alpha| \sigma_R$

Sums of random variables

The expectation of the linear combination of two random variables, such as the sum of two stock returns making up a portfolio, is $E(X_1 + X_2) = E(X_1) + E(X_2)$, if the returns are independent of each other. So, the expectation of a sum of random variables is just the sum of expectations of the random variables.

Portfolios of random variables

For a portfolio consisting of n assets with the ith asset having portfolio weight w_i and expected return R_i, the expected return of the portfolio is just $E(R_P) = E\left(\sum_{i=1}^{n} w_i R_i\right) = \sum_{i=1}^{n} w_i E(R_i)$

The expected variance of the portfolio is $\sigma_{R_p}^2 = \text{var}\left(\sum_{i=1}^{n} w_i R_i\right)$

This is a little complicated so we will just start with two assets in the portfolio, 1 and 2. The proportion of asset R_1 in the portfolio w_1, and the proportion of R_2 is w_2. Then

$$\sigma_{R_p}^2 = \text{var}(w_1 R_1 + w_2 R_2) = E(w_1 R_1 + w_2 R_2 - w_1\mu_1 - w_2\mu_2)^2 =$$
$$E\left(w_1^2(R_1 - \mu_1)^2 + w_2^2(R_2 - \mu_2)^2 + 2w_1 w_2(R_1 - \mu_1)(R_2 - \mu_2)\right)$$

Since the expectation of a constant times a random variable is just the constant times the expectation of the random variable, we can bring the constants w_1 and w_2 out of the expectation operator.

$$\sigma_{Rp}^2 = w_1^2 E([R_1 - E(R_1)])^2 + w_2^2 E([R_2 - E(R_2)])^2 + 2w_1 w_2 E[[R_1 - E(R_1)][R_2 - E(R_2)]]$$

The squared variances from the mean are just the variances of the assets. The cross term is the covariance of asset 1 with asset 2:

$$\sigma_{Rp}^2 = w_1^2\sigma_1^2 + w_2^2\sigma_2^2 + 2w_1 w_2 COV_{1,2}$$

where the covariance is related to the coefficient of determination through

$$COV_{1,2} = \rho_{1,2}\sigma_1\sigma_2$$

so we can also write $\sigma_{Rp}^2 = w_1^2\sigma_1^2 + w_2^2\sigma_2^2 + 2w_1 w_2\rho_{1,2}\sigma_1\sigma_2$

Example The Fed is meeting this afternoon to set interest rate policy. There are three possible states of nature: they will leave the Fed Funds rate unchanged, they will raise it 50 bp or they will cut it 25 bp. What is the expected outcome?

In order to determine this you must assign probabilities to each occurrence. You believe that:

Scenario	Probability of Occurrence
+50bp	0.15
0bp	0.80
-25bp	0.05

The random variable is the change in interest rates, and the expectation of the change in interest rates is the sum of the weighted random variables, with the weights being the probabilities. Then $E(\Delta r) = 0.15(50bp) + 0.8(0bp) + 0.05(-25bp) = +6.25bp$.

Example What are the expected return and variance of a portfolio consisting of 50% of asset 1 with an expected return of 5%, and 50% of Asset 2 with an expected return of 2%?

The standard deviations of the assets are $\sigma_1 = 10\%$, $\sigma_2 = 30\%$. Work this for three cases:
   a) $\rho = 1$;
   b) $\rho = 0$ and
   b) $\rho = -1$.

For the return calculation, we just take weighted expectations.

So $E(R_P) = 0.5(5\%) + 0.5(2\%) = 3.5\%$. This return will be the same for each of the three cases; only the portfolio variance will be affected.

Case a: $\sigma_{R_P}^2 = w_1^2\sigma_1^2 + w_2^2\sigma_2^2 + 2w_1w_2\rho_{1,2}\sigma_1\sigma_2 = 0.5^2 0.1^2 + 0.5^2 0.3^2 + 2(0.5)(0.5)1(0.1)(0.3) = 4\%$ so σ_p

Expected Return of Portfolio with n assets $\qquad E(R_p) = \sum_{i=1}^{n} w_i E(R_i)$

$= 20\%$.

Case b: $\sigma_{R_P}^2 = w_1^2\sigma_1^2 + w_2^2\sigma_2^2 + 2w_1w_2\rho_{1,2}\sigma_1\sigma_2 = 0.5^2 0.1^2 + 0.5^2 0.3^2 + 2(0.5)(0.5)0(0.1)(0.3) = 2.5\%$ so $\sigma_p = 15.81\%$.

Case c: $\sigma_{R_P}^2 = w_1^2\sigma_1^2 + w_2^2\sigma_2^2 + 2w_1w_2\rho_{1,2}\sigma_1\sigma_2 = 0.5^2 0.1^2 + 0.5^2 0.3^2 + 2(0.5)(0.5)(-1)(0.1)(0.3) = 1\%$ so $\sigma_p = 10\%$.

We see from the above that including just two uncorrelated assets (case b) resulted in a lower variance than would occur when there is a positive association between the assets (case a). But using assets with negative correlation resulted in the lowest portfolio variance. In fact, it is possible to choose the weights so that the portfolio variance is zero.

(Note: Independence implies zero correlation, but zero correlation does NOT imply independence.)

Distributions

We have already begun to think about distributions in our craps game, but it is now time to discuss properties of the **normal** and **lognormal distributions**.

If a random variable X has the probability density function $f(x) = \dfrac{1}{\sqrt{2\pi\sigma^2}} e^{-(x-\mu)^2/2\sigma^2}$, with $-\infty < x < \infty$,

then X is said to be "normally distributed." The **normal distribution** has these important properties:

Mean of Normal Distribution	μ
Variance of Normal Distribution	σ^2

The notation $X \sim N(\mu, \sigma^2)$ is used to indicate that X has a normal distribution with mean (expected value) of μ and dispersion about the mean (expected variance) of σ^2. The first graph below shows the normal distribution with a mean of zero and a standard deviation of 1. The second graph shows the effects of decreasing the standard deviation on the shape of the normal distribution.

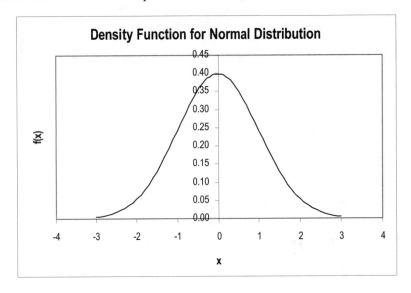

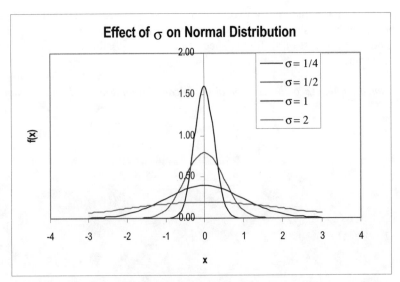

As the dispersion increases, the normal curve flattens out and the maximum height decreases. This is because the area under the curve must always equal 1 (remember this is the total probability.)

If we have a set of data to analyze, one of the first questions to ask is how the data are distributed. If you can assume that the data follow a normal distribution, then things are much easier because much is known about the properties of normal distributions. The normal distribution is completely specified with just two parameters. You can rank normally distributed portfolios using just their means and standard deviations. But what if your data are not normally distributed? Just apply the **central limit theorem**.

Central limit theorem

Suppose X_i is independently and identically distributed (IID, or i.i.d.) with mean μ and standard deviation σ. Then $\dfrac{1}{n}\sum_{i=1}^{n} X_i$ is distributed as $N(\mu,\sigma^2)$ as n→∞.

The random variable $Z = \dfrac{\overline{X} - \mu}{\sigma / \sqrt{n}}$ is normally distributed, even if X is not, provided that n is sufficiently large. Another way to put it: The distribution of a sum of IID drawings approaches a normal distribution. This is very useful since, in finance, we often have large quantities of data, which may or may not be normally distributed. But, the central limit theorem says that transforming the random variable X to Z should result in a distribution that is close to normal.

As an application, recall the distribution of the craps simulation with two independent random variables, both having identical distributions. The fact that n random variables X have identical distributions is critical in the use of the central limit theorem; the dice enjoy this property. Let's test it out: The distribution for two dice did not look very normal. But what if we had a new game, a sort of a "super craps" where we have 10 dice or even 20? What would the distribution of outcomes look like then? Even for three dice, the distribution starts to look more like a normal distribution than with n=1 or n=2:

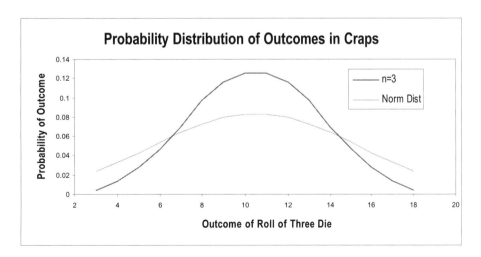

Lognormal distribution

A hedge fund manager might ask you: "How are prices on equities distributed?" or "How are returns on equities distributed?" To answer these questions, we always have to assume some underlying distribution when building our models, since we can only observe samples of data at a certain time. However, making the wrong assumptions can be disastrous to our models. The historical return of the S&P 500 index is about 8% and its standard deviation 16%. If you assume that the S&P 500 is normally distributed, you would expect that 68.42% of the returns will lie within one σ of the mean, 99.5% of returns will lie within 2σ of the mean and 99.7% of the returns will lie within 3σ of the mean. This means that you expect returns worse than μ – 3σ = 8%-3(16) = -40% or returns better than μ + 3σ = 8%+3(16) = -56% only 0.3% of the time.

Many studies have been performed to test the normality of financial markets and have found that the extreme cases occur much more frequently than would be expected. The actual distribution is said to be "fat-tailed." (More recent papers suggest using different distributions such as the "truncated Levy distribution," but further discussion of this is beyond the context of this book.) If we are thinking about prices, we see right away that we can't use the standard normal distribution, which ranges from -∞ to +∞, because stock prices have a lower limit of $0. So, it is common practice to use a **lognormal distribution** for stock prices, since the log function has the desirable property of approaching zero from the right. Most financial variables are assumed to be lognormally distributed, which means that the logs of the variables are normally distributed. The lognormal probability distribution has mean μ and standard deviation σ. The lognormal probability density function is given by

$$f(x) = \frac{1}{\sigma x \sqrt{2\pi}} e^{-(\ln(x)-\mu)^2 / (2\sigma^2)} \text{, } x > 0$$

A lognormal distribution is plotted below.

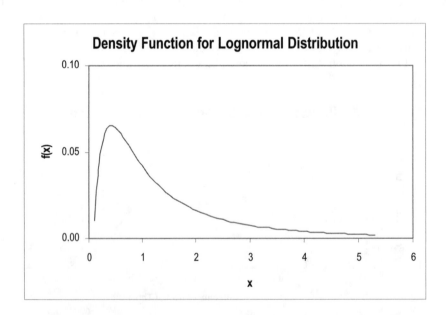

Scaling Returns and Standard Deviations with Horizon If you know the monthly standard deviation of a stock, how do you annualize it? If you know a stocks' annual return, what was the average return per day? These are typical interview questions. It turns out that returns and variances scale with horizon, but standard deviation scales with the square root of time. If you have a one-month return of 0.5%, you can just multiply by 12 months to annualize it to an annual 6% return. A variance of 1% is annualized to a 12% annual variance. But the standard deviation is multiplied by $\sqrt{t} = \sqrt{12}$ in this case. If you have annual standard deviation data and wish to convert it to daily values, divide by the square root of the number of trading days in a year, generally taken to be 250.

Regression Analysis

Regression analysis is used for building models and forecasting trends. It can also be used for explanatory analysis. Common packages used include Excel, Mathematica, Matlab, Minitab, S Plus and SAS. If you find yourself about to interview with a company that uses a statistical package unfamiliar to you, the web has many free resources to guide you through tutorials.

To motivate the following discussion, suppose we have a list of annual returns and standard deviations for common U.S. mutual funds. This type of analysis, where data are all at one point in time, is called a **cross-sectional analysis**. For example, say we want to estimate the standard deviation of a mutual fund that is not in the sample. We make a lot of assumptions in doing this. The first step is to plot the data in order to get a visualization of the relationship, if any, between the returns and standard deviations. (Any time you make an analysis like this, ask yourself if there should be a relationship – and what kind? Positive or negative correlation? In the above case, should there be a relationship between risk and return? The **CAPM** (Capital Asset Pricing Model) define? says yes.)

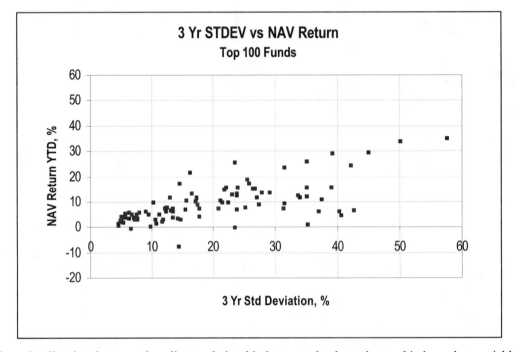

The figure implies that there may be a linear relationship between the dependent and independent variables.

Note: An apparent relationship between two variables does not necessarily imply causality.

We could just as easily have plotted σ on the y-axis as the dependent variable using return as the independent variable. Does return cause risk? It seems to rain often on the weekends. Do weekends cause rain? Does rain cause weekends? You see where this can go. Another way to say it is: *Just because you can write something down for the right-hand side of a regression equation does not imply that the right hand "causes" the left.* (For more on this, look up "Granger Causality" in a good econometrics book.)

Continuing with our data, we can perform linear regression analysis to derive a function that yields σ as a function of r. Here is how it works: Take a series of observations, generated from some random experiment or observation. Here, we have used a subset of the mutual fund data for simplicity in calculations.

Stdev	Return
4.57	1.33
12.26	7.2
25.67	18.8
33.81	12.12
42.15	22

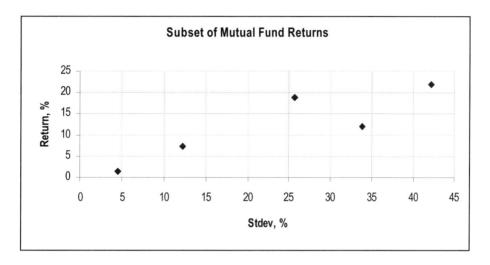

The data do not fall on a straight line (nor would any other actual market data), but we can draw a line by eye to estimate the trend of the data. The problem with drawing by eye, though, is each person will get a different answer, and we want the best straight line possible. This is achieved using linear regression. Following is a fit of the data.

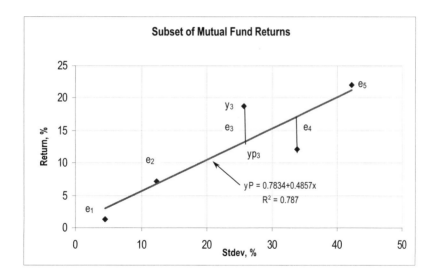

Each observation of the standard deviation ("x") has two corresponding responses ("y"): the observed response and the predicted response. The trend line, since linear, is of the form $y_p = a + bx$. For the third point, for example, the observed value is y_3. There is also a value predicted by the trend line, yp_3. The difference between the observed value and the predicted value at x_i is called the *deviation* δ_i, or *error* e_i. Both x and y are random variables. We sum the squares of all deviations (total variation in y, SST), and minimize this total error by differentiating the resulting expression. In the following, n is the number of data points.

$$\sum_{i=1}^{n} \delta_i^2 = \sum_{i=1}^{n} \left(y_i - y_{pi}\right)^2 = \sum_{i=1}^{n} \left(y_i - \left(a + bx_i\right)\right)^2 = \sum_{i=1}^{n} y_i^2 - 2\left(a + bx_i\right)y_i + \left(a + bx_i\right)^2$$

To minimize, differentiate the sum of squared deviations with respect to both unknowns, a and b, and set the resulting expressions to zero. We find

$$\frac{\partial}{\partial a} \sum_{i=1}^{n} \delta_i^2 = \sum_{i=1}^{n} \left(-2y_i + 2a + 2bx_i\right) = -2\sum_{i=1}^{n} \left(y_i - a - bx_i\right) = 0$$

$$\frac{\partial}{\partial b} \sum_{i=1}^{n} \delta_i^2 = \sum_{i=1}^{n} \left(-2y_i x_i + 2ax_i + 2bx_i^2\right) = -2\sum_{i=1}^{n} \left(x_i y_i - ax_i - bx_i^2\right) = 0$$

$$\frac{\partial}{\partial a} : \sum_{i=1}^{n} a + b\sum_{i=1}^{n} x_i = \sum_{i=1}^{n} y_i$$

$$\frac{\partial}{\partial b} : \sum_{i=1}^{n} x_i + b\sum_{i=1}^{n} x_i^2 = \sum_{i=1}^{n} x_i y_i$$

but since the sum of a, n times, is just n times a, we get finally:

$$\frac{\partial}{\partial a} : na + b\sum_{i=1}^{n} x_i = \sum_{i=1}^{n} y_i$$

$$\frac{\partial}{\partial b} : \sum_{i=1}^{n} x_i + b\sum_{i=1}^{n} x_i^2 = \sum_{i=1}^{n} x_i y_i$$

Solving this linear system of equations for a and b gives:

$$b = \frac{\sum_{i=1}^{n} x_i \sum_{i=1}^{n} y_i - n\sum_{i=1}^{n} x_i y_i}{\left(\sum_{i=1}^{n} x_i\right)^2 - \sum_{i=1}^{n} x_i^2} , \quad a = \frac{\sum_{i=1}^{n} y_i - b\sum_{i=1}^{n} x_i}{n} = \bar{y} - b\bar{x}$$

1391890763L   1391725130/

Applying this to our example:

	stdev	return		
i	x	y	x y	x^2
1	4.57	1.33	6.0781	20.8849
2	12.26	7.2	88.272	150.3076
3	25.67	18.8	482.596	658.9489
4	33.81	12.12	409.7772	1143.1161
5	42.15	22	927.3	1776.6225
Sum	118.46	61.45	1914.023	3749.88

Then, $b = \dfrac{118.46(61.45) - 5(1914.023)}{118.46^2 - 5(3749.88)} = 0.4857$, $a = \bar{y} - b\bar{x} = 0.7834$

The fitted trend line is $y = 0.7834 + 0.4857x$. This means that y (standard deviation) increases by 0.4857 for each unit change in x (return). The value of a is the intercept that is the value of y even when x is zero. This has the meaning of "risk free return" in this context. This technique is the same one used to estimate the coefficients α and β in the CAPM.

We must also compute the error of the regression. There are two components: the variation in the data explained by the regression equation, and the portion that is not explained. The first term is called **SSR (the sum squared of error due to regression)** and the second, **SSE (the sum of squared errors)**.

The sum of SSR and SSE is **SST (the sum squared total error)**. If we divide SSR by SST we have R^2, which runs between 0 and 1, and means the percentage of variation of the data explained by the regression equation. The higher the R^2 the better. $SSR = \displaystyle\sum_{i=1}^{n} \left(Y_{pred} - \bar{Y} \right)^2$ here, we take $Y = a + b\,X_i$ for each point, subtract the average value of observed Y from it and this gives SSR. SST is defined as the squared differences of observed ys from the mean, $SST = \displaystyle\sum_{i=1}^{n} \left(Y_i - \bar{Y} \right)^2$ We find SSR = 222.43 and SST = 282.73 so

	stdev	return				
i	x	y	x y	x^2	SSR	SST
1	4.57	1.33	6.0781	20.8849	86.24745888	120.1216
2	12.26	7.2	88.272	150.3076	30.82379348	25.9081
3	25.67	18.8	482.596	658.9489	0.92413422	42.3801
4	33.81	12.12	409.7772	1143.1161	24.15640912	0.0289
5	42.15	22	927.3	1776.6225	80.38296958	94.2841
Sum	118.46	61.45	1914.023	3749.88	222.5347653	282.7228

R^2		78.7%

that R^2 = 78.7%.

The idea behind linear regression analysis is that there is some population y that depends on the observed x. Since the observations are just sample drawings from a distribution that is unobservable, we expect some error in our trend line – different samples of data will result in different regression equations. There are many ways to fit a line (for example, by eye or by using Mean Average Deviations (MAD)).

Linear Regression is the technique of estimating the unobserved population *response y* with the "Best", "Linear", "Unbiased" "Estimator", or **BLUE**.

Tests for significance of statistical variables

One final thing of great importance: If you do perform a regression and you get some function of the form $y = a + b\,x$, you have to evaluate whether the regression coefficients a and b that you have calculated are statistically significant. This is done using the **t-statistic**. The t-statistic basically tells you how many standard deviations your calculated value is from some other chosen value, usually the assumed value for the underlying population. Because the regression coefficients are calculated on a sample population, it is always possible that they are very different from the actual values. It is also possible that they all might equal zero.

Steps:
1. State the **null hypothesis** H_0. An example would be that the actual intercept is zero.
2. Choose the **level of significance** α such as 0.05 (this value of α means that you want to be $1-0.05 = 95\%$ confident).
3. Decide whether you want a **one-tailed** or a **two-tailed** test. In a one-tailed test you are concerned with whether your target is greater or less than some target. Two–tailed tests are used in situations where you want to test whether the coefficient is different from some target, so you would accept positive or negative deviations from the target. For two-tailed tests, you must use $\alpha/2$.
4. Calculate the **degrees of freedom (dof)** for the sample. For simple linear regression, since you are calculating two regression coefficients, the dof is n-2.
5. Using your desired level of significance α, dof and number of tails for your test, look up the corresponding t-statistic in tables or by using Excel. This is called the **critical t-value,** or $t_{critical}$.
6. Calculate the t-statistic according to the following formulas depending on which variable you are testing. This is called t_{calc}.
7. Interpret the results. If $|t_{calc}| > t_{critical}$ reject the null hypothesis – the variable is significant. If $|t_{calc}| = t_{critical}$ accept the null hypothesis.

Rule of thumb: For a significance level of 0.05, the critical t-value is 1.96, which can be rounded to 2.0 for large samples of data.

Significance of regression correlation coefficient $t_{calc} = \left| \dfrac{r_{yx}\sqrt{n-2}}{\sqrt{1-r_{yx}^2}} \right|$

Significance of regression coefficients a and b $t_{calc} = \left| \dfrac{a-\alpha}{s_a} \right|, t_{calc} = \left| \dfrac{b-\beta}{s_b} \right|$

Example   Let's test our mutual fund data with a significance level of 5% and two tails. We have n = 5 data points so *dof* = 3. Then $t_{crit} = 3.61$.

We had $R^2 = 0.787$ so $r_{yx} = 0.8871$ (square root of R^2, just different notation). Then $t_{calc} = \left|\dfrac{0.8871\sqrt{5-2}}{\sqrt{1-0.787}}\right|$

$= 2.43 < 3.61$. We accept the null hypothesis and conclude that our R^2 is not significantly different from zero. Now are the regression coefficients significantly different from zero?

$$t_{calc} = \left|\frac{0.783-0}{3.995}\right| = 0.196 < t_{crit}, \; for\; b, t_{calc} = \left|\frac{0.4857-0}{0.1459}\right| = 3.329 > t_{crit}$$

So the intercept is not statistically significantly different from zero, while the slope is. What this actually means is that the value found for a is only 0.196 standard deviations away from zero and the value of b is 3.329 standard deviations from zero, supporting the idea that a is not significantly different from zero, and so forth. Such results are typical in the CAPM. Fund managers will often claim to beat their benchmark, which could be the S&P 500. If you regress Fund Performance = $a + b$ Market Performance, you will often find that a is not significantly different from zero. But this is the value that fund managers are supposed to add for the fees they collect, so significance tests are very important.

Other types of regression models

Depending on the nature of the relationship of the dependent to independent variables, it may be more appropriate to fit quadratic forms $y = a + bx + cx^2$, exponential forms $y = \alpha e^{\beta x}$ or logarithmic forms. The best way to decide what model to use is to just plot y as a function of x. Also, of course, always use common sense in your judgment. If you are building a model to forecast corporate bond prices as a function of spreads to treasuries and you find that the bond prices depend on the square of the spread, ask yourself if this is reasonable and what could be driving it. Your regression results are only as good as the analysis and data going into them.

Multiple regression, linear or not, is used in cases of more than one explanatory factor. If you have a large set of data and many potential explanatory factors, there are techniques such as best subsets regression, principal components or factor analysis that may be used. For such series the appropriate statistical test to use is the **F-test**, which tests a group of factors all at once to see whether they are statistically significant. Then individual t-tests may be used on each regression coefficient as before. Also, be wary interpreting a high R^2 to imply a high degree of explanatory power.

Time series data

Many financial data series are examples of **time series** – data collected for the same variable over time. Other data is **cross-sectional** – data summarized at a single point in time for different variables (such as end-of-year mutual fund performance for a large collection of funds.) Suppose we have historical weekly prices of the S&P 500 over a certain period of time and want to build a model to predict future prices.

Time Series of S&P500 Prices 1988-2002

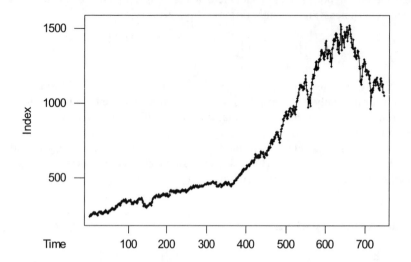

The time series plot seems to imply a trend of the form $y = a + b\,t$. A regression model on the data yields $a = 74.81$, $b = 1.687$ so Index $= 74.81 + 1.687\,t$, and $R^2 = 85.4\%$. For financial data, this R^2 is huge. But is this model "correct?"

```
Predictor         Coef       SE Coef            T          P
Constant         74.81         11.03         6.78      0.000
Time           1.68700       0.02551        66.14      0.000

S = 150.6        R-Sq = 85.4%     R-Sq(adj) = 85.4%

Analysis of Variance

Source            DF            SS            MS          F          P
Regression         1      99254693      99254693    4374.31      0.000
Residual Error   746      16927007         22690
Total            747     116181700
```

The model means that if this week's closing value of the index is 1052.7, the value for the next time period will increase by $74.81 + 1.687 = 76.49$. Problems with this model: it has a constant "trend" term of 1.687 so the prediction is the index will always be increasing. This is probably unlikely in the short run but may be reasonable over the long run. A more serious problem is that in building this particular model, we have completely ignored the fact that S&P 500 index values are highly correlated over time. The autocorrelation function looks like:

ACF function of S&P500 Price Series

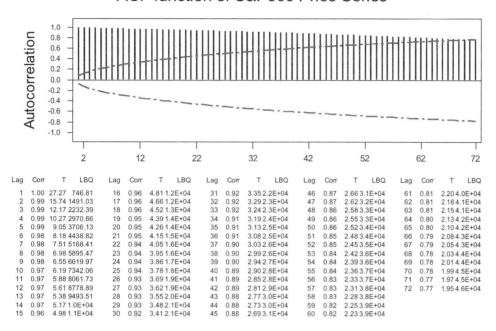

Lag	Corr	T	LBQ	Lag	Corr	T	LBQ	Lag	Corr	T	LBQ	Lag	Corr	T	LBQ	Lag	Corr	T	LBQ
1	1.00	27.27	746.81	16	0.96	4.81	1.2E+04	31	0.92	3.35	2.2E+04	46	0.87	2.66	3.1E+04	61	0.81	2.20	4.0E+04
2	0.99	15.74	1491.03	17	0.96	4.66	1.2E+04	32	0.92	3.29	2.3E+04	47	0.87	2.62	3.2E+04	62	0.81	2.18	4.1E+04
3	0.99	12.17	2232.39	18	0.96	4.52	1.3E+04	33	0.92	3.24	2.3E+04	48	0.86	2.58	3.3E+04	63	0.81	2.15	4.1E+04
4	0.99	10.27	2970.66	19	0.95	4.39	1.4E+04	34	0.91	3.19	2.4E+04	49	0.86	2.55	3.3E+04	64	0.80	2.13	4.2E+04
5	0.99	9.05	3706.13	20	0.95	4.26	1.4E+04	35	0.91	3.13	2.5E+04	50	0.86	2.52	3.4E+04	65	0.80	2.10	4.2E+04
6	0.98	8.18	4438.82	21	0.95	4.15	1.5E+04	36	0.91	3.08	2.5E+04	51	0.85	2.48	3.4E+04	66	0.79	2.08	4.3E+04
7	0.98	7.51	5168.41	22	0.94	4.05	1.6E+04	37	0.90	3.03	2.6E+04	52	0.85	2.45	3.5E+04	67	0.79	2.05	4.3E+04
8	0.98	6.98	5895.47	23	0.94	3.95	1.6E+04	38	0.90	2.99	2.6E+04	53	0.84	2.42	3.6E+04	68	0.78	2.03	4.4E+04
9	0.98	6.55	6619.97	24	0.94	3.86	1.7E+04	39	0.90	2.94	2.7E+04	54	0.84	2.39	3.6E+04	69	0.78	2.01	4.4E+04
10	0.97	6.19	7342.06	25	0.94	3.78	1.8E+04	40	0.89	2.90	2.8E+04	55	0.84	2.36	3.7E+04	70	0.78	1.99	4.5E+04
11	0.97	5.88	8061.73	26	0.93	3.69	1.9E+04	41	0.89	2.85	2.8E+04	56	0.83	2.33	3.7E+04	71	0.77	1.97	4.5E+04
12	0.97	5.61	8778.89	27	0.93	3.62	1.9E+04	42	0.89	2.81	2.9E+04	57	0.83	2.31	3.8E+04	72	0.77	1.95	4.6E+04
13	0.97	5.38	9493.51	28	0.93	3.55	2.0E+04	43	0.88	2.77	3.0E+04	58	0.83	2.28	3.8E+04				
14	0.97	5.17	1.0E+04	29	0.93	3.48	2.1E+04	44	0.88	2.73	3.0E+04	59	0.82	2.25	3.9E+04				
15	0.96	4.98	1.1E+04	30	0.92	3.41	2.1E+04	45	0.88	2.69	3.1E+04	60	0.82	2.23	3.9E+04				

This means that prior values have significant influence on future values. We can perform another type of regression called a time series analysis by regressing today's value on last week's value. This is called an **AR(1) regression** – Auto Regression of Lag 1 (period.) Simply plotting the index as a function of the prior weeks' index level indicates a high correlation. The form for this model is $Y_t = \alpha + \beta Y_{t-1} + \varepsilon_t$.

Regression of S&P500 on Lagged Index

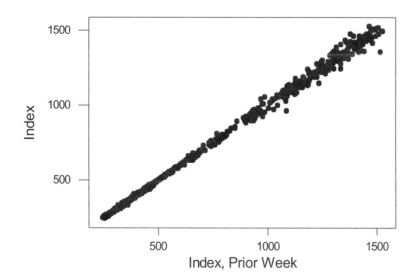

Running the regression of y_t (index at time t) against y_{t-1} (prior week's) gives an R^2 of almost 100%.

```
Predictor          Coef       SE Coef              T           P
Constant          2.331         1.543           1.51       0.131
C3             0.998234      0.001908         523.21       0.000

S = 20.55       R-Sq = 99.7%      R-Sq(adj) = 99.7%
```

This high degree of autocorrelation caused the R^2 in the trend analysis to be overstated. The autocorrelations must be removed before performing standard regression if you do not wish to get spurious results.

Random walks

It may be that the series is just a **random walk**. The form we will use for the random walk is the AR(1) equation. Of course, other models involving two lags (AR(2)), 12 lags (AR(12)), etc., are appropriate depending on the data.

In the AR(1) model $Y_t = \alpha + \beta Y_{t-1} + \varepsilon_t$

The first two terms are the part that depends on the past (predictable), and the last term on the right is the random error that is not predictable from the past. The errors must be normally distributed with mean of zero and standard deviation of σ^2 and independent of Y_t, Y_{t-1} and so forth. In this expression, β is the "drift" term. The four following plots compare the effect of different βs on the trend.

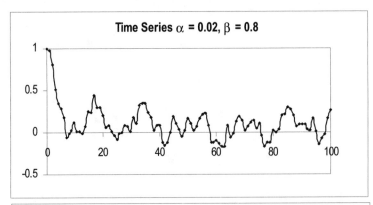

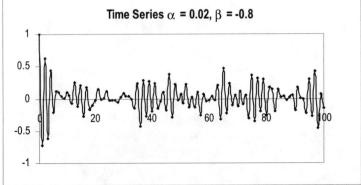

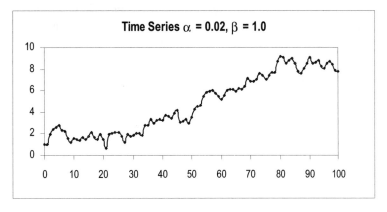

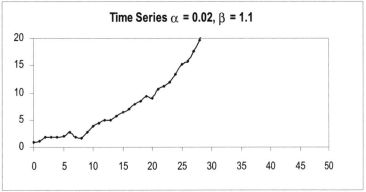

The series of the first time series seems to wander off quite a bit in one direction or other, but something appears to be pulling it back to the mean when it wanders off too far. This is the concept of **mean-reversion** – on average, the expected values of Y_{t-1} and Y_t are both μ. Substitution of this definition into the AR(1) expression gives:

$$\mu = \alpha + \beta\mu \ \text{ so } \ \mu = \frac{\alpha}{1-\beta}$$

Subtracting μ from both sides of the AR(1) equation gives $Y_t - \mu = \beta(Y_{t-1} - \mu) + \varepsilon_t$

In the first picture, the average of the data is 0.11. We calculate $\mu = \dfrac{0.02}{1-0.8} = 0.1$ The AR(1) equation for the first series is $Y_t = 0.02 + 0.8\ Y_{t-1} + \varepsilon_t$ Here, $Y_t - \mu = 0.8(Y_{t-1} - \mu) + \varepsilon_t$ which means that an above-average Y_t will tend to be followed by another above-average Y_t (but in a decreasing way since $\beta < 1$) until a large enough error occurs to make Y_t below average. Then, a below-average Y_t will tend to be followed by another below-average Y_t until a large positive error comes along. This behavior produces the "wandering" behavior characteristic of series that exhibit mean-reversion.

In the second picture, the actual mean is 0.01 and the calculated mean is 0.011. For this series $Y_t - \mu = -0.8(Y_{t-1} - \mu) + \varepsilon_t$ so an above-average Y_t tends to be followed by a below-average Y_t. This behavior causes the oscillation evident in this graph.

The third series appears to just wander off, with no evident mean-reversion. The mean is, in fact, undefined since $\beta = 1$. If β is even just close to one, the series is pretty much just driven by the random error since we have $Y_t - \mu \cong (Y_{t-1} - \mu) + \varepsilon_t$. This is the classic definition of the random walk.

In the final series, the growth is explosive. This will occur any time that $|\beta| > 1$.

Summary Characteristics of AR(1) Series
Mean Reversion $0 < \beta < 1$
Oscillation $-1 < \beta < 0$
Random Walk $|\beta| = 1$
Explosive Series $|\beta| > 1$

Now that we know all of this, what do you think of our time-series regression model for the S&P 500? Is the S&P500 just a random walk or is it predictable?

There is much more that can be said about the very important fields of statistics and econometrics, but hopefully this will give you a good start.

Sample Questions and Answers

Questions

1. You flip a coin 10 times. What is the probability of only three heads occurring? What is the probability of three heads occurring in a row? *(Actual interview question, J.P. Morgan.)*

2. If you believe that there is a 40% chance of earning a 10% return on a stock, a 50% change of losing 5% and a 10% chance of losing 20%, what is the expected gain/(loss) on the stock?

    $\beta \approx 0.99$

3. A trader comes to you with a model for forecasting the performance of the S&P 500. His model asserts that S&P 500$_t$ = a + 0.99 S&P 500$_{t-1}$ with an R^2 of 0.99. He wants to start trading on this basis right away. What would you say about his model? *(Actual interview question, Lazard Freres.)*

4. What is linear regression? *(Actual interview question, hedge fund.)*

5. If the monthly standard deviation of a stock is 1%, what would the annual standard deviation be?

6. A portfolio manager is considering two stocks. Stock A has an annual expected return of 10% and an expected standard deviation of 20%. Stock B has an annual expected return of 15% and an expected standard deviation of 30%. What proportion of the portfolio should consist of stock A if the portfolio should have an expected return of 12%? What will the standard deviation of this portfolio be? What should the manager do if she wishes to minimize the volatility of the portfolio?

7. A portfolio manager has chosen a stock for a client which has an average historical return of 2%/month and a standard deviation of 15%/month. What are the annual values?

8. A regression of a time series of monthly American Airline returns (R_{AA}) on the variables fuel prices (FP) and average passenger revenue/mile (PR) results in the following equation:
    R_{AA} = 0.056 - 0.0036 FP + 0.0118 PR
    where there are 120 data points, the standard error of the intercept is 0.035, the standard error of the coefficient of fuel price is 0.001 and the standard error of the passenger revenue/mile is 0.005. Which variables, if any, are significant?

9. If in the above regression we had found R_{AA} = 0.056 + 0.0036 FP + 0.0118 PR what would you conclude regarding the suitability of this model?

10. Consider a mutual fund prospectus that claims the fund's manager "beat the market" each year over the past ten years by two percent. Assume that the standard deviation of the market over this period has been 20% on average. What do you think about his claim?

11. A portfolio manager has chosen for a client a stock with an average historical return of 2%/month and a standard deviation of 15%/month. What are the annual values?

12. What is the probability that the rate of return of this stock will fall below zero for a given month? What range of values would be expected using a 95% confidence interval?

13. You have compiled estimates of annual returns and standard deviations for a certain time series of interest. Your boss claims that using more frequent data, such as daily data, will improve your estimates. What would you say to this?

14. How do you calculate the logarithmic value of a stock return? Why would you do this?

15. You purchase a stock for $100. The next day it goes to $200 and the following day back to $100. What are the average, mean and logarithmic returns over this period and what do you conclude about logarithmic returns on the basis of this example?

Answers

1. For the first question, you want a combination. How many ways can you choose three items from a set of 10? We have to use a combination here because the interviewer did not ask about a specific order. So $x = 3$ and $n = 10$ in $_nC_x = \dfrac{n!}{x!(n-x)!} = \dfrac{10!}{3!(7!)} = \dfrac{10*9*8*7!}{3!7!} = \dfrac{720}{6} = 120$ so the probability is $120/2^{10} \sim 0.117$

    For the second problem it might be easier to list all of the ways three heads in a row can happen. Another way to think of this is by thinking of each flip as "heads-TRUE" or "heads-FALSE". In this case, a binomial distribution is appropriate. You will get a distribution that looks like $\{H^{10}T^0,$ $H^9T^1, H^8T^2, ..., H^2T^8, H^1T^9, H^0T^{10}\}$ or in general H^xT^{n-x} where x runs from 0 to n and n is the number of flips. The coefficients of the H^xT^{n-x} are the binomial coefficients, $_nC_x = \begin{pmatrix} n \\ x \end{pmatrix}$ is the number of combinations of x items taken n at a time. If we are interested in just three heads, we have n = 3 and x = 10, or 120. For the second question, you might want to ask the interviewer if there are only to be three heads total in the sequence or if you could have three heads, then a tail, then some other combination of heads and tails. Never be shy to ask for more information.

    If she says "just three heads in a row and no other heads." then the answer is easy. You can just enumerate cases to find that out of the possible result like {HHHTTTTTTT},{THHHTTTTTT}, {TTHHHTTTTT}, {TTTHHHTTTT},{TTTTHHHTTT},{TTTTTHHHTT},{TTTTTTHHHT} or {TTTTTTTHHH}. There are only eight ways to do this out of a possible 2^{10} total possibilities so the probability would be $8/2^{10}$.

2. $0.40(10\%)+0.50(-5\%)+0.1(-20\%) = -0.5\%$.

3. Since $(1-\beta)$ in the denominator is close to zero, you can answer this one buy asking the interviewer, "How do you know it is not just a random walk?" (You can also go into more detail about Granger causality and econometric tests that might be performed.)

4. Focus on BLUE. A sketch is a good idea, too. You can also derive the equations, that is, if you can.

5. You multiply by the square root of t (here, the square root of 12) by monthly standard deviation to get 3.46%/year.

6. For this question, the expected return is just the weighted average of the individual returns. The formula is $E[R_P] = w R_A + (1-w)R_B$ so we have $12\% = w\,10\% + (1-w)\,20\%$ for $w = 0.8$, just a linear relationship. To answer the volatility question, we need to know the covariance between stocks A and B, since $\sigma_{R_p}^2 = w^2\sigma_A^2 + (1-w)^2\sigma_B^2 + 2w(1-w)\rho\sigma_A\sigma_B$

If the correlation is -1, we will have a variance-minimizing portfolio. If the goal is to minimize volatility, w would change: we have $\sigma_{R_p}^2 = w^2\sigma_A^2 + (1-w)^2\sigma_B^2 - 2w(1-w)\sigma_A\sigma_B$. Differentiation of this expression with respect to w gives $-0.3(1-w) + 0.2w = 0$ or $w = 0.6$.

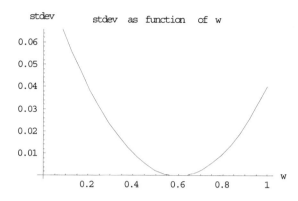

stdev as function of w

Here, the portfolio variance (and hence standard deviation) is then $0.6^2 *0.2^2 + 0.4^2 *0.3^2 - 2 *0.6 *0.4* 0.2 *0.3 = 0$.

7. To annualize, remember that mean and variance scale with the horizon. Standard deviation scales with the square root of horizon. Then, the annual return based on a monthly return is 12*monthly return = 12*2% = 24%. The estimated annual volatility is $\sqrt{T}\sigma = \sqrt{12}\ 15\% = 51.96\%$.

8. Since n is reasonably large, we can use the rule of thumb that the computed t-value should be compared to $t_{critical} = 2.0$. For the intercept, the computed t-value is 0.056/.035=1.6 so the intercept is not significantly different from zero. For the coefficient of fuel price, the t-value is |-.0036|/0.001 = 3.6 so this coefficient is significant; the coefficient of passenger revenue/mile is also significant because 0.0118/0.005 = 2.36 > 2.

9. Since fuel price is an expense it should have an adverse effect on revenue and would therefore be expected to have a negative coefficient; since it does not in this regression, we suspect a problem with this form. Perhaps we have serial correlation or just a bad model.

10. In order to determine if someone has truly "beaten the market," we have to evaluate the t-statistic. The variable of interest is the excess return $R_e = R_{fund} - R_{market}$. In order for the difference between the returns to be statistically significant, the return excess must be greater or equal to two times the standard deviation:

$$E(R_f - R_m) \geq 2\sigma(\overline{R}_f - \overline{R}_m) = \frac{2\sigma(R_f - R_m)}{\sqrt{T}}$$

The variance of the excess return is:

$$\sigma^2(R_f - R_m) = \sigma^2(R_f) + \sigma^2(R_m) - 2\rho_{f,m}\sigma(R_f)\sigma(R_m)$$

If we assume that the fund is about as risky as the market, then $\sigma(R_f) \sim \sigma(R_m)$ and

$$\sigma^2\left(R_f - R_m\right) \approx 2\sigma^2(R) - 2\rho_{f,m}\sigma^2(R) = 2\sigma^2(R)(1-\rho)$$

Solving for ρ gives $E\left(R_f - R_m\right) \geq \dfrac{2\sigma\left(R_f - R_m\right)}{\sqrt{T}} \geq \dfrac{2\sqrt{2\sigma^2(R)(1-\rho)}}{\sqrt{T}}$

$$\rho = 1 - \frac{1}{2}\left(\frac{\sqrt{T}\,E\left(R_f - R_m\right)}{2\sigma(R)}\right)^2$$

If $T = 10$ years, the variance of the market is 20% and the expected excess return is 2%, then $\rho = 0.9875$. This means that the fund's manager would have to have beaten the market while maintaining very high (almost 99%) correlation with it. It turns out that a 10-year period is not nearly long enough to claim persistence of positive excess returns. If we solve for T assuming that the average market return is 8% and standard deviation is 20%, we see that it takes at least 25 years for the market return to even be significantly different from zero. And, we have to take survivor bias into account: Was the manager managing the same fund over the entire period? Did the objectives change? Were unsuccessful funds dropped, and their negative returns not included in the "successful" returns? Also, often managers will stray from stated fund objectives. If this is supposed to be an "income fund", for example, obtaining a high return by perhaps using leverage through short selling and/or derivatives may violate the stated objectives of the fund and risk tolerance of the investors.

11. To annualize, remember that mean and variance scale with the horizon. Standard deviation scales with the square root of horizon. Then, the annual return based on a monthly return is 12*monthly return = 12*2% = 24%. The estimated annual volatility is $\sqrt{T}\sigma = \sqrt{12}\ 15\% = 51.96\%$.

12. Probability that the return will fall below zero in a given month is calculated as $\Pr(z<0)$ where $z = (0 - R)/\sigma = (0-0.02)/0.15 = -0.13333$. $N(z) = \text{NORMSDIST}(-0.13333) = 0.4469$, or 44.69%. Since we want a 95% confidence interval, we have $\alpha = 0.05$ and, for a two-tailed test, $\alpha/2 = 0.025$. The z value for which the cumulative normal distribution $= 0.025$ is -1.96 so the interval is $(r-1.96\sigma,\ r+1.96\sigma) = (0.02-1.96*0.15,\ 0.02+1.96*0.15) = (-0.274, 0.314)$.

13. Increasing the frequency of data does not improve precision. The boss's statement implies that we will be able to increase our estimate of the true, unobserved population mean by more frequent sampling, that is, the error $\{R-E(R)|$ will decrease. This is not true. Consider the following cases: case 1, using 10 years of annual observations, and case 2, using 10 years of daily observations.

<u>Case 1: Ten Years of Annual Observations</u> The estimate of annual mean return, assuming

constant deviation, is $\dfrac{1}{10}\sum\limits_{i=1}^{10}(R_i - E(R)) = \dfrac{1}{10}\sum\limits_{i=1}^{10}\delta_i = \bar{\delta}$

<u>Case 2: Ten Years of Daily Observations</u> The estimate of annual mean return, assuming constant

deviation, is $\dfrac{1}{10*365}\sum\limits_{i=1}^{10*365}(R_i - E(R)) = \dfrac{1}{3650}\sum\limits_{i=1}^{3650}\delta_i = \bar{\delta}$

What would improve is our estimate of the standard error. For the daily observations, this would

be equal to $\dfrac{1}{\sqrt{365}}\sigma_{annual}$ However, we would just get back the annual variance when we

annualize by multiplying by the square root of 365. Conclusion: there is no improvement in estimate of mean return obtainable by using more frequent sampling.

14. Some background: For stock prices, we assume a logarithmic distribution rather than normal distribution, but we assume returns are normally distributed and iid (independently and identically distributed). So why do we use logarithmic returns? Ignoring any dividends, the return on a stock is calculated as $(P_i - P_{i-1})/P_{i-1} = (P_i/P_{i-1}) - 1$. For example, if we buy a stock for \$100 and sell it for \$105, the holding period return is $(105/100) - 1 = 5\%$. Instead, we can use logs to calculate the returns: $r = \ln(P_i/P_{i-1}) = \ln(1.05) = 0.0487 = 4.87\%$. If we set $x = (P_i/P_{i-1})$ then expanding $\ln(x)$ in a Taylor Series about the point 1 gives

$$\ln(x) \cong \ln(1) + (x-1) - \frac{1}{2}(x-1)^2 + \frac{1}{3}(x-1)^3 - \frac{1}{4}(x-1)^4 + \cdots$$

Taking just the first term, for x close to 1, we have the approximation $\ln(x) \sim x-1$ or $\ln(P_i/P_{i-1}) \sim (P_i/P_{i-1})-1$.

15. Make a table:

Period	Price, $	r_i, %	$R_i = 1 + r_i$	$Ln(r_i)$
1	100	100%		
2	200	-50%	200%	0.6931
3	100		50%	-0.6931
Average			125%	0

The mean return is defined as the expectation of the returns, $\mu = E(R) = \sum\limits_{i=1}^{2}(R_i - \bar{R})$ Thus, $\mu = (200-125)+(50-125) = 75-75 = 0\%$.

The compound return is $R_m = R_1 R_2 = 2\,(\frac{1}{2}) = 1$ so that $r_m = 1 - R_m = 0$.

The average of the logarithmic returns is zero, which is as it should be: you bought the stock, it went up, and then it returned to the original price, resulting in no net gain.

Summary of Formulas

Linear Regression
$$b = \frac{\sum_{i=1}^{n} x_i \sum_{i=1}^{n} y_i - n \sum_{i=1}^{n} x_i y_i}{\left(\sum_{i=1}^{n} x_i\right)^2 - \sum_{i=1}^{n} x_i^2}, \quad a = \frac{\sum_{i=1}^{n} y_i - b \sum_{i=1}^{n} x_i}{n} = \bar{y} - b\bar{x}$$

Expectations of Random Variables For α constant, $E(\alpha X) = \alpha E(X)$
Expectation of a constant $\quad E(\alpha) = \alpha$
Variance of Random Variable $\quad \sigma^2(\alpha R) = \alpha^2 \sigma_R^2$
Variance of a constant $\quad \text{Var}(\alpha) = 0$
Variance of a linear combination $\quad \text{Var}(\alpha + \beta X) = \text{Var}(\alpha) + \text{Var}(\beta X) = \beta^2 \sigma_X^2.$

Mean
$$\bar{x} = \frac{\sum_{i=1}^{n} x_i}{n}$$

Expected return of portfolio of assets $E(R_P) = E\left(\sum_{i=1}^{n} w_i R_i\right) = \sum_{i=1}^{n} w_i E(R_i)$

Number of Permutations of x objects chosen from n $\quad _n P_x = \dfrac{n!}{(n-x)!}$

Number of combinations of x objects chosen from n $\quad _n C_x = \dfrac{n!}{x!(n-x)!} = \dfrac{1}{x!} {_n P_x}$

Correlation between x and y
$$r = \frac{\sum_{i=1}^{n} (x - \bar{x})(y - \bar{y})}{(n-1)\sigma_x \sigma_y}$$

Coefficient of Determination $\quad \rho = r^2 \qquad 0 \le \rho \le 1$

Covariance between two assets $\quad COV_{1,2} = \rho_{1,2} \sigma_1 \sigma_2$

Central Limit Theorem if n is sufficiently large then

$$\sqrt{n}\bar{X} \sim N(\mu, \sigma^2), \quad \frac{\bar{X} - \mu}{\frac{\sigma}{\sqrt{n}}} \sim N(0,1)$$

Expected Return of Portfolio with n assets

$$E\left(R_p\right) = \sum_{i=1}^{n} w_i E\left(R_i\right)$$

Variance of Portfolio with Two Assets

$$\sigma_{R_P}^2 = w_1^2 \sigma_1^2 + w_2^2 \sigma_2^2 + 2 w_1 w_2 COV_{1,2}$$

$$\sigma_{R_P}^2 = w_1^2 \sigma_1^2 + w_2^2 \sigma_2^2 + 2 w_1 w_2 \rho_{1,2} \sigma_1 \sigma_2$$

Probability Density Function of Normal Distribution $\quad f(x) = \dfrac{1}{\sqrt{2\pi\sigma^2}} e^{-(x-\mu)^2/2\sigma^2}$

Properties of Normal Distribution $X \sim N(\mu, \sigma^2)$

Mean of Normal Distribution	μ
Variance of Normal Distribution	σ^2

Significance of regression correlation coefficient $\quad t_{calc} = \left| \dfrac{r_{yx}\sqrt{n-2}}{\sqrt{1-r_{yx}^2}} \right|$

Significance of regression coefficients a and b $\quad t_{calc} = \left| \dfrac{a-\alpha}{s_a} \right|, t_{calc} = \left| \dfrac{b-\beta}{s_b} \right|$

The probability density function of lognormal distribution $\quad f(x) = \dfrac{1}{\sigma x \sqrt{2\pi}} e^{-(\ln(x)-\mu)^2/(2\sigma^2)}$ **, x>0**

DERIVATIVES

Introduction to Derivatives

A **derivative** is a financial claim whose value is derived from the value of the underlying contract. A gold futures contract is a derivative that depends on the underlying value of gold, while an option on a Eurodollar futures contract depends on the value of the underlying Eurodollar futures contract. Derivatives are also referred to as **contingent claims**, and range from a simple forward contract to highly complex options that depend on the price history of the underlying asset. Derivatives can be purchased on exchanges or custom-tailored to the parties' needs as OTC (over-the-counter) transactions. Derivatives exist to enable market participants to transfer risk, to take a position, or to exploit market mispricings. Market participants who wish to transfer risk are called **hedgers**. Those participants taking a view in the market are called **speculators**. And those who exploit profit opportunities, which may arise from a variety of reasons, are called **arbitrageurs**.

Derivatives play a vital and crucial role in capital markets. In this chapter, we will define and value derivatives, including forwards, futures, swaps and options. As long as you can find a willing counterparty, it seems that you can get a derivative on almost any underlying contract. As of 2000, the list of futures and options authorized by the Commodity Futures Trading Commission (CFTC) included a bankruptcy index; wood and fertilizer futures; and catastrophe, health and homeowners insurance derivatives. There are futures on degree-days in Atlanta as well as on gas and electricity. Credit derivatives are becoming increasingly important, accounting for almost $700 billion by mid-2001, according to the Bank for International Settlements (BIS).

Although modeling and pricing derivatives is important, it is equally important to understand and be able to manage the inherent risk. Sometimes, the unexpected does happen, and catastrophic losses can occur.

Forward Contracts

The **forward contract** is the most basic form of derivative. It is an agreement between two parties (the "counterparties") to make a trade at some future date. One party is S, the seller who agrees to deliver the underlying. The other party is B, the buyer, who agrees to take delivery of the underlying. The seller is also called "short" the contract and the buyer is "long" the contract. The agreement is binding on both parties since a contract is drawn up and executed upon entering the contract. Forward contracts are traded over the counter. The counterparties determine the nature and quality of the asset to be delivered, when delivery will take place (the expiration date of the forward), where delivery will take place and how pricing will be carried out. The OTC contract is custom-tailored to meet the needs of the counterparties.

Forward contracts enable market participants such as farmers to hedge their price risk. If a farmer has corn in the ground in May that he anticipates selling next July, he may worry that the price will fall before he can get the corn to the market. To hedge away this undesirable price risk, he can arrange to lock in a forward price today. The forward price he locks in may or may not be the price that actually prevails in July, but he has locked in a guaranteed price. On the other hand, the counterparty is speculating that the ultimate price for corn in July will be higher than the contracted price. The counterparty does not own the asset and so is not subject to the same price risk as the farmer. The forward contract establishes a shifting of price risk from the farmer, who does not wish to bear it, to the speculator, who does wish to take this risk on.

Entering a forward contract can help the farmer eliminate the unknown, but will not guarantee a profit. Because a forward contract is essentially a private transaction between two individuals, the creditworthiness of each party is a big factor. A forward transaction is a zero-sum game: one party's loss is the other's gain, so if the losing party decides to default on the contract, the other party is subject to loss. Usually, the contracts are non-transferable, which greatly reduces liquidity. No money changes hands at contract initiation. The payoff occurs only at expiration.

An example of such a contract is when you sell an item on eBay. If someone bids on the item, assuming they have met all of the conditions you have set (such as reserve price), you are bound to deliver the item at the end of the auction, and they are bound to pay for it at the ending price. The "contract" specifies what will be delivered, where it will be delivered and how delivery is to take place, in addition to how payment should be made. In a way, the buyer is agreeing on a forward price for your item. If the buyer defaults, you have some recourse through eBay, and if you default by refusing to deliver the item, the buyer can get recourse through eBay. The items are unique so that if you change your mind, the buyer can't go to another seller to get the identical item at the identical price. And if the buyer changes their mind, you can't easily transfer their contract to another. (You could contact the next bidder on the list, but probably wouldn't get as high a price.)

An example of short selling is if you decide to sell books on Amazon.com. Suppose that you notice that a particular Adobe Photoshop book is selling on the site for $31. You decide to offer one for sale at $29 even though you don't own the book, because coincidentally, you recently saw a street vendor selling the books for $20. If you sell the book, you plan to get one from the street vendor to deliver. In theory, this is a smart strategy because the vendor has to hold the inventory, and you get cash first to purchase the asset. In practice, though, what if the street vendor is not there on the day you wish to purchase the book? Or the vendor raises the price on the book? Or, even, is out of the book? You still have to deliver the book and thus will have to go to a bookstore to purchase it, possibly just breaking even, or even suffering a loss.

Forwards are traded on a diverse array of underlying assets including **financial assets** such as stocks, stock indices, interest rates and currencies; **grains and oils** including coconut, corn and soybean oil; **commodities** such as live hogs, sugar, coffee and orange juice; **natural resources** such as heating oil, gasoline, coal and crude oil; and **metals** such as gold, platinum and copper. We will find that futures have much in common with forwards, but they also have very important differences.

Valuing forward contracts

Suppose the **spot price** (the present price in the market) of corn today is $1.82 per bushel and Mr. McDonald the farmer can lock in a July **forward price** of $2.05 per bushel. Entering into the contract, the farmer is guaranteed -- no matter what -- a price of $2.05 per bushel in July, say, after he harvests his corn. (The contract size for corn is 5,000 bushels.) If the July spot price turns out to be $2.50 per bushel, the farmer will be disappointed, because he could have received $2.50 per bushel but has agreed to accept $2.05. Locking into this forward price causes him to lose out on the potential excess profit over the forward price (per contract size) of $(2.50 − 2.05)*5,000 = $2,250. He will, though, have the $2.05*5,000 = $10,250 per contract size realized from the sale of his corn. (This is the meaning of the statement, "Forward contracts don't guarantee a profit; they just guarantee a price.")

On the other hand, what if corn prices fall to $1.70/bushel by July? The farmer gets a bad price for his corn, $1.70*5,000 = $8,500 but has a gain from his forward position of $(2.05-1.7)*5,000 =$1,750. Total value of his portfolio of corn and forward contract is $10,250. Either way, he has received a net per-bushel price of $2.05, as guaranteed by the forward contract.

Is there a link between the forward price and the spot price? Market participants will want to understand this relationship so they can decide whether to enter into a forward contract.

Because the forward contract is derived from an underlying asset, it can be priced by appealing to the no-arbitrage agreement. We classify our underlying assets as those that can be stored, those that cannot be stored, and those that make cash payments such as coupons and dividend payments. Define spot price as the current price of the underlying. What is the relationship of the forward price to the underlying spot price?

$$t = \text{time } 0 \leq t \leq T$$
$$T = \text{expiration or maturity date of contract}$$
$$S_t = \text{spot price of underlying at time } t$$
$$F_{t,T} = \text{forward price at time } t \text{ for maturity } T$$
$$r = \text{risk-free interest rate}$$

We can use no-arbitrage arguments to form a relationship between S_t and $F_{t,T}$. Suppose that an arbitrageur ("arb" for short) can take either side of the contract. The arb (say, a large investment bank) can borrow and lend money at the risk-free rate r and has no transaction costs. The spot price of the asset today is S_t. The arb's counterparty (a grain elevator, say) quotes a forward price $F_{t,T}$. If the arb thinks that the forward price is too low, that is, the arb believes the actual spot price in July will be higher than $F_{t,T}$, how could the arb profit? (This type of question is always answered by remembering the mantra, "Buy low, sell high.") The arb could short 5,000 bushels of corn in the spot market today receiving S_t, and take the income and put it in the bank, earning a rate r for the period. At the same time, the arb goes long on one forward corn contract, agreeing to purchase the corn in July for $F_{t,T}$. Let's make a chart of the arb's cash flows.

Reverse Cash and Carry Arbitrage			
	time		Comments
Transaction	t	T	
Sell corn in spot market	S_t	$-S_T$	purchase spot for delivery
Invest proceeds in bank	$-S_t$	$e^{r(T-t)}S_t$	interest on deposit
Long forward contract	0	$S_T - F_{t,T}$	profit/(loss) on forward leg of transaction
Total	0	$-F_{t,T}+e^{r(T-t)}S_t$	

The above shows that we require the following relationship to hold:

$$F_{t,T} = S_t e^{r(T-t)}$$

It doesn't matter what the ultimate spot price at maturity (S_T) is: the arb is hedged no matter what. This parity relationship must hold in order to preclude any arbitrage. Although the spot and forward price will vary over time, at maturity, they must converge.

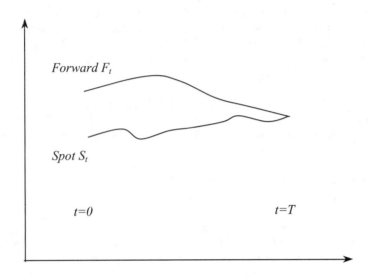

Now what if the arb anticipates that the ultimate spot price will be lower than the forward price? How can the arb profit in this case? The answer is to execute a **cash and carry arbitrage**.

As a numerical example, suppose that the risk-free rate is 5% and **time to expiry** (time to expiration date) is one year. The current spot and forward prices are $S_0 = \$1.985$/bushel, $F_{0,1} = \$2.34$/bushel. The arb sees an arbitrage opportunity when comparing the current futures price $F_{0,1}$ with the expected spot $S_0 e^{0.05(1-0)}$. Since $S_0 e^{0.05(1-0)} = \$1.985\ e^{0.05(1-0)} = \$2.0868 < F_{0,1} = \$2.34$, profit could be made by entering into a forward agreement to deliver corn in one year at the forward price of \$2.34/bushel. In order to be hedged, the arb borrows money at the rate r to finance the purchase of corn in the spot market at S_0. This corn will be sold at maturity for price S_T. The chart of the arb's cash flows appears below.

Cash and Carry Arbitrage			
	time		Comments
Transaction	t	T	
Buy corn in spot market	$-S_t$	S_T	purchase spot for delivery
Borrow money at rate r	S_t	$-e^{r(T-t)}S_t$	for purchase of spot, has to be paid back at T
Short forward contract	0	$F_{t,T}-S_T$	profit/(loss) on forward leg of transaction
Total	0	$F_{t,T}-e^{r(T-t)}S_t$	

Settlement of contract

At maturity, the contract is usually settled by delivery of the agreed upon underlying, if the underlying is some physical asset such as corn, oil or gold. For financial assets such as an exchange rate or forward on the S&P 500, it is not feasible to deliver the actual index, so such contracts are settled in cash. This will be discussed further in the section on futures.

Payoff graphs

Ignoring any transactions costs, let's examine the profit and loss for the corn contract with a July strike of $2.05.

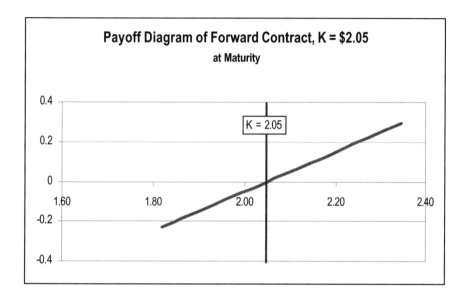

The payoff received will be $S_T - K$. This idea and payoff diagram are important because they will be built upon to develop more complex derivatives.

Valuing forward contracts with additional cash flows

The formula developed to price forward contracts $F_{t,T} = S_t e^{r(T-t)}$ can be extended to include contracts on underlyings that involve storage costs, require insurance, or pay dividends. The combination of all costs (storage, insurance, etc.) is called **the cost of carry**.

For example, if you sell a forward contract to deliver 100 ounces of gold three months from now, you will have to store the gold until delivery. The contract specifications will probably require insurance as well. If s is the total annual cost to store the gold, we can create a cash flow table just as we did before to develop the theoretical price of the forward. You will purchase gold at current spot price S_t by borrowing money at the rate r, as before, but this time you will also need to borrow enough to finance the annualized cost of carry s.

Cash and Carry Arbitrage with Storage Costs			
Transaction	t	T	
Buy gold in spot market	$-S_t$	S_T	purchase spot for delivery at time T on forward
Purchase storage and insurance	$-s$	0	
Borrow money at rate r	S_t+s	$-e^{r(T-t)}(S_t+s)$	for purchase of spot, has to be paid back at T
Sell forward contract (short contract)	0	$F_{t,T}-S_T$	profit/(loss) on forward leg of transaction
Net Proceeds	0	$F_{t,T}-e^{r(T-t)}(S_t+s)$	

We could do the same kind of thing for reverse cash and carry arbitrage. So, it must be the case that, at equilibrium, to preclude arbitrage we must have

$$F_{t,T} = (S_t+s)e^{r(T-t)}$$

Example The spot price of gold is currently \$308.20/troy ounce. The size of a gold contract is 100 troy ounces. If the three month risk-free rate is 1.6%/year and annual cost of carry is \$0.025/troy ounce, what is the three-month forward price of gold?

Answer $S_t = \$308.2$, $s = 0.025$ so $F_{t,T} = \$(308.2+0.025)e^{0.016(0.25)} = \$309.46$.

If the underlying pays a continuous dividend, δ, this can be accounted for in the same way. Although most stocks pay discrete dividends, this model may be appropriate for large indices of stocks such as the S&P 500 or DJIA (Dow Jones Industrial Average). The dividend yield is usually quoted in the financial press. For example, on May 9, 2002, the reported trailing 12-month dividend yield was 1.85% for the DJIA and 1.4% for the S&P 500. If you own the underlying asset, you are entitled to, and will receive, the dividend during the period you own the asset. Future dividends are factored into the current spot price. These dividends will be reinvested at the risk-free rate. (We will discussion this further in the following section.)

Summary of forward contracts

Pros:
- Can be custom-tailored.
- No up-front cost to enter the contract (which is settled at maturity).

Cons:
- Illiquid, cannot be easily reversed.
- Traded over-the-counter, so prices are not observable.
- Exposure to counterparty credit risk – counterparty can just walk away from an adverse position.
- No clearinghouse to regulate and monitor.

Futures Contracts

The futures market overcomes the illiquidity and credit risk problems of the forward market. In the forward market, a contract is drawn up between the buyer (B) and seller (S). If one of these parties later changes their minds and wishes to exit the contract, they can't just transfer their obligation to a third party. In a futures contract, a clearing house (CH) acts as the middleman. The seller S sells to the clearing house CH and then the clearing house sells to the buyer. The intercession of the clearinghouse makes the credit problem go away because each party just deals with the clearing house, usually a large institution such as a bank or large brokerage firm. The credit rating of the clearing house is the concern, not the credit ratings of the counterparties. The contracts are standardized so that they can be traded on large exchanges such as the CBOT, NYMEX and the CME. For example, a futures hedger would call her broker and order one August soybean contract. The contract size, delivery locations, delivery date and grade of soybeans are already set. The only variable is price. Prices are not set but "discovered" in the market.

The clearing house overcomes the credit risk problem observed in the forward market by requiring each counterparty to deposit an **initial margin** before any trading can occur. This initial margin can consist of cash and/or stocks and other tradable securities, and is monitored daily. When the balance in the margin account dips below some threshold amount, called the **maintenance margin**, the investor gets a call and is asked to deposit funds sufficient to bring the account back up to the initial margin level. If the investor does not do this, the clearing house will close out the investor's account, selling off any assets. The sale will not necessarily occur at a price that is in the investor's favor.

The daily monitoring of the futures position is called **marking-to-market**. At the end of each day, the positions are evaluated and cash transferred into or out of each investor's account according to the daily profit/loss position. This process is what lessens the potential for default, and is equivalent to closing out the futures position at the end of each day and establishing a new one at that day's closing price.

Closing out the futures position

It is amusing to imagine a trader waking up on the day after contract expiration to find a truck pulling up to his house to make delivery of 40,000 pounds of pork bellies. Most market participants never intend to take physical delivery of the underlying, but rather close out their positions prior to expiry by entering a reversing trade on the same underlying with the same maturity. For example, if Tanya has a contract to buy 100 tons of August soybeans, prior to expiry she can call her broker and put in an order to sell 100 tons of August soybeans. (Note that there is no requirement to match this trade with her original counterparty, David. The clearinghouse takes care of the transaction and David may well hold his contract to maturity, or reverse it at some other time with someone else taking the other side.) At expiry, these contracts net each other out.

The question now is: how do we price a futures contract? And, perhaps even more interesting: are futures prices good predictors of future spot prices? That is, does $F_{t,T} = E(S_T)$?

To begin to answer these questions, consider three categories of underlyings: (i) those that can be stored and have large inventories, (ii) those that can be stored and have moderate inventories and (iii) non-storable commodities such as currencies, stock indices and interest rates (these may pay dividends or interest).

We can make the same no-arbitrage argument we did in the forward contract section to preclude arbitrage. For assets having cost of carry only with no dividends or interest payments, the **spot-futures parity** relationship is:

$$F_{t,T} = (S_t + s)e^{r(T-t)}$$

If we consider cash and carry arbitrage on an underlying that pays a discrete dividend D at time t_d, we find

$$F_{t,T} = (S_t + s)e^{r(T-t)} - \delta e^{r(T-t_D)}$$

Assuming that $s = 0$ for such assets, we have:

Cash and Carry Arbitrage with Discrete Dividend δ			
Transaction	t	t_D	T
Buy spot	$-S_t$	0	S_T
Borrow money at rate r	S_t	0	$-e^{r(T-t)}S_t$
Sell futures contract (lock in price)	0	0	$F_{t,T} - S_T$
Receive Dividend	0	δ	0
Reinvest Dividend at r	0	$-\delta$	$\delta e^{r(T-tD)}$
Net Proceeds	0	0	$F_{t,T} - e^{r(T-t)}S_t + \delta e^{r(T-tD)}$

This model could easily be extended to account for multiple discrete dividends δ_i paid at times t_i. The general spot-futures parity relationship including discrete dividends is then:

$$F_{t,T} = S_t e^{r(T-t)} - \sum_{i=1}^{n} \delta_i e^{r(T-t_i)}$$

The futures price is reduced by presence of dividends, as it should be. The spot price of the asset would include expectations of future dividends, and when a stock pays a dividend D, its price is immediately reduced by δ to reflect this.

For a constant dividend yield at the continuously compounded annual rate δ, we have

Cash and Carry Arbitrage with Continuous Dividend δ		
Transaction	t	T
Buy spot	$-S_t e^{-\delta(T-t)}$	S_T
Borrow money at rate r	$S_t e^{-\delta(T-t)}$	$-S_t e^{(r-\delta)(T-t)}$
Sell futures contract (lock in price)	0	$F_{t,T} - S_T$
Net Proceeds	0	$F_{t,T} - e^{(r-\delta)(T-t)}S_t$

Thus, Spot-Futures Parity with Continuous Dividend is

$$F_{t,T} = S_t e^{(r-\delta)(T-t)}$$

The above relationship implies that dividends act like negative interest rates. In fact, if dividends are paid at the rate r, the futures price should be exactly the spot price. This leads to an interesting application of currency. Assuming that an investor in foreign country F can borrow funds at that country's risk free rate r_F, and a domestic investor can borrow at the domestic country's risk free rate r_D. How would spot-futures parity work?

Interest rate parity

In the preceding example, we apply the principle of **interest rate parity**, which relates spot and expected exchange rates between the two countries to spot and expected interest rates. If E_0 is the current exchange rate between the domestic currency and the foreign currency, and F_0 is the forward rate agreed upon today that will apply at maturity, then E_0 and F_0 are linked through the ratio of expected interest rates over the period T via:

$$F_0 = E_0 \left(\frac{1+r_D}{1+r_F} \right)^T \text{ simple compounding}$$

$$F_0 = E_0 e^{(r_D - r_F)T} \text{ continuous compounding}$$

Note that if one country pays a higher interest rate than another, it must be balanced by the exchange rates. If interest rate parity did not hold (you guessed it) arbitrage would occur.

As an example, suppose that Pablo is the treasurer of the Mexican cement company Cemex. Most of his supplies come from plants based in Mexico (currency symbol MXN), so he will suffer no exchange rate risk on his Mexican-based costs. But suppose that he also has some factories in Argentina. He is worried about his exposure to anticipated inflation of the Argentinean peso for next year's manufacturing costs. Since he will have to pay these costs in the local currency, he will need to buy Argentinean pesos (ARS). He can buy them today and invest them at the local rate, or lock in a futures contract today. Suppose the one-year risk-free rate in Mexico is 7% and the one-year rate in Argentina is 10%. If today one Argentinean peso costs 2.98 Mexican pesos, what is the expected exchange rate in one year? If interest rate parity holds, the futures rate that he could lock in today should be $F_0 = 2.98 \left(\frac{1+0.07}{1+0.10} \right)^1 \frac{MXN}{ARS}$ or 2.89

MXN/ARS. The expectation is that the Argentinean currency will weaken relative to the Mexican peso over the next year, so it will cost fewer pesos to buy one Argentinean peso next year. The table of cash flows for cash-and-carry arbitrage looks like the following (based on one unit of foreign currency; the domestic currency is Mexican peso, the foreign is the Argentinean peso; and S_t is used for the spot exchange rate, $F_{t,T}$ for the future exchange rate):

		t		T	
Cash and Carry Arbitrage with Foreign Currency					
Line	Transaction	DOMESTIC	FOREIGN	DOMESTIC	FOREIGN
1	Buy one Unit of Foreign Currency @ r_F	$-S_t e^{-rf(T-t)}$	$e^{-rf(T-t)}$	0	0
2	Borrow Domestic Currency	$S_t e^{-rf(T-t)}$	0	$-S_t e^{(r-rf)(T-t)}$	0
3	Invest unit of FX at r_F	0	$-e^{-rf(T-t)}$	0	1
4	Sell FX futures contract	0	0	$F_{t,T}$	-1
5	Net Proceeds	0	0	$F_{t,T} - S_t e^{(r-rf)(T-t)}$	0

In the above, Pablo wants to have one unit of Argentinean currency in one year's time. He will invest this Argentine peso in an Argentine bank to earn the local one year rate of 10%, thus today he must have purchased $1*e^{-rf(1)} = .$ $e^{-0.1}$ ARS = 0.9048 ARS. But he has to pay for this with Mexican pesos, so it will cost current rate 2.98 MXN/ARS * 0.9048 ARS = 2.6964 MXN. He has to borrow this at the domestic rate $r = 7\%$. This is represented in lines 1, 2 and 3 under time "t" in the above table. At the same time, he sells an FX futures contract for one Argentine Peso at the rate calculated by interest rate parity 2.89 MXN/ARS. Now, what happens after one-year's time?

His Argentinean currency has grown to 1.0 ARS in the bank. He has to pay back his loan, 2.6964 MXN, at 7%, or $2.6964e^{0.07(1)} = 2.89$ MXN. (Note: this is the rate we calculated using interest parity, so it works.) His futures contract is worth whatever the current exchange rate is, $F_{t,T}$. So his position is $F_{t,T} - 2.89$ MXN. He breaks even if the spot exchange rate is 2.89 MXN/ARS. If it is lower, say, 2.80 MXN/ARS, he loses on his futures contract because he has agreed to pay 2.89. His loss is 0.09 MXN/ARS. But, he is paying less for his materials, so his net cost is what he locked in: 2.89 MXN/ARS. If the exchange rate is higher (the Argentinean peso strengthened against the Mexican peso), he wins because he locked in a rate of 2.89, however, he has to pay more for his supplies. The difference $F_{t,T}-2.89$ will help offset these additional costs. In terms of formulas:

$$F_{t,T} = S_t e^{(r-r_F)(T-t)}$$

This is interesting because this formula looks exactly like the formula for the futures price with a continuous dividend, except r_F is used instead of δ. In fact, since Pablo is receiving r_F, the foreign interest rate functions just like a continuously compounded dividend. You can trade on intermarket spreads, borrowing money from one FX futures market and lending in another.

Trading strategy

For all cases, the appropriate trading strategy in the futures market is: if the futures prices exceed the right hand side (expected future value of spot plus cost of carry) then sell futures and buy the spot. If the futures price is lower than the right hand side of the equation, then buy the futures and sell the spot. The rule "buy low, sell high" applies.

Implied interest rate

In any of these formulas, we can invert them to solve for **implied interest rates** (often called the **implied**

$$F_{t,T} = (S_t + s)e^{r(T-t)}$$

repo rate), cost of carry, etc. For example, for an asset with cost of carry, we had
Taking natural logs of both sides allows us to solve for the implied risk-free rate as

$$r = \frac{1}{(T-t)} \ln\left(\frac{F_{t,T}}{S_t + s}\right)$$

Payoff diagram of futures position

In theory, the payoff graph will look just like the payoff graph for a forward, since payoff = F_T-S_T, but due to marking to market and margin requirements, the daily profit/loss of the portfolio will appear different. However, the payoff diagram for a single day should look like the payoff diagram for a forward. Suppose a trader Mike enters a September high-grade copper contract. The contract size for copper is 25,000 lbs and price is quoted in cents per lb. The current spot price ("cash price") is 72.05 and the September futures price is 73.70. Even though the contract is priced to provide equilibrium between the expected spot price in September and the futures price, so that theoretically the contract should have zero value when entered, there are margin requirements. Suppose that the initial margin requirement is $10,000 and the maintenance margin on this contract is $7,500. Mike would then have to deposit $10,000 in cash or other "marginable securities" into his account. The following table shows a hypothetical table of daily positions over the next five days. The initial futures position is worth $0.7370/lb times the contract size 25,000 lbs = $18,425.

Day	Futures Price, $/bu	Account Balance	Comments
0	0.737	$10,000	Initial margin
1	0.730	$9,825	Δ =$(0.73-0.737)*25,000 = -$175
2	0.727	$9,750	Δ =$(0.727-0.730)*25,000 = -$75
3	0.723	$9,650	Δ =$(0.723-0.727)*25,000 = -$100
4	0.729	$9,800	Δ =$(0.729-0.723)*25,000 = +$150
...	...	...	
15	0.640	$7,575	
16	0.635	$7,450	Margin call – trader must deposit $2,550
17	0.635	$10,000	
...	...	...	
30	0.750	$12,875	
31	0.760	$13,125	Trader closes out position

Note that when the account balance exceeds the initial margin balance (as in days 30 and 31 above) the excess margin may be withdrawn or kept in the account, where it will generally be invested in interest-earning money market funds.

At first glance, it appears that Mike made a nice profit of $13,125 - $10,000 = $3,125 on the position, but the actual profit/loss over the period is (0.760-0.737)*25,000 = $575 since he had to inject an additional cash flow of $2,550 into the account (note that $13,125 - $10,000 - $2,550 = $575). This illustrates one of the fundamental differences between futures and forwards, since, had he purchased a forward instead, he would have had a net gain of only $575. There is no marking to market on forward contracts.

Swaps

Swaps are agreements to exchange assets. There are interest rate swaps, currency swaps, equity swaps and commodity swaps. The swap market is huge. According to the Bank for International Settlements, U.S.-dollar denominated interest rate swaps accounted for almost $33 billion dollars in notional, approximately 50% of the total notional amount for all OTC derivatives in the first half of 2001. Outright forwards and forex (foreign exchange) swaps were the second largest, at almost $15 billion, and currency swaps accounted for about $2.3 billion.

Swaps, of whatever flavor, may be used to transform a company's liabilities to better match their assets, to borrow more cheaply in a different market, or to gain exposure to a desired market. As an example, a finance company such as Ford Credit or GE Capital makes fixed-rate loans to customers purchasing vehicles (cars, trucks, ambulances, fire trucks.) These loans are the company's assets and are funded by borrowing at a floating rate such as LIBOR and/or, perhaps, the commercial paper rate. They may also float huge bond issues that must be paid back at the agreed-upon fixed rate. These loans are the company's liabilities. If the funding cost of the bonds is lower than the interest income they receive, they profit; if not, they lose money. This spread between funding costs and interest income on customer loans is what drives companies' income and profitability.

Imagine that the finance company has a five-year bond issue that they are legally obliged to repay at 5%. Imagine also that they have a portfolio of car loans yielding 6%. The income from these loans can finance the debt payment on their borrowings. There are at least two potential risks to profitability here. First, there is a mismatch between the maturities of the assets and liabilities. The liability is for five years but the average car loan may be for three years or less, because even if people borrow for five years, there are always prepayments or trade-ins on new vehicles that reduce the average loan life to about two and a half years. And even if no new loans were issued at all for the first two and a half years, when new loans are made, they will likely be made at a different rate. If interest rates have fallen over this period, say, to 4%, then the company is in trouble. They still have the fixed 5% liability, but now there is a loss due to the gap between asset and liability. Of course, new loans are made continuously and new debt is incurred as well.

The second risk is called **basis risk**. This occurs when the liabilities are funded at one benchmark and the assets at another. For example, if a finance company borrows at three-year LIBOR plus some spread, but lends at the three year treasury rate plus some spread, and if these rates do not move identically over time, then the spreads between borrowing and lending will vary – again, potentially impacting profitability.

To solve these problems a company might enter into an interest-rate swap to trade their loan income to some counterparty for a fixed payment with a maturity matching their liabilities. This is called a **fixed-for-fixed** or **fixed-fixed** type of swap. Or, they might swap out their debt obligation for one that floats with some benchmark rate such as LIBOR plus a spread. This is called **pay fixed receive floating interest rate swap**. In fact, GE Capital and Ford Credit are the two largest users of interest rate derivatives. (Pricing of swaps will be covered in the fixed-income section.)

Options

An **option** is a derivative on an underlying asset such as a stock, index, Eurodollar futures contract, commodity, or interest rate. In some ways options are similar to forwards and futures, but in other ways they're significantly different. In contrast to futures and forwards, options cost more money upfront to buy. This cost is called the **option premium**. The buyer of the option has the right but not the obligation to exercise the option, while the seller of the option *is* obligated to perform. This is unlike the forward contract where, once entering the contract, both parties are obligated to deliver.

Options are traded on most major exchanges. They are used for hedging purposes, for speculation and by arbitrageurs. A **speculator** is an investor who wishes to take a position on a particular asset without actually owning the asset. Since options on an underlying can be purchased at a fraction of the cost it would take to acquire a long position in the underlying, options provide **leverage**. Leverage magnifies the returns, both positive and negative, which is the reason that some people say that options are very risky. Options range from the simple, "plain vanilla" flavors such as simple puts and calls on a stock, to the exotic such as binary options, barrier options, Asian options and compound options. The value of such exotic options depends not just on the value of the underlying at expiry, but also on the price path over the entire time period. There are options on currencies, options on interest rates, options on futures, options on swaps and even options on options. (While you're reading this, someone is probably engineering an option on an option to acquire an option.)

The work that we have already done to understand forwards and futures provides us with a good foundation to begin our discussion of options. Pricing options is far more complex than pricing either a forward or a future. In forwards and futures, we were able to develop a price due to an appeal to futures-spot parity (or forward-spot parity) and the no-arbitrage arguments. The prices we developed depended only on the risk-free rate, assumed to remain constant over the period, and on any dividends or costs of carry. We didn't concern ourselves with the actual path that the spot took over time, we locked in a price that we wanted and, at expiry, our profit was determined by the difference of the futures price with the spot at some point in time, whether positive or negative.

In contrast, with options we pre-select a price or level in advance (the **strike** price) as well as an expiration time. In order to model the behavior of the option, we need a model of the dynamics of the underlying. The model for the movement of the underlying asset is fairly complicated and is known as the **Black-Scholes partial differential equation**, which will be developed and solved in the following. We can apply the model, with modifications, to interest rates, stock indices and other options as well.

To begin, we consider two investors, Angus and Yukiko.

Suppose Angus owns 10,000 shares of Lucent that he purchased for $80/share. Later, the stock plummets to $4. Angus has lost (at least, on paper) ($4-$80)/share*10,000 shares = -$760,000. Angus originally bought Lucent with the expectation that the stock price would appreciate and, because it is a significant portion of his retirement portfolio, wonders what he could have done differently.

If Angus had expected Lucent shares to fall, he could have sold this stock short, with the agreement that he would repurchase it later. But short-sellers are exposed to the risk that the stock will rise instead of fall. One way or another, he will own 10,000 shares of Lucent at some point and will be exposed to the potential loss of not only his initial investment, but also potentially much more if the stock rises while he is short.

To make things simple, assume that Angus already holds Lucent stock that he does not wish to sell (say, he is an employee and is prohibited from selling), but he does seek protection against a price decline wiping out his retirement portfolio. In this case, he can purchase a protective **put**. If puts aren't traded on Lucent, he can form combinations of assets to create a **synthetic put**. The protective put is a form of insurance that allows Angus to lock in a minimum price that he will realize for his stock. Like other forms of insurance, Angus has to pay for this protection.

Another investor, Yukiko, believes that IBM will rise but does not have the funds to make an outright purchase of the stock. Instead, she can benefit from the rise, if it plays out, by purchasing a **call option** on the stock.

An option allows the purchaser to control a large block of shares with a minimal investment. This is why purchasers of derivatives are said to be using leverage. Let's look at IBM. Suppose that on April 15 the stock price is $85.35. Yukiko believes that the stock could rise to $90 within the next month. She could just buy the stock, hoping that the expected rise occurs. If she wishes to buy 100 shares, she would have to invest $8,535 up front. Additionally, there is the potential of completely losing the entire investment, should the stock become valueless. A better option for the investor might be to purchase a call option on the stock. A call option provides the purchaser with the right, *but not the obligation*, to exercise the contract at the agreed upon strike price at (or by, depending on the terms of the option) the expiration date. A call option provides the investor with the desired exposure to the stock without actually having to own the stock. Reproduced below is a table of actual IBM calls.

Stock Price, last	Expiry	Strike Price	Call Price	Put Price
85.35	Apr	80	5.70	0.50
85.35	Apr	85	2	1.75
85.35	Apr	90	0.30	5.10
85.35	Apr	95	0.05	10.10
85.35	May	80	7	1.70
85.35	May	90	1.60	6.40
85.35	Jul	80	8.60	3.40

Call and put options on stocks trade in standard blocks of 100 shares per contract. The investor selects the type of option wanted, call or put, from the list of available strike prices and expiry dates. If you buy a call (are long a call), or sell a put (are short a put), you are bullish on the stock (expect the stock price to rise). Puts are purchased and calls are sold when an investor is bearish on the stock (expects the stock price to fall).

In purchasing options, then, Yukiko must make three decisions. First, Yukiko has already decided on the *expected direction of price movement for her investment*: she expects the stock to rise. So, she will purchase a call. Second, she has a *time period for the expected price movement*: she expects the stock to rise in the next month. So she wants a May call, since it is now April. Finally, she has an *expected value for the terminal stock price*: $90. This totally specifies the option contract. She is buying a "May 90 call."

She now just has to decide if the option is priced attractively. (We will see much more on option pricing in the following. For now, assume that she feels that the option prices are fair.) The call prices are shown in the table above. For the May 90 call, the price (also called the **option premium**) is $1.60. This is the price, per share of the specified contract size, to purchase the option. Since the contract size for stocks is 100 shares, she will pay, upfront, $1.60/share * 100 shares = $160.

This is the concept of leverage: for just $160, a fraction of the $8,535 it would have cost to purchase the stocks outright, Yukiko now controls 100 shares of IBM stock (in this case, she is paying just 1.87% of the purchase price). She will receive all of the benefits of a rise in share price without having to actually purchase the shares. The downside is that she only receives these benefits while the option is "alive" (before expiration).

The $90 is called the **exercise price** or **strike price**. Options on stocks expire the Saturday of the third week of the stated contract month, but since the stock markets are not open on Saturday, effectively, this means the third Friday. Yukiko's call gives her the right, but not the obligation, to purchase the stock at the price of $90 at the expiration date of the contract. If the stock price is below $90 when the option expires, she will not exercise her option, since she would not want to buy the stock at $90 when it is trading for less in the open market. That's the importance of "but not the obligation" in the definition of a call option. On the other hand, suppose that the stock price is above $90 at the expiry date, say, $95. Then she can buy the stock at $90, making a gross profit of $95-$90 per share, for a net profit of $100\ n\ (S_t\text{-}K) - n$ *Premium* where *n* is the number of option contracts she holds. If she just holds a single contract, she will make $500. On an initial investment of $160, she has a realized return of (500-160)/160 = 212.5%. Had she made an outright purchase of the stock, her return would have been (95-85.35)/85.35 = 11.3%. Her return is enhanced a great deal by leverage.

A table of possible payoffs for a strike price of $90 is shown below.

Stock Price at Expiry S_t	Payoff of Call, K = $90
86	0
87	0
88	0
89	0
90	0
91	1
92	2
93	3
94	4

If we let K = exercise price and S = stock price at expiry then the value of a call option at expiry (**payoff of the call**), neglecting transactions costs, is then seen to be:

$C = max(S_t\text{-}K,0).$

Because she had to pay $1.60/share to enter the transaction, this also has to be factored in. The breakeven of this call is then

Stock Price at Expiry(per share)	Payoff of Call (per share) (1)	Call Premium (per share) (2)	Payoff including Premium (1) + (2)
86	0	(1.6)	(1.6)
87	0	(1.6)	(1.6)
88	0	(1.6)	(1.6)
89	0	(1.6)	(1.6)
90	0	(1.6)	(1.6)
91	1	(1.6)	(0.6)
92	2	(1.6)	0.4
93	3	(1.6)	1.4
94	4	(1.6)	2.4

Then the breakeven point of a call is the value of S that satisfies S-(K+Prem) = 0, or, S = K + Prem, here, S = 90+1.6 = 91.6. The premium effectively raises the strike price by the same amount. The call payoff diagram is plotted below.

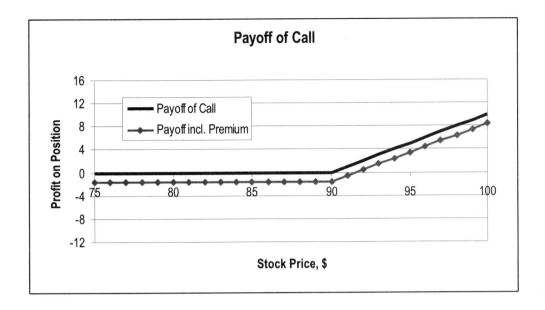

Contrast being long the call to outright purchase of stock at $85.35:

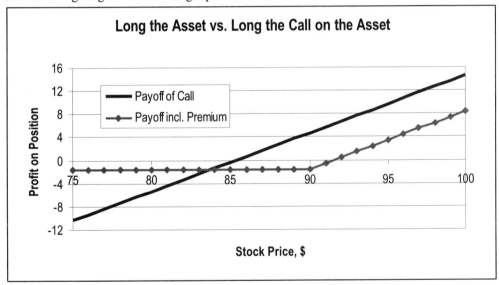

Note the "hockey stick" appearance of the option payoff diagram. The futures and forwards payoff diagrams were just 45 degree angled lines that would pass through the exercise price (which would correspond to the agreed-upon forward or futures price at initiation of the contract) which is also the payoff diagram of being long the asset shown above. The slope of the angled line for the call and put options is also 45 degrees, meaning there is a one dollar change in profit for each one dollar change in stock price. But there is downside protection here, caused by the fact that the holder of a call option that is **out of the money** (lower than the strike price) can just walk away from their position, unlike the holder of the forward or futures contract. The call option holder has the right, but not the obligation, to exercise. This feature makes the risk of the call "asymmetric" -- the investor can participate in upward movements of the stock, but loses no money (other than the option premium) if the stock price declines. The upside is lower than it would have been without the call, but with the call, the maximum loss that can occur is the loss of the call premium.

As seen above, the call premium effectively raises the strike price, so the investor will not realize a profit until the stock price is above the sum of the strike price and premium. Contrast this to outright ownership of the stock where a profit will be made at any price above the purchase price of $85.35. The downside, though, is the investor is only entitled to this protection from the call until expiry. If the stock price is below the exercise price at expiry, the investor is out the entire premium, even if the stock opens the following Monday above the expiry price. That is, even if the investor is correct about the direction of movement and the amount, if the timing is off by even one day, they'll lose the entire investment.

Put options

These are purchased if the investor thinks the asset price will decline. The **put option** gives the purchaser the right, but not the obligation, to sell the asset at the agreed-upon price. Consider Enron.

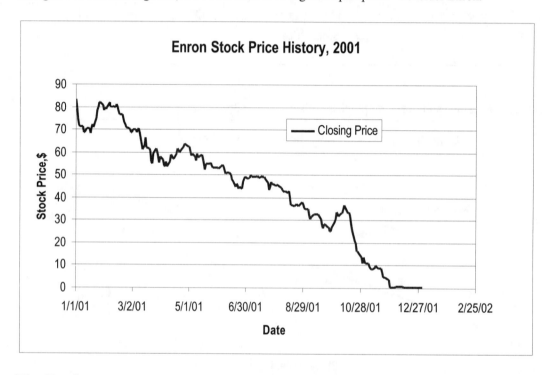

What if an investor, Hans, had somehow known, back in the first half of 2001, that this stock would suffer such a precipitous decline by the end of the year? What if he had purchased put options with a strike price of $80 in January? Then he would have had the right to sell the stock at expiry at $80 at expiry and taken as his profit the difference between $80 and the stock price at expiry. And, of course, this could have been without ever actually owning the stock. If the investor had not owned the stock, he would have been buying derivatives for purpose of "speculation." If he had owned the stock and bought the put as an insurance policy, it is called "hedging." This particular strategy is called a **protective put strategy** and is discussed in the following section on combinations of options.

Possible payoffs depend on the difference between the strike price, and the stock price at expiry. For a strike of 80 with a premium of $2:

Stock Price at Expiry(per share)	Payoff of Put (per share) (1)	Put Premium (per share) (2)	Payoff including Premium (1) + (2)
76	4	(2)	2
77	3	(2)	1
78	2	(2)	0
79	1	(2)	(1)
80	0	(2)	(2)
81	0	(2)	(2)
82	0	(2)	(2)
83	0	(2)	(2)
84	0	(2)	(2)

The put makes money if the stock price declines below the strike price. The payoff of the put at expiry is given by $P = \max(K-S_t,0)$. Considering the premium that must be paid, the breakeven point is calculated as the value of S that satisfies the equation $K - S - Prem = 0$, or $S = K - Prem$. In this example, $S = 80-2 = 78$. We can see this in the table above as well.

The payoff diagram looks like the following:

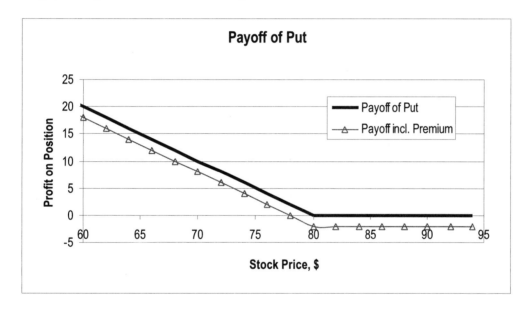

The payoff of the put is $\max(K-S_t,0)$. With the premium, the breakeven point is $S = K-Prem$. Comparing the profit from just holding the stock to the payoff from the put:

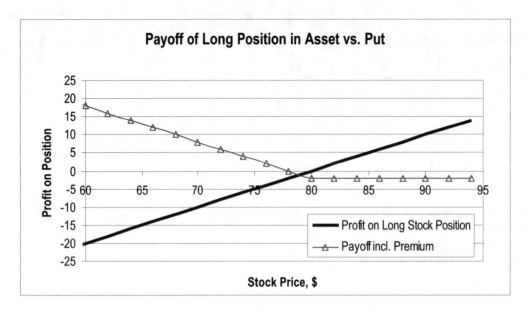

So if the stock closes above the strike price, the put expires worthless and the investor is out the premium. The investor breaks even if the stock closes at K-Prem. If the stock closes below this point, the investor profits. The maximum profit that can be made on the put will occur if the stock price goes to zero, in which case the profit = K (less the premium).

American vs. European options

In the scenarios described above, the investor can only exercise the option at the expiry date. These types of options are called "European options." For these options, though, the investor doesn't have to wait until expiry to either lock in profits or get out of the position: they can execute a reversing trade, effectively closing out the position. For example if someone owned Jan 80 puts on Enron and that expired in October, but didn't want to wait that long (perhaps because they thought that there might be a rebound and wanted to lock in profits), they could just sell their put.

There are also options that can be exercised at any time prior to expiry. These are called "American options" and are the most common. They are worth more than their equivalent European options, since the opportunity to exercise at any point is worth something. In fact, it can be shown mathematically that $V_{American} = V_{European}$. Theoretical prices for European options are calculated with the Black-Scholes equation (shown later). For American options, numerical techniques such as Monte Carlo analysis, trees, or finite difference methods must be used. This is because the price is path-dependent.

What gives an option value?

We will see that the value of an option can be decomposed into two sources of value: **intrinsic value** and **time value**. Intrinsic value is what we have if the option is **in the money**: for a call, this means that the strike price is below the asset price; for a put, this means the strike price is above the asset price. Even if the options are **out of the money** (call: strike price above asset price; put: strike price below asset price), they still have value because there is always the chance, given enough time, that the asset price can move sufficiently to place the option into the money (have positive value). The most important factor influencing this is the volatility of the underlying asset. The more volatile the asset (in this example, we used a stock as the underlying asset, but the underlying could be something else, such as an index, interest rate, exchange rate, commodity or swap), the greater the chance that the price can approach the exercise price.

Looking again at the table of IBM option prices, we can easily see how much of the price is due to intrinsic value and how much is due to time (and volatility).

Stock Price, last	Expiry	Strike Price	Call Price (1)	Status of Call	Intrinsic Value =max (S-K,0) (2)	Time Value (1) – (2)
85.35	Apr	80	5.70	In the Money	5.35	0.35
85.35	Apr	85	2	Near the Money	0.35	1.65
85.35	Apr	90	0.30	Out of the Money	0	0.30
85.35	Apr	95	0.05	Out of the Money	0	0.05
85.35	May	80	7	In the Money	5.35	1.65
85.35	May	90	1.60	Out of the Money	0	1.60
85.35	Jul	80	8.60	In the Money	5.35	3.25

Looking at the series of calls with strike prices of 80,where the intrinsic value is constant, it can be seen that the time value decreases as we get closer to expiry. In fact, the time value decays exponentially. It's also interesting that the time value for May differs between the 80 and 90 calls. One would expect this to be constant, but remember this also includes effects of volatility. It's harder for the stock to go to 90 than to 80, where the stock is already in the money. Graphs of time value of European calls and puts follow, with the top curve being the highest time to expiry and the lowest curve the value at expiry.

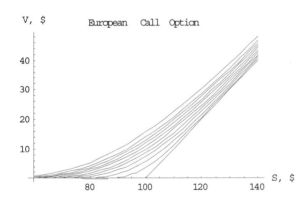

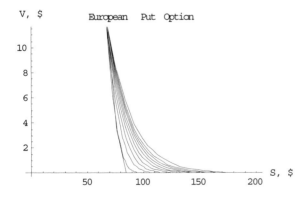

The option price should be highly correlated with the price of the underlying. This should be the case for options on the same asset as the underlying, such as Lucent puts on Lucent stock. In such a case, when the option is in the money, the slope of the option curve is +/- $45^?$ at maturity: a $1 change in the underlying causes a $1 change in the option. If there is a mismatch between the underlying and the hedging instrument, basis risk will occur. A **cross-hedge** is when you want to hedge an underlying, but perfectly correlated derivatives don't exist, so you do the best you can. An example is using calls on the gold contract to hedge silver, or using the S&P 400 to hedge the S&P 500. The risk-free rate is also an important parameter in option pricing.

What are options used for?

Many users of options are **hedgers**. They wish to reduce exposure to sources of risk, or correct mismatches between their liabilities and assets. They are usually exposed to sources of risk that they don't wish to take on, and use options to redistribute this risk to willing parties. These users include market participants such as farmers, commodity purchasers, multinational corporations, airlines, banks and other major creditors. One example of a hedger would be Ford Motor Company, which requires large supplies on precious metals such as palladium. The cost of materials can easily be 50 to 60 percent of their revenue and, because competition squeezes profit margins, Ford is very sensitive to cost. At one time Ford made large purchase of derivatives in an attempt to hedge against price increases of palladium (however, the price moved against them and they lost millions. Angus, the owner of Lucent stock in our example a the beginning of this chapter, would be a hedger if he purchased a protective put to hedge against price declines of his stock.

Other users of derivatives are known as **speculators**. Unlike hedgers, speculators aren't trying to hedge themselves against future price movements, but rather they're taking a position on a stock movement. The investor Yukiko described at the beginning of this section is a speculator.

Put-call parity

There is an important and fundamental relationship between the price of the underlying asset and a put and call with the same strike price and time to expiry. If you buy a portfolio consisting of the asset at price S, a put at strike price K and expiry T_{expiry}, and sell a call with the same strike and expiry, then

$$S + p - c = Ke^{-rt}$$

This relationship is called **put-call parity** and is used for purposes such as detecting arbitrage opportunities and price mismatches, the creation of synthetic securities, and in calculating "fair value" of derivatives prices. (To remember that the equation is "S + p" and not "S–p", just think "S and P," as in S&P 500.)

To see this, suppose that you borrow an amount Ke^{-rt} to finance the purchase of one share of the asset at price S and one put at price p. You sell one call at the same strike price and expiration date as the put. The money that you borrowed is to be paid back at expiry at the rate r. This is a risk-free position requiring zero net cash outlay because:

At time $t=0$, you are long $S+p$. It is financed with the cash Ke^{-rt} and the call premium c.

At time $t=T_{expiry}$, the asset is now at price S_t and you have to pay back the K dollars you borrowed earlier. There are three possible states of nature:

(1) *The stock price is equal to strike price K.* In this situation, the call and put expire worthless and you have to pay back K. But the stock is worth K. Sell the stock and pay the loan. Net cash outlay = $0.

(2) *The stock price S_t is below strike price K.*
Value of portfolio at expiry:

Stock: S_t
Call: 0 Expires worthless since $S_t < K$.
Put: $K - S_t$
Loan: $-K$ Have to pay back K.
Total: $S_t + (K - S_t) - K = 0$

(3) *Stock price S_t is above strike price K.*
      <u>Value of portfolio at expiry:</u>
      Stock: S_t
      Call: $-(S_t - K)$ You sold the call so payoff is *max(S_t-K,0)*.
      Put: 0 *Expires worthless since $S_t > K$.*
      Loan: $-K$ Have to pay back K.
      Total: $S_t - (S_t - K) - K = 0$

No matter what the price of the asset at expiry, you are perfectly hedged. All we need to do to complete this is to figure out the value of the portfolio at the time of purchase and set it equal to zero, since we can't have a risk-free profit. We pay back K so must have borrowed Ke^{-rt}. This is equal to the value of the portfolio $S+p-c$. If it were not, we would have an arbitrage possibility. Such "no-arbitrage" arguments are proved by squeezing from both sides as follows:

Case 1: $S+p-c > Ke^{-rt}$. We would sell the portfolio and invest the proceeds $(S+p-c)$ in the bank. At the end of the period, our account would be worth $(S+p-c)e^{rt}$. We would have to make good on our short sale of S and p and purchase of call, but we have already seen that this portfolio is perfectly hedged and worth K. So we would have a risk-free profit $(S+p-c)e^{rt}-K > 0$.

Case 2: $S+p-c < Ke^{-rt}$. We would buy the portfolio by borrowing $S+p-c$. At the end of the period, we would pay back $(S+p-c)e^{rt}$ from our loan, but since the portfolio is worth K, we have a risk-free profit $K - (S+p-c) e^{rt} > 0$.

With put-call parity, we see how to create synthetic positions. For example, if puts aren't traded on a certain stock, they can easily be synthesized by solving the put-call parity equation for p:

$$p = Ke^{-rt} + c - S$$

So you would buy a call and sell the stock short. If you were prohibited from selling your own company's stock short, like Angus in the discussion at the beginning of this section, you would buy a put, short the call and lend K:

$$p - c - Ke^{-rt} = -S$$

Once we know the strike price, price and volatility of the underlying, time to expiry and either the call or put price calculated from Black-Scholes, we can use put-call parity to get the price of the put or call.

Interview tip: Make sure you can draw the payoff diagrams of put-call parity and identify it when it appears on an interview question. For example, you could be asked a question including the following: "Suppose you borrow money and use it to buy a put and sell a call …" If an interviewer makes this statement in a question, they're trying to see whether you recognized that they had synthetically created a stock. If Angus wanted to purchase a put on Lucent but it wasn't available, or maybe a call was available for the month he wanted but a put was not, he could create one synthetically by forming a portfolio of stock, call and risk-free borrowings.

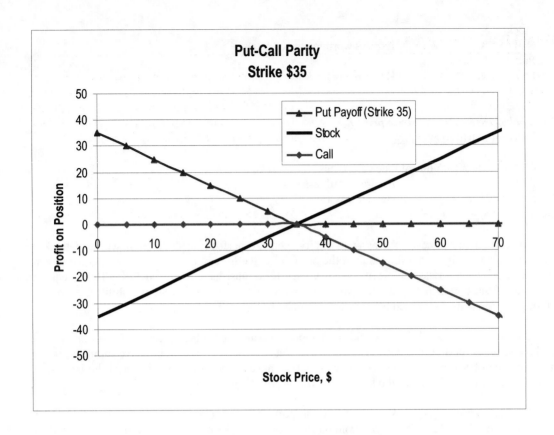

Combining Options

The previously discussed most basic vanilla options may be combined to form an endless variety of derivatives that can be tailored to match investor's desired objectives. In the following we cover several such combinations, incluuding covered calls and puts, straddles, strangles, bull and bear spreads, butterflies, caps, floors and collars. We begin with the simplest combinations: covered calls and puts. However, in order to understand what a covered call or put is, we must first discuss naked calls and puts.

Naked calls and puts

If you don't own the asset, but sell the call anyway, this is called selling (writing) a naked call. This is a highly speculative strategy. The investor is taking the view that the stock will not move much, or will even decline. If the stock rises, the call writer can be exposed to large, potentially infinite, losses. See the payoff box below where some poor soul sold 10 naked calls with a strike price of 35 on Cisco Systems expiring March 2000.

Stock Price at expiry	Short Call Payoff (per contract), K = $35 (1)	Premium Received $1.5/contract (2)	Strategy Payoff, per contract (1) + (2)
25	0	1.5	1.5
30	0	1.5	1.5
35	0	1.5	1.5
40	(5)	1.5	(3.5)
45	(10)	1.5	(8.5)
50	(15)	1.5	(13.5)
55	(20)	1.5	(18.5)
60	(25)	1.5	(23.5)
65	(30)	1.5	(28.5)
70	(35)	1.5	(33.5)
75	(40)	1.5	(38.5)
80	(45)	1.5	(43.5)

Writing naked calls on Cisco Systems would have been a bad strategy prior to 3/15/99, as shown below. Suppose, anticipating a price decline, or a sideways move at the least, Betty wrote 10 naked calls on 11 Sep 99 at $35 with expiry in March 2000. If the stock closed at $70, Betty would lose $35 per share per contract, or $3,500 per contract. Only a small portion of this is offset by the $150 option premium she received.

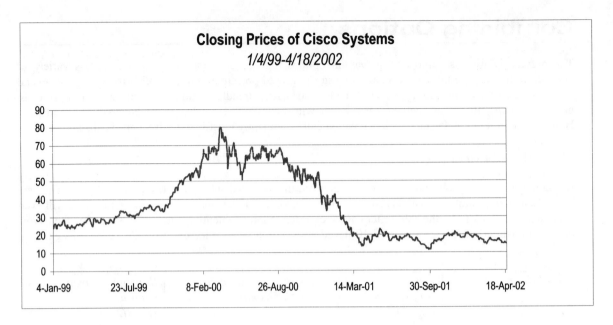

Closing Prices of Cisco Systems
1/4/99-4/18/2002

However, if the stock price really did decline, as it did after March 15, 2000, a writer of naked calls could pull in the premium rent for as long as someone else was willing to buy the calls. Of course, in this case, Betty would have made much more money buying puts.

The payoff to the writer of the naked call is just the negative of the payoff on the call, *-max(S-K,0)*. This also shows why they say that options are a "zero-sum game" -- the writer's loss is exactly the buyer's gain, and vice-versa.

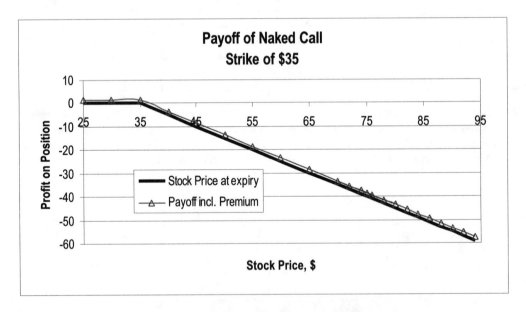

Payoff of Naked Call
Strike of $35

The converse of writing naked calls is writing naked puts. Here you sell a put on a stock you don't own. If the stock has a meltdown, you are potentially exposed to a large loss. If you had sold puts on Cisco Systems in early Feb 2000, you are exposed to the entire exercise price times 100 shares/contract, times the number of contracts sold if the stock price declines. This payoff has the same relationship to the put as the naked call does to the call. Payoff naked put = - *max(K-S,0)*. Again, a zero-sum game between the buyer and seller of puts.

Protective puts

If the investor is long the asset and purchases a put on that asset, such as the hedger Angus with his Lucent stock, he is said to have purchased a protective put. This strategy provides a form of insurance. If the stock price declines to less than K, the investor can exercise the put and effectively get K for the stock. He loses some money $(S_0 - K)$ but not as much as he would have without the put.

Straddles

The basic derivatives can be combined to form derivatives that more closely match the risk profile, or desired risk profile, of the hedger, or the desired payoff of the speculator. Consider a speculator, Harold, who expects a big move in a stock but has no idea which way the market will go. (Harold has heard that there will be a dividend change, for example, but doesn't know if there will be an increase or cut to the dividend. A dividend increase or decrease could be caused by several occurrences, including a management change, a lawsuit coming to a close, or a promising new drug nearing the end of its development.) In such a situation Harold could buy both a put and a call. If the two options have the same exercise price and expiry date, you have purchased a straddle. Following are the payoff table and diagram for a straddle with exercise price $35 (assuming that the premiums are $3 and $2 to purchase the call and put, respectively):

Stock Price at expiry	Call Payoff K = $35 (1)	Put Payoff K = $35 (2)	Premium (per contract) (3)	Strategy Payoff, per contract (1) + (2)+(3)
0	0	35	(5)	30
5	0	30	(5)	25
10	0	25	(5)	20
15	0	20	(5)	15
20	0	15	(5)	10
25	0	10	(5)	5
30	0	5	(5)	-
35	0	0	(5)	(5)
40	5	0	(5)	-
45	10	0	(5)	5
50	15	0	(5)	10
55	20	0	(5)	15
60	25	0	(5)	20
65	30	0	(5)	25
70	35	0	(5)	30
75	40	0	(5)	35
80	45	0	(5)	40
85	50	0	(5)	45

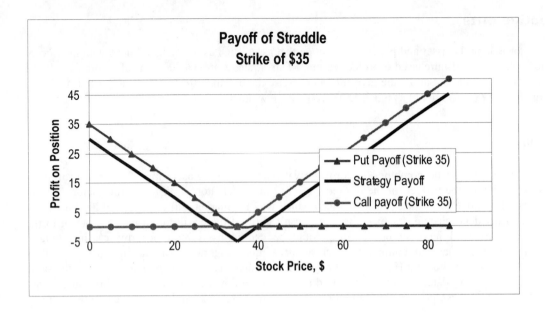

Note that due to the premium there are two break-even points, and hence there is a small range at which the strategy will lose money. The higher the premium paid, the greater this range. Payoff = payoff due to put + payoff due to call less premium = $max(K-S,0) + max(S-K,0) - Prem\ call - Prem\ put$.

Naked straddle

A person engaging in this strategy does not expect the stock to move very much either way. A naked straddle consists of the simultaneous sale of both a call and a put with the same exercise price and expiry date. The payoff is the reverse of the straddle. If the stock does move, the trader is exposed to potentially infinite losses.

Stock Price at expiry	Call payoff (Strike 35)	Put Payoff (Strike 35)	Premium Received	Strategy Payoff
0	0	-35	5	(30)
5	0	-30	5	(25)
10	0	-25	5	(20)
15	0	-20	5	(15)
20	0	-15	5	(10)
25	0	-10	5	(5)
30	0	-5	5	-
35	0	0	5	5
40	-5	0	5	-
45	-10	0	5	(5)
50	-15	0	5	(10)
55	-20	0	5	(15)
60	-25	0	5	(20)
65	-30	0	5	(25)
70	-35	0	5	(30)

75	-40	0	5	(35)
80	-45	0	5	(40)
85	-50	0	5	(45)

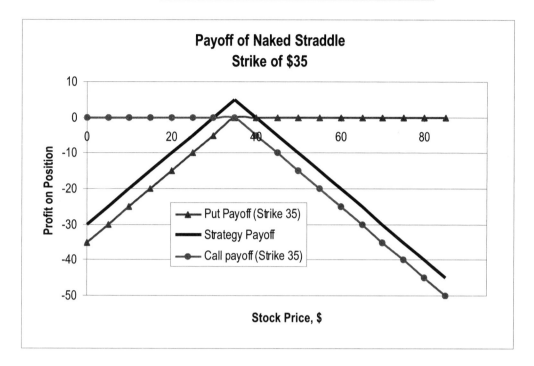

The seller of a naked straddle is exposed to a potentially infinite loss if the closing price is not near the strike. A small profit can be made even if the asset closes slightly above (below) the strike, because the small payoff on the call (put) will be counterbalanced by the premiums received.

The naked straddle was the favorite trading strategy of Nick Leeson, the infamous Barings Bank trader whose losses led to the collapse of the bank. Leeson sold 37,000 straddles on the Nikkei 225 index. He sold most of his straddles at exercise prices ranging from 18,500 to 20,000 during a period (November to December 1994) when the index was trading between 19,000 and 20,000. Examination of historical data shows that the index was fairly flat during that period. Then, the Kobe earthquake hit Japan. By the time the regulators stepped in and closed Leeson's positions, the Nikkei had dropped to 17,465. In total, his options positions lost $7 billion. (We'll further discuss the Barings case in the Risk Management section of this book.)

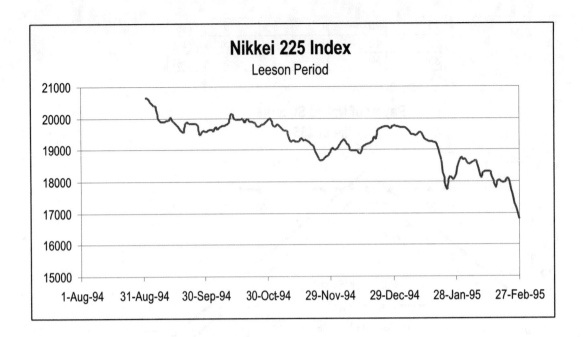

Spreads

Other possibilities involve spreads. These can be spreads in time (calendar spreads) or spreads in strike price (bull and bear spreads, box spreads, condors, butterflies, strangles and so on.) Spreads can be constructed using calls or puts.

An example of a **calendar spread** is when an investor buys a call at strike K with expiry t_1 and sells the same call with expiry t_2. The reason for doing this is the call premium income from selling the call at t_2 helps to finance the call premium for the purchase of the call at t_1.

A **bull spread** may be used when an investor is bullish on a particular asset. Here, the investor may purchase a call with a low strike price K_1 and expiry t_1 and sells a call with a higher strike price K_2 and expiry t_1. This strategy will produce a profit if the stock price rises. The sale of the call at the K_2 helps to finance the purchase of the call at K_1.

For example, Tom buys a July 70 call on copper and sells a July 72 call on copper. The cost for the July 70 call is 4.05 cents/lb and the cost for the July 72 call is 2.65 cents/lb. One contract is 25,000 lbs. Thus Tom will have to pay $1,012.50 for the July 70 call but this is partially offset by the $662.50 he will receive from selling the July 72 call. The total upfront cost to enter the position is then $350. The current spot price of copper is 72.05 cents per pound. Let's look at a hypothetical scenario for Tom's portfolio.

Copper Price cents/lb	$\max(S_t - 70,0)$	$\max(S_t - 72,0)$	Profit on Strategy cents per lb ((1)-(2))	Profit Including Call Premiums	Value of Total Position $
65	0	0	0	-1.4	-350
66	0	0	0	-1.4	-350
67	0	0	0	-1.4	-350
68	0	0	0	-1.4	-350
69	0	0	0	-1.4	-350
70	0	0	0	-1.4	-350
71	1	0	1	-0.4	-100
72	2	0	2	0.6	150
73	3	1	2	0.6	150
74	4	2	2	0.6	150
75	5	3	2	0.6	150
76	6	4	2	0.6	150
77	7	5	2	0.6	150

Tom will make a profit, ignoring transactions costs, as long as the copper closes above the lower strike price $K_1 = 70$. However, if the copper closes above the higher strike price, he is obliged to sell, capping his profit at $K_2 - K_1$ at 72-70 = 2 cents per pound, times contract size 25,000 = $500. Including transactions costs of (350), his maximum profit is then $150. The maximum possible loss is just the loss of the net option premium (350).

Caps

Another possibility, most often used with interest rate options, is a **cap**. A cap is an upper bound k on the underlying. Suppose that Blake, a corporate treasurer, has agreed to pay LIBOR plus a spread of 10 bp on a notional amount of $10,000,000. To protect himself against the possibility that LIBOR might rise substantially in the future, Blake might purchase a cap, which sets a maximum on the amount he will pay. If he buys a cap that sets the maximum level of LIBOR he will pay as $k = 5\%$, then the payoff would be $\min((5\%,r\%) + 10\text{ bp})*\$10,000,000$.

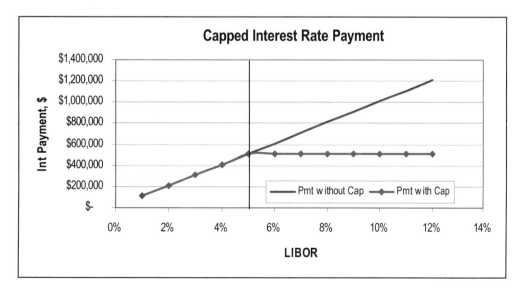

The cap has the potential to save Blake a lot of money if interest rates rise significantly. The most he will pay is $510,000 when the cap strike is met or exceeded. However, caps may be expensive to purchase.

r, %	Capped Payment	Capped Rate Plus Spread	Rate Plus Spread	Payment	Capped Payment
1%	1%	1.100%	1.100%	$ 110,000	$ 110,000
2%	2%	2.100%	2.100%	$ 210,000	$ 210,000
3%	3%	3.100%	3.100%	$ 310,000	$ 310,000
4%	4%	4.100%	4.100%	$ 410,000	$ 410,000
5%	5%	5.100%	5.100%	$ 510,000	$ 510,000
6%	5%	5.100%	6.100%	$ 610,000	$ 510,000
7%	5%	5.100%	7.100%	$ 710,000	$ 510,000
8%	5%	5.100%	8.100%	$ 810,000	$ 510,000
9%	5%	5.100%	9.100%	$ 910,000	$ 510,000
10%	5%	5.100%	10.100%	$ 1,010,000	$ 510,000
11%	5%	5.100%	11.100%	$ 1,110,000	$ 510,000
12%	5%	5.100%	12.100%	$ 1,210,000	$ 510,000

Floors

Blake's counterparty Yaz may purchase a floor to set the minimum interest they will receive. Suppose Yaz buys a floor set at 3%. If rates are above this floor rate, Yaz will receive whatever LIBOR is. But if LIBOR falls below $k = 3\%$, Yaz receives k. The floor sets the minimum interest and the cap sets the maximum.

Collars

This strategy is similar to a bullish call spread. Here, the investor buys the stock (or underlying asset if different from stock), buys a put at an out of the money strike K_1, and sells a call at an out of the money strike K_2. The maximum profit is capped at $K_2 - S_t$ and the maximum loss is capped at $S_t - K_1$. The capping of maximum loss and gain gives the collar its name. The strategy is bullish and the more out of the money the call strike price is, the more bullish the strategy.

For example, Eddie purchases an Intel stock at $28 per share and a June 25 Intel put at $0.55, and sells a June 32.5 Intel call at $0.50. The total outlay will be the purchase of 100 shares at $28 each and the put premium at $55. But this is partly offset by the income from the sale of the call, which yields $50 for a total outlay of $2,805. The transactions costs will be double those for just single options as well. The payoff diagram is shown below.

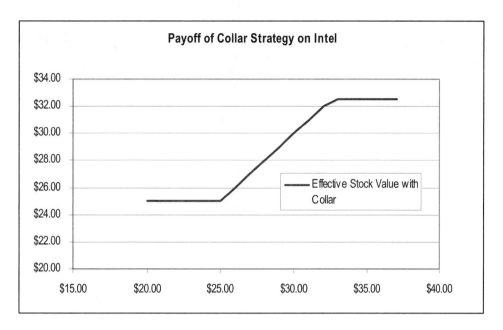

Swaptions

A swaption is an option on a swap. It gives the holder the right, but not the obligation, to enter into a swap at predetermined terms sometime in the future. The holder of the swaption pays a premium for the rights to this option but has the flexibility to not enter the swap later if conditions are unfavorable. For example, suppose a treasurer wants to enter a swap to receive fixed and pay floating. The fixed rate that is received is dependent on the expected future yield curve, as we shall see later. If rates are expected to rise, the treasurer will receive a higher fixed rate. She might enter a swaption so that she will have the flexibility of choosing whether or not to enter the swap at a later date. If interest rates rise, she will exercise the swaption but if they fall, the swaption will be allowed to expire worthless. and she will transact the interest rate swap at prevailing market rates.

Option Valuation I: Introducing Black-Scholes

Because option prices depend on the prices of the underlying (assumed to be a stock in the following), we need some way to model stock price movements over time. Once we have this model, we can price a European call in the usual way at expiry as *max(S_t-K,0)*. We can then just use put-call parity to price the put. But what if we want to price more complex path-dependent options such as knock-in or Asian? In the following section, we build up the Black-Scholes equation used in option pricing.

Suppose we have an option on some underlying asset S. If the value of the option can be assumed to depend only on the value of S and time t, then we can describe the random walk followed by V by the **Black-Scholes equation**:

$$\frac{\partial V}{\partial t} + \frac{1}{2}\sigma^2 S^2 \frac{\partial^2 V}{\partial S^2} + rS\frac{\partial V}{\partial S} - rV = 0$$

This equation may be used to value any derivative security as long as the derivative's price depends only on the values of S and t and satisfies the assumptions of the Black-Scholes equation. It is tremendously important as it can be modified to include assets paying dividends and interest rate options, for example.

In the following, we will derive this equation, solve it and discuss validity in the real world. We start by defining the path a stock price might take over time.

Derivation of Black-Scholes

Many models of asset behavior assume that the asset follows some form of random walk. The **Wiener process** is often used to model this behavior. It supposes that the asset price behaves something like a particle that is impacted by a number of small shocks. In physics this behavior is referred to as Brownian motion. The generalized Wiener process for a variable x is: $dx = a\,dt + b\,dz$. In this equation, dx is the expected change in the variable x over a short interval of time, with a random shock term given by the variable dz. Here, z is a random drawing from a standardized normal distribution with mean of one and variance zero, a and b are constants known as the **drift rate** and the **variance rate**, respectively. So the variable x changes due to the change in drift ($a\,dt$), which corresponds to the expected ("deterministic") growth rate of the asset, and the unexpected ("stochastic") component $b\,dz$, which could be an economic shock, earnings surprise or news, etc. Note that a and b can also be dependent on x and t. In this case, we have the generalized Ito process:

$$dx = a(x,t)\,dt + b(x,t)\,dz$$

This would be more appropriate if the drift and/or variance rate cannot be expected to remain constant.

Application to Stock Prices To apply this to stocks, replace the random variable x by S. We then have $dS = a\,dt + b\,dz$. This model means that the stock price is expected to change by some constant drift rate over time and some constant variance. But this is not appropriate as shareholders expect some constant return over time, which is not captured by this model. (That is, they require dS/S to be constant, not dS itself.) We can see this from the forward model $S = S_0 e^{\mu t}$. If there is no volatility, stock prices are expected to grow at the expected rate of return μ. This implies $\dfrac{dS}{S} = \mu dt$. The $b\,dz$ term captures the volatility. A reasonable assumption for b is that, over a short period of time, the volatility of the return is constant. We capture this with the standard deviation σ. (The shareholder's expectation of realizing the return μ is just as uncertain at *any* stock price. Is this reasonable? The analyst should decide if the expected return of, say, 20% on Lucent stock is just as probable when the stock has slipped to $5/share as it was when the stock was priced much higher, but the drivers for such extreme changes in a company's fundamentals would likely require changes to the investor's expectations as well.) Then the random term $b\,dz$ of dS/S becomes $s\,dz$. The final equation is then $\dfrac{dS}{S} = \mu\,dt + \sigma\,dz$

This decomposes the stock return into the sum of two components: the expected growth rate and the random volatility effect $\sigma\,dz$. Furthermore, the distribution of dS/S is normal, with mean μ and standard deviation σ. Let's put this into practice using Excel to see what this model will do for us.

Suppose we have a stock with expected return 10% and annualized standard deviation 20%. If the stock price is currently $5, we can generate sample paths for the stock over the interval dt by sampling repeatedly from a normal distribution with this mean and standard deviation and substituting into the formula above. We can perform this by sampling z_1 from a normal distribution with mean zero and standard deviation of one using the transformation $z_2 = u + \sigma z_1$. The normal distribution z_1 can be obtained in Excel using the function **NORMSINV(z)** where z is the random draw on the interval (0,1), which can be generated using **RAND()**. Then z_2 represents dS and the new stock price is obtained as $S + dS$.

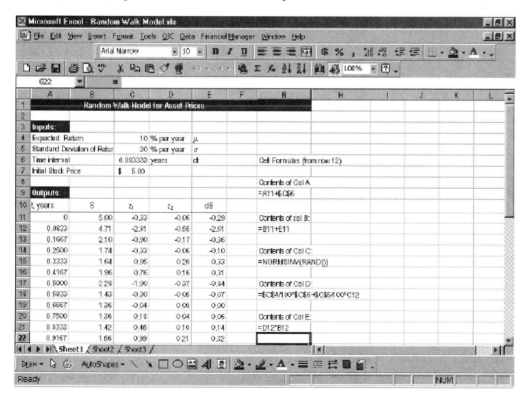

Generating several such paths results in a probability distribution for the ending stock price. Some sample runs are shown in the following graph. (Here, *dt* was chosen as one month so every 12 data points corresponds to one year.) The ending values ranged from $0.5 to over $50.

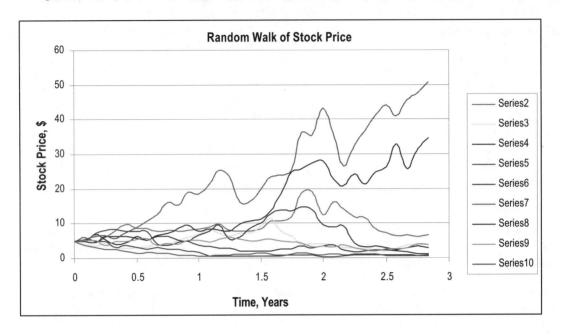

Putting it all together

The Ito process for asset price movement might not seem very useful, but it is the building block for the Black-Scholes model. Suppose that *f* is some smooth function depending on two independent variables *S* and *t*. We can write an expression for *f* by expanding in a Taylor Series. We find:

$$df = f(S + dS, t + dt) - f(S,t) = \frac{\partial f}{\partial S} dS + \frac{\partial f}{\partial t} dt + \frac{1}{2!}\left(\frac{\partial^2 f}{\partial S^2} dS^2 + 2 \frac{\partial^2 f}{\partial S \partial t} dSdt + \frac{\partial^2 f}{\partial t^2} dt^2 \right) + \cdots$$

Here we truncate the series after the second-order terms. This is valid for any such function *f*, but let's consider an option specifically. Then *S* could be the path that the asset follows and *t* could be time. To clarify that we are now considering an option, replace *f* by *V*.

We had an expression for *dS* from the Ito process, $dS = \mu Sdt + \sigma Sdz$. Squaring this gives

$$dS^2 = (\mu Sdt + \sigma Sdz)^2 = \mu^2 S^2 dt^2 + 2\mu Sdt\sigma Sdz + \sigma^2 S^2 dz^2$$

To simplify, we examine the relative size of each of the terms. Since *dt* is supposed to be small, dt^2 will be even smaller. What about the *dz* term? This is of the order of the square root of *t*. The reason for this is that the variance of the stock return must scale with *t*, so *dz* must scale with the square root of *t*. Then $\sigma^2 S^2 dz^2$ will be of size *dt* and $2\mu Sdt\sigma Sdz$ will be of size

$$dt\sqrt{dt}$$

Dropping terms smaller than size *dt* yields $dS^2 \sim \sigma^2 S^2 dt$.

The expression for dV now becomes $dV = \dfrac{\partial V}{\partial S}(\mu S dt + \sigma S dz) + \dfrac{\partial V}{\partial t}dt + \dfrac{1}{2!}\left(\dfrac{\partial^2 V}{\partial S^2}\sigma^2 S^2 dt\right) + \cdots$

Rearranging to group terms involving dt and terms involving dz gives

$$dV = \left(\mu S \frac{\partial V}{\partial S} + \frac{1}{2}\sigma^2 S^2 \frac{\partial^2 V}{\partial S^2} + \frac{\partial V}{\partial t}\right)dt + \sigma S \frac{\partial V}{\partial S}dz$$

The above equation gives the random walk followed by the option value V. If the derivatives were known, we could generate random paths just like we did for the asset in the simple Weiner model. We have more work to do, however, before we can actually use this to price an option.

We construct a portfolio consisting of one option, V, and some as yet unspecified quantity of the underlying asset S. For now, call this quantity $-\Delta$. If Π is the value of our portfolio with these holdings, then $\Pi = V - \Delta S$. Let a small quantity of time Δt pass. The value of our portfolio is now $d\Pi = dV - \Delta\, dS$. (The asset value and option value changed, but the quantity held is assumed to be held constant over this short time interval.) We have already developed expressions for dS and dV. Substituting them into the above equation gives:

$$d\Pi = dV - \Delta dS = \left(\mu S \frac{\partial V}{\partial S} + \frac{1}{2}\sigma^2 S^2 \frac{\partial^2 V}{\partial S^2} + \frac{\partial V}{\partial t}\right)dt + \sigma S \frac{\partial V}{\partial S}dz - \Delta(\mu S dt + \sigma S dz)$$

Collecting factors of dt and dz, we can write the equation as the sum of a deterministic term (the dt term) and a purely random term (dz):

$$d\Pi = \left(\mu S \frac{\partial V}{\partial S} + \frac{1}{2}\sigma^2 S^2 \frac{\partial^2 V}{\partial S^2} + \frac{\partial V}{\partial t} - \Delta\mu S\right)dt + \left(\sigma S \frac{\partial V}{\partial S} - \Delta\sigma S\right)dz$$

We now make use of a slick trick to eliminate the random component. Just force the coefficient of dz to zero by choosing

$$\sigma S \frac{\partial V}{\partial S} - \Delta\sigma S = 0.$$

This is the case if $\Delta = \dfrac{\partial V}{\partial S}$.

Note: The variable Δ is a very important one in options pricing. It represents the change in value of the option for a change in value of the underlying asset. It is known as **Delta**.

So, our equation is now $d\Pi = \left(\mu S \dfrac{\partial V}{\partial S} + \dfrac{1}{2}\sigma^2 S^2 \dfrac{\partial^2 V}{\partial S^2} + \dfrac{\partial V}{\partial t} - \dfrac{\partial V}{\partial S}\mu S\right)dt = \left(\dfrac{1}{2}\sigma^2 S^2 \dfrac{\partial^2 V}{\partial S^2} + \dfrac{\partial V}{\partial t}\right)dt$

Just one more step and we're there. We now invoke the no-arbitrage argument. Remember that we constructed the portfolio Π consisting of one unit of the option V and an amount $-\Delta$ of the asset. The funds for the portfolio Π could also be invested in the risk-free asset, in which case the portfolio value would grow at the rate Πrt. The change in value of the portfolio would be $d\Pi = \Pi rdt$ over a small interval of time dt. This equality must hold, because if the change in portfolio value $d\Pi$ were greater than Πrdt, an arbitrager could borrow funds at the rate r to purchase the portfolio Π, making a risk-free profit. If, however, the portfolio grows slower than the risk-free rate, the arbitrageur would short the portfolio and invest the proceeds at the risk-free rate, again earning a risk-free profit. So we have

$$\left(\frac{1}{2}\sigma^2 S^2 \frac{\partial^2 V}{\partial S^2} + \frac{\partial V}{\partial t}\right)dt = \left(V - \frac{\partial V}{\partial S}S\right)rdt$$

Since dt is small, but non-zero, we can divide both sides by it. Rearranging gives

$$\frac{\partial V}{\partial t} + \frac{1}{2}\sigma^2 S^2 \frac{\partial^2 V}{\partial S^2} + rS\frac{\partial V}{\partial S} - rV = 0$$

This is the famed **Black-Scholes model for option pricing**. It says that the option value depends on the underlying stock price S; the risk free rate r; the time to expiry t and the asset volatility σ. Notice that the expected growth rate of the stock μ is not a part of the equation; it canceled out. This is an important feature of the Black-Scholes equation.

The Black-Scholes equation can only be used to value European options. In summary, the assumptions underlying the Black-Scholes model are:

1. The investor can borrow and lend at the risk-free rate r.
2. The asset volatility remains constant over evaluation period.
3. Short sales are permitted.
4. No transactions costs or other market frictions.
5. The options are European.
6. No dividends are paid.

The Black-Scholes equation can be modified to handle the case where a continuous dividend is received at the rate D. In this case, we solve

$$\frac{\partial V}{\partial t} + \frac{1}{2}\sigma^2 S^2 \frac{\partial^2 V}{\partial S^2} + (r-D)S\frac{\partial V}{\partial S} - rV = 0$$

For a foreign currency, we saw in the section on forwards that holding a foreign currency is just like receiving a continuous dividend at the rate r_f. Then the Black Scholes equation is

$$\frac{\partial V}{\partial t} + \frac{1}{2}\sigma^2 S^2 \frac{\partial^2 V}{\partial S^2} + (r-r_f)S\frac{\partial V}{\partial S} - rV = 0$$

Solution of the Black-Scholes equation

Note that the Black-Scholes equation is second order in S and first order in time. Thus it requires two boundary conditions in S and one condition in time for solution. For example, for a European call, the time condition would be: At expiry, $V = max[S-K,0]$ where K is the strike price. For a put, the condition would be $V = max[K-S,0]$. The value of a call is then:

$C(S,t) = SN(d_1) - Ke^{-rt}N(d_2)$ where N is the cumulative normal distribution for a standardized random variable.

$$d_1 = \frac{\ln\left(\frac{S}{K}\right) + \left(r + \frac{1}{2}\sigma^2\right)(T-t)}{\sigma\sqrt{T-t}}, d_2 = d_1 - \sigma\sqrt{T-t}$$

In the above, the parameters σ and r are quoted on an annual basis. T is the time to expiry, in years and t is the time of evaluation. The corresponding equation for a put can be obtained by just using the Put-Call Parity relationship: since $p = Ke^{-rt} - S + c$ we have

$$p = Ke^{-rt}\left(1 - N(d_2)\right) - S\left(1 - N(d_1)\right)$$

Note: **As shown above, there is no need to remember the equations for both puts and calls. Just memorize one, and you can derive the other.**

Using Black-Scholes

The Black-Scholes model may be used in two ways: to value options by substituting values into the right-hand side of the equation, and to solve for the implied volatility by substituting current option price and solving iteratively for the volatility that will yield this price. Black-Scholes was derived on the basis of what may appear to be many unrealistic assumptions. Let's see how well it works in practice by taking actual stock and option prices from the newspaper and trying to price them. Right away, we see problems in that we don't know exactly what risk-free rate to use. This goes back to the idea that you can't actually borrow and lend at the same rate, and ordinary investors won't be able to borrow at the lowest rates. Even so, we'll use the T-bill rate that most closely matches the time to expiry of the option. There also is a day-count calculation that needs to be made in order to be really precise. More important, we don't know what asset volatility to use. If we use the historical volatility, we are operating under the assumption that future conditions are identical to the past, a very dangerous assumption.

Nevertheless, let's push forward and see just how sensitive the model is to changes in expectations about volatility. Here is a table of current options prices for IBM. Remember that options expire on the third Friday of the quoted month in calculating the time to expiry.

Table of Options on IBM Stock

S, last	Expiry	Strike Price	Call Price	Put Price
85.35	Apr	80	5.70	0.50
85.35	May	80	7	1.70
85.35	Jul	80	8.60	3.40
85.35	Apr	85	2	1.75
85.35	Apr	90	0.30	5.10
85.35	May	90	1.60	6.40
85.35	Apr	95	0.05	10.10

A model can quickly be built in Excel. The risk-free rates we will use are: 1.70% for April, 1.66% for May and 1.71% for July. It doesn't matter what units we use for r and σ, but they must match the units used for t. We will use annualized versions. We will also assume a volatility of 33.5% for the stock.

Results of Black-Scholes Model, σ = 33.5%, S = 85.35

Expiry	Strike Price	Call Price	B-S Result	Abs. Error, %	Put Price	B-S Result	Abs. Error, %
Apr	80	5.70	5.62	1.5	0.50	0.23	53.85
May	80	7	6.59	5.9	1.70	1.13	33.48
Jul	80	8.60	8.78	3.09	3.40	3.10	8.98
Apr	85	2	1.99	0.06	1.75	1.61	7.81
Apr	90	0.30	0.39	30.47	5.10	5.00	1.88
May	90	1.60	1.54	3.98	6.40	6.07	5.2

| Apr | 95 | 0.05 | 0.04 | 22.09 | 10.10 | 9.65 | 4.46 |

So, the model didn't seem to do very well. It priced the call reasonably well when the strike was close to being at-the-money, but did worse the farther we got from a strike near 85. The puts did worse. This was just one example, but it is accepted that the Black-Scholes model seems to do reasonably well pricing options at the money, but does not do so well for out of the money options or options that are deep in the money. (If you wish to know more about this apparent anomaly, look under "volatility smiles" in *Options, Futures, and Other Derivatives*, by John C. Hull, and in *Pricing Derivative Securities*, by Eliezer Z. Prisman.) Black-Scholes can provide an estimate for prices of options and warrants and the like, but you can't argue with the market. If you find what you feel is a mispriced option, all you can do is hope that the market will correct itself. Or it could be that the model is missing something important that the market is pricing into the option.

A better use for Black-Scholes might be to determine what volatility the market is pricing into the asset. Thus, it can be solved iteratively, inputting the option price and solving for the implied volatility. Using the above call prices, we use Excel's "solve" function to determine the market's view of the volatility. The results are tabulated below.

Implied Volatility for IBM Calls

Expiry	Strike Price	Call Price	Implied Volatility, %
Apr	80	5.70	36.76
May	80	7	38.94
Jul	80	8.60	32.28
Apr	85	2	33.52
Apr	90	0.30	30.66
May	90	1.60	34.24
Apr	95	0.05	34.86

Using Excel's solver to solve for implied volatility:

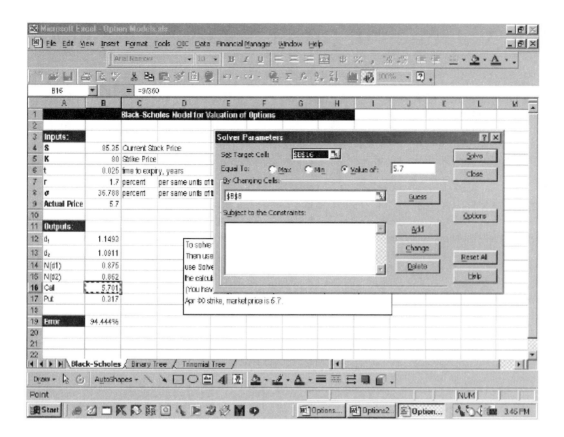

Modification of Black-Scholes (the Merton Model)

We can easily modify the Black-Scholes equation to handle payment of dividends, but only in those cases where the dividends can be assumed to be paid at a continuous rate. That is, as opposed to a discrete dividend, which is the norm for individual stocks, where dividends may be paid quarterly. What kind of dividends might be paid continuously? It might be appropriate to assume that stock market indices can be modeled this way. All we have to do to modify the Black-Scholes equation to handle the continuously-paid dividend, paid at the rate δ (δ is a percent per year, such as 1.38% currently for the S&P 500 index), is replace S in the equation by $S^{-\delta t}$. Then we have

$$C(S,t) = S^{-\delta t} N(d_1) - Ke^{-rt} N(d_2)$$

Note that d_1 and d_2 will be slightly modified to account for the dividends, where

$$d_1 = \frac{\ln\left(\dfrac{S}{K}\right) + \left(r - \delta + \dfrac{\sigma^2}{2}\right)(T-t)}{\sigma\sqrt{T-t}}, \quad d_2 = d_1 - \sigma\sqrt{T-t}$$

Option Valuation II: Other Solution Techniques

More complex options demand more complex strategies. These strategies include valuation by binomial trees, trinomial trees, finite difference methods, the control variate technique, and Monte Carlo analysis. These methods are particularly well-suited for handling path dependent options and situations that the Black-Scholes equation cannot handle, such as discrete jumps in dividends and stochastic volatility and interest rate shocks. We can also model interest rate options such as caps, collars and floors using these methods. We cover many of these techniques, with examples, in the following section.

Binomial tree method

The **binomial tree method** was developed as a simple strategy to use in teaching the Black-Scholes equation. The method gained popularity due to its simplicity of use, flexibility and ability to handle more complex problems. It is easy to understand and implement on a spreadsheet. We consider a stock at a current price $S = S_0$ and ask what the price might be in some discrete time period Δt, say, one day or one month. We assume that the stock price can either go up or go down – it can only move in one of two ways, which is why this is called the binomial method. More complex methods, such as the trinomial method, allow for the possibility that the stock can move sideways – the price stays the same. (The trinomial method will be introduced later.) Binomial and trinomial trees are heavily used in interest rate and interest rate option modeling. Below is a diagram of the stock price movement over a single time period:

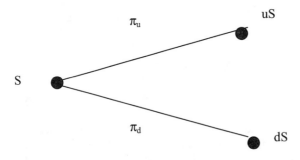

In the preceding figure, π_u and π_d are the probabilities of an upward and a downward move, respectively. These probabilities are constant as the tree evolves through time. Since there are only the two possible states of nature, $\pi_u + \pi_d$ must equal one. These probabilities are chosen so that the random walk that evolves using the binomial method will have the same mean and variance as the random walk $dS = \mu S dt + \sigma S dz$. (That is, the mean return from the stock over time Δt is μ and the variance of the return is $\sigma^2 \Delta t$.) This can be accomplished by setting

$$u = e^{\sigma\sqrt{\Delta t}}, d = \frac{1}{u} \text{ and } \pi_u = \frac{e^{rt} - d}{u - d}, \pi_d = 1 - \pi_u = \frac{u - e^{rt}}{u - d}$$

After a time Δt, the stock price S should grow to $Se^{r\Delta t}$. This must be equal to $\pi_u uS + (1-\pi_u)dS$. Note also that the spread between uS and dS is $2\sigma\Delta t$.

Example Going back to our IBM stock, $S = 85.35$, $\mu = 10\%$ and $\sigma = 33.5\%$. If $\Delta t = 0.0833$ years, what are the possible stock price movements?

$$u = e^{.335\sqrt{.0833}} = 1.1015, d = \frac{1}{1.1015} = 0.9078 \text{ and}$$

$$\pi_u = \frac{e^{0.1*.0833} - 0.9078}{1.1015 - 0.9078} = 0.5192, \pi_d = 1 - \pi_u = 0.4808$$

The stock price after the upward movement is then uS = 1.1015*85.35 = 94.01 and the price after the downward movement is dS = 77.48. Let's take the tree out for three time intervals (one quarter):

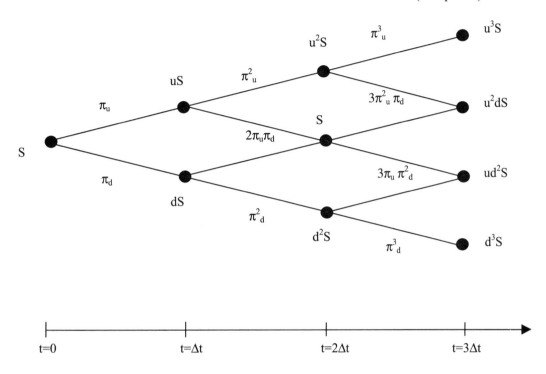

Note that at each time step nΔt, there are (n+1) nodes. Thus there are two possible stock prices, uS and dS, after one time step and so on. The stock price at any node can then be represented as $S_{i,n}$ where i is the number of up-moves and n is the number of time steps. The highest stock price at step nΔt is $S_{n,n} = u^n S$; the lowest is $S_{-n,n} = d^n S$ and so forth. Below is the tree with nodes identified in the $S_{i,n}$ notation.

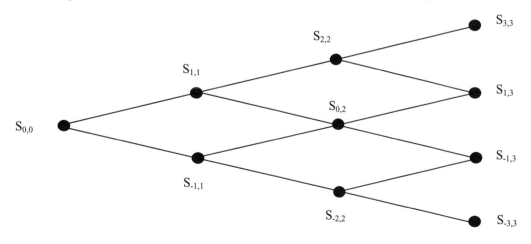

So to get to point $S_{2,2}$ we would take two time steps and two up moves. Point $S_{1,3}$ is reached after three time steps and one up move. On the tree, we would actually have to make two up moves followed by a down move to reach $S_{1,3}$, since $S_{1,3} = u^2 dS$, but recall that $u = \dfrac{1}{d}$ so $u^2 d = u^2 \dfrac{1}{u} = u$.

The probabilities of up- and down-moves π_u and π_d are constant in this model. Because we are using constant volatility, the tree is symmetric about the x-axis as we move forward. These trees can also be built for fixed income securities, in which case it may be desirable to use time-dependent volatility. Such trees will show a drift. For this example, the evolution of stock prices over time, and consequent probabilities, is thus:

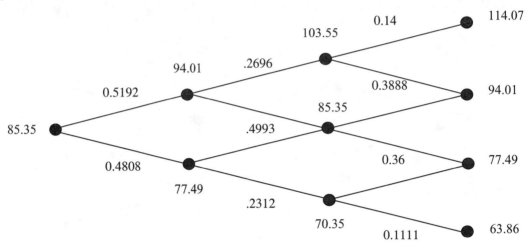

This method is easy and powerful. It can quickly be implemented in a spreadsheet.

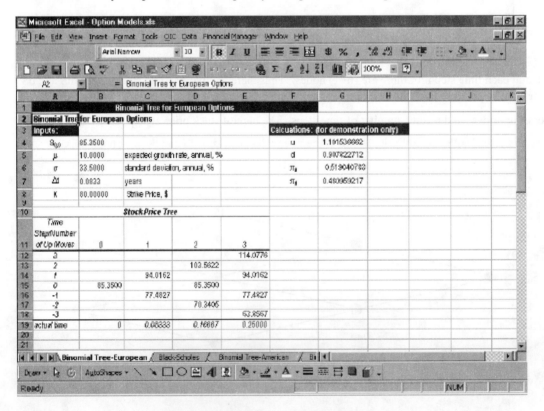

Use of binomial tree to price European call and put options

Now, let's apply this method to price a three-month European call on the option. In order to do this, we construct a tree for the call value by simply working backward from the ending value of the tree. Each node is evaluated in turn using the option valuation formula $C = \max(S_{i,n}-K,0)$. We are interested in determining the value of the call today – that is, $C_{0,0}$. Suppose the strike price is $80. The call values at the last time step would be:

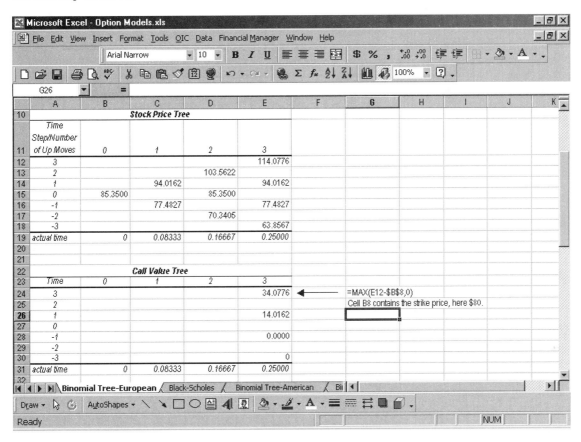

The next step is to work backward from time step 3 to time step 2. Each option value at preceding nodes is calculated from the option values at the following nodes. This just requires discounting. Remember that if we are at node $S_{2,2}$ (highlighted in the figure below), the only possible moves are to $S_{3,3}$ or $S_{1,3}$. We got there using probabilities π_u and π_d. At node (i,j) the call value $C_{i,j}$ is computed as

$$C_{i,j} = e^{-r\Delta t}\left(\pi_u C_{i+1,j+1} + \left(1-\pi_u\right)C_{i-1,j+1}\right)$$

So the formula for $C_{2,2}$ is just $C_{2,2} = (\pi_u C_{3,3} + (1-\pi_u) C_{1,3})e^{-r\Delta t}$.

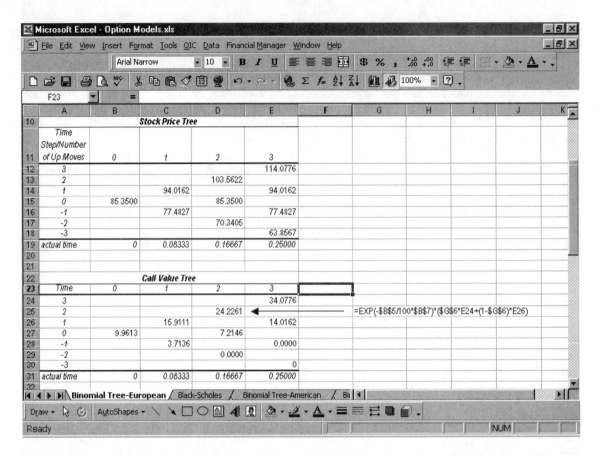

The remaining call values at time steps 1 and 0 are calculated the same way, to find that $C_{0,0}$ = \$9.9613. This compares to the actual value from the Black-Scholes model of \$9.88. The Binomial Method did not give the exact answer because Δt was relatively large (one month). We can increase accuracy by choosing many more time steps, so that Δt would be much smaller. The number of time steps can be determined via the formula $n = T/\Delta t$. So if we are using one-week increments, n = 0.25 year/(1/48 year) = 12, using the simplifying assuming 4 weeks/month. We would get a price of \$9.89 for the call using a one-week increment. Pricing puts is done the same way, but the option value at expiry is calculated using max(K-S,0) instead of max(S-K,0). We use the same underlying stock price tree. Here is the put value tree:

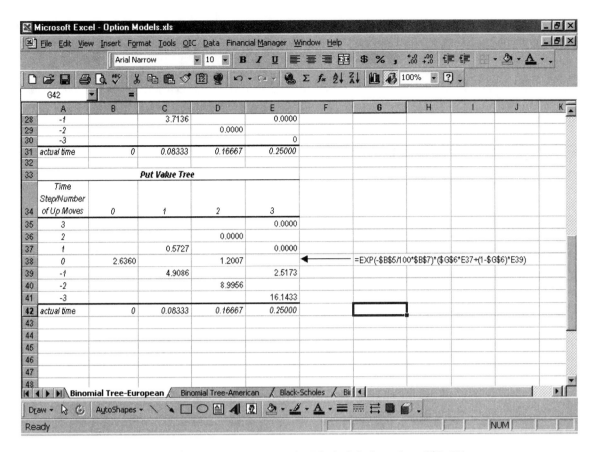

The calculated option price of $2.6360 compares to the Black-Scholes price of $2.551.

Summary

The steps in the binomial tree valuation method for European options:

1. Construct the tree for the underlying asset movement, using probabilities and up and down moves calculated with $u = e^{\sigma\sqrt{\Delta t}}, d = \dfrac{1}{u}, \pi_u = \dfrac{e^{rt} - d}{u - d}, \pi_d = 1 - \pi_u = \dfrac{u - e^{rt}}{u - d}$

2. Calculate the option value at expiry. Then, working backward, calculate the option value at preceding nodes, using the present value of option values at succeeding nodes that you would reach from the node you are at.

Valuation of American puts and calls

The preceding options were European: that is, they could only be exercised at expiry. There would be no advantage to building a binomial tree over just using the Black-Scholes equation if we were only going to value European options. The power of the tree comes in when we want to value more complex options, such as American and path-dependent options, because we can make a decision at each node. We can also pay discrete dividends, whereas Black-Scholes can be modified to value only continuous dividends. Exercising options prior to expiry is called "early exercise", and the ability to do this makes American options more valuable than European options. As stated previously, it can be proven mathematically that

$V_{American} \geq V_{European}$. It can also be shown that it is *never* optimal to exercise a call option early on a non-dividend paying stock. (A put, though, is a different matter.) Let's go back to our example of above. We can use the same stock price tree and the same option value at expiry, but as we move backward, we have to make a choice. There are two possibilities at each node. We can either hang on to the option, as we know its value is the PV of the option values at the two nodes that will be generated from the node we are at. Or, we can exercise the option. We decide between the two possibilities just by comparing the two values of the different decisions.

The starting point is the same put tree we had before, but with only the values at expiry filled in:

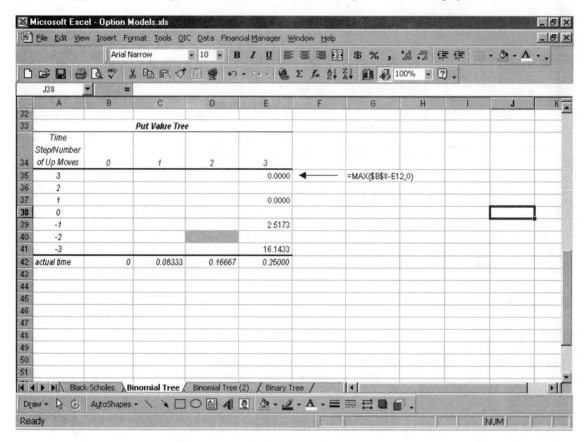

Let's calculate the value of the option at the highlighted point, $S_{-2,2}$. We calculated this previously as $P_{-2,2} = (\pi_u P_{-1,3} + (1 - \pi_u) P_{-3,3}) e^{-r\Delta t} = (0.51904*2.5173 + 0.48095*16.1433)e^{(-0.10*0.0833)} = \$8.9955$. This is the value of the option if held to expiry at this point in (s,t) space, and is called the **option alive price**. We must compare this value to the immediate value of the put option if exercised. Since the stock value at this point was \$70.3405, the put value here is $\max(K-S,0) = \max(80-70.3405,0) = \$9.6595$. This, symmetrically, is called the **option dead price**. In this case, since $\$9.6595 > \$8.9955$, we would choose to exercise the option immediately rather than waiting one more time step for the value to grow by $r\Delta t$. So, we must replace the put value in this cell by the value \$9.6595. We do this for all remaining values in this time step, i.e., $S_{2,0}$ and $S_{2,2}$. The value of the put is \$2.7871, compared with \$2.551 for the European put.

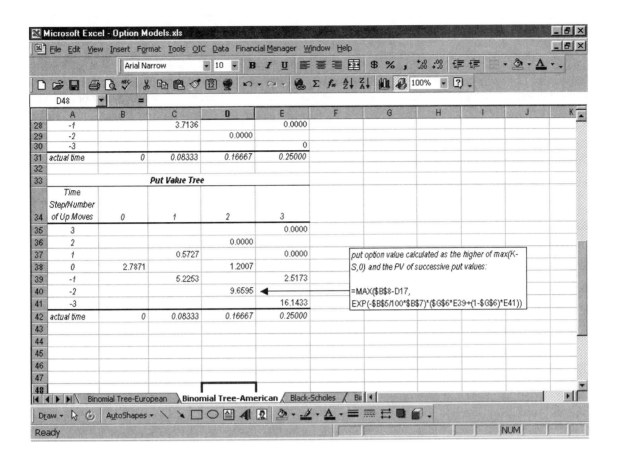

Trinomial method for option valuation

This is similar to the binomial method, but a stock can make one of three possible moves at each stop: it can move up, down or sideways.

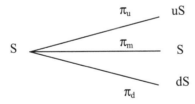

The only modifications we need to make are to our formulas: We have $\pi_u + \pi_m + \pi_d = 1$, with π_u and π_d as usual, and π_m the probability of a "middle" move, or no change in stock price. Since again we want the expectations of the change of the asset return and volatility over a small time increment to be μ and σ, the equations we get are:

Expected return of $dS/S = \pi_u u + \pi_m(0) + \pi_d d = E[\mu\, dt + \sigma\, dz] = \mu\, \Delta t$
Expected variance of $dS/S = E[(\mu\, dt + \sigma\, dz)^2] = \pi_u u^2 + \pi_m(0) + \pi_d d^2 = \mu\, (\Delta t)^2 + \sigma^2\, \Delta z^2 = \mu\, (\Delta t)^2 + \sigma^2\, \Delta t$
Also, $\pi_u + \pi_m + \pi_d = 1$.

Finite difference method for option valuation

This is a more sophisticated method for option valuation than the binomial method, but more difficult to implement. This method has a very obvious link to the governing stochastic partial differential equation. In the following, we will value the American put option, since we are already familiar with this option, and our answer may be checked against the analytic solution.

Recall our derivation of the Black-Scholes equation $\dfrac{\partial V}{\partial t} + \dfrac{1}{2}\sigma^2 S^2 \dfrac{\partial^2 V}{\partial S^2} + rS\dfrac{\partial V}{\partial S} - rV = 0$

We mentioned that this was a stochastic, non-linear partial differential equation. To solve it for the option value $V(S,t)$ requires specification of two boundary conditions in S and one time condition in t. There are some tricks that may be employed to make the solution easier (which we will cover later). The idea behind the solution is to form a numerical approximation of the solution $V(S,t)$, which will differ from the "true" answer by some error. We seek to make this approximation error as small as possible. We will not solve the equation exactly, but numerically, by making approximations of each derivative. This turns the equation from one that is continuous in S and t to one that is discrete, known only at certain "grid points" in the (S,t) space. This is called **discretization**, where we subdivide the payoff space $V(S,t)$ into $M+1$ stock prices such that $\Delta S = (S_{max} - S_{min})/M$, and $N+1$ times so that $\Delta t = T_{expiry}/N$. Then the option $V(i,j)$ is a function of time $t = j\,\Delta t$ and underlying stock price $i\,\Delta S$.

The steps are:

1. Discretize the domain.
2. Write the finite-difference equation (FDE) of the governing PDE and the boundary conditions
3. The FDE is applied at each node at which the solution is unknown (all interior points).
4. Solve the resulting system of linear equations.

First, decide on the range of stock prices we want. In the binomial method, these just evolved from our choice of time, u and π_u: we didn't *set* the range of possible stock prices in advance. In the **finite difference method**, we start by choosing a range for S, (S_{min}, S_{max}). The range will, of course, depend on the parameters' volatility, risk-free rate and time to expiry. The payoff space would then look something like the following:

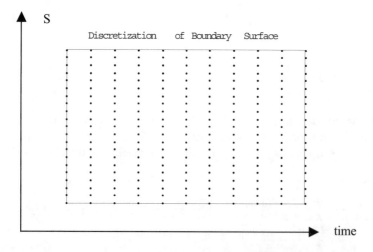

Each dot represents a different point (S,t). The points to the very left are $t = 0$ and the points to the far right are for $t=T_{expiry}$. The points along the lower edge, running from left to right (or $t=0$ to $t = T_{expiry}$) are the minimum stock price S_{min} that we chose, while the points along the extreme upper edge all have the value S_{max}. Letting the variable i represent the number of steps in the variable S, we have S at each point as S_{min} + $i\Delta S$, as i runs from 0 to M in increments of one. For example, if we choose S_{min} = 50 and S_{max} = 100 with M = 5 as the number of stock steps, we have ΔS = (S_{max} − S_{min})/M = (100-50)/5 = 10. Then, $S = S_{min} + i\Delta S$ =50 + 10i for i = 0 to 5. This means that we will calculate option values at the discrete values of S equal to 50, 60, 70, 80, 90 and 100. If we want the option value at some intermediate value of S, such as S = 85, we should define our grid so that we can generate this S, say, by changing M to 10. This will give ΔS = 5 and allow us to have a grid point at S = 85. (More complex techniques exist that allow for non-uniform grid spacing such as 50, 60, 70, 80, 84, 85, 86, 87, 90 and 100, where we cluster points about some stock price of intense interest, and use wider spacing outside of this range. But, here, we only cover uniform grid sizes – a constant spacing ΔS.)

Similarly, we choose a value for the total number of time steps, N, required to progress from t = 0 to t = T$_{expiry}$. Then the discrete time interval size, Δt = T$_{expiry}$/N with t = j Δt, with j = 0 to j = N incrementing by one each time. If we are valuing an option that expires in three months' time, we might choose N = 3 so that we have a time step each month Δt = 0.0833 year. We define t = 0.0833 j with j = 0 ... 3, so t = 0, 0.08333, 2*0.08333, 3*0.0833. Then we represent V(S,t) as $V(S,t) \cong V(S_{min} + i\Delta S, j\Delta t) = V_{i,j}$, i=0,…,M; j = 0, …, N.

Now that we have defined our (S, t) domain, we discretize the continuous *SDE*. This is done by replacing the derivatives with their numerical equivalents. We take each derivative in turn.

$$\frac{\partial V}{\partial t} \cong \frac{\Delta V}{\Delta t} = \frac{V(S,t+\Delta t)-V(S,t)}{\Delta t} = \frac{V_{i,j+1}-V_{i,j}}{\Delta t}$$. Note here we hold stock price constant by holding the variable i, which represents S, constant. We only let time vary.

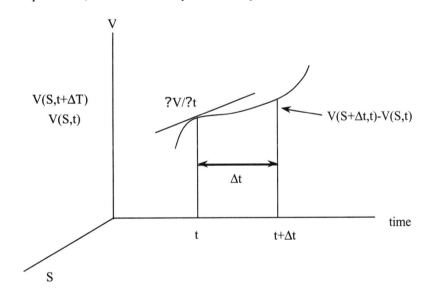

The second derivative of V with respect to S is calculated by holding time (j) constant and expanding about the point (i,j) as $\frac{\partial^2 V}{\partial S^2} \cong \frac{V_{i+1,j}-2V_{i,j}+V_{i-1,j}}{\Delta S^2}$. We move one increment ΔS from i to i+1, and one increment from i in the opposite direction to i-1. This is called the "central difference operator".

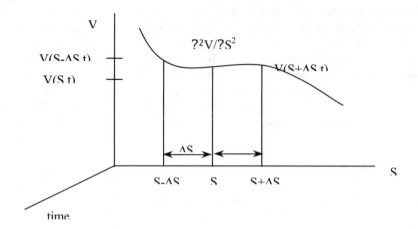

For $\dfrac{\partial V}{\partial S}$ we can use the centered difference operator as well. For first derivatives this has the form

Finally, we replace V and S by $V_{i,j}$ and $S_{i,j}$ respectively. Substituting all of these difference operators into the Black-Scholes equation gives:

$$\frac{\partial V}{\partial S} \cong \frac{V_{i+1,j} - V_{i-1,j}}{2\Delta S}$$

$$\frac{V_{i,j+1} - V_{i,j}}{\Delta t} + \frac{1}{2}\sigma^2 S^2_{i,j}\left(\frac{V_{i+1,j} - 2V_{i,j} + V_{i-1,j}}{\Delta S^2}\right) + rS_{i,j}\left(\frac{V_{i+1,j} - V_{i-1,j}}{2\Delta S}\right) - rV_{i,j} = 0$$

To make things easier, we will solve for $V_{i,j+1}$ (the known) in terms of the unknowns, $V_{i,j}$. This will generate a linear system of equations.

$$V_{i,j+1} = V_{i,j} - \frac{1}{2}\sigma^2 \Delta t(S_{min} + i\Delta S)^2\left(\frac{V_{i+1,j} - 2V_{i,j} + V_{i-1,j}}{\Delta S^2}\right) - r\Delta t(S_{min} + i\Delta S)\left(\frac{V_{i+1,j} - V_{i-1,j}}{2\Delta S}\right) + r\Delta t V_{i,j}$$

Collecting common terms,

If we define

$$V_{i,j+1} = V_{i-1,j}\left(-\frac{1}{2}\sigma^2\Delta t\,\frac{(S_{min} + i\Delta S)^2}{\Delta S^2} + \frac{r\Delta t(S_{min} + i\Delta S)}{2\Delta S}\right) +$$

$$V_{i,j}\left(1 + \frac{\sigma^2\Delta t(S_{min} + i\Delta S)^2}{\Delta S^2} + r\Delta t\right) +$$

$$V_{i+1,j}\left(-\frac{1}{2}\sigma^2\Delta t\,\frac{(S_{min} + i\Delta S)^2}{\Delta S^2} - \frac{r\Delta t(S_{min} + i\Delta S)}{2\Delta S}\right)$$

$$a_i = -\frac{1}{2}\sigma^2 \Delta t \frac{(S_{min} + i\Delta S)^2}{\Delta S^2} + \frac{r\Delta t(S_{min} + i\Delta S)}{2\Delta S}$$

$$b_i = 1 + \sigma^2 \Delta t \frac{(S_{min} + i\Delta S)^2}{\Delta S^2} + r\Delta t$$

$$c_i = -\frac{1}{2}\sigma^2 \Delta t \frac{(S_{min} + i\Delta S)^2}{\Delta S^2} - \frac{r\Delta t(S_{min} + i\Delta S)}{2\Delta S}$$

Then the finite difference equation is

$$a_i V_{i-1,j} + b_i V_{i,j} + c_i V_{i+1,j} = V_{i,j+1}, j = 0, \cdots, N-1, i = 1, \cdots, M-1$$

Since the known value $V_{i,j+1}$ depends on a sequence of unknown values at preceding times, this method is known as the **implicit method**. It is very robust and is the preferred technique to use, although it does require solution of a system of linear equations at each time step.

We write it at each of our interior grid points, for $i = 1, \ldots M$-1 and $j = 0, \ldots N$-1. This then generates a linear system of M-1 equations that must be solved at each of the N-1 time steps. The right hand side is known; the left hand side is a matrix equation for our desired option values at the preceding time step. Notice in the above that we kept r and σ constant. We can modify this expression by using $r_{i,j}$ and $\sigma_{i,j}$ if we wish to allow the risk-free rate and stochastic volatility to evolve through time, perhaps modeling the effect of volatility shocks on the option -- which is beyond the scope of this book, but can easily be done.

Specification of boundary conditions

For a call: Assuming that S_{min} and S_{max} are sufficiently large and small enough, respectively (meaning "far from" K), we have S_{max} deep in the money and S_{min} deep out of the money, regardless of time to expiry. This can be shown mathematically using the Black-Scholes equation and taking limits: for S_{max}, the value of the option approaches the stock price as the stock price goes to infinity; for S_{min}, the value of the option is zero.

For A Put: Here, the value of the option is K as stock price approaches zero. If the option is deep out of the money ($S_{max} >> K$), the option is valueless.

The boundary conditions must be correct. They diffuse from the boundaries into the interior so if they are incorrect, the solution will also be incorrect.

Time Condition: We begin at expiry, since we know that $V_{i,N} = \max(S_{i,N}-K,0)=\max(S_{min} + i\,\Delta S-K,0)$ for a call; $V_{i,N} = \max(K-S_{i,N},0)=\max(K-(S_{min} + i\,\Delta S),0)$ for a put.

Whether we have a call or a put, the system of equations that must be solved is the same. The only difference is in the application of the boundary conditions.

Numerical example: American put

For our IBM stock, because we have S known as $85.35, and we only have to calculate out for three months, we choose a range that we expect the stock price to take on over the time period. An idea is to center the range about the strike price. Because we actually already have a hint at the answers from the binomial model, let's use that. The price ranged from 63 to 114, but to use easy numbers we will choose

$S_{min} = 0$ and $S_{max} = 170$. We need to choose the grid so that there is a stock price at the current price. This would require very fine spacing, so we will content ourselves by using \$85 instead in this illustration. It is a good idea to have the current stock price in the center of the range you generate, making sure that S_{min} and S_{max} are far enough away from S and K. We will take 20 stock price steps, so $\Delta S = 170/20 = \$8.5$, and three time steps so $\Delta t = 0.25/10 = 0.025$ year.

Recall $r = 10\%$ and $\sigma = 33.5\%$. The grid looks like this:

i	j=0	j=1	j=2	j=3	j=4	j=5	j=6	j=7	j=8	j=9	j=10
0	$V_{0,0}$	$V_{0,1}$	$V_{0,2}$	$V_{0,3}$	$V_{0,4}$	$V_{0,5}$	$V_{0,6}$	$V_{0,7}$	$V_{0,8}$	$V_{0,9}$	$V_{0,10}$
1	$V_{1,0}$	$V_{1,1}$	$V_{1,2}$	$V_{1,3}$	$V_{1,4}$	$V_{1,5}$	$V_{1,6}$	$V_{1,7}$	$V_{1,8}$	$V_{1,9}$	$V_{1,10}$
2	$V_{2,0}$	$V_{2,1}$	$V_{2,2}$	$V_{2,3}$	$V_{2,4}$	$V_{2,5}$	$V_{2,6}$	$V_{2,7}$	$V_{2,8}$	$V_{2,9}$	$V_{2,10}$
3	$V_{3,0}$	$V_{3,1}$	$V_{3,2}$	$V_{3,3}$	$V_{3,4}$	$V_{3,5}$	$V_{3,6}$	$V_{3,7}$	$V_{3,8}$	$V_{3,9}$	$V_{3,10}$
4	$V_{4,0}$	$V_{4,1}$	$V_{4,2}$	$V_{4,3}$	$V_{4,4}$	$V_{4,5}$	$V_{4,6}$	$V_{4,7}$	$V_{4,8}$	$V_{4,9}$	$V_{4,10}$
5	$V_{5,0}$	$V_{5,1}$	$V_{5,2}$	$V_{5,3}$	$V_{5,4}$	$V_{5,5}$	$V_{5,6}$	$V_{5,7}$	$V_{5,8}$	$V_{5,9}$	$V_{5,10}$
6	$V_{6,0}$	$V_{6,1}$	$V_{6,2}$	$V_{6,3}$	$V_{6,4}$	$V_{6,5}$	$V_{6,6}$	$V_{6,7}$	$V_{6,8}$	$V_{6,9}$	$V_{6,10}$
7	$V_{7,0}$	$V_{7,1}$	$V_{7,2}$	$V_{7,3}$	$V_{7,4}$	$V_{7,5}$	$V_{7,6}$	$V_{7,7}$	$V_{7,8}$	$V_{7,9}$	$V_{7,10}$
8	$V_{8,0}$	$V_{8,1}$	$V_{8,2}$	$V_{8,3}$	$V_{8,4}$	$V_{8,5}$	$V_{8,6}$	$V_{8,7}$	$V_{8,8}$	$V_{8,9}$	$V_{8,10}$
9	$V_{9,0}$	$V_{9,1}$	$V_{9,2}$	$V_{9,3}$	$V_{9,4}$	$V_{9,5}$	$V_{9,6}$	$V_{9,7}$	$V_{9,8}$	$V_{9,9}$	$V_{9,10}$
10	$V_{10,0}$	$V_{10,1}$	$V_{10,2}$	$V_{10,3}$	$V_{10,4}$	$V_{10,5}$	$V_{10,6}$	$V_{10,7}$	$V_{10,8}$	$V_{10,9}$	$V_{10,10}$
11	$V_{11,0}$	$V_{11,1}$	$V_{11,2}$	$V_{11,3}$	$V_{11,4}$	$V_{11,5}$	$V_{11,6}$	$V_{11,7}$	$V_{11,8}$	$V_{11,9}$	$V_{11,10}$
12	$V_{12,0}$	$V_{12,1}$	$V_{12,2}$	$V_{12,3}$	$V_{12,4}$	$V_{12,5}$	$V_{12,6}$	$V_{12,7}$	$V_{12,8}$	$V_{12,9}$	$V_{12,10}$
13	$V_{13,0}$	$V_{13,1}$	$V_{13,2}$	$V_{13,3}$	$V_{13,4}$	$V_{13,5}$	$V_{13,6}$	$V_{13,7}$	$V_{13,8}$	$V_{13,9}$	$V_{13,10}$
14	$V_{14,0}$	$V_{14,1}$	$V_{14,2}$	$V_{14,3}$	$V_{14,4}$	$V_{14,5}$	$V_{14,6}$	$V_{14,7}$	$V_{14,8}$	$V_{14,9}$	$V_{14,10}$
15	$V_{15,0}$	$V_{15,1}$	$V_{15,2}$	$V_{15,3}$	$V_{15,4}$	$V_{15,5}$	$V_{15,6}$	$V_{15,7}$	$V_{15,8}$	$V_{15,9}$	$V_{15,10}$
16	$V_{16,0}$	$V_{16,1}$	$V_{16,2}$	$V_{16,3}$	$V_{16,4}$	$V_{16,5}$	$V_{16,6}$	$V_{16,7}$	$V_{16,8}$	$V_{16,9}$	$V_{16,10}$
17	$V_{17,0}$	$V_{17,1}$	$V_{17,2}$	$V_{17,3}$	$V_{17,4}$	$V_{17,5}$	$V_{17,6}$	$V_{17,7}$	$V_{17,8}$	$V_{17,9}$	$V_{17,10}$
18	$V_{18,0}$	$V_{18,1}$	$V_{18,2}$	$V_{18,3}$	$V_{18,4}$	$V_{18,5}$	$V_{18,6}$	$V_{18,7}$	$V_{18,8}$	$V_{18,9}$	$V_{18,10}$
19	$V_{19,0}$	$V_{19,1}$	$V_{19,2}$	$V_{19,3}$	$V_{19,4}$	$V_{19,5}$	$V_{19,6}$	$V_{19,7}$	$V_{19,8}$	$V_{19,9}$	$V_{19,10}$
20	$V_{20,0}$	$V_{20,1}$	$V_{20,2}$	$V_{20,3}$	$V_{20,4}$	$V_{20,5}$	$V_{20,6}$	$V_{20,7}$	$V_{20,8}$	$V_{20,9}$	$V_{20,10}$
actual time	0.0000	0.0250	0.0500	0.0750	0.1000	0.1250	0.1500	0.1750	0.2000	0.2250	0.2500

The stock prices are:

i	Stock Price Grid										
0	0	0	0	0	0	0	0	0	0	0	0
1	8.5	8.5	8.5	8.5	8.5	8.5	8.5	8.5	8.5	8.5	8.5
2	17	17	17	17	17	17	17	17	17	17	17
3	25.5	25.5	25.5	25.5	25.5	25.5	25.5	25.5	25.5	25.5	25.5
4	34	34	34	34	34	34	34	34	34	34	34
5	42.5	42.5	42.5	42.5	42.5	42.5	42.5	42.5	42.5	42.5	42.5
6	51	51	51	51	51	51	51	51	51	51	51
7	59.5	59.5	59.5	59.5	59.5	59.5	59.5	59.5	59.5	59.5	59.5
8	68	68	68	68	68	68	68	68	68	68	68
9	76.5	76.5	76.5	76.5	76.5	76.5	76.5	76.5	76.5	76.5	76.5
10	85	85	85	85	85	85	85	85	85	85	85
11	93.5	93.5	93.5	93.5	93.5	93.5	93.5	93.5	93.5	93.5	93.5
12	102	102	102	102	102	102	102	102	102	102	102
13	110.5	110.5	110.5	110.5	110.5	110.5	110.5	110.5	110.5	110.5	110.5
14	119	119	119	119	119	119	119	119	119	119	119
15	127.5	127.5	127.5	127.5	127.5	127.5	127.5	127.5	127.5	127.5	127.5
16	136	136	136	136	136	136	136	136	136	136	136
17	144.5	144.5	144.5	144.5	144.5	144.5	144.5	144.5	144.5	144.5	144.5
18	153	153	153	153	153	153	153	153	153	153	153
19	161.5	161.5	161.5	161.5	161.5	161.5	161.5	161.5	161.5	161.5	161.5
20	170	170	170	170	170	170	170	170	170	170	170
	j=0	j=1	j=2	j=3	j=4	j=5	j=6	j=7	j=8	j=9	j=10
actual time	0.0000	0.0250	0.0500	0.0750	0.1000	0.1250	0.1500	0.1750	0.2000	0.2250	0.2500

This schematic shows that we will be interested in the option value at $i = 10$, since this corresponds to our stock price of \$85. We will generate a table of option values evolving backward in time from the farthest right column (expiry) to the current time (extreme left column).

The next step is to write our equation at each node of the grid. We start with the ending (expiry) boundary at $j=N$, because this is the only point at which we know the option value.

First, compute the option values at expiry, recall $K=80$:

i	S	V=K-S
0	0	80
1	8.5	71.5
2	17	63
3	25.5	54.5
4	34	46
5	42.5	37.5
6	51	29
7	59.5	20.5
8	68	12
9	76.5	3.5
10	85	0
11	93.5	0
12	102	0
13	110.5	0
14	119	0
15	127.5	0
16	136	0
17	144.5	0
18	153	0
19	161.5	0
20	170	0

The Linear System of Equations For each j, we have

$$a_i V_{i-1,j} + b_i V_{i,j} + c_i V_{i+1,j} = V_{i,j+1}, j = 0, \cdots, N-1, i = 1, \cdots, M-1$$

Starting with j = N-1 (one time step prior to expiry), then,

$$a_i V_{i-1,N-1} + b_i V_{i,N-1} + c_i V_{i+1,N-1} = V_{i,N}, i = 1, \ldots, M-1$$

Since we have M=20, this equation must be written at 19 interior points.

$$i = 1 : a_1 V_{0,N-1} + b_1 V_{1,N-1} + c_1 V_{2,N-1} = V_{1,N}$$

$$i = 2 : a_2 V_{1,N-1} + b_2 V_{2,N-1} + c_2 V_{3,N-1} = V_{2,N}$$

$$\vdots$$

$$i = 18 : a_{18} V_{17,N-1} + b_{18} V_{18,N-1} + c_{18} V_{19,N-1} = V_{18,N}$$

$$i = 19 : a_{19} V_{18,N-1} + b_{19} V_{19,N-1} + c_{19} V_{20,N-1} = V_{19,N}$$

It may seem that we have two more unknowns than equations, but recall that $V_{0,N-1}$ and $V_{20,N-1}$ are boundary conditions. Then our equations become

$$i = 1 : b_1 V_{1,N-1} + c_1 V_{2,N-1} = V_{1,N} - a_1 V_{0,N-1}$$

$$i = 2 : a_2 V_{1,N-1} + b_2 V_{2,N-1} + c_2 V_{3,N-1} = V_{2,N}$$

$$\vdots$$

$$i = 18 : a_{18} V_{17,N-1} + b_{18} V_{18,N-1} + c_{18} V_{19,N-1} = V_{18,N}$$

$$i = 19 : a_{19} V_{18,N-1} + b_{19} V_{19,N-1} = V_{19,N} - c_{19} V_{20,N-1}$$

$$
\begin{bmatrix}
b_1 & c_1 & & & & & & \\
a_2 & b_2 & c_2 & & & & & \\
& a_3 & b_3 & c_3 & & & & \\
& & \ddots & \ddots & \ddots & & & \\
& & & \ddots & \ddots & \ddots & & \\
& & & & \ddots & \ddots & \ddots & \\
& & & & & a_{18} & b_{18} & c_{18} \\
& & & & & & a_{19} & b_{19}
\end{bmatrix}
\begin{bmatrix}
V_{1,N-1} \\
V_{2,N-1} \\
V_{3,N-1} \\
\vdots \\
\vdots \\
\vdots \\
V_{18,N-1} \\
V_{19,N-1}
\end{bmatrix}
=
\begin{bmatrix}
V_{1,N} - a_1 V_{0,N-1} \\
V_{2,N} \\
V_{3,N} \\
\vdots \\
\vdots \\
\vdots \\
V_{18,N} \\
V_{19,N} - c_{19} V_{20,N-1}
\end{bmatrix}
$$

The matrix of coefficients is tri-diagonal. There are special solvers available for such matrices (for example, LU factorization.) Although the coefficients a_i, b_i and c_i must be calculated for each i, it only has to be done once. For storage efficiency, once the inverse of A is known, it can be stored.

For our parameters, we solve the matrix to get the option values at j=9 (0.025 year to expiry) as:

i	$V_{i,9}$	$V_{i,10}$
0	80	80
1	71.3005	71.5
2	62.8005	63
3	54.3005	54.5
4	45.8005	46

5	37.3005	37.5
6	28.8007	29
7	20.3038	20.5
8	11.8490	12
9	3.8722	3.5
10	0.3912	0
11	0.0463	0
12	0.0063	0
13	0.0010	0
14	0.0002	0
15	0.0000	0
16	0.0000	0
17	0.0000	0
18	0.0000	0
19	0.0000	0
20	0	0

Now we have to solve the same system of equations again, but this time for $j = 8$. However, before we do, we must evaluate the optimal option strategy at each i. The values in the column $V_{i,9}$ above are for the "option alive". Compare $V_{i,9}$ to the value of immediate exercise $\max(K-S,0)$ at each i. Replace the option value with $\max(V_{i,9}, \max(K-S_{i,9}))$. For example, at $i=1$ we have $V_{i,9} = 71.3005$. The stock price is $S_{min}+i\Delta S = 0 + 1*8.5 = \$8.5$, so the put is worth $\$80-8.5=71.5$ (as shown.) This is higher than $\$71.3005$, so replace $V_{i,9}$ with 71.5. Once all option values at this step are evaluated, re-solve the system of equations. Repeat until you reach $j=0$. This process yields a put value of $\$2.6657$, shown in the following, which compares well to our Black-Scholes value of $\$2.647$. Our value should be higher than Black-Scholes, because the ability to have early exercise is worth something. (In fact, it is worth approximately $\$2.667-\$2.647$.)

i	Results										
0	80	80	80	80	80	80	80	80	80	80	80
1	71.2884	71.2884	71.2884	71.2884	71.2884	71.2884	71.2884	71.2884	71.2884	71.3005	71.5
2	62.8005	62.8005	62.8005	62.8005	62.8005	62.8005	62.8005	62.8005	62.8005	62.8005	63
3	54.3005	54.3005	54.3005	54.3005	54.3005	54.3005	54.3005	54.3005	54.3005	54.3005	54.5
4	45.8005	45.8005	45.8005	45.8005	45.8005	45.8005	45.8005	45.8005	45.8005	45.8005	46
5	37.3005	37.3005	37.3005	37.3005	37.3005	37.3005	37.3005	37.3005	37.3005	37.3005	37.5
6	28.8014	28.8013	28.8012	28.8012	28.8011	28.8010	28.8010	28.8009	28.8008	28.8007	29
7	20.3181	20.3159	20.3145	20.3133	20.3121	20.3107	20.3092	20.3076	20.3058	20.3038	20.5
8	12.0582	12.0263	12.0058	11.9888	11.9704	11.9503	11.9283	11.9042	11.8779	11.8490	12
9	6.0764	5.9051	5.7210	5.5214	5.3040	5.0667	4.8074	4.5236	4.2127	3.8722	3.5
10	2.6657	2.4796	2.2818	2.0707	1.8446	1.6015	1.3387	1.0528	0.7391	0.3912	0
11	1.0745	0.9501	0.8244	0.6981	0.5726	0.4494	0.3309	0.2206	0.1234	0.0463	0
12	0.4145	0.3480	0.2845	0.2250	0.1704	0.1216	0.0798	0.0462	0.0215	0.0063	0
13	0.1571	0.1254	0.0968	0.0718	0.0504	0.0330	0.0196	0.0100	0.0040	0.0010	0
14	0.0595	0.0452	0.0331	0.0231	0.0151	0.0092	0.0050	0.0023	0.0008	0.0002	0
15	0.0227	0.0165	0.0115	0.0076	0.0047	0.0026	0.0013	0.0006	0.0002	0.0000	0
16	0.0088	0.0061	0.0041	0.0025	0.0015	0.0008	0.0004	0.0001	0.0000	0.0000	0
17	0.0035	0.0023	0.0015	0.0009	0.0005	0.0002	0.0001	0.0000	0.0000	0.0000	0
18	0.0014	0.0009	0.0005	0.0003	0.0002	0.0001	0.0000	0.0000	0.0000	0.0000	0
19	0.0005	0.0003	0.0002	0.0001	0.0001	0.0000	0.0000	0.0000	0.0000	0.0000	0
20	0	0	0	0	0	0	0	0	0	0	0
	j=0	j=1	j=2	j=3	j=4	j=5	j=6	j=7	j=8	j=9	j=10

We can do the same thing for a call, and we find a value of $\$9.5773$, which should match Black-Scholes ($\$9.622$) since we would not exercise the call early. (*Tip*: in Excel, you can use the **MINVERSE** and **MMULT** functions to invert and multiply the matrices, respectively.)

The explicit method

The preceding method required solution of a linear system of equations at each time step. Graphically, what we were doing was solving for three unknowns from one known $V_{i,j+1}$.

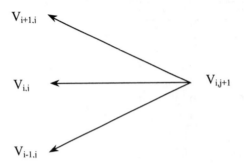

When we evaluated the derivatives $\dfrac{\partial V}{\partial S}$ and $\dfrac{\partial^2 V}{\partial S^2}$, we evaluated them at j. If we assume that the derivatives

$$\frac{V_{i,j+1}-V_{i,j}}{\Delta t}+\frac{1}{2}\sigma^2 S^2_{i,j}\left(\frac{V_{i+1,j+1}-2V_{i,j+1}+V_{i-1,j+1}}{\Delta S^2}\right)+rS_{i,j}\left(\frac{V_{i+1,j+1}-V_{i-1,j+1}}{2\Delta S}\right)-rV_{i,j}=0$$

stay constant over the small time interval Δt, then we can evaluate them at j+1. Then we have:

Simplifying and collecting terms to solve for $V_{i,j}$ gives

$$V_{i,j}=V_{i-1,j+1}\frac{1}{1+r\Delta t}\left(-\frac{1}{2}r\Delta t\left(\frac{S_{min}+i\Delta S}{\Delta S}\right)+\frac{1}{2}\Delta t\sigma^2\left(\frac{S_{min}+i\Delta S}{\Delta S}\right)^2\right)+V_{i,j+1}\frac{1}{1+r\Delta t}\left(1-\Delta t\sigma^2\left(\frac{S_{min}+i\Delta S}{\Delta S}\right)^2\right)$$

$$+V_{i+1,j+1}\frac{1}{1+r\Delta t}\left(\frac{1}{2}r\Delta t\left(\frac{S_{min}+i\Delta S}{\Delta S}\right)+\frac{1}{2}\Delta t\sigma^2\left(\frac{S_{min}+i\Delta S}{\Delta S}\right)^2\right)$$

If we define:

$$d_i=\frac{1}{1+r\Delta t}\left(-\frac{1}{2}r\Delta t\left(\frac{S_{min}+i\Delta S}{\Delta S}\right)+\frac{1}{2}\Delta t\sigma^2\left(\frac{S_{min}+i\Delta S}{\Delta S}\right)^2\right)$$

$$e_i=\frac{1}{1+r\Delta t}\left(1-\Delta t\sigma^2\left(\frac{S_{min}+i\Delta S}{\Delta S}\right)^2\right)$$

$$f_i=\frac{1}{1+r\Delta t}\left(\frac{1}{2}r\Delta t\left(\frac{S_{min}+i\Delta S}{\Delta S}\right)+\frac{1}{2}\Delta t\sigma^2\left(\frac{S_{min}+i\Delta S}{\Delta S}\right)^2\right)$$

Then, $V_{i,j}=d_iV_{i-1,j+1}+e_iV_{i,j+1}+f_iV_{i-1,j+1}$

Since all values on the right hand side are known, $V_{i,j}$ may be solved by straight forward evaluation. The problem with the explicit method is such ease of use has a high cost: the method leads to negative probabilities and is unstable except for carefully chosen ΔS and Δt. Usually, these steps must be chosen very small or the method will blow up. The schematic for the solution is:

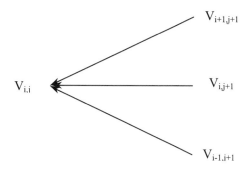

(*Tip*: To make the problem easier to solve, a commonly used transformation is to use ln(S) instead of S in the PDE.)

Monte-Carlo analysis

Like the name suggests, **Monte Carlo analysis** involves a form of "gambling." Well, random draws of normalized distributions, anyway. How is this done? We just generate paths for the stock price and then evaluate the call value at expiry, using $C = \max(S-K,0)$. We average all of the call values computed. The more simulations, the better the approximation will be, but this is a time-consuming analysis. Since we are generating an actual path for the stock prices, we can model American options and the other path-dependent variants. Monte Carlo may be slow to run, because you are doing many simulations and keeping track of the asset paths, but it is pretty easy to implement. The steps to value a European option are:

Step 1. Generate random paths for the asset using the lognormal random walk incrementing t by Δt to expiry.
Step 2. At the end of each path, evaluate the payoff of the option at expiry using $C = \max(S-K,0)$ or $P = \max(K-S,0)$.
Step 3. Compute the average of all such payoffs.
Step 4. Calculate the option value at the current time by discounting the average payoff by e^{-rt}.

In this model, we use the lognormal distribution rather than the previously derived $dS = \mu S dt + \sigma S dz$. If we use a normal distribution, it would imply that a stock could have a negative price. This is not the case. (Although stock *returns* may be normally distributed.) In order to derive the stochastic process for an asset which is lognormally distributed, recall the expression $df = \sigma S \dfrac{\partial f}{\partial S} dz + \left(\mu S \dfrac{\partial f}{\partial S} + \dfrac{1}{2}\sigma^2 S^2 \dfrac{\partial^s f}{\partial S^2} \right) dt$

f is just some function of S and t. Suppose we take $f = log\, S$. Then, $\dfrac{\partial f}{\partial S} = \dfrac{1}{S}$ and $\dfrac{\partial^2 f}{\partial S^2} = -\dfrac{1}{S^2}$. The

expression for df becomes $d(\log S) = \sigma S \dfrac{1}{S} dz + \left(\mu S \dfrac{1}{S} + \dfrac{1}{2}\sigma^2 S^2 \left(-\dfrac{1}{S^2} \right) \right) dt = \left(\mu - \dfrac{1}{2}\sigma^2 \right) dt + \sigma dz$

This expression can be integrated to give an expression for S:

$$\int_{t=0}^{T} d(\log S)\, dt = \int_{t=0}^{T} \left(\mu - \frac{1}{2}\sigma^2 \right) dt + \sigma dz = S_T = S_0 \exp\left(\left(\mu - \frac{1}{2}\sigma^2 \right) T + \int_{t=0}^{T} \sigma dz \right)$$

Over a small time interval Δt this is $\Delta t = \exp\left(\left(\mu - \dfrac{1}{2}\sigma^2 \right) \Delta t + \sigma \sqrt{\Delta t} N(z) \right)$ where N(z) is just a draw from a normal distribution.

Below is a plot of 100 simulations of our IBM option, over a one year period, using $S_0 = \$85.35$, $r = 1.7\%$, $\sigma = 33.5\%$ and $K = 80$. The computed call value was \$14.577, which is exactly equal to the theoretical solution of \$14.577. The put was calculated as \$7.876.

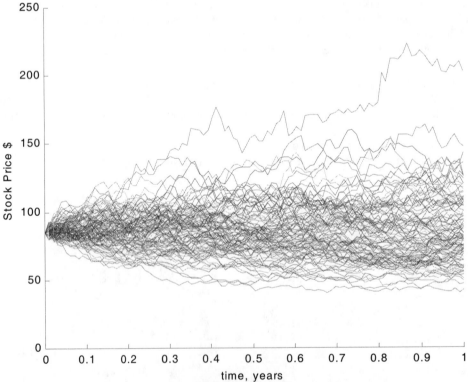

Monte Carlo Simulation of Stock Prices X =80 r =0.017 vol =0.335T =1 years.

Option Sensitivities – The Greeks

How will the calculated option value change in response to a change in the price of S, time, risk-free rate or volatility? The sensitivity of an option to changes in these parameters is very easy to calculate. Common option sensitivities of interest include delta, theta, vega and rho.

Delta

Recall the solution of the Black-Scholes equation for a call: $C(S,t) = SN(d_1) - Ke^{-rt}N(d_2)$ with

$$d_1 = \frac{\ln\left(\frac{S}{K}\right) + \left(r + \frac{1}{2}\sigma^2\right)(T-t)}{\sigma\sqrt{T-t}}, d_2 = d_1 - \sigma\sqrt{T-t}$$

If we differentiate the above equation with respect to S, we get $\frac{\partial C}{\partial S} = N(d_1)$

In derivation of the Black-Scholes equation, we set $\frac{\partial C}{\partial S} = \Delta$ to remove the stochastic term. This implies that $N(d_1) = \Delta$. Plotting delta for a call with a strike of $80, we find that options deep into the money take on the maximum delta of one (this is the maximum value, which makes sense because the limit of the Black-Scholes equation as $S \to \infty$ is just S, and $dS/dS = 1$.) At the low end, when the option is deep out of the money, the delta takes on its minimum value zero. Again this makes sense because C would be zero and there is virtually no chance that, so far out of the money, the call value would change with a small change in S. Call delta rises as the strike price is approached from the left. This means that the call value will increase with an increase in the stock price, again as we expect.

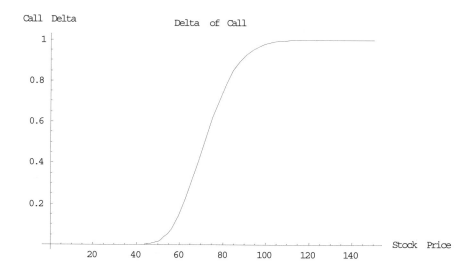

For the put, we have the reverse situation. Using Put-Call parity, we have $p = Ke^{-rt} - S + c$ Substitution of the expression for c gives $p = Ke^{-rt}(1 - N(d_2)) - S(1 - N(d_1))$. Differentiation with respect to S results in $\frac{\partial p}{\partial S} = N(d_1) - 1 = \Delta$ of a put. Note:

$\Delta_p = \Delta_c - 1$

This is an important relationship. Essentially, $N(d_1)$ represents the cumulative probability that the call will finish above the strike K, in the money. So $1 - N(d_1)$ should be the cumulative probability that the call will finish below K, out of the money. This is the probability that the put will be exercised.

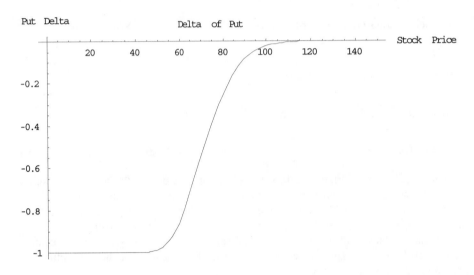

Let's see if this makes sense. Deep out of the money, the put has a value of zero. We expect the delta to be zero here, and it is. Deep into the money, as S? 0, the value of the put should be constant at K. As the stock price increases, the put will lose value so the sign should be negative. (Either $\frac{\partial p}{\partial S} < 0$ or $\frac{\partial p}{-\partial S} > 0$, whichever is easier to think about.)

Delta has already been seen to be a critical component of hedging. Know these definitions and behaviors. Delta for both puts and calls is far more sensitive near the money than deep out of or in the money.

Numerical estimation of delta

Delta can be estimated by computing the call price at two different stock prices close to the strike price where you want to calculate delta. All other variables are held constant.

To calculate delta at $S = 80$, April,

$$\Delta = \frac{\partial C}{\partial S} \cong \frac{\Delta C}{\Delta S} = \frac{C(S + \Delta S, t, \sigma, t) - C(S - \Delta S, t, \sigma, t)}{2\Delta S} = \frac{C(85, t) - C(75, t)}{85 - 75} = \frac{10.392 - 2}{10} = 0.839.$$

This means that the call value will increase by \$0.839 for each change of \$1 in the stock price at this point. This value of Δ makes sense, because the option is close to being at the money and delta should be near one at the money. In the formula, S is the stock price about which you wish to evaluate the parameter, and ΔS is the small increment that you vary the stock price by (\$80 and \$5, respectively, in this example.)   The analytical value of delta for a European call and put can be calculated by straightforward differentiation to yield:

Delta of Call $D_{call} = e^{-\delta(T-t)}N(d_1)$

Delta of Put $D_{put} = e^{-\delta(T-t)}(N(d_1)-1)$ (δ = dividend rate)

Gamma

This gives the second derivative of the option value with respect to S; or, the rate of change of delta.

$$\gamma = \frac{\partial^2 V}{\partial S^2}$$

$$\gamma = \frac{\partial^2 V}{\partial S^2} \cong \frac{V(S+\Delta S,t,\sigma,r)-2V(S,t)+V(S-\Delta S,t,\sigma,r)}{\Delta S^2}$$

The numerical approximation may be used as an approximation to γ.

Using $\Delta S = 5$, we find for the call that:

$$\gamma \cong \frac{C(80+5,t)-2C(80,t)+C(80-5,t)}{\Delta S^2} = \frac{10.392-2(5.7)+2}{5^2} = 0.0397.$$

This also makes sense because, close to the money, the delta approaches a constant value of one and so the second derivative should be approaching zero. The theoretical value of gamma for a call and put are:

$$\gamma_{call} = \frac{e^{-D(T-t)}N'(d_1)}{\sigma S\sqrt{T-t}}$$

$$\gamma_{put} = \frac{e^{-D(T-t)}N'(d_1)}{\sigma S\sqrt{T-t}} = \gamma_{call}$$

where $N'(x) = \frac{1}{\sqrt{2\pi}}e^{-\frac{1}{2}x^2}$

Rho

Rho is the sensitivity of the option to the risk-free interest rate: $\rho = \frac{\partial V}{\partial r}$. This definition is easy to remember since both rho and rate begin with the letter "r." We hold all parameters constant except for the risk-free rate r.

For a call, $\rho_{call} = K(T-t)e^{-r(T-t)}N(d_2)$
For a put, $\rho_{put} = -K(T-t)e^{-r(T-t)}N(-d_2)$

For the April 80 call, we used $r=1.7\%$ and found $C = \$5.701$. If we increase r to 2.7 %, $C = 5.718$. Then

$$\rho = \frac{\partial C}{\partial r} \cong \frac{\Delta C}{\Delta r} = \frac{C(S,t,\sigma,r+\Delta r)-C(S,t,\sigma,r)}{\Delta r} = \frac{C(S,\sigma,t,2.7\%)-C(S,\sigma,t,2.7\%)}{2.7\%-1.7\%} = \frac{5.718-5.701}{.01} = 1.7$$

This is an interesting parameter to evaluate, since we have assumed that interest rates remain constant over the life of the option. It is also interesting to evaluate vega (which we will later in this chapter) for the same reason, though note that vega is a dangerous parameter to evaluate because volatility is unobservable and, as such, we really don't have a good idea of what value to use. Volatility is one of the main factors influencing most option prices, too.

Theta

Theta gives the sensitivity of the option to time: $\theta = \dfrac{\partial V}{\partial t}$. Theta will be most sensitive when the option is close to the money, with sensitivity decreasing as the option approaches expiry. Consider the April 80 call and the May 80 call. If we hold interest rate constant at 1.7% and volatility constant at 36.788% with $\Delta t = 30$ days, then the April call is $5.701 as before, and the May call would be $7.323. These are calculated using Black-Scholes, as before. If we use the definition of theta we should get close to the same answer:

$$\theta = \frac{\partial V}{\partial t} \cong \frac{\Delta V}{\Delta t} = \frac{V(S,t+\Delta t,\sigma,r)-V(S,t,\sigma,r)}{\Delta t} = \frac{7.323-5.701}{30/360} = \$19.4/\text{year}$$

Analytical Solutions for a call and a put:

$$\theta_{call} = -\frac{\sigma S e^{-\delta(T-t)} N'(d_1)}{2\sqrt{T-t}} + \delta\, S\, N(d_1) e^{-\delta(T-t)} - rKe^{-r(T-t)}N(d_2)$$

$$\theta_{put} = -\frac{\sigma S e^{-\delta(T-t)} N'(d_1)}{2\sqrt{T-t}} - \delta\, S\, N'(-d_1) e^{-\delta(T-t)} + rKe^{-r(T-t)}N(-d_2)$$

To estimate the option price after two months, $C(S,69/360,\sigma,r) = C(S, 9/360, \sigma,r) + \theta\,\Delta t = \$5.701 + \$19.4 (60/360) = \$8.945$. Black-Scholes gives $C(\$85.35,69/360, 36.788\%,1.7\%)=\$8.567$.

Vega

Vega ($\varpi = \dfrac{\partial V}{\partial \sigma}$), option sensitivity to change in volatility, can be remembered because vega and volatility both start with the letter "v".

$$\varpi = \frac{\partial V}{\partial \sigma} \cong \frac{\Delta V}{\Delta \sigma} = \frac{V(S,t,\sigma+\Delta\sigma,r)-V(S,t,\sigma,r)}{\Delta\sigma}$$

Vegas of calls and puts:

$$\varpi_{call} = S\sqrt{T-t}\,e^{-D(T-t)}N'(d_1)$$

$$\varpi_{put} = S\sqrt{T-t}\,e^{-D(T-t)}N'(d_1)$$

Notes on the derivation: The preceding derivation for the delta of a call is more complicated than it looks. We have to do

$$\frac{\partial C}{\partial S} = \frac{\partial}{\partial S}\left(SN(d_1) - Ke^{-rt}N(d_2)\right)$$

$$= N(d_1) + S\frac{\partial}{\partial S}N(d_1) - Ke^{-rt}\frac{\partial}{\partial S}N(d_2)$$

since

$$N(d_1) = \frac{1}{2}\left(1 + Erf\left(\frac{r + \frac{1}{2}\sigma^2(T-t) + \ln\left(\frac{S}{K}\right)}{\sqrt{2}\sigma\sqrt{T-t}}\right)\right)$$

then the partial derivative with respect to S is:

$$\frac{\partial}{\partial S}N(d_1) = \frac{e^{-\left(\frac{\left(r + \frac{1}{2}\sigma^2(T-t) + \ln\left(\frac{S}{K}\right)\right)^2}{2\sigma^2(T-t)}\right)}}{\sqrt{2\pi}\,S\sigma\sqrt{T-t}}$$

With similar calculations for $N(d_2)$,

Substitution into the expression for $\dfrac{\partial C}{\partial S}$ gives $= N(d_1) + S\dfrac{\partial}{\partial S}N(d_1) - Ke^{-rt}\dfrac{\partial}{\partial S}N(d_2)$

The calculations get fairly ugly, but it can be shown that $\dfrac{\partial C}{\partial S} = N(d_1)$

Exchange-Traded Options

We have talked a great deal about options on stocks but need to mention options on interest rates and treasury bond futures, to name just a couple of other types. These must be covered separately because, in everything we have discussed so far, we have assumed that interest rates remain constant. If this were the case then we wouldn't have options on interest rate products. In fact, interest rates can and do change significantly over small time periods. We will have entire chapters on interest rate products but wish to introduce here a few of the more important exchange-traded derivatives, which include options on treasury bond futures and options on eurodollar futures.

If you look in the financial pages of papers such as *The Wall Street Journal*, you will see listed futures options contracts on grains, oilseeds, metals, food, fibers, livestock, petroleum, currencies and interest rates. The interest rate products include T-Bonds, T-Notes and Eurodollar futures, as well as more specialized futures. We know how to value futures, but how do we value options on futures?

Let's start with the **Eurodollar futures**. Eurodollar Futures, or EDFs, are traded on the Chicago Mercantile Exchange in addition to other exchanges such as SIMEX and LIFFE. First, let's go over some terminology: a **Eurodollar** is defined as U.S. currency that is held by a bank outside of the U.S. These banks can include foreign branches of U.S. banks. Eurodollars may be held to settle international transactions. Futures and options on futures with the same strikes and expiry settle on the same day. The option is settled in cash.

We can derive an equation for valuing options on futures just like we did for valuing options on stocks. Recall the futures-spot parity formula $F = Se^{r(T-t)}$. The futures price F depends on the price dynamics of the underlying spot. The evolution of the spot price can be modeled by the geometric Brownian Motion equation already discussed, in which $\frac{dS}{S} = \mu dt + \sigma dz$

Black's model

The volatility of the futures price can be obtained by application of Ito's lemma to the preceding equation,

we find $\sigma_F = \frac{1}{F}\sigma S \frac{\partial F}{\partial S} = \frac{1}{F}\sigma Se^{r(T-t)} = \sigma$

Hence, the volatility of the future is the same as the volatility of the underlying. Then the dynamics of the futures price is given by

$$\frac{dF}{F} = \mu_F dt + \sigma dz$$

where μ_F is the expected return on the futures.

If $V(F,t)$ represents the value of a futures option, form a portfolio consisting of a long position in α units of the underlying futures and a short position in one option on the futures. Then the value of the portfolio Π at initiation is $\Pi = \alpha \cdot -V = -V$ because the value of a futures position is zero at initiation. What is the change in value $d\Pi$ over a short interval of time dt? Just differentiate to get

$$d\Pi = -dV + \alpha \, dF$$

Now $dV = \left(\dfrac{\partial V}{\partial t}+\dfrac{1}{2}\sigma^2 F^2 \dfrac{\partial^2 V}{\partial F^2}+\mu_F F \dfrac{\partial V}{\partial F}\right)dt + \sigma F \dfrac{\partial V}{\partial F}dz$

So $d\Pi = -\left(\dfrac{\partial V}{\partial t}+\dfrac{1}{2}\sigma^2 F^2 \dfrac{\partial^2 V}{\partial F^2}+\mu_F F \dfrac{\partial V}{\partial F}\right)dt - \sigma F \dfrac{\partial V}{\partial F}dz + \alpha\left(F\mu_F dt + F\sigma dz\right)$

As before, we can eliminate the random dz term by collecting terms and setting the coefficient of dz to zero. Then,

$$d\Pi = -\left(\dfrac{\partial V}{\partial t}+\dfrac{1}{2}\sigma^2 F^2 \dfrac{\partial^2 V}{\partial F^2}+\mu_F F \alpha\right)dt + \alpha\left(F\mu_F dt\right) = -\left(\dfrac{\partial V}{\partial t}+\dfrac{1}{2}\sigma^2 F^2 \dfrac{\partial^2 V}{\partial F^2}\right)dt$$

This implies that $\alpha = \dfrac{\partial V}{\partial F}$

The change in portfolio value $d\Pi$ over a small increment of time dt is expected to grow at the risk free rate so we invoke the condition that $d\Pi = \Pi r dt$ to get

$$d\Pi = -\left(\dfrac{\partial V}{\partial t}+\dfrac{1}{2}\sigma^2 F^2 \dfrac{\partial^2 V}{\partial F^2}\right)dt = r\Pi dt = -rV dt$$

Rearranging,

$$\dfrac{\partial V}{\partial t}+\dfrac{1}{2}\sigma^2 F^2 \dfrac{\partial^2 V}{\partial F^2} - rV dt = 0$$

If we compare this equation to the one we derived for options paying a continuous dividend such as an FX option, we had

$$\dfrac{\partial V}{\partial t}+\dfrac{1}{2}\sigma^2 S^2 \dfrac{\partial^2 V}{\partial S^2} + \left(r-r_f\right)S \dfrac{\partial V}{\partial S} - rV = 0$$

The equation we derived for the option on the futures is the same as the equation for an option on an asset paying an interest rate r_f if the risk-free rate r is equal to r_f. So the formula for options on futures is actually a bit simpler than the ones we have already dealt with. We already know how to price calls and puts on more complicated derivatives. All we have to do to modify our solutions for options on futures is to replace r_f (or D) in the formulas by r:

Value of Call Option on Future $C = Fe^{-r(T-t)}N(d_1) - Ke^{-r(T-t)}N(d_2)$

Value of Put Option on Future $P = -Fe^{-r(T-t)}N(-d_1) + Ke^{-r(T-t)}N(-d_2)$

(Where d_1 and d_2 are as before but F replaces S.)

Note that put-call parity is given by $P + Fe^{-r(T-t)} - c = Ke^{-r(T-t)}$

Another observation that should be made is that when $F=K$, the put and call prices are identical.

The preceding is called **Black's model** for valuing futures options. Black's original paper was written to value futures on commodities, so in this spirit, let's try one.

Example   On May 14 the futures price of one contract of #2 yellow corn (contract size 5,000 bushels) is 215 cents/bushel. If the cost of carry is 1.7% per annum and volatility is 22.84% per annum, what should be the price of a call and a put with strike of 200 cents/bu? Use T = 60/360.

In this example, since the call is in the money, the price should be at least 15 cents per bushel, plus the two-month time value of the option. Using Black's formula with $F = 215$, $K = 200$ and the other parameters as specified, gives us $d1 = 0.8219$, $N(d1) = 0.794$, $d2 = 0.7287$ and $N(d2) = 0.767$. Then c is calculated as 17.375 cents/bushel. The price of the put is calculated from put-call parity,

$$P = Ke^{-r(T-t)} + c - Fe^{-r(T-t)} = (K-F)e^{-r(T-t)} + c = (200-215)e^{-.017(\frac{60}{360})} + 17.375 = 2.42 \text{ cents/bu.}$$

People trade options on futures rather than the futures themselves because the options are settled in cash, rather than physical delivery of the underlying. It is hard to deliver a portfolio of the S&P 500 stocks, but the option is just closed out in cash.

Eurodollar futures contract

The underlying on the **Eurodollars future contract (EDF)** is the three-month interbank lending rate (LIBOR) to be received over three months on a deposit with a face value of $1 million. Eurodollar futures contracts are unique in that the futures price F is constructed so that $100 - F = LIBOR_3$ (with $LIBOR_3$ the three-month LIBOR rate expected to prevail at maturity). The contract settles in cash at maturity, which is the second London business day prior to the third Wednesday of the maturity month. Maturity months are commonly March, June, September and December, but can be other months as well. For example, on May 14 we see the following sample of Eurodollar futures prices:

Maturity Month	Futures Price	Implied LIBOR₃, %
June	98.01	1.99
July	97.91	2.09
Aug	97.77	2.23
Sept	97.6	2.4
Dec	96.98	3.02

The contract is valued as $10,000(100 – 0.25(100-Z))$ where Z is the futures price. The LIBOR rate is $(100-Z)$ percent.

The underlying on an EDF contract is three month LIBOR, so these contracts increase in value when bond prices increase (rates drop), and decrease when bond prices drop (rates increase). It can be seen that a call on an EDF contract is equivalent to a put on LIBOR, and a put on an EDF contract is the same as a call on LIBOR, since the call pays off $\max(0,F-K) = \max(0,(100 - Z) - K) = \max(0,LIBOR-K)$. This is the payoff of a put on LIBOR with a strike rate of $K\%$. So if a speculator anticipates interest rates to rise in the short-term, he would purchase a put on the EDF contract. If interest rates are expected to fall in the short term, a call on the EDF futures contract can be purchased.

Another important feature of the EDF contract is the price of a one basis point move in the contract. We can see from the formula $V = \$10,000(100 - 0.25LIBOR)$ that if LIBOR changes by one basis point, the contract changes in value by $25. ($V = \$1,000,000 – 2,500LIBOR$, if LIBOR changes by 0.01, multiplier of 2500 changes by 25.) This gives a quick way to calculate the change in value of a contract.

For example, if the July contract is purchased today, the holder is entitled to receive interest of 2.09% annualized on his investment of $1,000,000 face. Thus, the holder will receive $1,000,000*0.25*0.0209 = $5,225 in interest. The contract is valued at $10,000(100 – 0.25(100-97.91)) = $994,775. (Note that this allows instant calculation of the interest to be received as just $1,000,000 – 994,775 = $5,225.)

What if the contract is purchased, but, at maturity, the futures price has moved to 97.95? How much profit/loss will the investor make? The change in futures price means that the three-month LIBOR rate prevailing in July will be 2.05%. The investor locked in 2.09% so profit can be calculated either as max(0,F-K) = max(0,97.95-97.91) = 0.04, or by thinking of the difference in interest the investor will receive: there is a difference of 4 bp =2.09-2.05 calculated above. So the investor will make .04*.25*1,000,000 = $100. Or, you could calculate the change in value of the contract: at expiry, it is worth $10,000(100 – 0.25(100-97.95)) = $994,875, which is $100 more than when the investor entered into it.

Short cut: The contract value changed by 0.04, or 4 bp. We know that 1 bp is equivalent to $25, so change = $100.

Options on Eurodollar futures

Now that we understand EDF contracts, we can discuss the call and put options on them. A call option on an EDF contract provides the holder with the right to enter into an EDF contract with a strike of K and maturity T. (A put option on an EDF contract works similarly.) The cost of the option is calculated using Black's model with F = futures price and K = strike price. For example, if we have a July call on a July EDF contract, we already know, from above, that the futures price F expressed in terms of LIOBR is 2.09%. Checking the financial section of the newspapers or the CME website, we see that July strikes of 97.5, 97.75, 98, 98.25 and 98.5 are offered for July. This corresponds to LIBOR strikes of 2.5%, 2.25%, 2%, 1.75% and 1.5%. For the current future rate of 2.09%, we will value the 2% strike, because this call is in the money and the value should be close to 0.09%. The EDF contract is valued using a day count convention of Actual/360 and put and call prices are expressed in the financial press as "% of 100" or bp. Thus, a listed call price of 0.22 means the cost is actually 22 bp times $25/bp = $550. So an investor who had purchased such a call option in the preceding example would have had a total loss of $100 - $550 = $450 because the expected change in rates, 4 bp, was not enough to cover the call option premium, 22 bp. This gives a good tool to measure breakeven.

Treasury bond futures

A similar analysis can be performed for Treasury Bonds and Treasury Notes, which have a contract size of $100,000 USD and are traded on the CBT. Treasury Bonds are quoted in percents of principal using 1/32 increments, thus, a quote of June 101-01 means 101 and 01/32 percent of $100,000 (or the contract has a face value of 101.0313% of $100,000). What if a treasurer wants to buy an option on this future? There are listed June futures contracts with strikes of 99 through 104 in increments of one. The value of a call option on the June T-bond future with strike of 101 should consist mainly of time value, since the option is close to being at the money. Let's try to value it: Here we use F = 101.0313, K = 101, T = 30/360, r = 1.78% and s = 6.5%. We get c = 0.7344 and p = 0.7031, which correspond to the listed call and put prices of "0-47" and "0-45", respectively.

Black-Scholes Model for Valuation of Options on Futures

Inputs:

F	101.0313	Current Futures Price
K	101	Strike Price
t	0.083333	time to expiry, years
r	1.78 percent	per same units of time as t
σ	6.186816 percent	per same units of time as t
Actual Price	0.7344	

Outputs:

d_1	0.0263		
d_2	0.0084		
N(d1)	0.510		
N(d2)	0.503	**Error**	
Call	0.7344		0.000%
Put	0.7031		
	0.703147		

Another common trading strategy, called the **TED spread**, involves a combination of Eurodollar futures and Treasury futures. The TED spread is a trade on the spread between treasuries and Eurodollar futures. This spread, which is the rate at which a U.S. Treasury bond is trading less the rate at which a Eurodollar futures contract is trading, is used to take a view on the relative credit quality between U.S. Treasuries and the highest-quality international banks. The simple building blocks we have covered here can be extended to price more complicated options, including floors, caps and caplets. Black's model also can be used to calculate the implied volatility of the futures. In fact, vendors often quote cap prices in terms of "black volatility," the implied volatility from Black's model, so it is a good tool to have on your desktop.

Exotic options

The simple "plain vanilla" options we have covered so far are just the beginning. Much more complex derivatives can be constructed. In most cases these exotic options are much more difficult to price, and the risks much more difficult to understand and manage. Proper hedging is very important. Exotic options include binary options, chooser options, compound options, quanto options, Asian options, lookback options, range options, rainbow options, barrier options, and on and on. There is a seemingly infinite variety of exotic options and we cannot possibly categorize them all here. These exotic options are generally traded over the counter, where a broker can custom-design them with the desired features of the buyer. In the following, we introduce only a handful of the more popular exotic options. (There is much, much more that could be written about exotics, including pricing and hedging them, than we have room for here.)

Binary options

A binary option, also known as a **digital option**, is a very simple derivative. The payoff on a binary call is just $1 if the asset price is above the strike price at expiry, otherwise it is zero. For a binary put, the payoff is $1 if the asset price is below the strike price at expiry, otherwise it is zero. The payoff diagrams are graphed below.

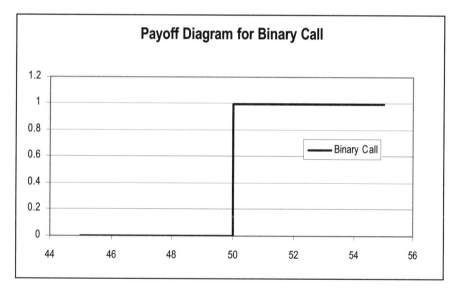

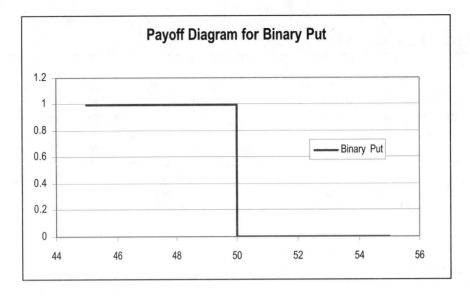

The above payoff function can be represented mathematically with slight modification by the **Heaviside function**, $H(x)$, which has a value of zero when it is evaluated with a negative argument, and a value of 1 otherwise. The payoff of the binary put is then $H(K-S)$ and for the call, $H(S-K)$. Why would someone buy this? A binary option is less expensive than the corresponding European call or put. If an investor thinks the asset price will rise, they will be better off buying a call. But if they don't think the stock price will rise much over the strike, they might prefer to buy a binary call.

Compound options

Options on options, compound call options allow you to exercise an option to purchase or sell either a call or put on S with strike price K_2 and expiry T_2. The option to purchase the call option itself has exercise price K_1 and strike T_1. Obtaining a price for this option is not difficult. Since the option still depends on the price movement of the underlying S, the Black-Scholes equation still applies. The time domain is broken into two parts: $(0, T_1)$ and (T_1, T_2). We already know how to value the option that you have the right to buy, whether call or put, by the standard solutions, to give either $C(S, T_1)$ or $P(S, T_1)$. These are evaluated at T_1 and compared to the strike price K_1. If the compound option is a call option to purchase a call option, then you would evaluate $\max(C(S, T_1) - K_1, 0)$ to decide whether to exercise the option or not; for a put option on a put option, then $\max(K_2 - P(S, T_1) - K_1, 0)$.

Barrier options

A barrier option is a call or put option with a twist: **Knock-in barrier options** are contingent upon the underlying asset reaching a chosen barrier, K, prior to expiry; **knock-out options** only have a payoff if the barrier K is not reached before expiry.

Knock-in barrier options include "up-and-in" and "down-and-in" variants. Knock-out options include "down-and-out" and "up-and-out." If the barrier feature is satisfied for whatever type of option you have, they are valued just like regular calls or puts. Of course, these type of options are path-dependent, so they might best be valued by techniques used in Monte-Carlo methods.

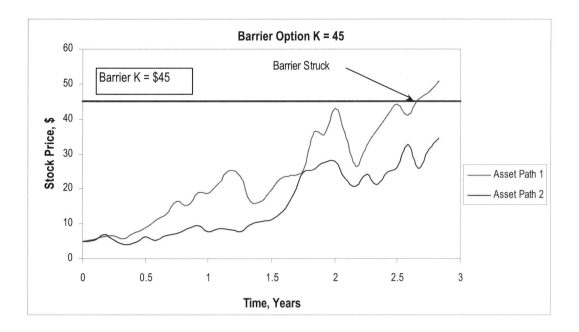

In the above diagram, we have two random asset paths that S might take, Asset Path 1 and Asset Path 2. K is the barrier. If this were an up-and-out option, then if S followed Asset Path 1, the option would expire worthless because it strikes K prior to expiry. Asset Path 2 would still be alive and valued at expiry just like a regular call or put. However, if this were an up-and-in option, only Asset Path 1 would be alive since it is activated once S crosses the barrier K. Asset Path 2 never reaches K over the time period, so expires worthless. We can do the same thing for down-and-out and down-and-in options.

Sample Questions and Answers

Questions

1(a). Referring to the IBM example at the beginning of this chapter, assume that IBM's current stock price is $85.35 when Yukiko buys the call, the risk free rate = 2%/year, and volatility = 35%/year. Ignoring transactions costs, what strategy would Yukiko employ if she expects the stock price to rise if she wants to maximize her profit? (Would she purchase a call, sell a call, purchase a put, sell a put?)

(b). How much money would she make on her strategy (over and above any costs of option premiums) if she buys a July 80 call and the stock closes at 90? Assume that the time to expiry is 99/360 days.

(c). If a July 90 call costs $4.527, how much is an July 90 put? Why?

(d). How much is the time value component of the July 90 put worth?

2.   What happens to the price of a call option if the underlying pays a dividend D? How about a stock split?

3.   People say that options are dangerous. Can you explain this?

4.   What is the value of a put option on an EDF future if the call price is $5.16 and the futures and strike price are 92.82?

5.   What is the implied three-month LIBOR starting in July if the July EDF futures contract price is 95.8?

6.   Is the current futures price of a commodity a good predictor of the expected future spot rate?

7.   How are spot prices and forward prices related?

8.   How would you use the Black-Scholes model to price a call option on an FX contract?

9.   You have a T-bond maturing in 6 days to a par of $1,000. The risk-free rate is 2.5% per annum and the strike price of a call option is 105 (quoted as % of par). What is the value of this option?

10. If the current exchange rate between the USD and British Pound is 1.80$/£, the one-year treasury rate in the U.S. is 2.5% and the one year risk-free rate in the UK is 4%, what is the forward exchange rate $/£ in one year? Please explain.

11. Suppose that the forward exchange rate in one year is actually 2 $/£. Is an arbitrage opportunity available? If so, how would you profit?

12. What does delta mean? How is it used?

13. If an option is deep in the money, what is it's delta? What is gamma?

14. "A call option on a Eurodollar Futures Contract is equivalent to a put option on LIBOR." True or false? Why?

15. The expected three-month LIBOR rate underlying a Eurodollars futures contract changes by 6 bp. What is the resulting change in value of the contract?

16. A treasurer expects short-term interest rates to rise, which would adversely impact his cost of funding. What should be his strategy?

17. You think that a stock price will rise in the next few months, but not very far over $40. What kind of option would allow you to profit from this move but be inexpensive?

18. Why would a person sell naked straddles on an index? Explain the expectations regarding movement of the underlying index.

19. If you are bullish on a stock, what kind of strategy might you adopt that will allow you to participate in some upside movement but be low cost?

20. What is implied volatility? Is it better to use implied volatility or historical volatility in pricing an option?

21. What is a volatility smile? What are the implications of this smile for the Black-Scholes model?

22. How is the delta of a call and put on an option related?

23. What is the difference between European and American options? Are the European options more expensive and more sophisticated?

24. Can Black-Scholes be used to value American puts? If not what would I use?

25. How do you perform Monte Carlo analysis in valuing an option?

26. Can Black-Scholes be used to value bond options?

27. What is Black's Model used for?

28. If you own Lucent stock and buy put options on it, are you perfectly hedged against price risk?

29. Assume that you can borrow money at the risk free rate. You use this money to buy one put option on a stock and you sell one call option. Suppose both the call and put are equal at $5. At the end of the day, the stock price has moved so that the call is now worth $6 and the put $4. How could you lose money (You were perfectly hedged at the beginning of the day?)?

30. You buy a knock-in put option with strike of $50. The stock closes at expiry at $49. What is the value of your option?

31. What's the maximum potential loss you could incur by selling a put on a stock?

32. If puts aren't offered on a stock but calls are, how would you synthetically create a position equivalent to a put?

33. What is a collar strategy and when might it be used?

34. What are the Greeks?

35. What is the gamma of a call option on a stock if the strike price is $100 and the stock is at $80?

36. A hedge fund uses a "delta neutral" strategy to hedge equities. Basically, they hold shares of the underlying and buy an appropriate number of puts as dictated by delta of the put (or sell Δc calls). Pros/cons?

37. You have sold 1000 shares of a stock short. The stock is currently at $100. How many call options at $11.01/call with a strike of $100 would be bought/sold to hedge this position if the delta of the call option is 0.589? Now, assume that the stock price moves to $120. What is your net position? How would you create a delta-gamma neutral portfolio?

Answers

1(a). To maximize profit on an expected rise in the stock's price, she should buy a call. She could also sell a put at the same time, and the premium she receives will help to finance the call premium that she must pay.

(b). Think you have to use Black-Scholes? That's only prior to expiry. Remember, a call or put option is priced as the sum of its intrinsic value plus time value. The time value decays exponentially to zero at expiry and we are left only with intrinsic value. The value of the call at expiry is $\max(0, S_T - K) = \max(0, 90 - 80) = \$10$, "the stock is in the money by $10." She sells it for $90 but paid $85.35, so her profit is $4.65. You can calculate HPR (holding period return) if you want.

(c). Use put-call parity to get P=$8.684. Since the current price of the stock is $85.35 and the strike of the put is 90, it is in the money by $4.65. So the value of the put should be *at least this*, if you have to estimate.

(d). $4.03. The difference between $8.684 and $4.65 is the time value of money.

2. The owner of the underlying asset gets the dividend, which was priced into S when the option price was calculated. When a stock pays a dividend D, the stock price drops exactly by D (well, theoretically it does.) Since the call option depends on the price of the underlying, there should be a jump – decrease – in the option price as well when the dividend is paid since the option is worth less. For stock splits, again theoretically, there should be no change in value at all. Suppose you hold one option on one hundred shares of a $100 stock. The stock splits so now there are 200 shares each worth $50. The underlying value has not changed at all (but it is one of the unexplained paradoxes of finance that stock prices do tend to jump on news of splits). You'd now have two option contracts and the strike price has to be adjusted to reflect the fact that the underlying price has halved. It has to. Imagine if the original strike was $100 and the stock was at $101. It would have been in the money. Then the stock splits so it is now worth $50/$50. Can you imagine the teeth gnashing in the executive suites if options were immediately worthless because the strike price didn't change along with the stock split?

3. Options involve a great deal of leverage and no one is forcing most traders to maintain a perfect hedge. In fact, the idea of a perfect hedge is probably impossible. There are all kinds of unanticipated risks that can occur if the unexpected happens. But options are not inherently dangerous. They're only dangerous when in the wrong hands, the risks aren't fully understood, or the proper internal controls aren't in place.

4. $5.16. Put and call prices are equal when the futures price and strike price are the same due to put-call parity on futures options. The strike and futures prices are discounted at the same rate r.

5. $\text{LIBOR} = 100 - Z = 100 - 95.8 = 4.2\%$.

6. Sometimes, but it all depends on supply and demand. If the market is at full carry, the futures price can be expected to be a good predictor of the future spot price.

7. Spot and forward prices are linked through spot-forwards parity. If this link did not exist, arbitrage opportunities would exist.

8. Just change r in the equation to r-r_f. Or, change D to r_f in the form for underlying paying a continuous dividend. You earn interest at the rate of r_f on your foreign investment and it acts as income just like a continuous dividend does.

9. This is a trick quick question: note the length of time to maturity (and don't talk about how you could apply Black-Scholes to bonds). Whatever the value of the bond right now, it has to converge to par in six days, so the call, having a strike of $1,050, would be out of the money with a great degree of probability.

10. We use interest rate parity here. The expected value of a future exchange rate is just the current rate multiplied by the ratio of $((1+r_d)/(1+r_f))t$ where t is the time over which you are analyzing the problem. Here $t = 1$ year, rd is the risk-free rate in the domestic country and rf the risk-free rate in the foreign country. Then, $E_1 = E_0((1+0.06)/(1+0.05))^1 = 1.817\$/£$.

11. Yes, there is an arbitrage opportunity available. Since the expected exchange rate is $1.817\$/£$ based on the risk free rate, you could make a risk-free profit by entering into a transaction to sell currency at $2.0\$/£$ and investing to earn the $1.817\$/£$.

12. Delta is the sensitivity of an option to a change in the price of the underlying. It is critical in hedging strategies as often we want to be "delta-neutral," to have one dollar change in the underlying, say, reflected in a one dollar change in value of the option.

13. When a call option is deep in the money, delta is zero. This means if the underlying changes, the option value won't change -- you are already so deep in the money that a small change won't do anything. (Gamma is also zero.)

14. True. By design, a call option on an EDF contract is equivalent to a put option on LIBOR (and a put option on EDF is equivalent to a call on LIBOR). If a strike price is, say, 95, then the value of a call contract is $\max(0,F-K)=\max(0,F-90)$ where F is the futures price at maturity, but $F = 100 -$ LIBOR so the value of the call contract would be $\max(0,(100-LIBOR)-K) = \max(0,10\% - K)$ so the call option acts like a put on LIBOR with a strike of $100-K = 10\%$.

15. 1 bp change is always equal to $25, so 6bp = 6(25) = $150.

16. He wants protection against an increase in interest rates, which means a put; and "short-term" rates means he wants, for example, Eurodollar futures. Thus, he would either buy a call on LIBOR or a put on an EDF contract.

17. You could buy a call but since you don't expect the price to move much over the strike price, you can still participate in the upside movement of the stock with a binary call option, which is cheaper.

18. Nick Leeson didn't expect the index to move much either way and thus expected premium income from both legs of the straddle. If the underlying does move much either way, though, you'll be exposed to potentially infinite losses.

19. You could invest in a bull spread, where you buy a call with a strike K_1 and sell one with a higher strike K_2. You get premium income from the sale of the call at a higher strike, but get to participate in upward movement between K_1 and K_2.

20. Implied volatility is the volatility that makes the model price equal to the observed market price. Historical volatility is the volatility that pertained in the past. In pricing options, we want to use the volatility that will pertain going forward. This, of course, is unknown, but implied volatility is the market consensus of the expected volatility and would be better to use than historical volatility.

21. A volatility smile is a graph of the implied volatility of the option vs. the strike price. When historical volatility is used to value an option, particularly for out-of-the-money and in-the-money options for equity, currency, index and commodity options, the calculated theoretical price is below the market price. If the volatility implied by the price is calculated, it is seen that this implied volatility is higher when the option is deep in or out of the money, and lower when the option is close to being at the money. This implies that the true distribution is probably not lognormal. The existence of the volatility smile is inconsistent with Black-Scholes and would tend to reject this model. Empirical evidence on asset returns shows that volatilities are neither constant nor deterministic functions. Rather, volatility evolves in a random process. However, almost all evidence points to volatility being mean-reverting, which means that we may be able to do reasonably well over the long run.

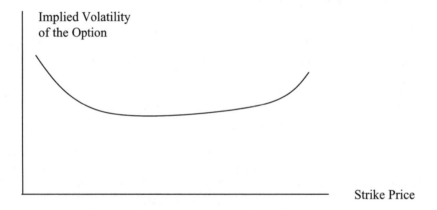

22. The delta of a call is $N(d_1)$ and delta of the put is $N(d_1)-1$. $N(d_1)$ is the cumulative probability distribution of hitting the strike price over the time period so the probability of closing below it must be the inverse $1- N(d_1)$.

23. A European option can only be exercised at the expiration date of the option, while American options can be exercised at any point up to expiry. This added "perk" has value, so American options are worth more than their European equivalents.

24. No, Black-Scholes can only handle European options. To value American options, path dependence must be modeled by some method such as a tree, Monte Carlo analysis or finite difference methods.

25. Monte Carlo analysis is a simulation technique that allows us to generate random paths for the stochastic variables. We can model effects such as jumps in asset prices, random interest rates and volatilities. Let's consider a simple American option. We can generate paths for the underlying

stock price according to the dynamic price process $\frac{dS}{S} = \mu dt + \sigma dz$ where z is a random variable drawn from a standardized normal distribution. At each point dt we examine the option value to see whether early exercise is optimal. If so, this path is terminated and the payoff determined. We average the payoffs of all payoffs and discount back to obtain an average payoff value.

26. Not without modification, because constant interest rate and constant volatility are assumed for Black-Scholes. In fact, we must deal with the entire term structure of interest rates in valuation of a bond or bond option, not just a single, constant variable. Volatilities also vary across the term structure, and both interest rates and volatilities are random functions of time which must also be captured. Another unusual feature of bonds that must be captured is that the volatility of a bond price should decrease with time, eventually becoming zero at maturity. This is very unlike a stock option.

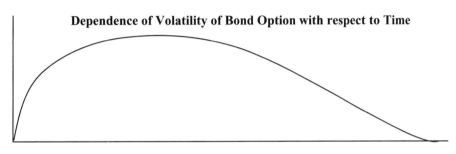

Dependence of Volatility of Bond Option with respect to Time

Time to Maturity of Option, T

27. Black's model is used for valuation of options on futures.

28. Not at all. You have purchased a protective put, which provides some protection against downward price movements. What if the stock falls from $100 to $80 but the strike price of your put is $78? You have no protection. Also, the stock could just move horizontally, so you can't use your put, though you don't have any capital gains, either. Perfect hedging requires also selling a call option and, as changes occur, dynamic rebalancing of the portfolio. Transactions costs and execution imperfections will also introduce frictions into the hedging model.

29. You can't just set up a hedge and forget it. Hedges have to be dynamically rebalanced as the price of the underlying changes. (Hedge fund interview question.)

30. That depends. You would have to know the price history of the underlying. Did it hit the barrier – that is, did it ever reach $50 prior to expiry? If so, it is alive and the value would be $\max(0, S_T - K) = \$1$.

31. If you write a put on a stock, the maximum loss you can incur will occur when the stock price goes to zero. In this case, you lose K, the strike price, times the number of contracts you wrote.

32. A synthetic put is created by selling the stock, buying a call and borrowing K at r for time t.

33. A collar strategy is similar to a bull spread and is used when the buyer is bullish on the underlying. The maximum loss and profit are capped. A corporate treasurer might buy a collar to limit the interest rates they pay on a swap.

34. The "Greeks" are partial derivatives that measure the sensitivity of option value to various underlying independent variables, such as risk-free rate, time, stock price, volatility and so on. Specifically, delta is the sensitivity of the option value to movements in underlying stock price. Vega is the sensitivity of the option value to changes in volatility of the underlying. Gamma is the second derivative of the change in option value with respect to price of underlying. Rho measures the impact of the change in the risk free rate on the option value, and theta gives the change in option value with respect to time.

35. Recall that gamma is equal to the rate of change of delta, or $d^2C/dS^2 = d\Delta/dS$. It indicates how fast delta is changing as the underlying is changing. Since delta is zero when the stock is deep out of the money, and 1 when the stock is deep in the money gamma will be zero unless you are close to the money. Because $80 is pretty far from $K = \$100$, we can assume that gamma is zero. A plot of Δ and Γ appears below.

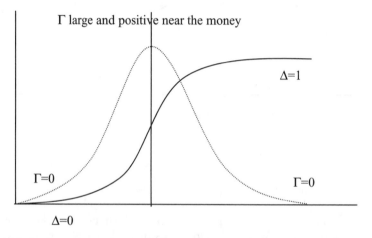

As a numerical check, you can use $r = 5\%$, $\sigma = 35\%$, $K = \$100$ and $t = 3$ months. The following data were calculated using the Black-Scholes model:

S	C
75	0.37237
80	0.863873
85	1.736368

Then gamma is estimated as $(c(75) - 2c(80) + c(85))/\Delta S^2 = (0.37237-2*0.863873+1.736368)/5^2 = 0.01524$.

36. Because real options have gamma as well as delta, using delta alone as a hedging measure probably isn't good enough. You can't just "set it and forget it," but must also consider gamma.

37. The number of contracts required to delta hedge is $-1/\Delta c*$(Number of Shares to Hedge)/(Contract Size) $= -1/0.589*(-1000)/100 = + 16.977$. You would buy 17 calls at a total cost outlay of $187.77. If the stock price moves to $120, the change in value of the call option should be equal

to the call delta times the change in price of underlying, or 0.589*$20 = $11.78. You have 17 call contracts, or $200.26. Because each call contract controls 100 shares of stock, the total change in value = $20,026. Your stock holdings have changed by 1,000 shares ($120-$100) = -$20,000, so you are a bit over-hedged. However, the *actual* call delta at S = $120 would change to 0.832, and the new call price is $25.465, so position change is ($25.465 - $11.01)*17*100 = $24,573.5. You should be tailing the hedge as the underlying changes. To create a delta-gamma neutral portfolio, you have to satisfy two equalities at the strike prices S_1 and S_2:

$N_s + \Delta_{S1} N_{S1} + \Delta_{S2} N_{S2} = 0$ *delta neutral position*

$\Gamma_{S1} N_{S1} + \Gamma_{S2} N_{S2} = 0$ $\qquad\qquad$ *gamma neutral position*

N_s is the number of shares held, N_{S1} is the number of contracts at price S_1 and N_{S2} is the number of contracts at price S_2. Suppose that $S_1 = \$100$ and $S_2 = \$120$. We have $\Delta_{100} = 0.589$ and $\Delta_{120} = 0.834$. Also, $\Gamma_{100} = 0.0225$, and $\Gamma_{120} = 0.0092$. Solving the gamma-neutral equation we find that $N_{S1} = -\Gamma_{S2} N_{S2}/\Gamma_{S2} = -0.0092/0.0225* N_{120} = -0.41 N_{S2:}$ this implies we will trade more contracts at a strike of $120 than at $100 in order to maintain gamma hedging. Now solve the delta neutral position equation for either N_{S1} or N_{S2}: we find $N_{S2} = (-(N_s + \Delta_{S1} N_{S1}))/\Delta_{S2} = (-(1000 + 0.589(-0.41 N_{S2})))/0.834$ so $N_{120} = -1686$ contracts and $N_{100} = 691.2$ contracts in order to maintain both delta and gamma neutral hedging.

Summary of Formulas

Spot-Futures Parity

$$F_{t,T} = S_t e^{r(T-t)}$$

Spot-Futures Parity with Cost of Carry

$$F_{t,T} = (S_t+s)e^{r(T-t)}$$

Spot-Futures Parity with Discrete Dividends

$$F_{t,T} = S_t e^{r(T-t)} - \sum_{i=1}^{n} D_i e^{r(T-t_{Di})}$$

Spot-Futures Parity with Continuous Dividend δ

$$F_{t,T} = S_t e^{(r-\delta)(T-t)}$$

Interest Rate Parity

$$F_0 = E_0 \left(\frac{1+r_D}{1+r_F} \right)^T \text{ simple compounding}$$

$$F_0 = E_0 e^{(r_D-r_F)T} \text{ continuous compounding}$$

Spot-Futures Parity for FX

$$F_{t,T} = S_t e^{(r-r_F)(T-t)}$$

Implied Repo Rate

$$r = \frac{1}{(T-t)} \ln\left(\frac{F_{t,T}}{S_t + s} \right)$$

Contango   Futures prices exceed expected future spot prices.

Full Carry   Futures prices are equal to the expected future spot price with carry costs $(S_t+s)e^{r(T-t)}$

Backwardation   Futures prices are below the expected future spot prices

Payoff of Call

$$C = max(S_t-K,0)$$

Payoff of Put

$$P = max(K-S_b,0)$$

American vs. European Options

$$V_{American} \geq V_{European}$$

Put-Call Parity

$$S + p - c = Ke^{-rt}$$

Payoff of Straddle $max(K-S_b,0) + max(S_t-K,0) - Prem\ call\ Prem\ put.$

Payoff of Interest Rate Cap $\qquad$ $max((r\%-k\%),0))*Notional\backslash What\ we\ will\ pay\ back\ for\ loan:$ $(min(r\%,k\%)+spread)*notional$

Model for Stock Price Movement $\qquad\qquad$ $\dfrac{dS}{S} = \mu\, dt + \sigma\, dz$

Generalized Ito Process $\qquad\qquad$ $dx = a(x,t)\, dt + b(x,t)\, dz$

Black-Scholes PDE $\qquad\qquad$ $\dfrac{\partial V}{\partial t} + \dfrac{1}{2}\sigma^2 S^2 \dfrac{\partial^2 V}{\partial S^2} + rS \dfrac{\partial V}{\partial S} - rV = 0$

Black-Scholes with continuous dividend D

$$\frac{\partial V}{\partial t} + \frac{1}{2}\sigma^2 S^2 \frac{\partial^2 V}{\partial S^2} + (r-D)S\frac{\partial V}{\partial S} - rV = 0$$

Black-Scholes on foreign currency paying r_f

$$\frac{\partial V}{\partial t} + \frac{1}{2}\sigma^2 S^2 \frac{\partial^2 V}{\partial S^2} + \left(r - r_f\right)S\frac{\partial V}{\partial S} - rV = 0$$

Solution of Black Scholes Equation

Call Value $\qquad\qquad$ $C(S,t) = SN(d_1) - Ke^{-rt}N(d_2)$

Put Value $\qquad\qquad$ $p = Ke^{-rt}\left(1 - N(d_2)\right) - S\left(1 - N(d_1)\right)$

If continuous dividends or FX rate δ:

Call Value $\qquad\qquad$ $C(S,t) = Se^{-\delta(t-t)}N(d_1) - Ke^{-rt}N(d_2)$

Put Value $\qquad\qquad$ $p(S,t) = Ke^{-rt}\left(1 - N(d_2)\right) - Se^{-\delta(T-t)}\left(1 - N(d_1)\right)$

Where

$$d_1 = \frac{\ln\left(\dfrac{S}{K}\right) + \left(r - \delta + \dfrac{\sigma^2}{2}\right)(T-t)}{\sigma\sqrt{T-t}}, \quad d_2 = d_1 - \sigma\sqrt{T-t}$$

The Greeks:

Delta $\qquad\qquad$ $\Delta = \dfrac{\partial V}{\partial S}$

Delta of Call $D_{call} = e^{-D(T-t)}N(d_1)$

Delta of Put $D_{put} = e^{-D(T-t)}(N(d_1)-1)$

Numerical Approximation of Delta

$$\Delta = \frac{\partial C}{\partial S} \cong \frac{\Delta C}{\Delta S} = \frac{C(S+\Delta S, t, \sigma, t) - C(S-\Delta S, t, \sigma, t)}{2\Delta S}$$

Gamma $\qquad \gamma = \dfrac{\partial^2 V}{\partial S^2}$

$$\gamma = \frac{\partial^2 V}{\partial S^2} \cong \frac{V(S+\Delta S, t, \sigma, r) - 2V(S,t) + V(S-\Delta S, t, \sigma, r)}{\Delta S^2}$$

$$\gamma_{call} = \frac{e^{-D(T-t)}N'(d_1)}{\sigma S\sqrt{T-t}}$$

$$\gamma_{put} = \frac{e^{-D(T-t)}N'(d_1)}{\sigma S\sqrt{T-t}} = \gamma_{call}$$

where $N'(x) = \dfrac{1}{\sqrt{2\pi}}e^{-\frac{1}{2}x^2}$

Rho

$$\rho = \frac{\partial V}{\partial r}$$

For a call, $\rho_{call} = K(T-t)e^{-r(T-t)}N(d_2)$

For a put, $\rho_{put} = -K(T-t)e^{-r(T-t)}N(-d_2)$

Numerical Approximation of rho

Option rho $\qquad\qquad \rho = \dfrac{\partial C}{\partial r} \cong \dfrac{\Delta C}{\Delta r} = \dfrac{C(S,t,\sigma,r+\Delta r) - C(S,t,\sigma,r)}{\Delta r}$

Theta $\theta = \dfrac{\partial V}{\partial t}$

$$\theta_{call} = -\frac{\sigma S e^{-\delta(T-t)} N'(d_1)}{2\sqrt{T-t}} + \delta S N(d_1) e^{-\delta(T-t)} - rKe^{-r(T-t)} N(d_2)$$

$$\theta_{put} = -\frac{\sigma S e^{-\delta(T-t)} N'(d_1)}{2\sqrt{T-t}} - \delta S N(-d_1) e^{-\delta(T-t)} + rKe^{-r(T-t)} N(-d_2)$$

Numerical approximation of theta

$$\theta = \frac{\partial V}{\partial t} \cong \frac{\Delta V}{\Delta t} = \frac{V(S,t+\Delta t,\sigma,r) - V(S,t,\sigma,r)}{\Delta t}$$

Vega

Sensitivity of Option to Change in Volatility $\varpi = \dfrac{\partial V}{\partial \sigma} \cong \dfrac{\Delta V}{\Delta \sigma} = \dfrac{V(S,t,\sigma+\Delta\sigma,r) - V(S,t,\sigma,r)}{\Delta\sigma}$

$$\varpi_{call} = S\sqrt{T-t}\, e^{-D(T-t)} N'(d_1)$$

$$\varpi_{put} = S\sqrt{T-t}\, e^{-D(T-t)} N'(d_1)$$

Exotic Options:

Binary (Digital) Option   *Payoff is either $1 or $0. For call, C = $1 if S>=K, $0 else. For put, P = $1 if S<=K, $0 else.*

Black-Scholes Equation for Options on Futures $\dfrac{\partial V}{\partial t} + \dfrac{1}{2}\sigma^2 F^2 \dfrac{\partial^2 V}{\partial F^2} - rVdt = 0$

Value of Call Option on Future $C = Fe^{-r(T-t)} N(d_1) - Ke^{-r(T-t)} N(d_2)$

Value of Put Option on Future $P = -Fe^{-r(T-t)} N(-d_1) + Ke^{-r(T-t)} N(-d_2)$

(Where d_1 and d_2 are as before but F replaces S.)

Put-Call Parity for Options on Futures $P + Fe^{-r(T-t)} - c = Ke^{-r(T-t)}$

Eurodollar Futures Contract   *V= $10,000(100 − 0.25(100-Z)) where Z is the futures price. The LIBOR rate is (100-Z) percent.*

Price Value of 1 bp change in LIBOR = $25

Finite Difference Approximation of Derivatives

$$\frac{\partial V}{\partial t} \cong \frac{\Delta V}{\Delta t} = \frac{V(S, t + \Delta t) - V(S, t)}{\Delta t} = \frac{V_{i,j+1} - V_{i,j}}{\Delta t}$$

$$\frac{\partial V}{\partial S} \cong \frac{V_{i+1,j} - V_{i-1,j}}{2\Delta S}$$

$$\frac{\partial^2 V}{\partial S^2} \cong \frac{V_{i+1,j} - 2V_{i,j} + V_{i-1,j}}{\Delta S^2}$$

Binomial Tree Formulas

$$u = e^{\sigma\sqrt{\Delta t}}, d = \frac{1}{u} \text{ and } \pi_u = \frac{e^{rt} - d}{u - d}, \pi_d = 1 - \pi_u = \frac{u - e^{rt}}{u - d}$$

Call Value at node (i,j) $C_{i,j} = e^{-r\Delta t}\left(\pi_u C_{i+1,j+1} + \left(1 - \pi_u\right)C_{i-1,j+1}\right)$

FIXED INCOME
SECURITIES

Bond and Fixed Income Market Issuers

A **bond** is a guarantee to pay a specified amount at maturity (par value), which is commonly $1,000 or $5,000. The bond may pay periodic interest or not, according to the type of bond. Bonds run the gamut from "risk-free" to highly speculative **junk bonds**. Corporations, agencies, municipalities and the government are among some of the primary issuers of bonds.

Bonds that pay periodic interest are called **coupon bonds**. The interest is generally semi-annual. If a bond is quoted as a "ten-year 6% bond" this means that it pays 6% of par per year, or $60. If the bond is semi-annual it pays $30/period. At first glance, valuation of bonds seems pretty simple: just discount the stream of cash flow payments to the present and this is the price of the bond. However, bonds can actually be more complicated to value than equities, making them fascinating to study.

Bonds are highly sensitive to interest rates. The risk of the bond is characterized by the major ratings agencies, which include Standard and Poor's, Moody's Investment Services and Fitch. The lower the rating, the higher the probability of default and so the greater the compensation required by the investor. A brief summary table of S&P's ratings is shown below.

Issuer Credit Rating (Long-Term)	Meaning	Classification
AAA	Highest rating given by S&P. Issuer has "extreme y strong" capacity to meet its financial commitments.	Investment grade
AA	Issuer has "very strong" capacity to meet its financ l commitments. Differs from AAA only slightly.	Investment grade
A	Issuer has "strong" capacity to meet its financ l commitments. More vulnerable to adverse effects th n AAA- or AA-rated issuers.	Investment grade
BBB	Issuer has "adequate" capacity to meet its financ l commitments. Risk of weakening under adverse economic conditions r change in situation.	Investment grade
BB	Issuer "less vulnerable" in near-term than other lower rated issuers, but faces "major ongoing uncertainties."	Highly speculative
B	Issuer currently has capacity to repay debt, but ability is likely to be impaired under unfavorable financial, economic or business conditions.	Highly speculative
CCC	"Currently vulnerable," dependent on favorable economic, financial and business conditions.	Highly speculative
CC	Issuer is "currently highly vulnerable."	Highly speculative
C	"Currently highly vulnerable to non-payment."	Highly speculative
R	"Under regulatory supervision owing to its financial condition."	Highly speculative
SD, D	Selective default or default.	Highly speculative
NR	Not Rated	

Government Bonds

Bonds issued by the U.S. government are generally considered "risk free" because they are backed by "the full faith and credit of the U.S. government." These bonds include Treasury bills, notes and bonds. They are sold at auction by the Federal Reserve Board acting on behalf of the U.S. Government.

A **Treasury bill** (commonly referred to as a **T-bill**) is a discount bond having a maturity of less than 270 days. T-bills, which converge to par at maturity, pay no interest so, technically, they are zero coupon bonds. T-bills are quoted in terms of yields and are distinguishable from other bonds because their bid price appears higher than the ask price. (Recall that the bid price is the price at which a securities dealer would buy the instrument from a seller; the ask price is the price at which the seller would sell the instrument. The dealer makes a profit on the bid-ask spread, so it looks unusual to have an apparently higher bid than ask.) For example:

Maturity	Days to Mat	Bid	Asked	Ask Yield
Aug 08 02	86	1.74	1.73	1.76

Treasury bills are priced according to the formula:

*Price = (1 - (Ask / 100 * Days to Mat / 360)) * (Face Value)*

The asked price of the Aug 08,02 bond above would then be (1 - (1.73 / 100 * 86 / 360)) * ($10,000)=$9,958.67.

A dealer would be willing to purchase a bond at the bid, or (1 - (Bid / 100 * Days to Mat / 360)) * (Face Value) = (1 - (1.74 / 100 * 86 / 360)) * ($10,000)= $9,958.43. Since T-bill yields are calculated on the basis of a 360-day year rather than a 365-day year, they aren't directly comparable to bonds quoted on a day count basis of 365 days/year. However, a simple calculation can correct this. The "ask yield" in the table is the bond's calculated **bond equivalent yield**, computed on the basis of a 365-day year. This is done by assuming that the bond is purchased for the asked price, and annualized over its life.

$$\text{Thus } r_{BEY} = \left(\frac{10,000 - P}{10,000}\right)\frac{365}{n} = \left(\frac{10,000 - 9,958.67}{10,000}\right)\frac{365}{86} = 1.76\%.$$

Treasury notes and **Treasury bonds** are generally coupon-bearing instruments. They are issued in denominations of $1,000 or greater and make semi-annual coupon payments. **Treasury notes** have maturities ranging from 2 to 10 years, while **Treasury bonds** have maturities exceeding 10 years. Treasury bonds, unlike Treasury notes, might also be callable. Prices for both, though, are quoted as a percentage of par in 32nds. For example, an Aug 04 Treasury note with a 3.25% coupon quoted at 100:07 would cost 100+7/32 % of par, or 100.21875 ($1,000) = $1,002.1875.

Agency bonds

Agency bonds are issued by federal agencies such as the Federal Home Loan Mortgage Corporation (FHLMC, often referred to as "Freddie Mac"), the Government National Mortgage Association (GNMA, "Ginnie Mae"), the Federal National Mortgage Association (FNMA, "Fannie Mae"), the Federal Farm Credit Bank, and the Student Loan Marketing Association ("Sallie Mae"). These organizations issue their own debt to provide liquidity to certain markets. If an agency is owned by the government (GNMA, for example), their bonds are default-free. However, if the agency is only sponsored, and not owned, by the government, their debt comes with default risk, because the bonds are not federally insured. It is generally assumed, though, that the government would not permit agencies that it sponsors to go into default, so these agency bonds will trade at only a slight spread to treasury bonds. Listings for agency bonds appear in papers such as *The Wall Street Journal.*

Municipal bonds

Whereas government bonds are issued by the federal government, **municipal bonds** (often called "munis") are issued by state and local governments. Governments issue munis on the basis of their taxing power, or on the basis of anticipated revenues from construction projects. Munis are exempt from federal taxes and may also be exempt from state and local taxes. If a muni is exempt from all three types of taxes, the bond is called **triple-tax exempt.** Investors buy munis for the tax advantages and, as a result, yields on munis can be lower than equivalently rated taxable bonds. The **taxable-equivalent yield** of a muni is calculated as:

$$Taxable\ Equivalent\ Yield = \frac{Municipal\ Yield}{100\% - Tax\ Bracket}$$. Recall that for a taxable bond, the net yield is the yield

after-tax, or $Net\ Yield = Taxable\ Yield(100\% - Tax\ Bracket)$

For an investor in the 35% tax bracket, a municipal bond yielding 6% is equivalent to a non-tax-exempt bond yielding 9.23%. This is an important feature of municipal bonds. The higher the tax bracket of the investor, the greater the benefit derived from a muni. Investors (such as pension funds) who are not subject to taxation would not benefit by investing in municipal bonds. Municipal bonds are rated by those ratings agencies that have a special category for munis.

General obligation bonds, also known as **GOs**, are issued on the basis of the taxation power of the issuing authority. Revenue may be brought in by tax on real estate (ad valorem tax), cigarettes and so on. In analysis of such bonds, the analyst needs to consider the taxable base and the tax rate.

Revenue bonds are issued on anticipated revenue that can be collected via tolls and user fees. Revenue bonds are commonly used to finance construction projects such as bridges, toll roads, airports and hospitals. With respect to rating revenue bonds, analysts are not concerned with the taxing capability of the issuing authority, since taxes are not the source of revenue. Instead, a study is performed to try to quantify the amount of expected revenue from the user fees.

Corporate Bonds

Issued by corporations as a way of raising capital, **corporate bonds** are usually more risky than treasuries or agencies. In order for agencies to rate a corporation's bond issue, the corporations must first put in a request with one of the agencies (only the major agencies rate corporate bonds). Once a bond issue is rated, the rating is updated quarterly. Because there is a cost for the rating service, most often, only the larger issues are rated. Certainly, ratings downgrades are bad. For example, due to S&P's opinion that industry fundamentals were deteriorating, in late 2001 the agency downgraded Ford Motor Company's rating to BBB+. Just two years earlier, the company was as high as A+. (Notice that BBB is the last category that can be considered "investment grade.") The following illustrates how this downgrade could increase the cost of debt issuance:

Say, a 5-year $8 billion bond rated A+ is currently trading at a spread of 90 bp to treasuries, while the spread of an equivalent BBB+ bond is 125 bp. The borrowing cost for the downgrade is seen as the spread

$v.0035$

(125 - 90 = 35bp) relative to Treasuries. A quick, crude calculation of the borrowing cost is then 35 bp times $8 billion = $28 million. If Ford wanted to go into the debt markets to raise an $8 billion bond issue, it would pay about $28 million for the downgrade in its rating. (This is not quite exact since we have to account for the time value of money. To be more exact, we assume that the $8 billion borrowing is assumed to be financed over a five-year period with semi-annual interest payments. We would calculate the difference between the PV of interest payments with a 90-bp spread to Treasury and the PV of interest payments with a 125-bp spread to Treasury.)

Yields have to increase with credit downgrades in order to compensate investors for the higher probability of default p. It is possible to calculate p by comparing prices of similar instruments with different ratings.

Suppose that 5-year treasuries are currently yielding 2%, a 5 year A+ corporate is yielding 5%, and a BBB+ bond is yielding 6.4%. The implied probability of default can be calculated using expectations theory. Let p be the probability of default and suppose that the recovery factor is zero. (In actuality, the investor can usually expect to get more than this.) Then there are two states of nature: default and non-default with probabilities p and $(1-p)$, and outcomes of -100% (complete loss) and the stated yield to maturity, respectively. For an investment of $100, the Treasury bond will return $102 in either state of nature. The corporate bond will return $0 in case of default or $105 in case of non-default. See sketches below.

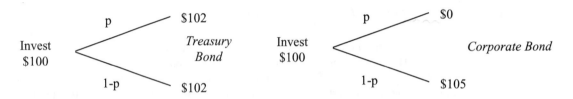

Then we must have $\$0p + \$105 (1-p) = \$102$ so that $p = 2.85\%$ is the probability of default on the A+ rated bond.

For the BBB+ rated bond, a similar analysis shows that the probability of default is (106.4 - 102)/106.4 = 4.14%. This is a very simple, back-of-the-envelope analysis. To calculate this more accurately, we would use binomial trees.

Mortgage-backed and other asset-backed securities

Consider a mortgage or auto lender. They have a large amount of small, illiquid loans on their balance sheet. Mortgages and auto loans are forms of loans termed **amortizing loans**, which means that each month the borrower makes a payment consisting of part interest and part principal. This is in contrast to loans such as credit card balances, where the borrower is only required to make a minimum monthly payment. Since mortgages typically have long maturities, the lender may reliquify its balance sheet by packaging the loans into pools or **tranches** and selling them to a third party. Credit card companies and other holders of receivables backed by assets (such as auto finance companies) can do the same thing. These tranches have different characteristics and credit quality. The loan originator usually receives a servicing fee, and both external and internal credit enhancements may be added to make the loans more attractive to buyers.

The greatest risk in a mortgage loan is **prepayment risk**. Borrowers can generally prepay with no penalty and may do so for a variety of reasons. Since the value of a bond is the present value of its future cash flows, these have to be able to be forecast with a high degree of accuracy if the bond is to be valued correctly. The tranches are generally arranged so that there is a set of tranches that receive interest and principal, and a residual tranche where the interest is accrued only. Factors that may encourage prepayments include a declining interest rate environment. If prepayments increase, the bondholders are exposed to early return of their principal, which must then be reinvested at lower rates. They are also subject to curtailment risk – the risk that the loan will be paid off early. Curtailment has the following impact on those receiving principal payments:

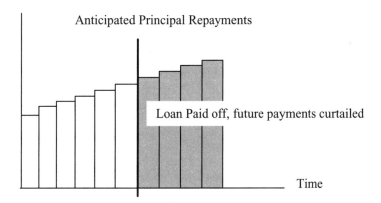

On the other hand, an increasing rate environment means that mortgage holders may have to delay payment, stretching out the duration of the pool. This risk is called **extension risk**. Analysts of amortizing-type loans must model the amount of expected prepayments in order to value the securities. This will be covered in greater detail in a later section.

Types of Fixed Income Securities

A **fixed coupon bond** pays a stated percentage of the bond face value at specified periods. Usually, these type of bonds pay interest on a semiannual basis. It is very easy to value this type of bond. However, since coupons *are* received, the investor is subject to **coupon reinvestment rate risk**. If interest rates have fallen since the bond was purchased, the coupon will be reinvested at a lower rate than initially anticipated. If rates have risen, however, the bondholder will profit as he receives a higher rate than initially anticipated.

Zero coupon bonds just accrue interest until maturity. No coupons are paid. Thus, there is no coupon reinvestment risk on a zero coupon bond, but there is substantially higher price risk. Investors may also suffer adverse tax consequences because, prior to maturity, interest has not been received, yet tax laws require write up of the basis of these bonds for a net negative income effect. Ten, thirty and even one-hundred year (century) zero coupon bonds may be purchased.

In contrast to the fixed rate bonds that pay a constant coupon rate, the payments of **floating rate bonds** can be set to some floating rate benchmark such as LIBOR. The investor receives a variable rate each payment period.

If a corporation issues a fixed rate bond, it is obligated to pay this coupon over the life of the bond. It funds the payment through other borrowings. If rates decline, the spread between the funding cost and the coupon will widen, adversely impacting profit. If the rate decline is large enough, the corporation may wish to "call the bond" away from the investors. The benefit of the call option does not accrue to the investor, as the corporation will call the bond when it is most convenient for them, not when it is most profitable for the investor. In order to be compensated for this additional risk, **callable bonds** carry a higher coupon than non-callable bonds. Generally, there is some lock out period during which the bond is not callable -- for example, during the first 10 or 15 years. Such a bond is said to contain an **embedded option** and thus cannot be valued by the technique of simply discounting expected future cash flows.

A **putable bond** contains an embedded put option. This benefit does accrue to the investor as it makes the bond more valuable. The bond indenture will contain a clause that states that the bond may be put back to the corporation if interest rates reach some specified level, say 6%. For example, an investor may hold a fixed rate bond paying 4%. If rates increase above the fixed rate, the value of the bond falls. The investor may sell the bond back to the corporation for the price implied by the contracted fixed rate, which will exceed the market price. This put option provides some insurance to the investor.

Convertible bonds provide the holder with a debt instrument that has equity-like features, thus, it is considered a hybrid security. The convertible bond provides the issuer a low cost source of financing, and gives the holder the option to convert the bond into equity -- so holders have the security of a prescribed cash flow when they hold the bond, and the ability to participate in upward price movements when converted into equity.

Quoting Bond and Fixed Income Prices

If you try to buy a bond at the price listed in the newspaper, you will find that it's not the price you will ultimately pay. Suppose you are trying to buy a $1,000 bond paying 10% interest with semi-annual payments. This means that the bondholder will receive 10%/2*$1,000 = $50 per period in coupon interest. Suppose that there are 180 days between coupon payments, and 60 days have elapsed since the last coupon payment. The owner of the bond is the one who is entitled to the interest, so if you purchase the bond, you will receive the full coupon payment of $50 in 120 days. But, for the first 60 days, the bond was owned by the seller, so you will pay the invoice price -- which is equal to the price quoted in the paper (the **clean price**) and the payment of accrued interest to that point, 60/180*$50 = $16.67.

Invoice Price = Clean Price + Accrued Interest

This makes sense since it provides a common way of comparing bonds with different maturities. It also explains why the price of a maturing bond is quoted as $1,000, not the expected $1,000 plus coupon. If you buy the above bond one day before maturity, you will receive the coupon of $50 the next day. Because you are receiving $1,050 of value, you would agree that $1,050 is the fair price for this bond. But this coupon actually belongs to the seller, so the net price of the bond is $1,000, as quoted.

Analyzing and Valuing Bonds and Fixed Income Securities

The pricing of a bond pretty much just requires calculation of discounted cash flows, where the cash flows are the expected coupons plus par at maturity, or simply par if the bond is a zero-coupon bond.

If a bond is quoted at face value, it is said to be **selling at par**. A par bond is simply a bond whose coupon is equal to its yield. A $1,000 face value bond selling or $1,000 is a **par bond**. If the price of the bond is higher than par, the bond is a **premium bond**; if lower, it is a **discount bond**. Thus:

$C = y$ Par Bond
$C < y$ Discount Bond
$C > y$ Premium Bond

The price of a bond is inversely proportional to its yield. We will go through detailed calculations in a later section of this chapter, but in general, the higher the coupon on the bond, the lower its price. For a given maturity, a zero coupon bond would normally be priced lower than any similarly rated coupon bond. The price of a bond will also depend on the characteristics of the bond. For example, if the bond is callable, it will generally be priced high enough to compensate the investor for the risk of early termination. The price of the bond should also embed any assumed credit risks, yield curve risks, liquidity risks, country risks and currency risks.

Typically, if the coupon paid is lower than the current yield curve rate (note that this is a simplification as we must consider term structure effects), the bond will be priced at a discount to par. If the coupon rate is comparable to current yields, the bond should be priced close to par. If the bond pays a coupon that is higher than the yield curve for that maturity, the bond sells at a premium.

Below is a table of current bonds, their coupons, yield curve rates and prices. Note that the two-year bond is priced above $100 because its coupon, 3.375%, is slightly greater than the yield curve rate of 3.24%. The 30-year bond is priced below par since its coupon of 5.375% is lower than the yield curve rate of 5.67. The five-year bond is priced fairly close to par.

Maturity, yrs	Yield, %	Price of Bond	Coupon
0.25	1.75	1.72	
0.5	1.9	1.86	
2	3.24	100.25	3.375
5	4.44	99.6875	4.375
10	5.13	98.0625	4.875
30	5.67	95.875	5.375

NPV of cash flows

We consider three bonds here: a premium bond, a par bond and a discount bond.
Assume that we have a two-year bond paying 6% semi-annual coupon. The investor will thus receive the series of cash flows shown below.

Time, yrs	Cash Flow
0	

0.5	$60
1.0	$60
1.5	$60
2.0	$1,060

The price of a bond is the present value of the expected cash flows. Then,

$$Price = \sum_{i=1}^{n} \frac{CF_i}{(1+r_i)^n} = \frac{CF_1}{(1+r_1)^1} + \frac{CF_2}{(1+r_2)^2} + \frac{CF_3}{(1+r_3)^3} + \frac{CF_4}{(1+r_4)^4}$$

If the yield curve is flat at 6% then the bond is a par bond because

$$Price = \frac{30}{\left(1+\frac{0.06}{2}\right)^1} + \frac{30}{\left(1+\frac{0.06}{2}\right)^2} + \frac{30}{\left(1+\frac{0.06}{2}\right)^3} + \frac{1030}{\left(1+\frac{0.06}{2}\right)^4} = \$1,000.$$

Suppose that the yield curve shifts up by 100 bp so that the six-month, one-year, one-and-one-half year and the two-year interest rate are 7%. The price of the bond is then:

$$Price = \frac{30}{\left(1+\frac{0.07}{2}\right)^1} + \frac{30}{\left(1+\frac{0.07}{2}\right)^2} + \frac{30}{\left(1+\frac{0.07}{2}\right)^3} + \frac{1030}{\left(1+\frac{0.07}{2}\right)^4} = \$981.63.$$

The effect of increasing interest rates lowers the price of the bond.

If the yield curve shifts down by 100bp uniformly, so that the flat rate is 5%, the bond will be priced at:

$$Price = \frac{30}{\left(1+\frac{0.05}{2}\right)^1} + \frac{30}{\left(1+\frac{0.05}{2}\right)^2} + \frac{30}{\left(1+\frac{0.05}{2}\right)^3} + \frac{1030}{\left(1+\frac{0.05}{2}\right)^4} = \$1,018.1, \text{ above par.}$$

The reason for this is coupon reinvestment. If the purchaser buys a 6% bond and the yield curve later shifts so that newly issued, similar bonds will pay 7%, the bond is worth less. On the other hand, the holder of a 6% bond benefits if rates drop, since the bond will be worth more than newly issued bonds. *Remember this because it's very important.*

Risks of Bonds

When coupons are received, they must be reinvested. The future rate at which they will be invested is unknown at the time of purchase. Thus, bonds are subject to interest rate risk, default risk and reinvestment risk. There are three commonly quoted measures of yield: the stated or nominal yield, the current yield, and the yield to maturity.

The **stated yield** is the quoted coupon in percentage terms. The 10-year bond with a 6% coupon has a nominal yield of 6%. The stated yields of the par, premium and discount bonds above are all 6%. The stated yield may or may not be the ultimate yield that the investor receives, but it guarantees the amount of income realized via the coupon.

Similar to a dividend yield, **current yield** is calculated by dividing the coupon payment by the price of the bond. The current yield of the par bond is $30/$1000 = 3%, the current yield of the premium bond is $30/1018.1=2.94% and the current yield of the discount bond is $30/981.63 = 3.06%.

If the yield curve is not flat, coupons will be reinvested at different rates. Suppose that the actual yield curve is:

Time, yrs	r, %
0	
0.5	4.5
1.0	5.5
1.5	6.5
2.0	7.5

The price of the bond is calculated as:

$$\Pr ice = \frac{30}{\left(1+\frac{0.045}{2}\right)^1} + \frac{30}{\left(1+\frac{0.055}{2}\right)^2} + \frac{30}{\left(1+\frac{0.065}{2}\right)^3} + \frac{1030}{\left(1+\frac{0.075}{2}\right)^4} = \$973.97$$

The **yield to maturity** is the single discount rate r that will give the same price. That is, we solve for y in the equation below:

$$\$973.97 = \frac{30}{\left(1+\frac{y}{2}\right)^1} + \frac{30}{\left(1+\frac{y}{2}\right)^2} + \frac{30}{\left(1+\frac{y}{2}\right)^3} + \frac{1030}{\left(1+\frac{y}{2}\right)^4}.$$

For this problem we find $y = 7.43\%$.

The **duration** of a bond is an important measure of interest rate risk but is limited as a stand-alone number (as shown in chapter two). Duration assumes a linear relationship between price and yield. The convexity of a bond is the second derivative of price with respect to yield and should be added to the price change calculated by using duration to give a more accurate price. Recall that the effective duration of a bond is a numerical estimate based on the change in calculated prices with respect to yields, so should not have the convexity problems of analytical duration. Also note that duration does not measure yield curve risk. To solve this problem, key rate durations should be used. To demonstrate this, recall the bonds we used in the bond fundamentals chapter in calculation of duration of a bond portfolio. We had Portfolio A, a "bullet" portfolio consisting of a 10-year, 8% coupon bond and Portfolio "B," a "barbell" portfolio consisting of a two-year, 5% bond and a 20-year, 12% bond. Suppose we also add a "ladder" portfolio consisting of all three bonds. We constructed duration-neutral portfolios by choosing the weights of bonds in portfolios B and C so that the overall duration of each portfolio matches the duration of the barbell, 6.71 years.

Bond	Mod Duration, years	Weights for Portfolio A	Weights for Portfolio B	Weights for Portfolio C
2 Year	1.86	0%	13.55%	10% (chosen)
10 Year	6.71	100%	0%	26%
20 Year	7.47	0%	86.45%	64%

When we had a parallel shift of the yield curve, all bonds had the same price change, but the duration alone was not enough to handle a non-parallel yield curve shift. To do this we use **key rate durations**.

Example Assume the key rate durations for a 2-year, 10-year and 20-year bond are as shown above. What is the effect on each portfolio of a 100bp decrease in the 2-year rate, 50 bp increase in the 10-ear rate and a 150 bp increase in the 20-ear rate?

Portfolio A
$\Delta P/P = -(w_2 D_2 \Delta P_2 + w_{10} D_{10} \Delta P_{10} + w_{20} D_{20} \Delta P_{20}) = -(0(1.86)(-0.01) + 1.0*6.71*0.005 + 0.0*7.47*.015) = -3.355\%$

Portfolio B
$\Delta P/P = -(w_2 D_2 \Delta P_2 + w_{10} D_{10} \Delta P_{10} + w_{20} D_{20} \Delta P_{20}) = -(0.1355(1.86)(-0.01) + 0*6.71*0.005 + 0.8645*7.47*.015) = -9.435\%$

Portfolio C
$\Delta P/P = -(0.10(1.86)(-0.01) + 0.26*6.71*0.005 + 0.64*7.47*.015) = -7.858\%$

Portfolio A performs best under these circumstances as it drops by the least amount.

Term structure of interest rates, spot rates and forward rates

Understanding the term structure of interest rates is absolutely critical in pricing bonds. Suppose the par yield curve is as shown below. This is constructed from newly issued bonds (which are usually issued at par), so that their coupons are the same as their yield to maturity:

Par Yield Curve			
Maturity, yrs	Yield, %	Price of Bond	Coupon
0.25	1.75	1.72	0
0.5	1.9	1.86	0
1	2.35	100	2.35
1.5	2.79	100	2.79
2	3.24	100	3.24
3	3.64	100	3.64
5	4.44	100	4.44

The indicated par yield curve is upward sloping. We can use this par-yield curve to derive the expected **spot rates**. The process we use is called **boot-strapping**. For example, the one-year bond has cash flows of $2.35/year or $1.175/period. The price is

$$P = \frac{1.175}{(1+r_{0.5})^1} + \frac{101.175}{(1+r_1)^2} = \$100.$$ $r_{0.5}$ is the periodic spot rate for an 0.5-year bond. Since the 0.5 year bond

pays no coupon, it is essentially a zero-coupon bond and so the given rate of 1.9%/year is the spot rate. We need to solve for the one-year spot rate by solving the equation above. We find

$$P_1 = 100 = \frac{1.175}{\left(1+\dfrac{0.019}{2}\right)^1} + \frac{101.175}{\left(1+\dfrac{r_1}{2}\right)^2}$$

$$\left(1+\frac{r_1}{2}\right)^2 = \frac{101.175}{100 - \dfrac{1.175}{\left(1+\dfrac{0.019}{2}\right)^1}}$$

$r_1 = 2.353\%$

For the 1.5-year bond, we use the rates $r_{0.5}$ and r_1 found above (this is what gives the process the name bootstrapping). This bond pays 2.79%/year so the coupon is 1.395/period. Then:

$$P_{1.5} = 100 = \frac{1.395}{\left(1+\dfrac{0.019}{2}\right)^1} + \frac{1.395}{\left(1+\dfrac{0.02353}{2}\right)^2} + \frac{101.395}{\left(1+\dfrac{r_{1.5}}{2}\right)^3}$$

$$\left(1+\frac{r_{1.5}}{2}\right)^3 = \frac{101.395}{100 - \dfrac{1.395}{\left(1+\dfrac{0.019}{2}\right)^1} - \dfrac{1.395}{\left(1+\dfrac{0.02353}{2}\right)^2}}$$

so $r_{1.5} = 2.798\%$.

Finally, for the 2-year bond, which pays an annual coupon rate of 3.375% or $1.6875/period we have:

$$P_2 = 100.25 = \frac{1.6875}{\left(1+\dfrac{0.019}{2}\right)^1} + \frac{1.6875}{\left(1+\dfrac{0.02353}{2}\right)^2} + \frac{1.6875}{\left(1+\dfrac{0.02798}{2}\right)^3} + \frac{101.6875}{\left(1+\dfrac{r_2}{2}\right)^4}$$

$$\left(1+\frac{r_2}{2}\right)^4 = \frac{101.6875}{100.25 - \dfrac{1.6875}{\left(1+\dfrac{0.019}{2}\right)^1} - \dfrac{1.6875}{\left(1+\dfrac{0.02353}{2}\right)^2} - \dfrac{1.6875}{\left(1+\dfrac{0.02798}{2}\right)^3}}$$

Then $r_2 = 3.212\%$.

Now an arbitrageur, seeing the yield curve, could decide to buy the two-year bond, guaranteeing a yield of 3.5% (assuming the bond doesn't default). Or, he could buy a one-year bond, and at the end of the one year, roll it over for another year. The investor should be indifferent between these alternatives. Thus, there must be some linkage between the two-year rate, the one-year rate, and the expected one-year rate, one year from today. The expected one-year rate, one year from now is called a **forward rate**. The notation we use is $_1f_n$, where 1 refers to the one-year rate and n is the number of years forward, so $_1f_n$ is the rate for n years prevailing in one year that can be locked in today.

For example, consider an investor who will invest for two years. Assume for simplicity that the two-year rate is 5%. The investor could either buy a two-year bond or buy a one-year bond and, at year-end, roll it over into a new one-year bond. Either choice should yield identical two-year returns. Even though the rate that will prevail in one year is unknown today, the market expectation of this rate is the forward rate, which can easily be calculated. If the one-year Treasury bond is trading at 4%, what is the implied one-year rate, one year forward $_1f_1$? It is calculated from $(1+r_2)^2=(1+r_1)(1+{_1f_1})$ where r_2 and r_1 are the two and one year spot rates respectively. Then,

$$_1f_1 = \frac{(1+r_2)^2}{(1+r_1)}-1 = \frac{(1+0.05)^2}{(1+0.04)}-1 = 6.01\%.$$

If the forward rate were other than this, arbitrage would occur. Suppose that the forward rate were 5.9%. Then the investor rolling the bond over would lock in $_1f_1$ today using a forward contract, and would receive

an effective two-year rate of $r_2 = \sqrt{(1+r_1)(1+{_1f_1})}-1 = 4.946\%$. Since 5% could be locked in by buying the

two-year bond, the one-year bond one year forward would be sold short. The effect of many traders selling this bond would cause its price to drop, raising its yield to the point where equilibrium would be achieved. This equilibrium would be at 6.01%. Check yourself on the following calculations:

Maturity, Years n	Spot Rate	Forward Rate $_1f_{n-1}$
1	4%	NA
2	5%	6.01%
3	6%	8.029%
4	7%	10.057%
5	8%	12.094%

By construction, spot rates must be equal to the product of short-term forward rates. For example, the four year spot rate of 7 % satisfies $(1+r_4)^4 = (1+r_1)(1+{_1f_1})(1+{_1f_2})(1+{_1f_3}) = (1+0.04)(1+0.0601)(1+0.08029)(1+0.10057)$, so for an upward sloping yield curve, the spot rates should lie below the forward rates. And, since par rates are somewhat of an average of spot rates, for an upward sloping yield curve, par yields will be below spot rates, as shown below.

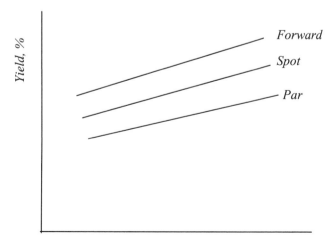

For a downward sloping yield curve, the situation is reversed. Here, the par yield is highest, then the spot, and finally the forward.

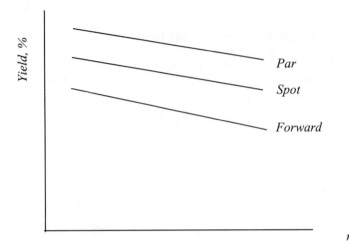

For a flat yield curve, the par, spot and forward rate curves are identical.

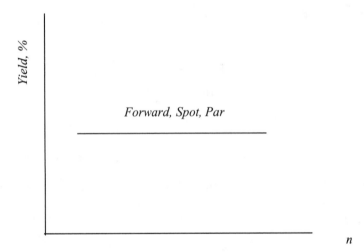

Want a memory trick to remember this? Imagine you are about to run an uphill race. You would have to pass the starting line before you finish, wouldn't you? P-ass S-tart to F-inish (P-ar, S-pot and F-orward on an upward sloping yield curve.) Running a downhill or even flat road race (downward or flat sloped) is the same thing: PSF.

Pure expectations theory of the term structure

This theory assumes the yield curve is a series of short forward rates, so the yield curve contains market expectations of future interest rate changes. If the market expects interest rates to rise, the yield curve will be upward sloping. If the market expects interest rates to fall, the yield curve will be downward sloping. Only if the market expects interest rates to remain unchanged will the yield curve be flat. The yield curve can twist as well. A study using principal components analysis showed that approximately 90% of the price change of bonds was due to changes in interest levels, 8.5% by a changing yield curve slope, and the remaining 1.5% by curvature of the yield curve.

Empirical evidence shows that forward rates are poor predictors of rates that ultimately prevail. They can, however, be used to assess relative value in various sectors. If the forward rates imply that the market expects two-year rates to rise 50 bp over the next three months, but you believe they will remain unchanged, it may be possible to make some profit in bonds of this maturity.

Fixed Income-Specific Derivatives

A brief introduction was provided to fixed-income derivatives in the derivatives chapter. Now we can go further into valuation of these derivatives. This is usually done using trees and Monte Carlo analysis.

A **zero** is defined as a theoretical bond with maturity T paying $1 at T. There are no coupons. Using Z_n for the price of a zero maturing n periods from today, zeros are the basic building block of bond pricing. Zeros are also called discount factors d_f.

Example   Using the table of bond prices, yields and maturities shown below, determine a price for bond E.

Bond	Maturity, n, years	Annual Coupon Rate	Yield, %	Price per $100 of par
A	0.5	2.0%	2.5%	99.75
B	1.0	3.0%	4.0%	99.029
C	1.5	3.5%	3.2%	100.436
D	2.0	4.0%	6.0%	96.2829
E	2.0	8.0%	?	?

The cash flows resulting from the bonds in the table above are:

Bond	0.5 years	1 year	1.5 years	2 years
A	101			
B	1.5	101.5		
C	1.75	1.75	101.75	
D	2.0	2.0	2.0	102.0
E	4.0	4.0	4.0	104.0

The implied discount rate for bond A:

$PV= 1/(1+df)$ $FV = Z_{0.5}FV$, where $Z_{0.5} =1/(1+df)$.   Then, $99.75 = Z_{0.5}(100+C)$, $Z_{0.5} = P_0/P_{0.5} = 99.75/101=0.98762$.

For Bond B, discounting cash flows back to present gives

$$\frac{1.5}{(1+r_{0.5})}+\frac{101.5}{(1+r_1)}=99.029, or\, 1.5Z_{0.5}+101.5Z_1=99.029$$

Thus, $Z_1 =\dfrac{P_0-CF_{0.5}Z_{0.5}}{CF_1}=\dfrac{99.029-1.5*0.98762}{101.5}=0.96106.$

For Bond C we have:

$1.75Z_{0.5} + 1.75Z_1 + 101.75Z_{1.5} = 100.436$, so

$$Z_{1.5}=\frac{P_0-CF_{0.5}Z_{0.5}-CF_1Z_1}{CF_{1.5}}=\frac{100.436-1.75*0.98762-1.75*0.96106}{101.75}=0.95357$$

For Bond D:

$2.0Z_{0.5} + 2.0Z_1 + 2.0Z_{1.5} + 102.0Z_2 = 96.2829$, so

$$Z_{2.0} = \frac{P_0 - CF_{0.5}Z_{0.5} - CF_1 Z_1 - CF_{1.5}Z_{1.5}}{CF_{2.0}} = \frac{96.2829 - 2.0*0.98762 - 2.0*0.96106 - 2.0*0.95357}{102}$$

$= 0.88704$

We can now price Bond E. We have:

$P = 4.0Z_{0.5} + 4.0Z_1 + 4.0Z_{1.5} + 104.0Z_2 = 4.0*0.98762 + 4.0*0.96106 + 4.0*0.95357 + 104.0*0.88704 =$ $103.86116. With this price, the YTM is calculated as 5.92%.

Also note that since the cash flow of Bond A is $101, this is like holding 101 zeros. This allows us to create synthetic zeros for any maturity desired, because buying one hundred six-month zeros is equivalent to buying $1/101*100 = 0.9901$ of Bond A.

In general:

$$Z_n = \frac{P - C\sum_{i=1}^{n-1} Z_i}{100 + C}$$

Bootstrapping the zero curve

We can use the prices of the zeros to construct the zero-coupon yield curve. The spot rates implied by these prices are:

$$\frac{1}{\left(1+\dfrac{y_{0.5}}{2}\right)} = Z_{0.5} = 0.98762 \text{ so } y_{0.5} = 2.507\%$$

$$\frac{1}{\left(1+\dfrac{y_{1.5}}{2}\right)^3} = Z_{1.5} = 0.95357 \text{ so } y_{1.5} = 2\left(\sqrt[3]{\frac{1}{Z_{1.5}}} - 1\right) = 3.195\%$$

$$\frac{1}{\left(1+\frac{y_1}{2}\right)^2} = Z_1 = 0.96106 \text{ so } y_1 = 2\left(\sqrt{\frac{1}{Z_1}} - 1\right) = 4.012\%$$

$$\frac{1}{\left(1+\frac{y_{2.0}}{2}\right)^4} = Z_{2.0} = 0.88704 \text{ so } y_{2.0} = 2\left(\sqrt[4]{\frac{1}{Z_{2.0}}} - 1\right) = 6.084\%$$

The general formula is $y_i = 2\left(\left(\frac{1}{Z_i}\right)^{\frac{0.5}{i}} - 1\right)$

Interest rate derivatives

These include forwards, swaps, caps, floors, collars, swaps, swaptions, mortgage-backed securities (MBS), collateralized mortgage-backed securities (CMBS), and collateralized mortgage obligations (CMOs).

A **forward contract** is an agreement today to take or make delivery at a future date. There is no cash flow at contract initiation. Forward rates let us lock in a future rate today. A forward contract would allow us to lock in the price we would pay for a one- year bond, one year from today. In order to price this all we need to know are the current prices of the one-year bond and the two-year bond.

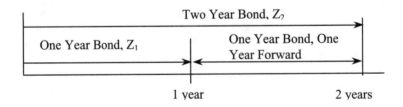

Then, $_1F_1$ is the price of the year bond, one year from now and this price is

$_1F_1 = \frac{Z_2}{Z_1} = \frac{0.8870}{0.9535} = 0.92298$. The implied one year forward rate can be calculated

$$\frac{1}{\left(1+\frac{y_1}{2}\right)^2} = {_1F_1} \text{ so } y_1 = 8.177\%$$

The following table shows the calculations. In general, the forward price of an *m*-year bond, *n* years forward is calculated as Z_m/Z_n.

	Maturity, Years				
Delivery, years	*0.0*	*0.5*	*1.0*	*1.5*	*2.0*
0.0	1	0.98762	0.96106	0.95357	0.88704
0.5		1	0.97311	0.96552	0.89816
1.0			1	0.99220	0.92298
1.5				1	0.93023
2.0					1

Note that in all of the above, we only use bonds that are option-free. Bonds that are callable, putable, etc., should not be used in construction of the yield curve.

Bond valuation using binomial trees

What about bonds with embedded options such as callable bonds and mortgages? We need more complex techniques. In valuing bonds with options, we need to know whether the bond price depends on the interest rate path, as opposed to simply depending on the level. For example, a callable bond may be callable when interest rates hit 6%. It won't matter how the rates get to this point, merely that they do. Such bonds can be priced using the backward induction technique of binomial trees. In contrast, mortgage-backed securities may depend on the prepayment history. If rates have been steady at 10% and then suddenly drop to 7%, there may be a surge of refinancings. If rates then move to 8% and then back to 7%, there may be fewer refinancings than before because many of those who would have refinanced have already done so. This is called **burnout**. The fact that the rate is at 7% is not as important as how it got there.

Binomial tree method for valuation of simple derivative instruments

While there are many complex methods for forecasting interest rates, here we will just use a simplified approach to **Black-Derman-Toy (BDT)**. (You should also be familiar with other models such as **Ho-Lee** and **Heath-Jarrow-Morton**.)

In this very simple version of BDT, we assume that interest rate volatility is constant. In practice, we should use the actual term structure of volatility, which would introduce some drift into our tree.

(*Tip*: We suggest that you go through the spreadsheet and try to build one for yourself. Construction of the spreadsheet will help you to understand the mechanics of the model, and to remember it during an interview. You might use your model to price some bonds you find in *The Wall Street Journal*. If you do, in an interview, you can mention that you have constructed a BDT model to estimate forward prices. You can say you did this because you (or a friend) wanted an idea of what interest rates were going to do, as you were debating whether to lock in a new mortgage now, or wait to see if rates fall even further. You whipped this model up one day on your Palm Pilot using live feeds from Bloomberg. Well, the last sentence may be a stretch, but you get the idea.)

In order to value a bond, we must first start with an expectation of how interest rates will evolve through time. We need to calibrate our tree to observed spot rates and have an estimation of interest rate volatility σ. This volatility should be calculated from the current yield curve. We begin by assuming that interest rates follow a random walk with the expected value in one year equal to the one-year spot rate, $_0f_1 = r_1$. After that, it is assumed that rates will either move up or down. If down, the forward rate will be $_1f_{1,-1}$ and if up, the rate will be $_1f_{1,1}$. (The new subscript represents the number of upmoves.) We relate the upmove to downmoves by requiring that $_1f_{1,1} = {}_1f_{1,-1}e^{2\sigma}$.

Suppose we are at time 0 and wish to value a two-year bond. We divide up the two-year period into subintervals. For simplicity here we use one-year subintervals. The starting interest rate is assumed to move up or down in the next time period.

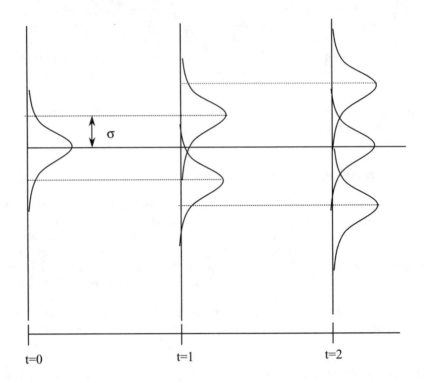

This tree is used to develop the possible interest rate paths that can be expected to prevail in the future. Next, the binomial tree to value the bond is constructed. $V_{i,j}$ is the value of the bond at time i after j upmoves.

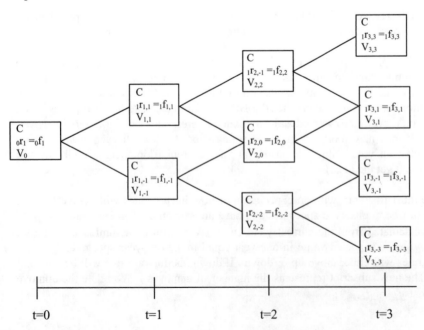

Let's value a three-year treasury bond with a coupon of 5%. To do this, we have to compute the forward rates consistent with the lognormal probability distribution for the volatility term structure. Assuming that volatility is constant at 10%, we have to begin with the current spot and forward rates. From the current on-the-run treasury yield curve, we had

Maturity, Years	Par Yield	Spot Yield	One Year Forward Rate
1	2.35%	2.35%	2.35%
2	3.24%	3.255%	4.168%
3	3.64%	3.666%	4.493%

Spot rates are calculated from par rates using bootstrapping and price of $100. For example, the two-year bond has a coupon of $3.24 per year so

$$100 = \frac{3.24}{1.0235} + \frac{103.24}{(1+r_2)^2} \text{ so } r_2 = 3.255\%.$$

$$\text{For } r_3: \quad 100 = \frac{3.64}{1.0235} + \frac{3.64}{(1+0.03255)^2} + \frac{103.64}{(1+r_3)^3} \text{ so } r_3 = 3.666\%$$

Next, calculate the forward rates as we have done earlier. $(1+0.03255)^2 = (1.0235)(1+_1f_1)$ so $_1f_1 = 4.168\%$, $(1+0.03666)^3 = (1+0.03255)^2 (1+_1f_2)$ so $_1f_2 = 4.493\%$.

Now we build a tree for the two-year bond. The reason we have to do this first is that the forward rates must be chosen to price the two-year bond. Once we have these, we will build the tree for the three-year bond.

At any node, the price is calculated by backward induction as

$$V_{i-1} = \frac{1}{(1+_1f_{i-1})} \frac{1}{2} \left(V_{i,up} + C_{i,up} + V_{i,down} + C_{i,down} \right)$$

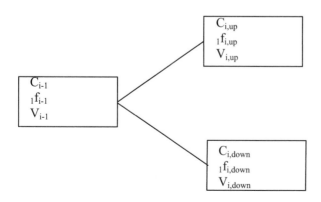

To value the two-year par bond (this bond pays a coupon of 3.24%), we have

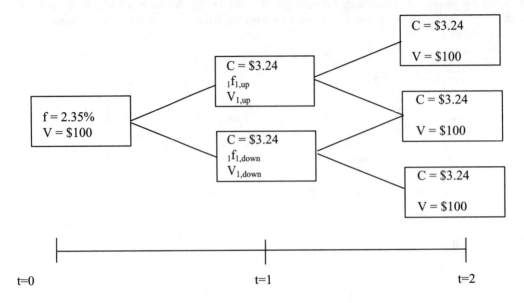

So, the value of the bond after one upmove, $V_{1,up} = \dfrac{1}{\left(1+{}_1f_{1,up}\right)}\dfrac{1}{2}\left(\$100+\$3.24+\$100+\$3.24\right)$

and after one downmove, $V_{1,udown} = \dfrac{1}{\left(1+{}_1f_{1,down}\right)}\dfrac{1}{2}\left(\$100+\$3.24+\$100+\$3.24\right)$

But, ${}_1f_{1,up} = {}_1f_{1,down}e^{2\sigma}$ so $V_{1,up} = \dfrac{1}{\left(1+{}_1f_{1,down}e^{2\sigma}\right)}\dfrac{1}{2}\left(\$100+\$3.24+\$100+\$3.24\right)$

We have three unknowns and only two equations. The third condition that we impose is the requirement that the bond trades at par at t=0, so we have

$$\$100 = \frac{1}{1.0235}\frac{1}{2}\left(\frac{1}{1+e^{2\sigma}f}(100+3.24)+3.24+\frac{1}{1+f}(100+3.24)+3.24\right)$$

$$\$204.7 = \frac{1}{1+e^{2\sigma}f}(100+3.24)+3.24+\frac{1}{1+f}(100+3.24)+3.24$$

$$198.22 = 103.24\left(\frac{1}{1+e^{2\sigma}f}+\frac{1}{1+f}\right)$$

This can be solved by trial and error using, for example, Excel's Solver.
We find that $f = f_{1,down} = 3.75325\%$ and $f_{1,up} = f\,e^{2\sigma} = 4.58423\%$. See spreadsheet below. Here, Solver was used to set the value of the bond at cell J9 to $100 by changing the value in the cell K20.

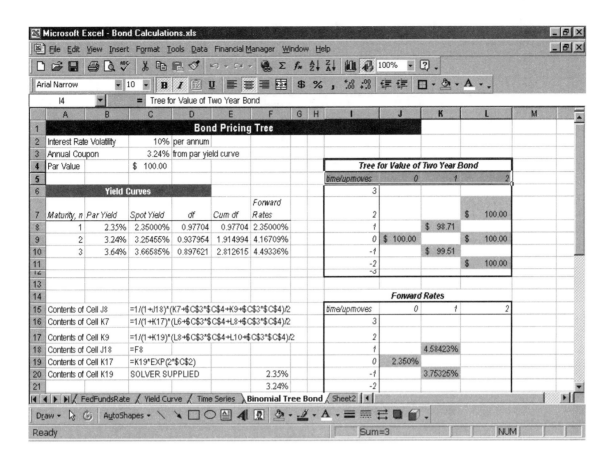

Now we price the three-year bond. The unknowns will be the values of the bond at $t=2$ and the forward rates there. Again we turn to the spreadsheet, using the year one forward rates that we just calculated.

Use the Solver to set the value of the bond at $t=0$ to zero by changing the contents of $_2f_{-2}$ (where it currently shows 3.582%; Remember to change the coupon to the three-year coupon in cell C3) results in:

Tree for Value of Three Year Bond				
time/upmoves	0	1	2	3
3				$ 100.00
2			$ 98.29	
1		$ 97.91		$ 100.00
0	$100.000		$ 99.22	
-1		$ 99.51		$ 100.00
-2			$ 99.99	
-3				$ 100.00

Forward Rates			
time/upmoves	0	1	2
3			
2			5.4405%
1		4.58423%	
0	2.350%		4.4543%
-1		3.75325%	
-2			3.6469%
-3			

That's it. We have the forward rates needed to price this bond or others.

To check, let's price a two-year, 6% coupon, option-free bond.
The tree is:

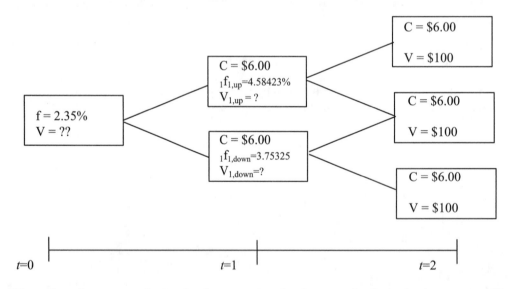

The only unknowns are the bond values at t=1 and, of course, the desired price at t=0. They are easily calculated:

$$V_{1,up} = \left(\frac{1}{1.0458423}\right)\frac{1}{2}(100+6+100+6)=\$101.35371. \text{ Similarly,}$$

$$V_{1,down} = \left(\frac{1}{1.0375325}\right)\frac{1}{2}(100+6+100+6)=\$102.16547. \text{ Now we can get the price at t=0:}$$

$$V_0 = \left(\frac{1}{1.0235}\right)\frac{1}{2}\left(101.35371+6+102.16547+6\right)=\$105.285.$$ Of course, we could have priced this bond with

a financial calculator. It should be just the PV of cash flows,

$$PV = \frac{\$6}{(1+r_1)} + \frac{\$106}{(1+r_2)^2} = \frac{\$6}{(1+0.0235)} + \frac{\$106}{(1+0.0325455)^2} = \$105.285.$$ Using forwards:

$$PV = \frac{\$6}{(1+r_1)} + \frac{\$106}{(1+r_1)(1+_1f_1)} = \frac{\$6}{(1+0.0235)} + \frac{\$106}{(1+0.0235)(1+0.0416709)} = \$105.285.$$ Finally, using the

prices of zeros we calculated:

$$PV = \$6Z_1 + \$106Z_2 = \$6(0.97704) + \$106(0.937954) = \$105.285.$$

With this prep work, we are now ready to value some options.

Example Take a three-year, 6% coupon bond callable at 102 after one year. The call decision rule is that the bond will be called if at any node the price exceeds $102. In this case, the bond will be called at $102. The call feature is an unattractive option to the bondholder, so the price of the bond with embedded call is worth less than an equivalent option-free bond. What is the price of the callable bond, and what is the value of the option? Resetting the tree with the 6% coupon, we get:

Tree for Value of Three Year Bond				
time/upmoves	0	1	2	3
3				$ 100.00
2			$ 100.53	
1		$ 102.31		$ 100.00
0	$106.638		$ 101.48	
-1		$ 103.97		$ 100.00
-2			$ 102.27	
-3				$ 100.00

Forward Rates				
time/upmoves	0	1	2	
3				
2			5.4405%	
1		4.58423%		
0	2.350%		4.4543%	
-1		3.75325%		
-2			3.6469%	
-3				

Note the price of the option free bond for later use: $106.638. Now, walk backward from t=3 in the value tree to see if the bond would be called. We see that it would be called at t=2 for the lower node. Replace this node with the call value, $102.

Tree for Value of Three Year Bond

time/upmoves	0	1	2	3
3				$ 100.00
2			$ 100.53	
1		$ 102.31		$ 100.00
0	$ 106.638		$ 101.48	
-1		$ 103.97		$ 100.00
-2			$ 102.27	
-3		102		$ 100.00

We now have to recalculate the values at t=1, but only the ones affected by the change. This is $V_{1,-1}$ which is now $0.5(101.48 + 6 + 102 + 6)/1.0375325 = \$103.84253$. Since this is higher than the call value of $102, replace it by $102 and recalculate $V_0 = 0.5(102 + 6 + 102 + 6)/1.0235 = \$105.52$. The spreadsheet formulas are easily modified to handle this. I put the call price in C5, then used formulas like =MIN(1/(1+K39)*(L28+$C$3*$C$4+L30+$C$3*$C$4)/2,C5) in K29, for example.

The investor holding this bond is essentially holding a portfolio that is long a three-year, 6% coupon bond and short a call option. So, $V_{callable} = V_{noncallable} - c$. The option value is thus equal to $V_{noncallable} - V_{callable}$ =$106.638 - \$105.52 = \$1.11773$. Note that Black-Scholes cannot be used to find the value of this option: The option here has value only if interest rates change, and Black-Scholes assumes a constant interest rate.

Example Consider a three-year, 6% coupon bond putable at $101 after one year. This works the same way except the decision rule is if the price drops below $101, the investor puts the bond back to the company. Here, all we do is change the MIN in the formulas above to MAX and change the strike price to 101.

Tree for Value of Three Year Bond

time/upmoves	0	1	2	3
3				$ 100.00
2			$ 101.00	
1		$ 102.54		$ 100.00
0	$ 106.747		$ 101.48	
-1		$ 103.97		$ 100.00
-2			$ 102.27	
-3		101		$ 100.00

The bond is now worth $106.747. This is higher than the price of the bond without the option, because the ability to put the bond back to the company has value to the investor. Then $V_{putable} = V_{nonputable} + p$ with p in this case worth $106.747-$106.638 = $0.109.

Example Take a three-year, 6% coupon bond callable at $102 and putable at $101 after one year. This works the same way except the decision rule is put the bond if the price drops below $101, and if the bond price goes above $102, the company will call it. Now that we have a tree, we can value just about any combination of these things. Recall that we started with:

Tree for Value of Three Year Bond

time/upmoves	0	1	2	3
3				$ 100.00
2			$ 100.53	
1		$ 102.31		$ 100.00
0	$ 106.638		$ 101.48	
-1		$ 103.97		$ 100.00
-2			$ 102.27	
-3				$ 100.00

The bond would be put at node (t=2,2 upmoves) so the $100.53 is replaced by $101. No change to the node t=2, 0 upmoves. The bond is called at the node t=2, -2 upmoves, so the $102.27 is replaced by $102. After this is done, we have

Tree for Value of Three Year Bond

time/upmoves	0	1	2	3
3				$ 100.00
2			$ 101.00	
1		$ 102.54		$ 100.00
0	$ 106.684		$ 101.48	
-1		$ 103.84		$ 100.00
-2			$ 102.00	
-3				$ 100.00

We now work with nodes at t=1. The bond is callable at these nodes, so replace their values with $102 to get:

Tree for Value of Three Year Bond

time/upmoves	0	1	2	3
3				$ 100.00
2			$ 101.00	
1		$ 102.00		$ 100.00
0	$ 105.520		$ 101.48	
-1		$ 102.00		$ 100.00
-2			$ 102.00	
-3				$ 100.00

Should this bond price be equal to the value of the bond with no options, less the call at $102, plus the put at $101? Let's see: $106.638-$1.11773+$0.109=$105.629. It's close but would be better with more steps/continuous compounding.

Interest rate caps

Now, suppose Tanya is a corporate treasurer who is paying LIBOR plus 250 bp on $100 million. She is concerned that rates will rise and wishes to control her costs. She can buy an **interest rate cap**, which is just a contract whereby she will pay LIBOR + spread up to some cap rate. Suppose the cap is 10%. What is the cap worth to her? Using the same three-year forward rate tree, we now add the spread 250 bp to each forward rate. We find:

Forward Rates

time/upmoves	0	1	2
3			
2			14.7236%
1		7.0842%	
0	4.8500%		10.0078%
-1		6.2533%	
-2			6.1469%
-3			

At the two-year point, it is possible that Tanya will be paying quite a high borrowing cost: 14.7236% of $100,000,000 is $14,723,600. For this cap, the contract holder pays only the cap rate 10% if the rates are higher than 10%, so replace the top and middle nodes at *t*=2 with the cap rate. Then, the forward rate tree is:

Forward Rates

time/upmoves	0	1	2
3			
2			10.0000%
1		7.0842%	
0	4.8500%		10.0000%
-1		6.2533%	
-2			6.1469%
-3			

This new tree could be used to value bonds. For example, the price of the three-year bond with this tree is $98.034 while the price of the uncapped bond is $96.03. The value of the cap is thus $2.004 per $100 face.

Interest rate floors

An **interest rate floor** provides a lower limit to the interest rate received. Floors work just like caps, except if the rate falls below some critical value, the floor rate is received. Actually, all receivers of LIBOR are receivers of floors where the floor is set at zero.

Other important concepts are **inverse floaters**, which pay a rate that varies inversely with some benchmark rate such as LIBOR, and Option Adjusted Spread (or OAS; spread over Treasuries that is designed to capture the higher yield that would have to be paid to an investor on callable bonds and other bonds with embedded options). Note that duration of the bond can easily be calculated using a tree: we just price the bond, then shock all interest rates by Δr, price again, shock by $-\Delta r$ and use the effective duration formula.

Interest rate swaps

Suppose Tanya is a net payer of floating rate LIBOR, as above, but now she has fixed rate liabilities. She is thus subject to basis rate risk, which is where the underlying does not match the hedging instrument. She may also have a mismatch between the tenor of her assets (floating rate LIBOR is usually reset every three or six months) and her liabilities (in this case, they are car loans with average maturities of three years). She also has credit and liquidity risk. The liquidity risk comes about because she has a large portfolio of thousands of small car loans, which can't be readily liquefied. In order to take care of the basis risk, remove the mismatch between asset and liability tenor and reliquify her portfolio, thus, she enters into an **interest rate swap**.

The swaps market is huge and growing by the day. One reason that people use swaps is for hedging, as in the example above. Another reason is **comparative advantage**: We will start with a very simple example of two U.S. companies. Suppose company X has obligations to pay floating rate LIBOR and company Y has obligations to make fixed coupon payments. Company X can borrow fixed at 7% or floating at LIBOR plus 100 bp, while company Y can borrow at a fixed rate of 6% or at floating rate of LIBOR plus 250 bp. Company X needs to borrow fixed and Y needs to borrow floating. Since X can borrow more cheaply in the floating rate market than Y can, X is said to have a comparative advantage in this market. Y, on the other hand, has a comparative advantage in the fixed rate market. A swap dealer can put these two together so they can swap interest rate payments. In an interest rate swap, parties agree to exchange payments on a stated notional amount for a stated period of time. So X will borrow at LIBOR + 100 bp and Y will borrow at 6%. X will make Y's fixed payments, and in return, Y will make X's LIBOR payments. The net effect will be that X gets Y's cheaper fixed rate cost, saving 1%, and Y will get the benefit of X's lower borrowing cost in the floating rate market, saving 150 bp. This type of swap is called **fixed-floating**. Company X is the "pay fixed," the "fixed payer," the "floating receiver," "long the swap," or has "bought the swap." Company Y, meanwhile, is the "receive fixed" party, the "fixed receiver," the "floating payer," "short the swap," or has "sold the swap." From X's viewpoint, the sway is a "pay-fixed, receive floating"; from Y's, it is "pay floating, receive fixed." The swap is a zero sum game. One party's gain is the other's loss. There are floating-floating swaps as well as fixed-fixed swaps.

A diagram of the swap is shown below.

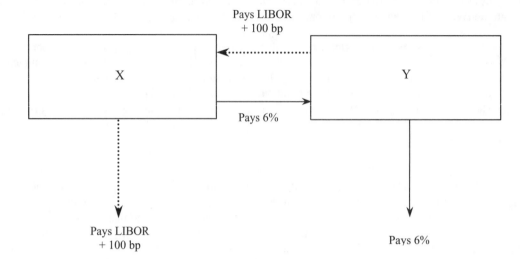

The net borrowing cost to X is –(LIBOR+100bp) + 6%, while the net borrowing cost to Y is -6%+(LIBOR + 100bp). X and Y both gain. Swaps can create value. Generally, however, a clearinghouse will act as middleman, taking a percentage of the net gain created by the swap. The clearinghouse verifies the creditworthiness of each party, finds potential matches and may even make markets themselves.

The swap is constructed to have a value of zero at initiation. (If not, one party would be disadvantaged and would never enter the transaction. Also, riskless arbitrage would be possible.) The notional (principal) is never exchanged. Only the payments are exchanged. In fact, in most cases the payments are netted. Since swaps are traded over the counter, if one party decides to default or otherwise terminate the swap early, the other party may suffer a cost. The process of early termination of a swap is called **unwinding the swap**. Although the swap has no net value at initiation, we will see that the value will change over the life of the swap.

Example   Company X and company Y swap interest rate payments on $1,000,000 notional for one year. X will pay floating rate LIBOR, to be reset every three months.   Y will pay semiannually at a spread to one-year Treasury, currently 2.25%. The LIBOR rate to be paid is the LIBOR rate prevailing three months prior.   What is the fixed rate paid by Y?   What is the net gain/loss of each party?   Current three-month LIBOR deposit rate is 2%.

In order to analyze a swap we need a way of forecasting future LIBOR rates. The cash flows from the floating rate payment are discounted to the present. The fixed rate k of the swap is calculated as that coupon rate that will make the present value of the fixed cash flows exactly equal to the PV of the floating rate. The fixed-rate payer essentially holds a portfolio of two bonds: short a coupon bond (coupon rate of k) and long a six-month bond holding LIBOR. Every six months the floating rate bond is rolled over. On the other hand, the floating-rate payer can be considered to hold a portfolio short a six-month floating rate bond and long a fixed rate bond. Generally, the floating rate payments are quoted at the reference rate ("LIBOR flat," for example), and any needed adjustments are made to the fixed rate side. In order to value the swap, then, we need to find a k that is some kind of an average of floating rates. Since there is a high correlation between Eurodollar Futures contracts and LIBOR, the forward rates implied by the EDF contracts can be used as a good approximation of the market's expectation of future rates.

Suppose the following data are known:

Maturity, Months	Notation	Eurodollar Spot Rate	Notation for Forward Rate	Forward Rate, 3 months forward Eurodollar
0			0x3	2.00%
3	r_3	2.00%	3x6	2.20%
6	r_6	2.10%	6x9	2.40%
9	r_9	2.20%	9x12	2.60%
12	r_{12}	2.30%	12x15	2.55%
15	r_{15}	2.35%	15x18	2.65%
18	r_{18}	2.40%	18x21	2.75%
21	r_{21}	2.45%	21x24	2.85%
24	r_{24}	2.50%	24x27	2.95%

The forward rates implied by the Eurodollar spot rates can be calculated in the usual way. Note that these rates are calculated using a simple day count on a 30/360 basis. For the three-month rate prevailing in three months, "3x6",we relate the current three month to the six month through the forward:

$$\left(1+\frac{90}{360}r_3\right)\left(1+\frac{90}{360}\,{}_3f_6\right)=\left(1+\frac{90}{360}r_6\right)^2 \text{ so}$$

$$_3f_6=\frac{360}{90}\left(\frac{\left(1+\frac{90}{360}r_6\right)^2}{\left(1+\frac{90}{360}r_3\right)}-1\right)=\frac{360}{90}\left(\frac{\left(1+\frac{90}{360}0.021\right)^2}{\left(1+\frac{90}{360}.02\right)}-1\right)=2.20\%$$

To value the swap, we first find the PV of the floating rate payments. Then we calculate the PV of the fixed rate payments and solve for the fixed rate.

Floating Rate Payments

Period i	(1) Annualized LIBOR	(2) Periodic LIBOR = $r_i/4$	(3) Forward Discount Factor Product $1/(1+r_i/4)^{i/3}$	(4) Expected Payment = (2)*Notional	(5) PV Expected Payment = (3)*(4)
3	2.00%	0.50%	0.9950	$ 5,000.00	$ 4,975.12
6	2.45%	0.61%	0.988967	$ 6,125.06	$ 6,057.49
9	2.65%	0.66%	0.982458	$ 6,625.19	$ 6,508.97
12	2.85%	0.71%	0.975508	$ 7,125.37	$ 6,950.86
Total					$ 24,492.44

For the fixed rate payments, we don't know the rate k yet, but we have the discount factors. For semiannual payments, the payment at 6 months is discounted by 0.98958211 as shown above, and for the payment at 12 months, the discount factor is 0.97732686. Then,

Fixed Rate Payments			
Period	Days	Discount	Payment
1	180.00	0.989582	$ 494,791.06
2	180.00	0.977327	$ 488,663.43
Total			$ 983,454.49

If the one-year treasury is trading at 2.250%, the swap cost is 55 bp over Treasury.

Since PV floating must equal PV fixed, and PV fixed $= kZ_6 Notional + kZ_{12} Notional = kNotional \sum_{i=1}^{n} Z_i$

Then $k = \dfrac{PV_{float}}{Notional \sum_{i=1}^{n} Z_i} = \$22,673.14/\$983,454.49 = 2.305\%$

The net gain/loss to each party at the initiation of the swap is zero. If we plot the expected LIBOR forward rates against the fixed rate, we see that the fixed rate is somewhat close to an average of expected LIBOR rates. In fact, the average of the four forward rates is 2.30%.

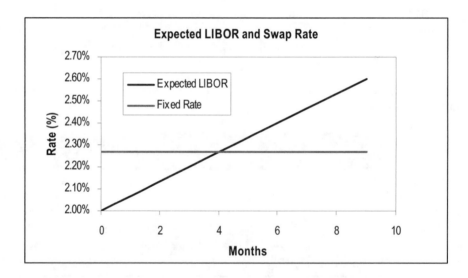

The expected payments are netted as follows. Suppose that LIBOR does not change from that expected on the first day -- that is, Eurodollar forwards are perfect predictors of forward rates.

However, after the swap is initiated, the future three-month LIBOR rates will likely deviate from those predicted by the Eurodollar forwards. If the floating rates are lower than expected, the fixed-rate payer will lose because he's paying more than he should. If interest rates rise, the fixed rate payer benefits.

Suppose that the LIBOR spot rates change by 25 bp immediately after the swap is initiated and stay that way through the life of the swap. Then we have:

Maturity, Months	Notation	Eurodollar Spot Rate	Notation for Forward Rate	Forward Rate, 3 months forward Eurodollar
0			0x3	2.00%
3	r_3	2.00%	3x6	2.70%
6	r_6	2.35%	6x9	2.65%
9	r_9	2.45%	9x12	2.85%
12	r_{12}	2.55%	12x15	2.80%

The PV of the floating rate payments is $24,492 and the fixed rate would be 2.49% to remain in equilibrium. But the contract requires that the fixed rate payer pay only 2.305%. So the PV of the fixed rate payment is $982,237*$k$ = $22,640$, for a net gain to the fixed payer of $1,852.

When interest rates rise, the fixed-rate payer benefits. When interest rates fall, the floating-rate payer benefits. Recall that as the floating rate payer is essentially long a bond, when rates rise, the value of the bond falls. The fixed-rate payer can also be thought of as holding a portfolio of Eurodollar futures contracts and short the bond, while the floating-rate payer would hold the other side of this position. So, if you are asked how to synthetically synthesize the payoffs of a swap, you would use these instruments in the construction. (This is an actual question on the CFA exam.)

Swaptions

Options on interest rate swaps are called **interest rate swaptions**. Swaptions are designed to have the same price behavior as a call on a bond -- if interest rates rise, the value of the swaption falls, and if interest rates fall, the value of the swaption rises. A buyer of a swaption has the right, but not the obligation, to enter into an interest rate swap. By convention, exercise of the swaption entitles the buyer to receive fixed and pay floating. Thus, the buyer has effectively purchased a call option on a bond, with the exercise price being the fixed swap rate. The seller of the swap has the other side of the transaction -- when the swaption is executed, the seller will pay fixed and receive floating. The buyer pays the premium of the swaption up-front, which is generally 0.20 to 0.45% of the notional amount. Swaptions can be either European or American.

For example, a finance company buys an American-style one-year swaption on an underlying 5-year interest rate swap with swap rate of 4%, floating rate LIBOR and notional amount of $1,000,000. The company then has the right to enter into an interest rate swap receiving 4% and paying LIBOR at any time over the next year. Assume that the premium paid is 0.3% of the notional, or $3,000. If swap rates drop over the course of the year, say to 3%, the buyer will find it advantageous to exercise the swap. The buyer will receive a higher than market rate of 4% in exchange for LIBOR. If this fixed rate is not needed for his balance sheet, the buyer can enter into another swap, as the payer of fixed and receiver of LIBOR:

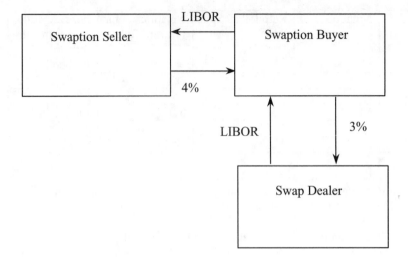

The net payment to the swaption buyer will be (-LIBOR+4%+LIBOR-3%) = 1% of notional or $10,000 per year. Over five years, this payment (assuming flat yield curve at 3%) has a net present value of $45,797. Less the original premium of $3,000 this yields a profit of $42,797.

If interest rates rise, the buyer of the swap will not find it advantageous to exercise the swap and it will expire worthless. The seller pockets the premium, which will help defray added costs on higher fixed rates that, perhaps, it is now paying out on other liabilities due to the rise in interest rates.

Mortgage-Backed Securities

When buyers borrow money to finance the purchase of their new home (take out a mortgage), they must make monthly interest and principal payments to the lending agency, which can be an entity such as FNMA, a bank or a credit union. These mortgage loans are considered to be amortizing: they contain both principal and interest rate payments. The interest payments are highest in the early years but, as principal is paid down, in later years the proportion of the payment going to interest diminishes. The interest rate can be fixed or floating, and generally, the borrower is free to make a higher than required payment. Suppose someone has a 30-year, $250,000 mortgage at a rate of 7.5%. The total mortgage payment is calculated as $1,748.04. Since the periodic interest rate is 7.5%/12 = 0.625%, the interest payment for the first month will be $1,562. The remaining $185.54 will be applied to reduce the principal to $249,814.5. The next interest payment will then be 0.00625* $249,814.5 =$1,561 and the remainder of the payment, $186.69, is applied to reduce the principal owed. And so on. An abbreviated table is shown following.

Principal	$ 250,000.00
Term of Loan	30 years
Coupon	7.50%
Periodic Payment	$1,748.04

Amortization Schedule

Month	Initial Principal	Payment	Interest Payment	Principal RePayment	Ending Principal
1	$ 250,000.00	$1,748.04	$1,562.50	$185.54	$ 249,814.46
2	$ 249,814.46	$1,748.04	$1,561.34	$186.70	$ 249,627.77
3	$ 249,627.77	$1,748.04	$1,560.17	$187.86	$ 249,439.91
4	$ 249,439.91	$1,748.04	$1,559.00	$189.04	$ 249,250.87
5	$ 249,250.87	$1,748.04	$1,557.82	$190.22	$ 249,060.65
6	$ 249,060.65	$1,748.04	$1,556.63	$191.41	$ 248,869.24
7	$ 248,869.24	$1,748.04	$1,555.43	$192.60	$ 248,676.64
8	$ 248,676.64	$1,748.04	$1,554.23	$193.81	$ 248,482.83
9	$ 248,482.83	$1,748.04	$1,553.02	$195.02	$ 248,287.81

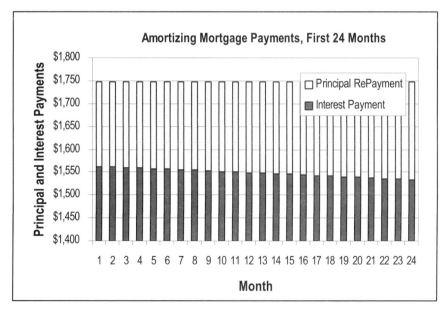

A typical lender might be Chase Manhattan Mortgage. Because mortgage loans are not uniform (lenders vary in their credit ratings, down payment amounts, term of loan, when originated, interest rate paid, etc.), Chase's pool of loans will consist of loans of varying maturities and coupons, so a weighted average coupon (WAC) and weighted average maturity (WAM) are used to describe the mortgage portfolio. The weights used are just the loan amounts.

For example, if the following three loans are in the portfolio:

Loan	Amount	Maturity, yrs	Coupon, %	Proportion of Portfolio
1	$250,000	30	7.5	39.62%
2	$231,000	25	8.25	36.61%
3	$150,000	10	6	23.77%
Total	$631,000			100%

The weighted average coupon is 0.3962(7.5%) + 0.3661(8.25%) + 0.2377(6%) = 7.42% and the weighted average maturity is 0.3962(30) + 0.3661(25) + 0.2377(10) =23.42 years.

The nature of these long-term assets renders Chase's balance sheet illiquid. Chase is also taking interest rate risk in that the maturity and rates of the instruments used to fund these loans most likely do not match the WAC and WAM of the asset portfolio. Should they wish to transfer this risk and reliquify their portfolio, they can package these loans into groups, or tranches, with specified payout and risk characteristics. These securities, which can be purchased by private investors, are backed by underlying real mortgages, so they are called **mortgage passthrough securities** or **mortgage-backed securities (MBS)**. Chase collects the payments from the homeowners at the first of the month, sits on them for about two weeks, and then passes on these payments -- less a servicing fee -- to the investors.

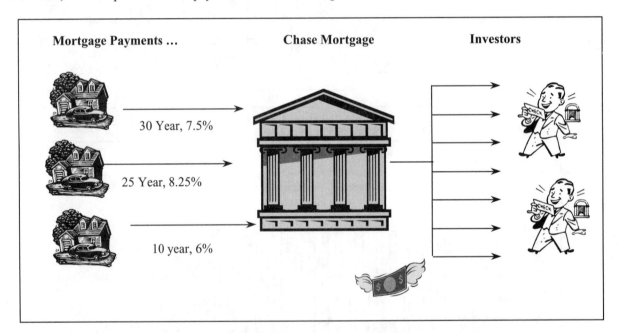

Incentives to prepay mortgages

In terms of the homeowner with the 30-year, 7.5% loan, if just 1% extra of principal is prepaid each year, there is a substantial impact on interest rate costs. As a result, the following strategy is often recommended: Instead of making one monthly payment, split it into two and pay every two weeks. You will have an extra payment, which will be applied to principal. Since the interest is calculated on the basis of principal, you will save substantial charges. The total loan to be paid off including interest is $629,293, of which only $250,000 is principal, so that leaves $379,293 in total interest paid. If one additional two-week payment is made at the end of each year, the loan will be paid off early -- after just about 28 years -- and you'll save $28,048 in total interest paid ($379,293 less $351,875). If somehow you could pay an additional amount at the beginning of each year as well (a double payment on Jan 1), the loan would be paid off in 27.5 years and almost $55,000 in interest would be saved. If just $100 extra is added to each payment per month, the loan would be paid off almost two years early and $38,841 in interest would be saved.

Homeowners also have incentives to refinance when interest rates drop low enough to overcome the refinancing costs. Homeowners paying 7.5% might refinance if interest rates drop to 6.25%, however, there is a chance that they might be unable to do so --because, for example, they have not had the mortgage long enough to build up required equity, they are anticipating even lower rates, they have no time to shop around, or they plan to sell their homes soon. Thus, lower interest rates alone, while extremely important, are not the sole factor influencing prepayments. If the economy is healthy and rates are low, new homeowners may enter the market, spurring sales of homes and, therefore, prepayment of the entire remaining principal. Home sales might also occur for different reasons, including layoffs, job relocations, job promotions, stock market gains, remarriage, divorce, death, retirement to a condo in Mexico, etc. Also, a mortgage loan might be paid off because the home was destroyed due to hurricane or fire. The holder of the passthrough security is holding a bond with an embedded call option where the call is on the entire principal due.

So mortgage passthrough securities are subject to a great deal of risk, although sellers may claim that they are risk free. It is true that they may only bear a small amount of credit risk, since the underlying is real property that can be foreclosed on. Even so, the investor is exposed to a great deal of interest rate and prepayment risk.

Prepayment assumptions

It is common practice to assume a **constant prepayment rate**, or **CPR**. This is an annualized rate. If CPR is 6% and the principal at the beginning of the year is $100,000, then (1-CPR) times the principal will remain at the beginning of the next year. Here it would be $940,000. Since mortgage payments occur monthly, we use the **single month mortality rate**, or **SMM**, to calculate the new principal at the beginning of each month. SMM and CPR are related through the formula

$Beg\ Principal(1\text{-}SMM)^{12} = Beg\ Principal(1\text{-}CPR)$

or, $SMM = 1 - (1 - CPR)^{\frac{1}{12}}$

How do we estimate the CPR? Large corporations such as Ford Motor Credit conduct studies on the historical performance on their own loans to estimate this, but it is common to use the Public Securities Association (PSA) prepayment assumption. This is a benchmark that can be modified based on specific industry data. This model assumes that mortgages prepay at a rate of 6%(t/30) for the first 30 months, and for 6% thereafter. That is,

$$CPR = \begin{bmatrix} 6\%\dfrac{t}{30}, t < 30months \\ 6\%, t \geq 30months \end{bmatrix}$$

This model implies that mortgage prepayments will ramp up from 0 to 6% in a linear fashion over the first 30 months and, thereafter, remain constant at 6%. A mortgage that prepays at this rate is said to be at 100 PSA. If the mortgage prepays faster, it will be greater than 100 PSA, and if it prepays at a slower rate, it will be lower than 100 PSA.

So, we have seen that there is a substantial amount of prepayment risk to investors in mortgage-backed securities. Specialized instruments such as Collateralized Mortgage Obligations (CMOs) have been designed to redistribute the prepayment risk in ways that might better match the desired asset/liability profile of the investor.

Collateralized mortgage obligations

In a **collateralized mortgage obligation**, or **CMO**, the mortgage payments are not simply passed through to the investor as they are in a mortgage-backed security. A CMO is a structured security consisting of prioritized tranches. Investors in CMOs buy bonds from the tranche providing the desired risk profile. For example, suppose that the CMO has been split into six tranches: *A, B, C, D, Z* and the **residual tranche** (see explanation below). When mortgage payments come in, the interest and principal are split.

All tranches except for the residual tranche receive interest payments on a pro-rata basis. The interest for the *Z* tranche is accrued (so it behaves like a zero coupon bond, hence the name), while the interest payments to the other tranches are made in cash. The residual tranche receives nothing.

Tranche *A* receives all principal payments, including prepayments, until it is paid down and retired. Once this happens, Tranche *B* starts to receive all principal payments until it, too, is paid down. At this point, Tranche *C* starts to receive payments. Once all of these tranches have been retired, Tranche *Z* starts to receive payments, which include the accrued interest payments. Only after all prior tranches have been retired does the residual tranche start receiving payments. It will receive any principal and interest payments that remain after all prior tranches have been retired. To make this clearer, think of a buffet where you are only allowed a single trip. People pay up front to enter the buffet, get their trays and silverware and get in line to load their plates. The first person loads up, and no one else can get anything until this first person has completed piling food on his plate. Then the second person loads up, and no one else can get anything until he is finished loading. And so on. The residual tranche is like the guy at the end of the line, who will be able to help himself to any leftovers. If there are enough people in front of him, he might not get anything, not even a tray. Think of the upfront payment as the purchase of the bond. People might pay more to go first. And think of the distribution of trays and silverware as interest payments, since everyone gets them (though, the *Z* tranche has to wait for more trays to come from the kitchen and only gets the promise of one until everyone else has left the buffet.)

Risks of CMOs

CMOs don't eliminate prepayment risk, but rather they redistribute it. In the early years, tranche A bears the most prepayment risk. Once it is paid down, Tranche B becomes the bearer of prepayment risk. Remembering that the value of any bond is just the present value of its expected future cash flows makes it clear that the uncertainty of the cash flows of the lower priority tranches is very high. Note that the residual tranche actually benefits if interest rates increase, as prepayments should decrease, and any cash accruals will be invested at higher rates. There is a greater chance that more funds will be left over to accrue to the residual tranche, so its price will increase with an increase in interest rates. Thus, the residual tranche has the unusual property of negative convexity.

Additional CMO structures

Though we only discuss two here, there are many other possible structures, including sequential pay tranches, floater tranches, inverse floaters, and planned amortization class bonds (PACs). It is also possible to have stripped mortgage-backed securities in terms of interest only (IO) and principal only (PO) tranches (For a detailed history of these securities, read *Liar's Poker*.)

Interest only strips: These securities pay off all interest received on the mortgages. Since the interest payment is very high at the early years and declines toward maturity as more principal is paid off, the cash flows look like the following:

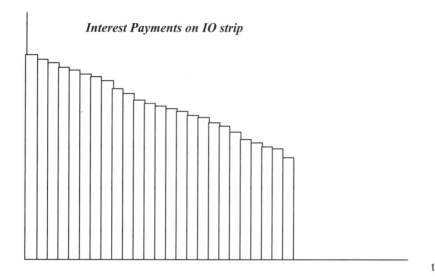

The value of the IO strip is then $V = \sum_{i=1}^{n} \dfrac{INT_i}{(1+r)^i}$

Principal only strips: These securities pay off all principal received on the mortgages. Since the principal payment is very low at the early years and increases toward maturity, the cash flows look like the following:

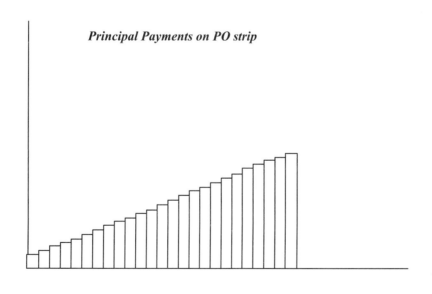

The value of the PO strip is $V = \sum_{i=1}^{n} \frac{P_i}{(1+r)^i}$ where P_i is the principal payment, including prepayments, at month i.

The sum of the value of the IO and PO strips must equal the value of the original (unstripped) bond. If the unstripped bond is worth $100, the IO strip may be worth $70 of that and the PO strip the remaining $30.

Risks of IO and PO strips: As interest rates fall, bonds increase in value since the expected future cash flows are being discounted at a lower rate. Since both IO strips and PO strips are bonds, they will benefit in the same way as straight bonds when rates fall. Beyond this, though, their resemblance ends. If interest rates drop low enough, homeowners have incentives to refinance and the principal may be returned earlier than originally anticipated. This shortens the average life of the bond and increases the value. Thus, PO strips benefit in two ways from a declining interest rate environment. The IO strip will be punished because, as interest rates fall, the average life extends and the payments are smaller and must also be reinvested at lower rates. If interest rates rise, both bonds decline in value as would any other bond. PO strips may experience an extension of expected average life since the assumed prepayment rate may slow, so they take a double hit in this case. Because the IO strip will be able to reinvest income at a higher than anticipated interest rate, the net effect could be neutral.

Valuation of mortgage-backed securities

In theory, valuing these securities should be straightforward, but in practice, it's one of the most difficult valuation problems in fixed income. The reason for this is the path-dependency of the cash flows. Although mortgage-backed securities work somewhat like bonds, unlike bonds they have no par value at the end of their lives (the last payment pays down remaining principal, which has been amortized over the life of the mortgage), and they have an implicit call option. They are similar, though, to callable bonds in which the strike price (which is the pay-off amount of the loan) changes through time in a deterministic fashion. In order to value a mortgage, we need an interest rate tree, a prepayment function and decision rules for cash flows. These are best-solved using Monte-Carlo simulation, although non-recombining trees are also used to capture the path dependency.

The solution technique that will be illustrated below uses the concept of non-recombining trees. The steps are:

Step 1: Calculate the fixed mortgage payment.
Step 2: Develop the interest rate paths.
Step 3: Develop a prepayment tree based on assumed prepayment model.
Step 4: Discount the cash flows back to the present.
Step 5: Value the mortgage value as the probability-weighted average of all present values computed using the preceding paths.

Example For simplicity, we will value a three-year mortgage making annual payments. (Of course, in reality, mortgages are monthly payments and they may span a time period of 30 years, so the problem would require a huge number of calculations.) We will work with $100 of principal.

Step 1: Calculate the periodic fixed payment based on the homeowner's fixed interest rate of 4.0%. To do this, realize that if the fixed payment is *P*, the present value of all future payments discounted by the fixed rate must be the present value of the loan, or $100 = \dfrac{Pmt}{1+r} + \dfrac{Pmt}{(1+r)^2} + \dfrac{Pmt}{(1+r)^3}$, $Pmt = \dfrac{100}{\dfrac{1}{1+r} + \dfrac{1}{(1+r)^2} + \dfrac{1}{(1+r)^3}} = \$36.03$. Another

way to do this is to use Excel as in $= PMT(4\%, 3, \$100)$. To see all details we can make an amortization schedule using the scheduled principal payment using PPMT and interest payment using CUMIPMT as:

Amortization Schedule for Mortgage					
Fixed Rate	4.0%				
Fixed Payment		($36.03)		PMT(B12,A18,B16)	
Year	Starting Principal	Interest Payment	Principal Repayment	Total Payment	Remaining Principal
1	100	-4.000	($32.03)	($36.03)	$67.9651
2	$67.97	-2.719	($33.32)	($36.03)	$34.6489
3	$34.65	-1.386	($34.65)	($36.03)	$0.0000

Step 2: Now that we have the fixed payment, we now construct the interest rate tree using any appropriate model. For this case, since we have a three-year mortgage, we can use the interest rate tree we have already derived for three-year rates:

Interest Rate Tree		
		5.44%
	4.58%	
2.35%		4.45%
	3.75%	
		3.65%
1 Year	2 Year	3 Year

There are four possible paths to consider, each with assumed equal probability of 1/4:

Path 1 Interest rates move uu, or 2.35% to 4.58% to 5.44%.
Path 2 Interest rates move ud, or 2.35% to 4.58% to 4.55%.
Path 3 Interest rates move du, or 2.35% to 3.75% to 4.55%.
Path 4 Interest rates move dd, or 2.35% to 3.75% to 3.65%.

Step 3: The prepayment model assumes that prepayment rate at any time t depends on the relationship between the fixed mortgage rate being paid and the prevailing rate r_t, but also on the relationship between the current rate r_t and the preceding rate r_{t-1}. This would be statistically developed using historical data or developed from some forecasting model that takes into account macroeconomic variables such as projected interest rates, inflation and housing demand. Suppose, for example, that you have come up with the prepayment at time t as

$P(r_t, r_{t-1}, t) = 10\ (max(y - r_t, 0) + max(r_{t-1} - r_t, 0))$

where y is the mortgage rate. Then in this case, $P(r_t, r_{t-1}, t) = 10\ (max(0.04 - r_t, 0) + max(r_{t-1} - r_t, 0))$.

Other models are possible -- this is just an example -- but any model should have the dual dependency feature like this one does.

Note that the nodes are labeled as follows where u is an upmove and d a downmove. Note that this tree is non-recombining since ud ? du.

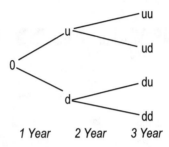

1 Year   2 Year   3 Year

Prepayment Calculations:

Using our assumed function, the rates are calculated as follows:

At u $P_u = 10(max(0.04 - r_u, 0) + max(r_0 - r_u, 0)) = 10(max(0.04 - 0.0458, 0) + max(0.0235 - 0.0458, 0)) = 0$. This means that if rates rise from 2.35% to 4.58% and to 4.58% relative to the fixed rate of 4%, there will be no incentive to refinance -- which makes sense. However, moving from (1,-1) to (2,-2) there may be some slight incentive to refinance, as $P(3.65\%, 3.75\%, 2) = 10(max(0.04 - 0.0365, 0) + max(0.0375 - 0.0365, 0)) = 0.045$ so 4.5% of people would refinance.

At d $P_d = 10(max(0.04 - r_d, 0) + max(r_0 - r_d, 0)) = 10(max(0.04 - 0.0375, 0) + max(0.0235 - 0.0375, 0)) = 0.025$. The refinancing incentive is driven solely by the drop in fixed rate from 4% to 3.75%.

At uu $P_{uu} = 10(max(0.04 - r_{uu}, 0) + max(r_u - r_{uu}, 0)) = 10(max(0.04 - 0.0544, 0) + max(0.0458 - 0.0544, 0)) = 0$.
Again, it makes sense that there is no incentive to refinance in such a rising-rate environment.

At ud $P_{ud} = 10(max(0.04 - r_{ud}, 0) + max(r_u - r_{ud}, 0)) = 10(max(0.04 - 0.0445, 0) + max(0.0458 - 0.0445, 0)) = 0.013$.

At du $P_{du} = 10(max(0.04 - r_{du}, 0) + max(r_d - r_{du}, 0)) = 10(max(0.04 - 0.0445, 0) + max(0.0375 - 0.0445, 0)) = 0$.

At dd $P_{dd} = 10(max(0.04 - r_{dd}, 0) + max(r_d - r_{dd}, 0)) = 10(max(0.04 - 0.0365, 0) + max(0.0375 - 0.0365, 0)) = 0.0045$.

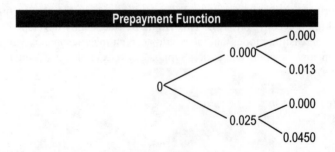

Prepayment Function

Step 4: We must calculate the cash flows at each node and then discount back to the present. The cash flows at each point consist of two flows: the normal, expected payment from people who do not refinance, and the payment from the people who do refinance. This adds to 100% of the people, so the cash flow at any node is equal to the mortgage payment, P, times the percentage of people who do not refinance, 1-p, plus the remaining principal balance, times proportion refinancing, times interest due, $(1 + y)$:
$CF = Pmt(1$-$p) + p\ Prin(1+y)$. Recall the table of principal balances by year:

Year	Starting Principal
1	100
2	$67.97
3	$34.65

At node u, no one is refinancing so we expect a cash flow of $36.035. At *node uu,* again no one refinances, so we get the normal payment $36.035.

At *node d*, something new happens. A total of 0.025% of people will refinance, so we have cash flows from those who do not refinance equal to $36.035(1-0.025), plus cash flows from the ones who do pay off the loan of 0.025*$100*1.04 = $37.734.

At *node uu*, no one is refinancing so we have the normal cash flow of $36.035.

At *node ud*, 0.013% of people will refinance, so the cash flow is $36.035(1-0.013)+$67.97*0.013*1.04 = $36.485.

At *node du*, 0.025% of people have already refinanced when rates dropped to *d*, so they are out of the pool. But no new people are refinancing – this is the meaning of the two terms (1-0.025) and (1-0) following.

Then the cash flows are: $36.035*(1-.025)(1-0) + 0 = $35.134.

At *node dd*, again we have to remove the 0.025 percent of people who refinanced after the first year, and we have an additional 0.045% of people refinancing and thus paying off the remaining principal of $67.97 early. Then CF_{dd} = $36.035(1-0.025)(1-0.045) + 0.045*$67.97*1.04(1-0.025) = $36.654.

Finally, at the end of the three-year period, we have to adjust for the amount of people remaining in the pool.

At *node uu*: no one has paid off, so we have CF_u = $36.035.
At *node ud*: CF_{ud} = $36.035*(1-0)(1-0.013) = $35.566.
At *node du*: CF_{du} = $36.035*(1-0.025)(1-0) = $35.134
At *node dd*: CF_{dd} = $36.035*(1-0.025)(1-0.045) = $33.553.

Cash Flows of the Mortgage Pool

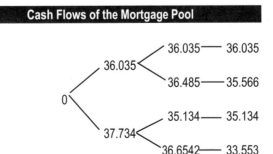

Finally, we are ready to discount back to present value along the appropriate interest rate path. We have four paths:

$$Node\ uu:\ PV_{uu} = \frac{36.035}{1.0235} + \frac{36.035}{(1.0235)(1.0458)} + \frac{36.035}{(1.0235)(1.0458)(1.0544)} = \$100.802$$

$$Node\ ud:\ PV_{ud} = \frac{36.035}{1.0235} + \frac{36.485}{(1.0235)(1.0458)} + \frac{35.566}{(1.0235)(1.0458)(1.0445)} = \$101.1057$$

$$Node\ du:\ PV_{du} = \frac{37.734}{1.0235} + \frac{35.134}{(1.0235)(1.0375)} + \frac{35.134}{(1.0235)(1.0375)(1.0445)} = \$101.6311$$

$$Node\ dd:\ PV_{dd} = \frac{37.734}{1.0235} + \frac{36.654}{(1.0235)(1.0375)} + \frac{33.553}{(1.0235)(1.0375)(1.0365)} = \$101.870$$

Step 5: The average value of the mortgage pool is then the sum of probability-weighted present values over all paths. Here we only have four paths and using $p_i = 0.25$ we have:
Value $=0.25(100.802 + 101.1057 + 101.6311 + 101.87) = \$101.35$ per $100.

Note: As an alternative valuation technique, we can also use the observed prices to calculate the implied prepayment function. This is done the same way we calculated the implied default rates on corporate bonds using observed prices over different ratings.

Sample Questions and Answers

Questions

1.   What is the bond equivalent yield of the following treasury bond:

Maturity	Days to Mat	Bid	Asked	Ask Yield
Oct 09 02	89	1.38	1.35	1.40

2.   Which bond would you choose for the portfolio of a high-net-worth client: a municipal bond yielding 7% or a corporate bond yielding 8.5%? Your client is in a 35% tax bracket. Which would you choose for the pension fund under management?

3.   An 8.5% coupon bond is quoted at 101.3 in the paper. The bond makes semi-annual payments and there are 180 days between coupon payments. If 75 days have elapsed since the last coupon payment, how much will you pay for the bond?

4.   You have two 10-year bonds available to sell to a client: one yields 7% and the other 9%. He says that obviously the bond yielding 9% is a better deal for him. Do you agree or disagree and why?

5.   What is the implied probability of default of a BBB+ rated corporate bond yielding 5%. A Treasury bond of the same maturity is yielding 3%, and the assumed recovery rate is 10 cents on the dollar.

6.   What is the price of a 7% coupon bond paying semi-annually if the yield curve is flat at 7%?

7.   How and why do you bootstrap a yield curve?

8.   What is the price of a 2-year, 6% bond if a 6-month, 2.5% bond is selling at 99; a one year, 3% bond is priced at 99.5; a one and one half year bond with a 4% coupon is priced at 101; and a 2-year bond with a 4.5% coupon is priced at 98? (All bonds make semi-annual coupon payments.)

9.   What is the spot yield curve implied by the above prices?

10.   If the yield curve is upward sloping, are the forward rates above or below the par yield rates?

11.   Are CMOs risk free?

12.   How will rising interest rates affect IO and PO prices?

13.   What are the risks inherent in an interest rate swap? How are payments made?

14.   I just initiated an interest rate swap where I will pay 7.5%/year on $10,000,000 notional with payments t be made semiannually on a 30/360 day count basis. I will receive LIBOR on the same notional amount with LIBOR used at the previous reset date. What is the value of the swap to me?

15.   Bruce, a corporate treasurer, is paying LIBOR. He's concerned that interest rates will increase. He would like to enter an interest rate swap but board regulations prohibit him from using swaps or selling anything short. What instruments could be used in order for him to replicate a swap?

16.   The following data are given for Eurodollar futures contracts on June 15, 2002:

Date	EDF
Sep 02	97.5
Dec 02	97.18

The Sep 02 contract expires 75 days from now. If current 75-day LIBOR is 2.15%, what would be the annualized no-arbitrage value for 255-day LIBOR? If the current 255-day rate is 2.4%, is an arbitrage possible? And if so, identify the trades you would make.

Answers

1. Treasury bills are priced according to the formula:

Price = (1 - (Ask / 100 * Days to Mat / 360)) * (Face Value) so the asked price of the Oct 09,02 bond above would then be (1 - (1.35 / 100 * 89 / 360)) * ($10,000)=$9,966.62.

$$r_{BEY} = \left(\frac{10,000 - P}{10,000} \right) \frac{365}{n} = \left(\frac{10,000 - 9,966.62}{10,000} \right) \frac{365}{89} = 1.369\%.$$

2.

$$Taxable\ Equivalent\ Yield = \frac{Municipal\ Yield}{100\% - Tax\ Bracket}.$$ Recall that for a taxable bond, the net yield is the yield

after-tax, or *Net Yield = Taxable Yield*$(100\% - Tax\ Bracket)$

For an investor in the 35% tax bracket, a municipal bond yielding 7% is equivalent to a non-tax-exempt bond yielding 10.76%. Since the net yield of the muni is superior to the corporate bond, you should choose the muni for the high-net-worth client. Pension funds are not subject to taxation so would not benefit by investing in the lower yielding muni.

3. The owner of the bond is the one who is entitled to the interest, so if you purchase the bond, you will receive the full coupon payment of $0.085/2*$1,000 = $42.5 in 105 days. But, for the first 75 days of the coupon period, the bond was owned by the seller. You will pay the invoice price, which is equal to the price quoted in the paper (the clean price) and the payment of accrued interest to that point

Invoice Price = Clean Price + Accrued Interest

The clean price is calculated as of 101 + 3/32 = 101.09375% of par, or $1,010.937, and the accrued interest is equal to 75/180*42.5 = $17.70833 so you will pay $1,028.645.

4.   Disagree. The price of a bond that makes periodic coupon payments and matures after n periods

is: $$P = \sum_{i=1}^{n} \frac{C}{(1+y)^i} + \frac{Par}{(1+y)^n}$$

Yield is nothing more than the mathematical value of y that solves the equation for P. In actuality, since interest rates change over time, the first coupon should be discounted by $(1+r_1)$ where r_1 is the rate over the time to the first coupon payment, the second coupon by the product $(1+r_1)(1+r_2)$ with r_2 being the rate prevailing over the period between the first and second coupon payment, and so on. Yield is that single, convenient measure that solves the above equation, so for example, for a four period bond,

$$P = \frac{C}{(1+r_1)} + \frac{C}{(1+r_1)(1+r_2)} + \frac{C}{(1+r_1)(1+r_2)(1+r_3)} + \frac{C}{(1+r_1)(1+r_2)(1+r_3)(1+r_4)} + \frac{Par}{(1+r_1)(1+r_2)(1+r_3)(1+r_4)} =$$

$$\frac{C}{(1+y)} + \frac{C}{(1+y)^2} + \frac{C}{(1+y)^3} + \frac{C}{(1+y)^4} + \frac{Par}{(1+y)^4}$$

This should give a clearer picture of what yield means. Now, bonds of the same maturity can have different yields. If $C = y$ the bond will sell at "par", or a price of 100 (which means, 100% of face, or $1,000 per $1,000 of face.) This is evident by plugging y in for C in the preceding price equations. If the bond sells for above par, it means that the coupon C exceeds the yield whereas if the bond sells for below par, the calculated yield will be higher than the coupon. Suppose that the coupon is $80 and the bond makes annual payments. The price of the bond yielding 7% will be $1,070.24 and the price of the 9% bond will be $935.82. A bond yielding 8% will be at par. The investor should make the decision on the basis of whether he thinks 10-year rates will rise or fall. Since the duration of the 7% bond is –68.660 and the convexity is 3.362, the total price change will be 65 for each percent change in yield. If 10 year rates fall to 7% from 8%, the price change of the bond will be $65 per $1,000 face. But the 9% yield bond price will fall by $64 in this case.

A higher yield may also mean that the 9% bond has higher risk than the 7% bond – perhaps it is a junk, or non-investment grade. It will be priced below par.

5.   In a simple one-period analysis, there are two states of nature: default and non-default. Let p be the probability of default and δ the recovery factor of 10%. The outcomes are $\delta \cdot \$105$ and the $105 that is expected if no default. Thus, we have:

So, $\$103 = (1-p)\$105 + p\,\delta\,\$105 = \$105 - p\,\$105 + p\,\delta\,\$105 = \$105 + \$105p(\delta - 1)$, thus $p = (\$105-\$103)/(\$105(1-\delta)) = \$3/\$94.5 = 2.116\%$.

6.   This is a par bond so it sells at 100% of face or $1,000.

7.   If you look in the financial press or on web sites for risk-free zero coupon yields in order to construct a spot yield curve, you may only find coupon-paying bonds. Bootstrapping is the process of taking the observed coupon bond price data and extracting implied prices of zero coupon bonds from it.

8.   Bootstrap the zero curve: we have the following cash flows:

t, years	0.5	1	1.5	2	Price
0.5	101.25				99

1.0	1.5	101.5			99.5
1.5	2	2	102		101
2.0	2.25	2.25	2.25	102.25	98

For the 0.5 year bond, we have PF = 1/(1+df)FV where 1/(1+df) = $Z_{0.5}$. Price = $Z_{0.5}(100+C)$ and so $Z_{0.5}$ = Price/(100+C) = 99/101.25=0.97778. The following zeros are found in a similar way using the formula:

For example, $99.5 = 0.97777(1.5) + 101.5(Z_1)$, so $Z_1 = (99.5 - (0.97777)(1.5))/(100+1.5) = 0.96584..$

$$Z_n = \frac{P - C\sum_{i=1}^{n-1} Z_i}{100+C}$$

		Bootstrapping Yield Curve			
t, years	Coupon	Price	Periodic Coupon	Zero	Spot Rate
0.5	2.5%	99	1.25	0.977778	4.5455%
1	3.0%	99.5	1.5	0.965846	3.5055%
1.5	4.0%	101	2	0.952086	3.3003%
2	4.5%	98	2.25	0.894715	5.6406%
2	6.0%	100.8428	3	0.894715	5.6406%

Then the price of the two year, 6% bond is $3(Z_{0.5}+Z_1 + Z_{1.5} + Z_2) + \$100\ Z_2 =$ $3(0.97778+0.965846+0.952086+0.894715) + \$100*0.894715 = \$100.8428.$

9.   The spot rates implied by these zeros are found by the general formula

$$y_i = 2\left(\left(\frac{1}{Z_i}\right)^{\frac{0.5}{i}} - 1\right),\ \text{for example,}\ y_{1.5} = 2\left(\left(\frac{1}{Z_{1.5}}\right)^{\frac{0.5}{1.5}} - 1\right) = 2\left(\left(\frac{1}{0.946504}\right)^{\frac{0.5}{1.5}} - 1\right) = 3.6991\%.$$

10.   Remember, PSF, Pass Start to Finish, Forwards above Par Yields, and Par Yields below Spot Yields.

11.   No. While an argument may be made that CMOs are default free (since the underlying asset can be repossessed), they are highly sensitive to prepayment risk.

12.   The higher interest rate decreases the present value of expected cash flows to PO so the value of the bond should drop. (Also, a rising rate environment will result in fewer prepayments, delaying payment to PO holders.) This also holds for the IO but, because prepays slow, could have more interest payments over the life of the IO. So the price could rise or fall depending on which effect dominates.

13.   Primarily counterparty risk. Payments are netted. For example, if the fixed rate payer is obligated to pay 6% on a notional of $100,000,000, and the floating rate payer has to pay LIBOR, which was 8% at the reset date, the net payment to the fixed payer would be (8% - 6%) $100,000,000 = $2,000,000. The floating rate payer may have incentive to walk away without paying, exposing the floating rate receiver to a loss of $2,000,000 and the PV of future expected payments.

14.   The value of the swap must be zero at initiation. The fixed rate is calculated from the PV of all floating rate payments using the expected forward LIBOR rates. If the value were not zero at initiation there would be no incentive on one side to do the deal.

15.   Portfolios of EDF futures contracts would give the same payoff.

16.   The implied 3-month LIBOR rates prevailing in Sep and Dec can be calculated from the observed EDF prices. For Sep-Dec the implied rate is 100-97.5 = 2.5%, and for

the period Dec-Mar the implied rate is $100 - 97.18 = 2.82\%$. The rate over the 255-day period now-Mar 03 is then calculated as:

$$\frac{360}{255}\left[\left(1+\frac{75}{360}0.0215\right)\left(1+\frac{90}{360}0.025\right)\left(1+\frac{90}{360}0.0282\right)-1\right] = 2.5247\%.$$ Since the actual rate of 2.4% is

lower than this, an arbitrage opportunity is possible. You would borrow at the low 255-day rate of 2.4%, then lend at the current 75-day rate. Buy both the Sep 02 and Dec 02 EDF contracts to lock in the rate you will receive.

Summary of Formulas

Price of T-bill $\qquad$ $Price = (1 - (Ask / 100 * Days\ to\ Mat / 360)) * (Face\ Value)$

Bond Equivalent Yield $\qquad$ $r_{BEY} = \left(\dfrac{10,000 - P}{10,000} \right) \dfrac{365}{n}$

$Taxable\ Equivalent\ Yield = \dfrac{Municipal\ Yield}{100\% - Tax\ Bracket}$

$Net\ Yield = Taxable\ Yield(100\% - Tax\ Bracket)$

$SMM = 1 - (1 - CPR)^{\frac{1}{12}}$

$CPR = \left[\begin{array}{l} 6\% \dfrac{t}{30}, t < 30 months \\ 6\%, t \geq 30 months \end{array} \right]$

Value of IO strip $\quad V = \displaystyle\sum_{i=1}^{n} \dfrac{INT_i}{(1+r)^i}$

Value of PO strip $\quad V = \displaystyle\sum_{i=1}^{n} \dfrac{P_i}{(1+r)^i}$

Bootstrapping Zeros and Spot Rate Curves:

$Z_n = \dfrac{P - C \displaystyle\sum_{i=1}^{n-1} Z_i}{100 + C}$ $\qquad\qquad$ $y_i = 2 \left(\left(\dfrac{1}{Z_i} \right)^{\frac{0.5}{i}} - 1 \right)$

EQUITY
MARKETS

Equity Valuation Overview

When you buy stock in a corporation, you exchange cash for a share of hoped-for future profits of the company. These profits can come via capital appreciation and/or the receipt of dividends. Unlike bondholders or other creditors, shareholders are not guaranteed any return. Should a company go bankrupt, its common shareholders will be at the very end of a long line of investors. So, there is substantial risk in the stock market -- but there is also the potential for significant returns. Modern portfolio theory holds that there is a relationship between the riskiness of an asset and the return demanded by investors: the riskier the asset, the higher the return it should earn. There are many economic theories aimed at evaluating an investor's risk profile, which is characterized by a quadratic utility function. The general assumption is that investors are risk-averse.

Regression Analysis

What is a fair price for an asset? What factors influence the price? Is the value we see in the pages of financial papers correct? How do we account for the riskiness of an asset? Although prices are discovered in the marketplace, there are some tools that we can employ to price an asset. Effectively, prices are driven by expectations of future earnings, so today's price is calculated as the discounted cash flow of expected future earnings. According to Benjamin Graham, who is widely considered the "dean of financial analysis" and "father of value investing," the *earnings power* of a firm is the ultimate source of value. So in order to price any asset, we must have a good understanding of its current and future growth prospects. (For more from father Graham, check out *Security Analysis*, the classic 1934 textbook that Graham co-authored with David Dodd and is still widely used today.)

We also must account for the inherent risk of an asset. This risk is embedded in the price of the asset through the correct choice of discount rate. How to choose this discount rate is a topic of discussion and debate that continues even today. While there is an entire chapter on risk later in this book, for now we will decompose equity risk into two sources: **systematic risk**, which all stocks are subject to and **unsystematic risk**, which is the company-specific portion of risk.

The efficient market hypothesis

First, we must summarize the **efficient market hypothesis (EMH)**, also called the **random walk theory**, which is a theory of how prices are set in the market, and is the foundation of modern portfolio theory. This hypothesis asserts that future prices are random. Although future prices might follow some mean path related to expected growth of corporate earnings, they fluctuate according to random events. There are three levels of the efficient markets hypothesis: the weak form, the semi-strong form, and the strong form.

The **weak form of the EMH** asserts that security prices include all publicly available trading data, including price/share, trading volume and short interest. Thus, studies of price history contain no information that can help predict future prices, so charting and other forms of technical analysis do not work. (The idea here is that since this information is publicly available, all investors have access to it, and so it would already be factored into the security price.)

The **semi-strong form of the EMH** asserts that security prices embed all known trading data as well as company fundamentals. Thus, no meaningful price behavior can be forecasted by forming relationships between accounting variables such as earnings/share, dividends/price and other financial ratios. (The idea here is similar to the weak form: such data can easily be obtained from sources like Bloomberg.com so would already be reflected in the price of the security.)

The **strong form of the EMH** asserts that security prices reflect all of the information it is possible to know about a company, both public and private, including trading variables, all accounting data and all information known only to insiders. The only variable that can impact the price of a security is new information, which by definition enters the market randomly and is unknowable. Under this form, stock prices follow a random walk. The strong form includes the weak form as well as the semi-strong form as shown below.

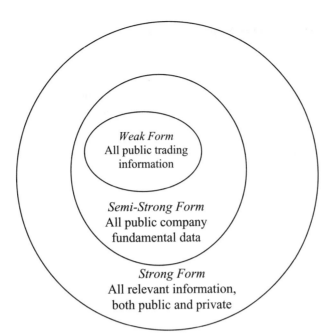

Dividend Discount Model

The value of any company is the present value of expected future cash flows that will accrue to investors. The investors include debt holders, preferred dividend holders and common equity shareholders. In order to value the price of the common stock, we have to work with cash flows expected to accrue to the common shareholders. So, the simplest possible model is the **dividend discount model**. Here, we just forecast the future flow of dividends and discount by the appropriate cost of equity capital to calculate the present value of the dividend stream. This gives the price of the stock. The first simple case is where the company pays a dividend that is expected to remain stable over time. This might be the case for a mature company. Then the price of the stock is calculated using the perpetuity model already developed:

$$P_{CS} = \frac{DIV}{r_{CE}}$$

In the above formula, DIV is the stable dividend and r_{CE} is the cost of equity capital, which is not observable. One way to estimate it is to use the CAPM. Another way is to ask management what their hurdle rate for new projects is. (Hurdle rate is the minimum return that they require before making an investment in something; also referred to as "required rate of return.")

Example Suppose that the Caterpillar Corporation (CAT) pays an annual dividend of $1.40 and its cost of equity capital is 15%. What is the price of the stock?

Answer: If investors expect a perpetual stream of $1.40 dividends and the cost of equity capital is expected to remain constant, then

$$P_{CS} = \frac{DIV}{r_{CE}} = \frac{\$1.40}{0.15} = \$9.33.$$

Gordon growth model

If the dividend is expected to grow forever at a constant rate g, the stock price will be higher than that calculated above. In this case, the price of the stock is calculated using

$$P_{CS} = \frac{DIV_0(1+g)}{r_{CE} - g}$$ where DIV_0 is the current dividend. In this case it can be seen that the spread

between the cost of equity capital and the growth rate of the dividend is the primary driver of stock price.

Example Suppose that the Caterpillar Corporation (CAT) pays an annual dividend of $1.40 and their cost of equity capital is 6.5%, but the dividend is expected to grow at a constant rate of 2.5%/year. What is the price of the stock?

Answer $P_{CS} = \frac{DIV_0(1+g)}{r_{CE} - g} = \frac{\$1.40(1+0.025)}{0.15 - 0.025} = \$11.48$

So how well did these models do in pricing Caterpillar? Since the actual price is currently $54.71, there must be something that these models are not capturing.

The Gordon growth model must be used with care. If the growth rate is higher than the cost of equity capital, a negative price per share will result. A company can't grow at a high rate for an infinite period of time, otherwise it would overtake the entire economy. We can construct more complex dividend discount models to account for companies that will be experiencing changing growth rates over time. (For example, we'd do this when a high-tech company expands rapidly for a period, then begins a transition period where sales might begin to stabilize, and eventually enters a mature period of stable growth. Such models include but are not limited to: the two-stage dividend discount model, the H Model and the three-stage dividend discount model.)

Also, note that these models only apply to companies that pay a dividend, or are expected to pay a dividend in the future, so can't be used to value start-ups and other companies that may not pay dividends. For such companies, we can use **multiples analysis** for valuation.

Multiples Analysis

Common multiples used in valuation include price/earnings, price/sales, dividend/price, and book value/market value. While multiples are easy to use, we have to be very careful because we don't know what the "right" multiple should be. To value a company using a multiple requires a set of "comparable" companies for comparison. Also, since no understanding or knowledge of the company fundamentals or outlook is required to use a multiple, multiples analysis, if misused, can give misleading prices. Nevertheless, let's try out a few of these ratios on some real companies.

Price/earnings ratio

The "earnings" here means net income per share. Net income is used because, theoretically, it's the income available to pay to investors. Net income is income net of operating expenses, taxes and negotiated debt capital that must be paid. Since net income is only reported quarterly (at least for U.S. companies it is), we have to use historical, or "trailing," income. Assume that the average number of shares held over the period Mar 31, 2001 to Mar 31, 2002 was 343.8 million, and the net income for this period was $715 million. Then earnings/share = $715 million/343.8 million shares = $2.08/share. If price/share was $54.71, then price/earnings = (price/share)/(earnings/share) = $54.71/$2.08 = 26.30. We use price/earnings multiples to compare to other stocks or indices, to either assess relative valuation or attractiveness of the stock, or to estimate price when other metrics aren't available. If we wanted to value a new company "similar" to Caterpillar, we might use the P/E ratio. Suppose the similar company has earnings/share of $1.50. Then its price would be calculated as 26.30($1.50) = $39.45. This could be done even if the company is not expected to pay any dividends.

Another way to calculate the price/earnings ratio is to recognize that companies can either pay their net income out to shareholders via dividends, or reinvest it in the company to fund new projects. The ratio of net income paid in the form of dividends is known as the payout ratio K. When companies are experiencing rapid growth, they generally plow their earnings back into the company. But as companies mature, they generally pay out a higher percentage of their earnings as dividends. Thus $DIV = K E$. The Gordon growth model can be modified to allow us to solve for price/earnings as:

$$P_{CS} = \frac{DIV_0(1+g)}{r_{CE}-g} = \frac{KE_0(1+g)}{r_{CE}-g} \ so \ \frac{P_{CS}}{E_0} = \frac{K(1+g)}{r_{CE}-g}$$

If $K = 66.7\%$ for CAT and the consensus estimate for long-term growth rate is 11%, then

$$\frac{P_{CS}}{E_0} = \frac{0.667(1+0.11)}{0.15-0.11} = 18.5.$$

This would imply a current price of 18.5(E_0 = 2.08) = $38.5.

Warning: It is not a good idea to use P/E ratios to value a stock, since there are so many variables involved. The P/E ratio is a quick estimate that assumes that the only factors influencing a stock's price are earnings/share. Even if the two companies we are comparing have totally different risk characteristics, it is possible to forecast the same P/E ratio for them. The P/E ratio is an easy metric to calculate, but should never be used in place of more sophisticated analysis. We might look at the trend of P/E ratios over time for a stock or index to try to get some idea of whether the market is under or over-priced, but even this will work only if the current environment is very similar to that which prevailed historically. We can see that price/earnings ratios are not stable over time as companies frequently manipulate their earnings through accounting games.

As an example of how we might actually use the P/E ratio in a useful way, consider the stock of TASER, a company that makes laser stun guns. (The following example is based on a May 28, 2002, *New York Post* article, "TASER Losing Its Zip," by Christopher Byron.) The stock was languishing around $6/share pre-9/11 but shot up to over $18/share after United Airlines placed an order for 1,300 guns. At $575/gun this is equivalent to about $750,000 in revenue. According to United's most recent financial statements, they have a fleet size of 543 aircraft, meaning they are buying 2.4 guns/plane.

Looking at TASER's financial statements, we see 12-month trailing earnings of about $608,000. With 2.8 million shares outstanding, this yields earnings/share of $0.21. Thus the P/E ratio is $18/$0.21 = 85. The Dow is currently trading at about 20 times earnings. Is a $750,000 sale to UAL sufficient to justify the increase in P/E of 85 from 28?

To find out, let's figure out how much revenue would have to be generated to justify the TASER multiple. With net profit margins of 7.59% this means that approximately $56,925 of net income spread over 2.8 million shares will add about 2 cents/share. If it is assumed that the company should trade at about the same multiple as the Dow Jones Industrial Average, a P/E of 20 means that the EPS should be $0.8875/share. How many guns would have to be sold to justify this? Revenue = $0.8875/share times 2.8 million shares/0.0759 = $32.7 million. This implies that about 57,000 guns would have to be sold per year to justify a P/E ratio of 20. How large is the market for TASER guns on airlines assuming that all airlines buy in the same ratio as United? There are about 15,000 commercial aircraft. Even if each buys 3 guns/plane, this implies a one-time sale of 45,000 guns. So the price must embed expectations of selling to other users such as police forces, for example.

Dividend/price

Otherwise known as **dividend yield**, the **dividend to price ratio** for Caterpillar would be $1.40/$54.17 = 2.58%. If the dividend yield and dividend are known, this allows us to estimate price. Studies have been performed on the dividend yield of the S&P500 and other indices in an attempt to forecast market tops and bottoms. A relatively high dividend yield implies that the market is undervalued, while a low dividend yield implies that the market is overpriced. If mean-reversion holds, the idea is that periods of low dividend yields should be followed by falling prices. The problem is that no one can predict exactly when this will happen.

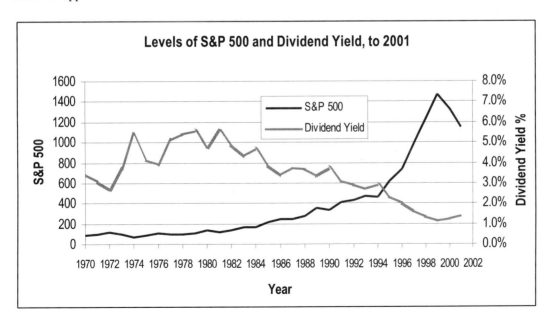

Price/sales

The **price to sales ratio** is often used because sales are the ultimate source from which net income and consequent dividends might be paid. Additionally, sales are considered to be less subject to accountings manipulation than earnings, so this ratio might be stable over time. The price/sales (P/S) ratio can be used for companies that don't yet have any reported earnings -- such as start-ups. Returning to the Caterpillar example, if we knew that the P/S ratio was 0.95 and we knew that its 12-month trailing sales was $20.0 billion, then the market cap would be calculated as $19 billion. If there are 343.9 shares outstanding, this leads to a price of $55.25/share.

The Price/Sales ratio might be a good valuation measure for TASER, which has no dividends so can't be priced using the dividend discount model. If price/sales for "comparable" companies (with respect to TASER, we might look for sector comparables in technology, and for industry comparables in Electronic Instrumentation & Controls) are obtained and averaged, we might find P/S = 2.29 for the industry, 5.46 for the sector and 3.41 for the S&P 500. If the 12-month trailing sales are $8 million/2.8 million shares = $2.85/share, this would give a P/S ratio for the company of $17.75/2.85 = 6.23. Price computed using comparables are tabulated below.

	P/S	Calculated Share Price
Industry	2.29	$6.54
Sector	5.46	$15.56
S&P500	3.41	$9.71
TASER	6.23	$17.75

Price/book value

The **price to book value (P/BV) ratio** compares the current price of a company's stock to its book value per share. The underlying idea is that the company is able to use its assets to generate earnings. For Caterpillar, the price/book value ratio for the quarter ended March 31, 2002, was 3.32. A firm's book value – assets less liabilities – can be obtained from a firm's balance sheet. This residual is what would remain to be distributed to shareholders. If the book value is $16.50/share, this would imply a share price of 3.32(16.50) = $54.78. The problem with using this ratio is that some assets, such as cash and marketable securities, are recorded at current market prices, while longer-term assets are recorded at historical acquisition cost. This will depress book value and overstate the P/BV ratio in many cases. For many service-based companies, such as consulting or software firms, assets include employee talent, which is not recorded on any balance sheet. As a result, book value will appear very low. In fact, for the first quarter of 2002, Microsoft had a price/book value ratio of 5.4. For a reported book value/share of $10.03, this would imply a price of $54.86 at a time when Microsoft's price had experienced a high price of $76/share. Service companies may have higher P/BV ratios since they have fewer **hard assets** (land, building and equipment). Growing companies making large capital expenditures might have lower P/BV ratios, but as these assets start to depreciate, the ratio should rise.

Price/cash flow

This ratio compares a company's stock price to its free cash flow per share. Free cash flow is the flow that would accrue to common shareholders after any capital expenditures or interest payments have been made, and any preferred dividends paid. Using accounting statements, the free cash flow can be determined. Because it's most likely harder for companies to manipulate actual cash flow than earnings, the price to cash flow ratio might be a better measure of earnings power than the P/E ratio. TASER's cash flow/share was \$0.28/share, which results in a price/cash flow measure of 63. By comparison, the industry, sector and S&P500 price/cash flow were 19.92, 30.7 and 20.54, respectively.

Other multiples: There are several other metrics by which performance may be measured. These include revenue/employee and net income/employee.

Return on an asset

The return on any asset is calculated as the sum of price appreciation over the holding period, plus net cash flows accruing to the investor. Thus, if an asset is expected to grow at a rate g over the holding period, an investment of P today will grow to $(1+g)P$ by the end of the holding period. The return will then be:

$$r = \frac{P(1+g)+D-P}{P} = \frac{D}{P} + g$$

If the consensus long-term growth expectations for Caterpillar are 11%, the current price is \$54.8, and a dividend payment of \$1.40 is expected over the year, neglecting compounding of the quarterly dividend, the expected return over the year would be calculated as:

$$r = \frac{\$1.40}{\$54.8} + 0.11 = 13.55\%.$$ This would give an expected price in one year of $1.1355(\$54.8) = \$62.2$ for the

stock. Note that it is the expected growth rate that drives this calculation, not the dividend payment, so if the growth rate is wrong, an investor could make the wrong decision.

CAPM

About 40 years ago, a relationship between a security's return and its risk was developed. This relationship is known as the **Capital Asset Pricing Model**, or **CAPM** for short. The CAPM posits that all security risk is captured in a parameter known as **beta**, and that there is a linear relationship between the excess return of the security to the excess return of the market. The investor should be compensated for risk. The greater the risk, the higher the return the investor should require. The CAPM is:

$$R_s = R_f + \beta(R_m - R_f)$$

In terms of excess returns,
$$R_s - R_f = \beta(R_m - R_f)$$

where

R_s = return on security, %
R_f = risk-free rate, %
R_m = return on market portfolio, %
β = measure of correlation between security and market portfolio

The CAPM can be used to estimate the required return on equity capital needed in security valuation (it would be the correct discount rate to use), or to determine relative attractiveness of a security. The validity of the CAPM is a fertile topic of academic debate, as are questions such as what to use as the proper risk free rate, what market portfolio should be used, whether a market portfolio even exists, whether beta is stable over time, and whether beta is alive or dead.

Risk-free rate

The risk-free rate chosen should correlate with the expected holding period of the investment. Some use the 3-month T-bill rate, but for corporate finance matters or investments meant to be held for longer periods, use longer-tenor maturities. For example, if one wants the required return on equity capital for a new capital expenditure expected to last for ten years, use the 10-year Treasury bond.

Market portfolio

The market portfolio is generally assumed to be unobservable. Theoretically, the market portfolio would encompass all possible investments. In practice, thought, it's usually taken to be the return on the S&P 500. If we are valuing large-cap U.S. stocks, this is probably acceptable. If you are using the CAPM to value risky investments in emerging markets, you should choose another index that is more appropriate to your investments.

Excess return

This is the return over the risk-free rate as in $R_s - R_f$, $R_m - R_f$. Historically, the excess returns over the S&P 500 index have averaged about 7%.

Beta

This measures the co-movement of the security with the market portfolio. By definition, beta (b) of the market itself is equal to one. Stocks that are perfectly correlated with the market, then, will have $b = 1$. Stocks that are riskier than the market will have betas exceeding 1, and stocks less risky than the market will have betas lower than one. The minimum value of beta is zero. A beta of 3 would mean that if the market had an excess return of 10%, the stock would be expected to have an excess return of 30%. Beta can be calculated via regression analysis or looked up from financial sources. Knowledge of beta can help in devising a portfolio with the desired risk and return characteristics.

Example Suppose that the risk-free rate is 5%, the market return is expected to be 12%, and the company's beta = 1.74. The required return on equity is calculated using the CAPM as

$R_s = 5\% + 1.74(12\% - 5\%) = 17.18\%$

or 12.18% over the risk-free rate.

Example Caterpillar's beta is reported as 0.73. It is expected to pay dividends of $1.40 over the next year and pays out 66.7% of net income as dividends. Is the stock an attractive buy at the current price of $55? Assume that the risk-free rate is 3% and the market will return 10%.

Answer In order to evaluate whether the stock is over or undervalued at the current price, we may use either of the following two methods. In the first method, we use the CAPM to calculate the required return on the stock, and use this as the denominator to calculate price. If the market price of the stock exceeds the price calculated, the stock is over-valued; if the market price is lower than the price calculated, the stock is over-valued.

In the second method, we use the market price to back-out the required return that is implied by the price. This required return is compared to the required return calculated from the CAPM. If the implied market return is lower than the CAPM required return, the stock is overvalued; if the implied market return is higher than the CAPM required return, the stock is under-valued.

Required return on equity capital using CAPM is $R_s = 3\% + 0.73(10\% - 3\%) = 8.11\%$. Then the price/share should be $P_{CS} = \dfrac{DIV_0(1+g)}{r_{CE} - g}$ where g is the internal growth rate of the company. This can be calculated by recognizing the fact that there are only a few ways for a company to grow internally: it can retain earnings and plow them back into new capital projects to earn the return on equity, or it can buy back shares priced below book value or sell stock above book value and invest the capital received.

Assuming that the company will plow back earnings, the internal growth rate g = return on equity times earnings retention ratio, or $g = ROE(1-K)$. Since $ROE = \dfrac{Net\ Income}{Common\ Equity}$ this can be decomposed into two sources of return. Since Earnings/Share = $\dfrac{Net\ Income}{Share}$ and Book Value/Share = $\dfrac{Common\ Equity}{Share}$ then $ROE = \dfrac{Net\ Income}{Common\ Equity} = \left(\dfrac{Net\ Income}{Share}\right)\left(\dfrac{Share}{Book\ Value}\right) = EPS/BV$.

Note: The above calculation is known as **Dupont analysis**, in which the return is decomposed into sources of return. Another useful form is to write

$$ROE = \left(\frac{Sales}{Assets}\right)\left(\frac{NetIncome}{Sales}\right)\left(\frac{Assets}{Equity}\right) = (AssetTurnover)(\Pr ofitM\arg in)(LeverageRatio)$$

Quick tip: To remember (S/A) (NI/S) (A/E), write out the first letters of each term (SANISAE) and remember, *"Southwest Airlines Announces: Nuts Increase Sales." (Film) At Eleven.*

Then $g = EPS/BV(1-K) = ROE(1-K)$. Since Caterpillar's *EPS* and *BV/share* are \$2.08/share and \$16.5/share, respectively, then *ROE* is calculated as 12.61% and thus $g = 12.61\%(1-.667) = 4.19\%$.

Finally, the price is calculated as $P = \dfrac{\$1.40(1+0.0419)}{0.0811-0.0419} = \$37.2/share$. Since the current market price is higher than this, it is not an attractive buy at this time.

Note: There are many perils in using this formula. For one thing, it assumes that the company has reached a mature growth stage and thus is assumed to grow at a constant rate, which may not be true if the company is planning, for example, acquisitions or diversifications. A sensitivity analysis should always be performed. Because the price is so sensitive to the spread between r_{CE} and g, we can calculate a range of prices. In fact, if r_{CE} is decreased by just one percent, the price would be \$49.95, whereas increasing g by just one percent results in a share price of \$50.43.

The Markowitz portfolio

If we plot all possible (risk, return) pairs of assets where risk is measured by standard deviation, we might get something like the following.

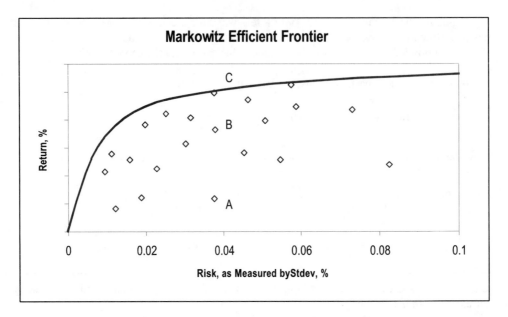

The solid line in the above graph is the **efficient frontier**: investors holding portfolios that lie along the efficient frontier have the optimal return for the risk they are willing to bear. If an investor was willing to tolerate a standard deviation of 4%, he could hold portfolio *A*. But this is suboptimal because there are portfolios such as *B* that offer a higher return for the same amount of risk. The highest return that could be earned would be if a portfolio *C*, which lies along the efficient frontier could be found. According to the theory, there are no portfolios that could be formed lying outside of the envelope described by the frontier. This goes back to the idea that investors are risk-averse.

The assumption is that investors are only concerned with mean return and risk of their portfolios. positive constant, which must be determined for each investor. The utility function describes a trade-off

Suppose that the utility function looks something like $U = E[R_P] - \frac{A}{2}\sigma^2[R_P]$ where A is some

between risk and return with higher utility derived from higher returns, but moderated by risk.

Overlaying sample utility functions for two different investors on the efficient frontier gives:

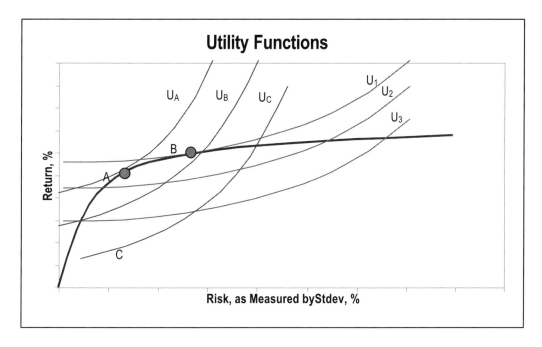

The indifference curves for a highly risk-adverse investor are shown above as U_A, U_B and U_C with $U_A > U_B > U_C$. This investor would be indifferent between any (risk, return) combination along any utility curve. It is assumed that the investor seeks to maximize his utility so, if he desires to hold the portfolio C on indifference curve U_C, he could earn higher utility for the same risk by holding portfolio A on indifference curve U_A. It is not possible to form portfolios with higher return for the same risk since these would lie outside of the efficient frontier. The optimal portfolio for this investor is where the highest utility curve is tangent to the efficient frontier. On the other hand, for the utility curves U_1, U_2 and U_3 of a less risk-averse investor, the optimal portfolio to hold is where the highest utility curve U_1 is tangent to the efficient frontier, which occurs at point B. The second investor will earn a higher return than the first investor, but must take on more risk to do so.

Derivation of CAPM

We regress the returns of a stock against the returns of the market. The slope of the regression line is β. For example, regressing Microsoft's returns against the returns of the S&P 500 over the past seven years results in the relation $R_{MSFT}-R_F = 0.0018 + 1.47 (R_{S\&P500}-R_F)$. This implies that $\beta = 1.47$ for this period. (We should also perform statistical analysis of the regression coefficients. We find that the t-statistic of the intercept is 0.15, so the intercept is not significant. The slope has a t-statistic of 9.1 so is significant. Since the standard deviation of the slope coefficient is 0.16, a 95% confidence interval is $1.144 = \beta = 1.79$.)

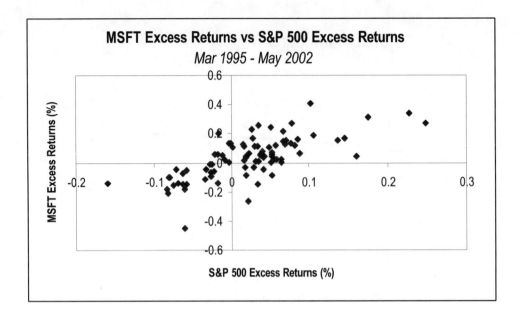

Recall that if we form a portfolio of securities, the expected return and variance of the portfolio can be calculated as

$$E[R_P] = R_f + \sum_{i=1}^{n} w_i \left(E[R_i] - R_f \right)$$

where

$$\sum_{i=1}^{n} w_i = 1, \ \sigma_{R_P}^2 = \sum_{i=1}^{n} w_i^2 \sigma_i^2 + 2 \sum_{i=1}^{n} \sum_{j=1}^{n} w_i w_j COV_{i,j}, \ i \neq j$$

Returning to our risk-averse investor, suppose he decides to hold only two assets: some fraction w_S of a single stock and $w_m = (1 - w_s)$ of the market portfolio. Can we derive his optimal portfolio?

The expected return of the portfolio will be $R_P = R_f + w_S(R_S - R_f) + w_m(R_m - R_f)$ and the variance will be $\sigma_P^2 = w_S^2 \sigma_S^2 + w_m^2 \sigma_m^2 + 2 w_s w_m COV(R_s, R_m)$. Differentiating with respect to w_s gives

$$\frac{\partial \sigma_P^2}{\partial w_s} = 2 w_s \sigma_S^2 + 2 w_m COV(R_s, R_m) \text{ and } \frac{\partial E[R_p]}{\partial w_s} = \left(R_s - R_f \right)$$

Assuming that at the optimal point $w_s = 0$ and $w_m = 1$, $\dfrac{\partial \sigma_p^2}{\partial w_s} = 2 COV\left(R_s, R_m \right)$

Also, at the optimal point, the marginal change in expected return for change in variance should be constant regardless of the security held, even for the market portfolio. Thus:

$$\left(\frac{\partial E[R_p]}{\partial \sigma_p^2} \right) = \frac{R_s - R_f}{2 COV(R_s, R_m)} = \frac{R_m - R_f}{2 COV(R_m, R_m)} = \frac{R_m - R_f}{2 \sigma_m^2}$$

This leads to the CAPM:

$$R_p - R_f = \frac{COV(R_s, R_m)}{\sigma_m^2}(R_s - R_f) = \beta_{sm}(R_s - R_f)$$

which implies that the only source of risk that the market will compensate the investor for is market risk, measured by the covariance of the asset return with the market. This is so because with proper choice of weights, it is possible to diversify away company-specific (unsystematic) risk: the market does not reward you for taking diversifiable risk. We will show this in the following section.

Please note that the CAPM is essentially a one-factor model, as it employs a single source of risk – the covariance of the return with the market return – as driving return. There are more complex models such as the APT factor model, which attempt to quantify return as the sum of sensitivities to various economic factors. The CAPM assumes that investors are "mean-variance" optimizers and that the market portfolio, whatever that may be, is the portfolio that gives the optimal return for a given variance. Another difficulty with the CAPM is that it provides a relationship between expected excess returns (ex-ante returns), but investors observe actual (ex-post) returns. For example, suppose we you want to calculate the standard deviation of returns on a stock. If the calculation is done ex-post, we would assume a distribution for the returns (such as a normal distribution) and, on the basis of expected mean returns, compute the probability of returns as different from the expected return. In an ex-post calculation, wee would use historical price data to compute returns and calculate standard deviation as previously discussed, $s^2 = \dfrac{\sum_{i=1}^{x}(x_i - \bar{x})^2}{n-1}$.

Equity Indexes

Most businesses are exposed to the same macroeconomic effects, including inflation, business cycles, interest rate changes, energy prices, and costs of manufacturing inputs. If all of these common factors are lumped together as F, we can measure the sensitivity of the individual firm to F by β_i. Firms are also exposed to firm-specific risk such as patent approvals, new technology integration, innovation and favorable litigation settlements. If this risk is represented by the term ε_i we can represent the expected excess return of the security over the risk-free rate as

$$R_s - R_f = \alpha_i + \beta_i(R_m - R_f) + \varepsilon_i$$

In this equation, the intercept α_i represents the return that would be expected in a neutral market where $R_m - R_f = 0$. $\beta_i(R_m - R_f)$ is the excess return resulting from market exposure, and ε_i is the firm-specific risk. The excess return is composed of two parts: the systematic excess return $\alpha_i + \beta_i(R_m - R_f)$ due to sensitivity to market factors, and the excess return attributable to unsystematic, firm-specific risk ε_i. This is known as the **index model** and is very similar to the CAPM, except for the term α_i. This form is also identical to the regression model obtained earlier by regressing MSFT returns on the S&P 500.

If we form an equally-weighted portfolio of n assets, the excess return of the portfolio is just the weighted sum of each individual excess return.

$$R_P - R_f = \sum_{i=1}^{n} w_i(R_i - R_f) = \frac{1}{n}\left(\sum_{i=1}^{n}\alpha_i + \beta_i(R_m - R_f) + \varepsilon_i\right) = \frac{1}{n}\sum_{i=1}^{n}\alpha_i + \frac{1}{n}\sum_{i=1}^{n}\beta_i(R_i - R_f) + \frac{1}{n}\sum_{i=1}^{n}\varepsilon_i$$

if $\alpha_P = \frac{1}{n}\sum_{i=1}^{n}\alpha_i$ and $\beta_P = \frac{1}{n}\sum_{i=1}^{n}\beta_i$

then

$$R_P - R_f = \alpha_P + \beta_P(R_m - R_f) + \frac{1}{n}\sum_{i=1}^{n}\varepsilon_i$$

The first two terms are the excess returns due to systematic market risk and the last are due to non-market (firm-specific) factors. The variance of $R_P - R_f$ is:

$$\sigma_P^2(R_P - R_f) = \beta_P^2\sigma_P^2 + \sigma^2(\varepsilon_p) = \beta_P^2\sigma_P^2 + \frac{1}{n}\sigma^2(\varepsilon)$$

Plotting this:

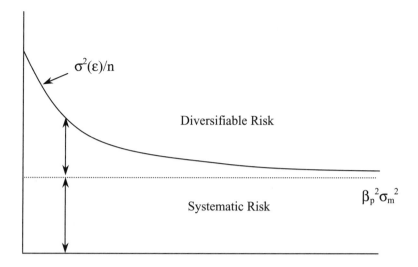

Studies have been performed that show holding n = 30 stocks should be sufficient to diversify the portfolio.

Hybrids

In addition to the standard debt and equity instruments, a company can issue hybrid instruments: debt instruments with exposure to equity, foreign exchange, commodities or currency markets. These hybrid instruments include **warrants, convertible preferred stock**, **convertible bonds**, dual currency bonds and PERCS (Preference Equity Redemption Cumulative Stock; a form of convertible preferred stock with an enhanced dividend).

Warrants

A warrant is the right to purchase stock at a later date at a specified price, called the subscription price. Warrants are often attached to debt offerings, but are detachable. If the subscription price is lower than the stock price, the warrant will have intrinsic value. Warrants are similar to call options, but the major differences are: (1) call options are traded on regular exchanges through clearinghouses and warrants are not; (2) the exercise of call options does not result in the issue of new stock, but exercise of warrants causes issuance of new stock, and so causes dilution of shares; and (3) warrants typically have long expiration dates, spanning several years, while common stock options (not withstanding LEAPS) may have expiries of less than one year. The famed Black-Scholes equation was actually originally developed as a means to value warrants.

Convertible preferred stock

Corporations can issue two types of stock: common and preferred. Preferred stock entitles the holder to preferred dividends. Preferred dividends are paid before any common stock dividends. The coupon rate quoted is the maximum the company will pay -- it may pay less if it doesn't have the money. Some preferred stock is convertible: it can be exchanged for common stock at the holder's option.

Convertible bonds

A corporation may also issue convertible bonds, which are bonds entitling the holder to the normal coupon payments and par value at maturity. Like convertible preferred stock, convertible bonds can be exchanged for common stock. And like a regular bond, a convertible bond has a stated coupon, payment schedule, par value and maturity. Corporations issue convertible bonds because they provide a low-cost funding alternative -- perhaps 400 to 700 basis points below the rates they would pay on straight bonds. Investors are willing to accept lower rates for the opportunity to participate in stock appreciation, and the issuing corporation benefits because most convertible bonds are callable, allowing the issuer to force conversion if so desired. Some convertible bonds are even putable.

Note: Since the process by which we value convertible bonds and convertible preferred stock is the same, we won't distinguish between the two in the following discussion.

Convertible bonds became popular among dot.com companies. According to *CFO Magazine*, dot coms issued $61 billion worth of convertibles issued in 2000. Start-up companies traditionally obtained new capital by issuing equity, which dilutes existing shares, or by issuing debt, which usually carries a high coupon rate. Convertible bonds provide a low-cost alternative to these types of companies. Effectively, in issuing convertible bonds, companies are selling stock at a premium, but receiving favorable accounting treatments. Companies that issue convertible bonds are hoping that their stock prices go up so they can call the bonds, forcing conversion and ending their interest payments.

When a corporation issues a convertible bond, the **term sheet** will specify a conversion price and a conversion ratio. (A term sheet is a binding contract detailing all of the terms of the convertible bond (or other instrument), including issue description, issue price, settlement date, call feature, conversion price, conversion ratio, and conversion premium.)

If you know the conversion price, you can figure out the conversion ratio, and vice versa. For example, if a company issues a corporate bond convertible into 50 shares of common stock, the conversion ratio is one bond per 50 shares of stock and the conversion price is $1,000/50 shares = $20/share. The only difficulty in valuation of convertible bonds is deciding upon an optimal conversion strategy. In order to value a convertible bond, we must compare the value of the bond as a straight debt instrument to the value of the equity it could be converted into.

Depending on the price of the underlying equity, convertible bonds may behave more like equity than debt. Some companies are turning to zero-coupon convertible bonds as an alternative to raising capital in the equity market. The dependence of the convertible bond value to the underlying equity value can be depicted in a graph composed of three regions as shown below.

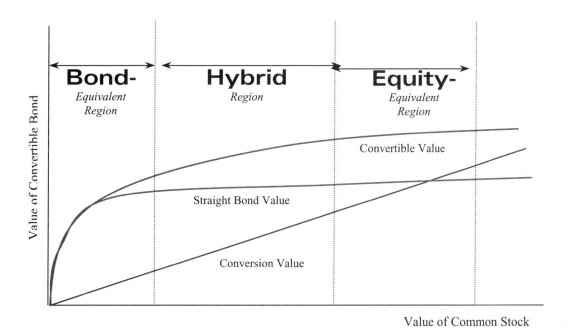

In the **bond-equivalent region**, the conversion price is well above the market price of common stock, so the bond trades like a straight debt instrument. In the **hybrid region**, the bond has characteristics of debt and equity: As the share price increases, the bond increases in value, but since it is trading at a premium, it does not increase at the same rate as the stock. In the **equity-equivalent region**, the common shares have appreciated above the conversion price and the bond then behaves similarly to equity.

To determine the optimal conversion strategy we will use the squeezing technique again: The investor would make a risk-free profit if he purchased the bond when the price of common stock was higher than the conversion price, because he could just buy the bond immediately, convert it and sell the stock. On the other hand, if the conversion price were lower than the current share price, he could short the bond and buy the shares. Thus, the optimal conversion strategy would be to convert the bond when the conversion price is equal to the share price.

$$Conversion\ \Pr ice = \frac{Par\ Value\ of\ Bond}{Conversion\ Ratio}$$

Stock splits and stock dividends will affect the conversion ratio and conversion price of a convertible bond, since more shares will exist. A 2 for 1 stock split will make the preceding bond convertible into 100 shares ($50 x 2), so the new conversion price will be $10 ($20 x ½). A 20% stock dividend will result in 10 more shares for each 50 held, so the conversion ratio will increase by 20% while the conversion price will decline to $16.67.

If the market value of the convertible bond is equal to the market value of the shares it can be converted into, the bond is said to be at *parity*. Most convertible bonds sell at a premium in order to induce investors to hold them (and that call option they sold the company is worth something.)

$$Parity\ \Pr ice\ of\ Bond = Market\ \Pr ice\ of\ Common\ x\ Number\ of\ Shares$$

Example   If common stock is selling at $70/share and the conversion ratio is 20 shares per bond, what price should the bond be to be at parity with the stock? It should sell at $70/share x 20 shares, or $1,400.

Valuing convertible bonds

Step 1: Determine the Minimum Value of the Convertible Bond.
This is the lowest value at which the bond should trade, and is found by comparing the value of the bond as a straight bond without the conversion feature to the parity value.
Step 2: Calculate the investment premium of the bond.
Step 3: Calculate the premium payback period.
Step 4: Calculate value of the embedded convertible bond option.

Example   An Internet start-up issued $500 million of 8-year, 7% convertible bonds when their current stock price was $155/share. The bonds were convertible into 5.263 shares of stock once the stock hit $190. Assume that the bonds are callable and that the stock pays no dividends. If bonds of similar credit quality were yielding 8%, what is the market conversion price, the market premium ratio, the premium payback period and the value of the embedded call option, given that the market price of the bond is $1,200? Assume that the par value of the bond is $1,000 and all coupons are paid annually.

Step 1: First, we must calculate the value of a straight bond (one without the convertible feature). The price of 8-year, 7% coupon bonds priced to yield 8% is 94.17% of par or $941.7. Next, we calculate the conversion value of the bond. We have the conversion ratio k already (but if we didn't, we would just calculate it as par/conversion price = $1,000/190 = 5.263). Then the conversion value of the bond is k times the current share price, 5.263 x $155 = $815.76. We have two prices, which one is right? The minimum price of the bond should be the larger of these two numbers – max (straight bond price, converted share value) = $941.7. If we priced the bond at the lower number $815.76, which assumes immediate conversion, an arb could buy this and have a straight bond worth $941.7.

Step 2: Next, we perform a premium analysis by comparing this bond to a straight bond. We need to figure out what we are really paying for the right to acquire shares.

$$\Pr emium\ Over\ Straight\ Bond = \frac{Market\ \Pr ice\ Convertible\ Bond}{Straight\ Value\ of\ Bond} - 1 = \frac{\$1,200}{\$941.7} - 1 = 27\%.$$

As a side note, we could also figure out the equivalent yield of this convertible bond compared to a straight bond yielding 8% as a way of indicating the premium paid.

So what are we paying per share by acquiring them via the convertible bond? If we converted now,

$$Market\ Conversion\ Price = \frac{Market\ Price\ of\ Convertible\ Bond}{k} = \$1{,}200/5.263 = \$228/share.$$

The conversion premium that we are paying is then the difference between the market conversion price and the current market price, $228 - $155 = $73. The market conversion premium ratio is the premium over the market price of the shares, $73/$155 = 47%.

Step 3: Is this a good deal? We are paying a premium to hold the convertible bond, but we will receive coupon interest on it. The breakeven point will occur where the difference between the coupon interest and the dividends we would receive had we just purchased the stock outright offsets the premium we pay to hold the bond. (In this case, there are no dividends, but the idea is presented anyway.) As a rule of thumb, the payback period should be between 3 and 5 years.

$$Premium\ Payback\ Period = \frac{Market\ Price\ of\ Bond - kP_{CS}}{Coupon\ on\ Bond - kDIV_{CS}} = \frac{\$1{,}200 - 5.263(\$155)}{\$70 - 0} = 5.48\ years.$$

Step 4: Finally, the value of the embedded call. If a convertible bond is neither callable nor putable, it is equivalent to a portfolio consisting of a straight bond plus a call option on the stock at the conversion price. So, $P_{convBond} = P_{straight}$ + call option. The call option can be valued by the Black-Scholes equation. For this bond, with $T = 8$ years, $S = 155$, $K = 190$, $r_f = 5\%$ and $\sigma = 35\%$, the value of the call is $68.35. Since one bond is convertible into 5.263 shares, the price of the convertible bond should be 941.7 + 68.35*5.263 = $1,301. If the bond is callable by the corporation, say, at any time after three years, the investor has essentially written a covered call at the conversion price with maturity three years or greater. The value of the bond is then $P_{convBond} = P_{straight}$ + Call Option – Value of Embedded Call.

Note that the Black-Scholes equation can be used to value the option on the underlying stock, but it cannot be used to value the embedded call. This is because the Black-Scholes equation relies on many assumptions that are not appropriate in valuing bonds. First, it assumes that volatilities are constant, which for bonds is incorrect. As a bond approaches maturity, the duration decreases and the volatility should decrease because the holder receives a known quantity – par – at maturity. Second, it assumes that short-term interest rates are constant, which will cause a significant error in valuation of interest rate sensitive securities. Finally, it is assumed that the distribution of terminal prices is lognormally distributed, with a price of zero as well as an infinitely high price possible, albeit with very low probability. A bond would never be worth more than its par value plus any accrued coupons, so Black-Scholes tends to overprice bond options. As a result, binomial trees should be used to value this option.

Note: Notice how the company in this example was able to raise $500 million by selling these convertible bonds. If all are eventually converted, they will dilute equity by issuing 5.263*$500,000,000/$1,000 par = 2.6 million new shares. Had the company simply sold the same number of shares at a public offering at the current market price of $155, it would have raised only $403 million.

Equity-Specific Derivatives

Equity derivatives include the familiar calls, puts and other combinations. These are valued in the usual way using Black-Scholes or interest rate trees. The foundation for these derivatives is found in chapter 3.

Stock index futures

Futures and forwards on stock indexes work just like the other forwards and futures we have seen, except that instead of physical delivery of a bond, stock or commodity, the contract is settled in cash. The value of the contract is calculated as *(Index Value)(Multiplier)* where the multiplier used depends on the index. For the S&P 500 and S&P 400 the multiplier is $250, for the DJIA it's $10, for the Russell 2000 it's $500 and for the NIKKEI the multiplier is $5.

Thus, the value of the long position at time t is $V_t = $ *(Index Multiplier)*$(F_t\text{-}F_{t\text{-}1})$ where F_t is the index level at time t. The value of the short position is $-V_t$. The multiplier makes it easy to calculate the change in value of position for a change in 1 unit of the underlying, it is just *Index Multiplier*.

Example An investor, Willie, believes that the DJIA will rise over the next three months and decides to purchase a future on the index. She deposits $5,000 in her margin account and instructs her futures broker to perform the transaction. A second investor, Tara, believes that the DJIA will fall over the next three months. She also deposits the margin funds into her account and requests execution of her trade. When the trades hit the futures pit in the CBOT, they are settled at 9925. There is no cash flow until the end of the trading day when the accounts are marked to market. Each day, Willie's account is settled according to $V_t = $ *(Multiplier)*$(F_t\text{-}F_{t\text{-}1})$ and Tara's according to $V_t = -$ *(Multiplier)*$(F_t\text{-}F_{t\text{-}1})$. Suppose that at the end of the first day, the value of the futures contract is 9935. The profit to Willie is $10(9935-9925) = $100 (as promised, $10 for every unit change in the index). Tara's account is debited $100 and her balance is now $4,900. The $100 is passed through the clearinghouse and credited to Willie's account, which now has a balance of $5,100. This process continues on a daily basis until the investors reverse out of their positions or the expiration date of the futures contract.

Suppose that one month passes and the futures contract is now trading at 10100. Willie decides to close out her position. She calls her broker and asks him to sell her position. Her total profit is the sum of the profit and loss over each day, but since *(Multiplier)*$(F_T\text{-}F_{T\text{-}1})+$ *(Multiplier)*$(F_{T\text{-}1}\text{-}F_{T\text{-}2})+ \dots +$ *(Multiplier)*$(F_1\text{-}F_0)$ is the same as *(Multiplier)*$(F_T\text{-}F_0)$, it can be calculated as *($10)*$(F_t\text{-}F_{t\text{-}1}) = $10(10100-9925) = $1,750. Willie walks away with her $6,750. If Tara also closes out her account on the same day, she would walk away with $5,000 + ($1,750) = $3,250. Alternatively, one or both of them can just wait until expiration. At this date, the futures price must converge to the spot price of the index. If the index is 9920 on this date, Willie will lose a total of $50 for the three-month period and Tara will realize a profit of $50. The daily ups and downs could be much more volatile, however.

Forwards on stock indexes work the same way, but cash is settled only at one time (expiry or closing out of the contract.) The net change in portfolio value should be the same whether settled in daily increments as it is in futures contracts or at one point as in a forward.

Stock index futures can be priced using spot-futures parity, $F = S_0 e^{(r_f - \delta)T}$

The dividend yield δ is estimated using historical data or taken from the financial press. For example, the DJIA the dividend yield as of May 13, 2002 was reported to be 1.86% compared to 1.57% one-year prior. If the current level $S_0 = 10109.66$ and the three-month risk free rate is 1.82%, what should be the futures price? $F = 10109.66 e^{(.0182-0.0186).25} = 10,108$.

Hedging with stock index futures contracts

Stock index futures were developed as a hedging vehicle for portfolios of equity securities. The most common scenario is that an investor is long a portfolio of equities and wishes to hedge against adverse price movements. He can hedge by shorting a number of equivalent forward or futures contracts. So his total portfolio consists of a long position in the equity portfolio, Q_P, and a short position in forwards or futures, Q_F. If the value of the portfolio changes by an amount Δ and if the hedge is perfect, the value of the total portfolio should be unchanged: $\Delta V_{CS} + \Delta V_F = 0$. The value of the equity position is the price times the number of shares, and the value of the futures contract is the contract multiplier times the number of contracts, N_F, times the contract size, times the futures price. So a change in price would result in a corresponding change in value of the hedged portfolio of:

$\Delta P_{CS} Q_{CS} + (Index\ Multiplier)(Contract\ Size) N_F \Delta F = 0$

$$\text{Then}\ \ N_F = -\frac{\Delta P_{CS} Q_{CS}}{(Index\ Multiplier)(ContractSize)\Delta F}$$

Defining $\beta_F = -\dfrac{\Delta P_{CS}}{\Delta F}$ we have $N_F = -\beta_F \dfrac{Q_{CS}}{(Index\ Multiplier)(ContractSize)}$

where β_F is the **futures hedge ratio**, obtained by a regression of historical futures price change to underlying price change of equities. The R^2 obtained in the regression indicates the effectiveness of the hedge, while $1-R^2$ is the basis risk of the hedge. Ideally, the portfolio of securities should be hedged with an instrument having $R^2 = 1$. This is not always possible and so there will be basis risk.

Example A portfolio manager has $100,000,000 worth of equity securities. Concerned about his upcoming performance-based bonus, he fears a loss in portfolio value over the next five months. He wants to hedge his portfolio to protect against an anticipated market fall. Since he has mostly large-cap, U.S. domestic stocks in the portfolio, he chooses the 6-month futures contract on the S&P 500 as his hedging vehicle. The current value of the index is 1074 and 6-month futures are 1090. The number of contracts required for a hedge are:

$$N_F = -\beta_F \frac{Quantity\ of\ Equities\ to\ be\ Hedged}{(IndexMultiplier)(ContractSize)} = -\beta_F \frac{\$100,000,000}{\$250(1090)} = -367\beta_F.$$

He runs a regression and determines β_F to be 0.85 so he will need to sell short $367(0.85) = 312$ futures contracts. (You must always round up or down to an integer number because you can't have a fraction of a contract.) Suppose at the end of five months, the S&P500 index is at 1065 and the futures contract is at 1080. What is his gain/(loss) on his portfolio, both hedged and unhedged?

Answer:

Unhedged

Initial value of equity portfolio		$100,000,000
Gain/(Loss) on stocks	$\left[\left(\dfrac{1065-1074}{1074}\right)\$100,000,000\right]0.85 =$	($712,291)
Net Value of Portfolio		$99,287,710
Net Gain/(Loss)		(71 bp)

Hedged (neglecting transactions costs)

Initial value of equity portfolio		$100,000,000
Gain/(Loss) on stocks	$\left[\left(\dfrac{1065-1074}{1074}\right)\$100,000,000\right]0.85 =$	($712,291)

Gain/(Loss) on futures position   (312)($250)(1090-1080)   = $780,000
Net Value of Portfolio $100,067,710
Net Gain/(Loss)   <u>7 bp</u>

The hedging instrument was not perfect so there is some basis risk: risk that at termination the spread between the spot price of the underlying and the futures price of the hedging instrument will not be zero. Also, this hedge should be rebalanced on a daily basis to track fluctuations in β_F. This is called tailing the hedge. But the manager did better than he would have, had he not hedged.

Equity swaps

Suppose an investor desires exposure to Japanese stocks for diversification of a $100,000,000 portfolio but does not wish to, or is unable to, make direct investments in Japanese equities. A corporate treasurer holds a position in the NIKKEI index, but is uncomfortable with this exposure and wishes instead to receive floating-rate LIBOR. (Perhaps this treasurer is required to make floating rate payments to yet another investor and wants to hedge these payments.) These two investors can each receive the exposure they desire by entering into an equity swap. The investor agrees to pay the treasurer LIBOR in exchange for receiving the return on the NIKKEI index on a notional amount, here agreed to be $100,000,000. No notional is exchanged in this transaction, and the payments are netted.

This is an OTC transaction and the cash flows would appear as follows:

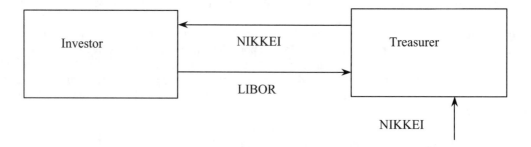

Suppose that the 3-month LIBOR on the date of the agreement is 5%. The return on the NIKKEI over the 3-month period is 10%. Then the treasurer would pay 0.1($100,000,000) = $10,000,000 to the investor. The investor must pay LIBOR/4*$100,000,000 = $1,250,000 to the treasurer. Since payments are netted, the treasurer pays $8,750,000 to the investor. The treasurer originally earned $10,000,000 on his long NIKKEI position. By paying $8,750,000 to the investor, he has a net return of 5% annualized, the LIBOR return he wanted. The investor, in turn, receives the full return from the NIKKEI, the exposure *he* wanted. What if the NIKKEI had lost 15% instead? The treasurer is bound to pay *r*NIKKEI so would receive $15,000,000 from the investor. The investor also has to pay LIBOR so the net position of the treasurer is his NIKKEI loss is covered, he gets LIBOR and the investor is fully exposed to the 15% loss on the NIKKEI, which is what he bargained for.

Sample Questions and Answers

Questions

1.   What should be the return on equity capital of TASER's stock if the risk-free rate is 5%, the expected return on the market is 10% and TASER's beta is 1.78?

2.   What should be next-year's price of TASER if the current ROE is 17.25%, the company pays out no dividends and the current price is $18?

3.   If the net income for the past 12 months was $650,000 and there are 2.8 million shares outstanding, what is the P/E ratio? If the company should be trading at the current P/E of the Dow (20), what would the price be?

4.   Based on a sector price/sales ratio of 6.54, total 12-month trailing sales of 8 million what should the price of TASER be?

5.   Kevin owns 100,000 shares of Ford Motor Company stock for his portfolio. Ford is currently trading at $17.72 with a beta of 1.05. He is concerned that the share price will fall over the next three months but is restricted by his employer from trading options on Ford stock, so he decides to hedge by using futures on the S&P 500. The current level of the S&P 500 is 1073.33. If the futures price is 1085, how many contracts would he have to buy or sell? If he closes out his position in two months when the index is at 1060 and the futures price is 1075, what is his gain/(loss) compared to the gain/(loss) he would have experienced without hedging? Assume zero transaction costs.

6.   Kevin quits and is now allowed to trade options on Ford. If the current risk-free rate is 5%, the annual volatility of Ford stock is 15% and he buys a 3-month put with a strike price of $17, how much does the put cost? How much should a call cost? Assume no dividends will be paid.

7.   Kevin wants to buy more Ford shares but wonders if they are overvalued. He has checked GM and Daimler-Chrysler's P/E ratios and they are 36.23 and 12.41, respectively. He can't calculate Ford's P/E ratio but uses the dividend-discount model to estimate the P/E using the current dividend of $0.40/year, dividend yield of 2.25% and expected growth rate of 5%. What is the P/E ratio on this basis? Assume Ford pays out 30% of its earnings in the form of dividends.

8.   Kevin's broker calls him and tells him about a new 10-year 6% convertible bond issued by Ford Motor Credit that will allow him to convert into Ford stock when Ford reaches $25/share. If he buys the bond, what effective price is he paying for the shares and how long will it take him to break even? Assume that Ford maintains the dividend yield of 2.25%, and the bond is selling at 110% of par (i.e., $1,100) and makes annual payments. The 10-year treasury bond is currently yielding 6.5%. Is this bond a good deal?

Answers

1.   Use the CAPM to find $R_s = R_f + \beta(R_m - R_s) = 5\% + 1.78(10\%-5\%) = 13.9\%$. This is the required return on equity capital that should be used in discounting future free cash flows to equity.

2.   Since the company pays no dividends, we can't use the model

$$P = \frac{DIV_0(1+g)}{r_{CE} - g} = \frac{KE_0(1+g)}{r_{CE} - g}$$

However, we can use the ROE. If we assume that TASER will grow only because it plows back earnings, the growth rate should equal ROE, in fact $g = ROE(1-K)$ but since K, the dividend payout

Thus $g = r = 17.25\%$.   Then $P_1 = P_0(1+g) = \$18(1.1725) = \$21.11$.

ratio, $= 0$ we have $g = ROE = 17.25\%$. Since $r = \dfrac{P_1 + DIV - P_0}{P_0} = \dfrac{P_0(1+g) + DIV - P_0}{P_0} = \dfrac{DIV}{P_0} + g$

3.　　Earnings/share = net income/number of shares outstanding = \$650,000/2.8 million shares = \$0.23/share, P/E = \$18/0.23 = 77.58. If price is 20 times earnings, the price should be \$4.6/share.

4.　　Price/Sales = 6.54, sales/share = \$8 million/2.8 million, so price = (P/S) (Sales) = 6.54(8/2.8) = \$18.68.

5.　　The quantity of equities to be hedged = number of shares times share price = 100,000 times \$17.72. The number of futures contracts for the hedge is calculated from

$$N_F = -\beta_F \frac{Quantity\ of\ Equities\ to\ Hedge}{(Contract\ Multiplier)(Contract\ Size)} = -1.05 \frac{\$\$1,772,000}{(\$250)(1085)} = -7.$$

Since he is long the stock he must short seven futures contracts.   After two months, he closes out his position. *(Note: actual answer above for N_F is –6.86 but you have to round to the nearest integer.)*

Unhedged Position

Initial Portfolio Holdings	\$1,772,000
Gain/(Loss) on stock**	(\$23,107.3)
Total position, unhedged	\$1,748,892.6
Effective Share Price	\$17.488
Net Gain/(Loss) per share	(\$0.231)

** *Need to estimate the return on the Ford stock using CAPM.*
Return on market = -1.24%, estimated return on Ford stock = -1.24%*1.05 = -1.3%, loss on stock is then (\$23,107.3).

Hedged Position
Here, he has the gain/(loss) of the futures position, equal to \$250*7*(1085-1075) = \$17,500, so his total position is \$1,768,501+\$17,500 = \$1,786,001. Effective share price is \$17.86 for a gain of 14 cents/share. His actual profit/(loss) could have gone either way, because he closed out of the hedge before maturity, was not tailing the hedge, and the correlation between Ford and the S&P 500 futures market may not have been stable over this period.

6.　　The correlation between an equity option and the underlying stock should be close to perfect when the same equity is used as a hedging vehicle. Since there are 100 shares per option contract whether call or put, he will need 1,000 put contracts. The Black-Scholes equation is used to value the put: using $T = 0.25$ we find $d1 = 0.7572$, $N(d1) = 0.776$, and so $p = \$0.179$. He will have to pay a total of 100 contracts (\$0.179/contract) = \$17.9 option premium.   The call can be valued using put-call parity: $S + p - c = Ke^{-rT}$ so $c = \$17.72 + 0.179 - 17e^{-0.05/4} = \$1.11$. This checks with the Black-Scholes equation as well.

7.　　Since $r = Div/Price + g = Div\ Yield + g = 2.25\% + 5\% = 7.25\%$, P/E $= K(1+g)/(r_{ce}-g) = 30\%(1.05)/(7.25\%-5\%) = 14$. On this basis he decides that the price for Ford seems reasonable.

8.   First, figure out the market price of the straight bond. This is most easily done with a financial calculator, although Excel can also be used. Price = 96.365% of par, or $963.65. Next figure out the conversion ratio k, which is k = (par value)/(conversion price of shares) = $1,000/$25 = 40 shares. So, if he bought the bond today, he could immediately convert into 40 shares, but, at the current price of $17.72, this wouldn't be optimal – because the value of these shares is only $708.8. This gives us the minimum price for the bond as max(value of straight bond, converted share value) = max(963.65,708.8) = $963.65.

The market premium of the bond is the (market price of the bond)/(straight value of bond)-1 = $1,100/963.65-1 = 14.14%. If you buy the shares by buying the bond and converting, the current price you would pay is (market price of convertible bond)/k = $1,100/40 = $27.5/share. The conversion premium is just the difference between the market conversion price and the current market price, $27.5 - $17.72 = $9.78/share.

We now need to decide whether this is a good deal or not. The premium payback period is (market Price of Bond - kP_{CS})/(Coupon on Bond - $kDIV_{CS}$). If current price is $17.72 and dividend yield is 2.25%, we calculate DIV as 0.0225*17.72 = $0.40, then premium payback period *is* ($1,100 – 40*17.72)/(0.06*$1,000 – 40*0.40) = 8.891 years. Because we typically expect the payback period to be within 3 to 5 years, the bond is not a good deal.

The convertible bond gives him an implicit call option on the underlying with a strike of $25. Using Black-Scholes with r_f = 6.5%, σ = 15% (assumed), S = 17.72 and K = 25, we get c = $5.782. But one bond can be converted into 40 shares. The price of the convertible bond should be the sum of the prices of the straight bond and the call option, the convertible bond should be priced at 963.65 + 5.782*40= $1194.93. The market price is lower than this, thus it is an indication that the bond may be a good deal when we consider the value of the call option.

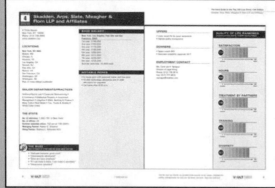

CURRENCY
AND
COMMODITY
MARKETS

Currency and commodity markets risks affect a wide variety of entities. Multinational corporations that do business in a foreign currency are exposed to currency risks. Companies that purchase a lot of raw production inputs, such as copper or palladium, are exposed to commodity risk. For example, airline companies are exposed to commodity risk because their profitability is highly dependent on jet fuel costs. Farmers, too, are exposed to commodity risk because they're exposed to price risk with respect to their crops. In order to hedge against currency and commodity risks, these and other types of businesses will typically look to the futures, forwards and swaps markets.

Currency Swaps

What is a currency swap?

A **currency swap** involves an exchange of interest payments and notionals in two different currencies. Suppose that a U.S. company (Vern) issued bonds in Japan. The company has foreign currency exposure because the proceeds of the bonds are in JPY and interest rate payments must be made in JPY. Should the company wish to hedge this exposure, it could buy a JPY forward contract for each interest rate payment date (paying in USD for the JPY that will be used to make the contracted JPY interest payments). However, this could get expensive. The result of this series of transactions is the transformation of a JPY-denominated liability into a USD-denominated liability. Or, perhaps the company simply prefers a U.S. dollar-denominated liability, rather than just needing it to hedge exposure to JPY. A practical solution to both scenarios is to enter into a currency swap. A currency swap is an OTC transaction that may be put together by a swaps dealer who will find a counterparty. Suppose a Japanese company (Ty) has issued bonds in the U.S. market and wishes to transform this debt into yen denominated liability. The swap dealer could match up Ty with Vern, making a swap. Currency swaps can be fixed-fixed, floating-floating or fixed-floating.

Mechanics of the Currency swap

Initiation: Both parties exchange notional (principal). If Vern exchanges $N_¥ = 100$ million yen, Ty will exchange the equivalent number of USD, calculated with the current spot rate, so Ty exchanges $N_{US} = S(0)$ $N_¥ = ¥100,000,000*0.008559$ USD/ ¥ =$805,900 where $S(0)$ is the current spot exchange rate. The effect of this exchange of principal at initiation is that each party gets rid of the currency they don't want and receives currency that they do want. Because the current spot rate was used, the value of the swap at initiation is zero. Note that the exchange of principal differentiates a currency swap from an interest rate swap, although there are currency swaps where exchange of principal is not required.

During swap period: At agreed-upon intervals, usually semi-annually, counterparties exchange interest payments. Vern must pay in USD and Ty must pay in ¥. If Vern is paying 6% USD, it will pay an annual rate of 6% of the USD notional it received, or $24,177 every six months. If Ty is to pay 3% on JPY notional per year, it will make payments of ¥1,500,000 to Vern. Recall that for an interest rate swap, the payments were netted. In contrast, for a currency swap, payments are usually made by both sides, otherwise netting could only occur if one currency were translated into the other.

Termination of swap: Counterparties give back the notional they received at the beginning of the swap.

Absolute advantage: One argument often put forward for the popularity of currency swaps is the idea of absolute, or comparative, advantage. Suppose that the companies Vern and Ty can borrow at the following rates in the U.S. and Japanese markets:

Company	Borrowing Rate in US Market	Borrowing Rate in Japanese Market
Vern	6.0%	3.0%
Ty	6.4%	5.2%

Recall that Vern wants USD and Ty wants ¥. Vern can borrow at lower rates in both markets than Ty can, because Vern is probably more credit-worthy than Ty. If Ty wants to borrow in the U.S. market, it would have to pay 6.4%, unless Ty can get Vern to borrow (and thus make the payments) for it. This is the motivation for the absolute advantage argument. Even though Ty still has to pay a higher rate than Vern in the U.S. market, the spread between the rate it pays and the rate Vern pays is only 0.4%, while in the Japanese market, the spread is 2.2%. So Ty appears to have a comparative advantage in the U.S. market and Vern in the Japanese market. Here's how the currency would work:

Each company borrows currency in the market in which it has the comparative advantage. Thus, Vern borrows in the Japanese market at 3% and Ty borrows in the U.S. market at 6.4%. Vern must borrow ¥100,000,000 and Ty, $805,900. The principal payments are exchanged. Now Vern has a USD-denominated loan and Ty has a Japanese-denominated loan. The diagram below shows one possible outcome of the agreement with an intermediary.

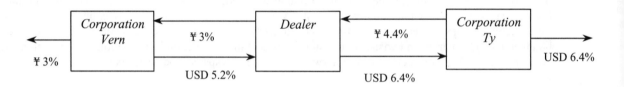

The net borrowing cost to Vern is 6%-5.2%+3%-3% = 0.8%. Use of the swap enabled Vern to effectively borrow U.S. funds at 5.2%, a savings of 0.8% over what it could have gotten had it gone to the market itself. For Ty's part, it is paying ¥4.4% when it would have had to pay 5.2%, so it saves 0.8%. The dealer makes a profit of ¥1.4% and pays USD 1.2%. If exchange rates remain stable, he has a net gain of 0.2%. The total value created is then 1.8%. This is typical of swaps with comparative advantage and it can be shown that the total net gains to be divided between all parties is $a - b$, where a is the largest market spread (here, Japanese market, 5.2% - 3% = 2.2%) and b is the smaller spread (US market, 6.4% - 6%). The distribution of this spread depends on who has the most leverage. In a case like this one, Vern should get more of the advantage than Ty.

Valuing currency swaps

Valuation of a currency swap is straightforward. All we need is the current spot rate and term structures of interest rates in each currency. The value of a swap where dollars are received and the foreign currency is paid is

$$V_{swap} = V_{domestic} - S_0 V_{foreign}$$

The "domestic" currency is the currency we want to calculate the swap in (also called the numeraire) and S_0 is the current spot exchange rate. The swap must be priced so that its value at initiation is zero. Then $V_{swap} = V_{domestic} - S(0) V_{foreign} = 0$.

Example Suppose that we wish to price a two-year JPY-USD swap with semi-annual interest payments. The current exchange rate is 0.008059 ¥/$ and the principals are ¥100,000,000 and $805,900. The intermediary to the swap will receive 4% in ¥ and pay 5% in USD, using continuous compounding. Assume flat term structures in U.S. and Japan. U.S. LIBOR is flat at 6% and Japanese LIBOR is flat at 3%. Just take the PV of each set of cash flows in each currency, then convert one to the other using the spot rate.

Japanese Cash Flows: semi-annual interest payment is 0.04/2*¥100,000,000 = ¥2,000,000. PV is then

$$PV = 2,000,000\left(e^{-0.5*0.03} + e^{-1.0*0.03} + e^{-1.5*0.03} + e^{-2.0*0.03}\right) + 100,000,000e^{-2.0*0.03} = ¥101,883,092.$$

US Cash Flows: semi-annual interest payment is 0.05/2*$805,900=$20,147.5.
PV is then

$$PV = \$20,147.5\left(e^{-0.5*0.06} + e^{-1.0*0.06} + e^{-1.5*0.06} + e^{-2.0*0.06}\right) + \$805,900e^{-2.0*0.06} = \$789,578.$$

Now if the numeraire is USD, the Japanese Yen PV is converted to USD at the current spot rate, thus, V_{swap} = $V_{domestic}$ - $S(0)$ $V_{foreign}$ = $789,578 – 0.008059USD/¥*¥101,883,092 = -$31,497.75.

Since the value of the swap must be zero at initiation, the payments would have to be adjusted by an iterative process (perhaps using Excel's Solver function or Goalseek function, which solves equations for the unknown x that satisfies the equation $f(x)$ = some value) until V_{swap} = 0.

Example Now suppose that the term structure of each currency is as shown below. Now what is the value of the swap to the intermediary?

Time, Months	R_{US}	R_{Japan}	Z_{US}	Z_{Japan}
6	4.5%	1.5%	0.97775	0.99253
12	5.5%	2.5%	0.94649	0.97531
18	6.5%	3.5%	0.90710	0.94885
24	7.5%	4.5%	0.86071	0.91393

The calculations are performed in the same way as in the previous example (we use the zero bond notation here just as a shortcut).

Japanese Cash Flows: semi-annual interest payment is 0.04/2*¥100,000,000 = ¥2,000,000. PV is then
$$PV = 2,000,000\left(Z_{0.5} + Z_1 + Z_{1.5} + Z_2\right) + 100,000,000Z_2 = ¥99,054,240.$$

US Cash Flows: semi-annual interest payment is 0.05/2*$805,900=$20,147.5. PV is then
$$PV = \$20,147.5\left(Z_{0.5} + Z_1 + Z_{1.5} + Z_2\right) + \$805,900Z_2 = \$768,032.$$

If the numeraire is USD, the Japanese Yen PV is converted to USD at the current spot rate, thus, V_{swap} = $V_{domestic}$ - $S(0)$ $V_{foreign}$ = $768,030 – 0.008059USD/¥*¥99,054,240 = -30,246.35.

Currency Swaps

Commodities can also be swapped and hedged. For example, in the 1980s, fuel costs accounted for about 30% of an airline's total operating costs but, due to hedging and introduction of fuel-efficient jets, now only account for about 16% of operating costs. Still, this is a substantial cost. Rising fuel costs can have a tremendous adverse impact on airlines' profit margins. A **commodity swap** works like this: An airline determines its periodic needs of the commodity and enters into an agreement with a dealer to pay a flat rate of X in return for some value Y, which is usually the average of some prior period's prices. This Y could, for example, be the average spot price for the prior month. If S_{avg} is higher than X, the airline makes a profit, which helps to offset the higher cost of buying in the spot market. If S_{avg} is less than X, the airline loses on the swap but makes up for it by being able to purchase fuel at a lower price in the spot market. It effectively locks in the price X.

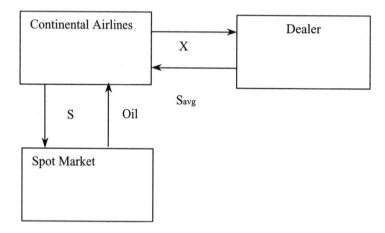

A commodity swap can be valued just like an interest rate swap. It can get more complicated, though, when the commodity is denominated in a different currency. Even so, you have all the building blocks needed to value such swaps.

Commodity futures pricing

Commodities futures pricing has been covered in some detail in the derivatives chapter. The general relationship for futures pricing is the spot-futures parity relationship developed there, $F_{t,T} = (S_t+s)e^{r(T-t)}$. However, be aware that behavior of commodity futures contracts differs from interest rate, stock index or currency contracts, in that physical delivery of the contract often occurs. This can result in market squeezes and corners that can make ultimate settlement price very different from the expected forward price.

Futures and expected spot prices

If we look at the prices of some different commodities we see something very surprising.

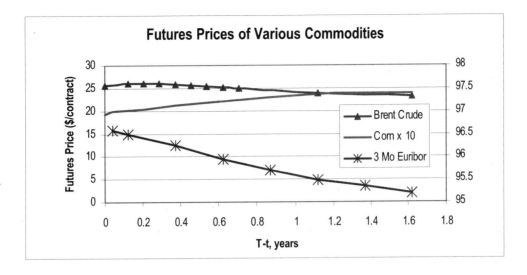

While the futures prices for corn increase with time, the prices for brent crude and the 3-Month Euribor Futures decrease with time. (Euribor, short for Euro Interbank Offered Rate, is the benchmark rate of the euro money market; it's the rate at which euro interbank term deposits are offered by one prime bank to another prime bank.)

Normally, for storable commodities, we expect prices to increase with time. The spread of futures prices to spot prices can be positive or negative. In cases where the futures prices exceed expected future spot prices, we say that the market is in **contango**. When futures prices are equal to the expected future spot price with carry costs $(S_t+s)e^{r(T-t)}$, the market is at **full carry**. If the futures prices are below the expected future spot prices, the market is said to be in **backwardation**.

Various economic theories have been advanced that explain this phenomenon. Consider the crude oil prices. Why should they decrease with time? Can we make a profit by buying oil futures and selling spot oil today? To answer this question we have to examine the market forces (supply and demand are the major forces) causing the decreasing futures price behavior. If supplies today are scarce (inventories are low), the spot price will go up. If it is anticipated that either demand will lessen or supplies will increase in the future, then futures prices can be lower than current spot prices. You can't make a profit because, to do so, you would have to have some spot oil to sell in the market today. If you already own it, you would be trying to sell it at the high price. If you don't own it, you will have to sell it short, but no one will lend it to you. What about the corn? This price increases with time, but in order to find out whether the futures prices are higher than the expected future spot prices, we would have to know the carry cost of the corn.

The apparently bizarre behavior of 3-month Euribor prices is simply a function of how these series are calculated. It turns out that the convention for quoting 3-month Euribor futures prices is $r_3 = (100-F_t)/100$ where r_3 is the 3-month interest rate that is expected to prevail and F_t is the futures price. For example, if we read a quote of 96.25 for Sept02, this just means that the expected 3-month rate starting in Sept02 is $r_3 = (100-96.25)/100 = 3.75\%$. We will have more to say about interest rates in a later section of this chapter. In conclusion, there are some situations where futures prices are good estimators of future expected spot prices, and other cases where they are not. You really have to be very familiar with the particular market of interest before trading futures.

Sample Questions and Answers

Questions

1.   Outline a currency swap between companies *A* and B given their borrowing rates in the U.S. and Mexican markets. What is the net value created by the swap?

Company	Borrowing Rate in US Market	Borrowing Rate in Mexican Market
A	6.0%	4.2%
B	7.0%	4.8%

2.   What is the value at initiation of a fixed-fixed 2-year JPY-USD currency swap? The counterparties make semi-annual interest payments. The current exchange rate is 125¥/USD and the notional is ¥100,000,000. The yen-receiver will receive annual coupons of 2% in ¥ and pay 4% in USD. The Japanese yield curve is expected to remain flat at 2.5% and LIBOR is expected to remain flat at 5%.

3.   What is the value of a fixed-fixed 2-year currency swap where one counterparty receives 5% USD on a notional of $1,000,000 and the other receives 6% on USD $1,000,000 using semi-annual payments and continuous compounding?

4.   Hildy, a designer on the show "Trading Spaces," is concerned about the possible price increase of black, interior latex paint. She wishes to lock in a future price for delivery in six months. The current price of her favorite designer brand paint is $24/gallon. She observes the following data (prices per gallon):

Spot Price (June 02)	Futures Price July 02	Futures Price Aug 02	Futures Price Sept 02	Futures Price Dec 02
$24	$22	$21	$20.05	$19

Is the market in contango, full carry or backwardation? Assume that the risk-free rate is 5% and the annual carrying costs (storage) for one gallon of paint are $0.50/gallon. What is the theoretical spot price in Dec 02? What could be an explanation for this behavior of futures prices?

5.   Could a profit be made in this market by short-selling the paint?

6.   The copper market is currently in backwardation and the economy is expected to slow. What do you expect will happen to the degree of backwardation in the copper market? Will copper prices become more or less volatile? What will happen to the link between copper spot prices and forward prices?

Answers

1.   For an effective swap, each country should borrow in the market in which it has a comparative advantage. *A* would borrow USD and *B* would borrow Pesos. Hopefully, this is the currency that each company wishes to trade. The net value created by the swap is the difference in the spreads in each market, or $(A\text{-}B)_{US} - (A\text{-}B)_{Mexican} = 1\% - 0.6\% = 0.4\%$. This is available to be divided between the two counterparties, usually weighted proportionate to their leverage. (That is, the company with the better credit rating gets more.)

One realization of the swap could look like this:

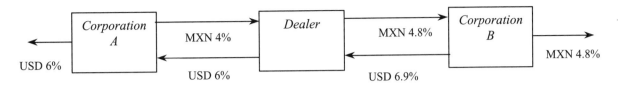

The net borrowing cost to *A* is MXN 4.0%, a savings of 0.2% over what it could have gotten had it gone to the market itself. For *B*'s part, it is paying USD6.9% when it would have had to pay 7.0%, so it saves 0.1%. The dealer makes a profit of USD 0.9% and pays MXN 0.8%. If exchange rates remain stable, he has a net gain of 0.1%. The total value created is then 0.4%.

2. The value of the swap at initiation is $V_{swap} = V_{domestic} - S_0 V_{foreign}$

where the "domestic" currency is the currency we want to calculate the swap in (also called the numeraire), and S_0 is the current spot exchange rate. The swap must be priced so that its value at initiation is zero. Then $V_{swap} = V_{domestic} - S(0) V_{foreign} = 0$.

The notional in ¥ is ¥100,000,000, so the notional in USD is $800,000. For flat term structures of U.S. LIBOR = 5% and Japanese LIBOR = 2.5%, we just take the PV of each set of cash flows in each currency, then convert one to the other using the spot rate.

Japanese Cash Flows: semi-annual interest payment is 0.02/2*¥100,000,000 = ¥1,000,000. PV is then
$$PV = 1,000,000\left(e^{-0.5*0.025} + e^{-1.0*0.025} + e^{-1.5*0.025} + e^{-2.0*0.025}\right) + 100,000,000 e^{-2.0*0.025} = ¥99,000,254$$
U.S. Cash Flows: semi-annual interest payment is 0.04/2*$800,000=$16,000. PV is then

$$PV = \$16,000\left(e^{-0.5*0.05} + e^{-1.0*0.05} + e^{-1.5*0.05} + e^{-2.0*0.05}\right) + \$800,000 e^{-2.0*0.05} = \$784,016.$$
Now if the numeraire is USD, the Japanese Yen PV is converted to USD at the current spot rate, thus, V_{swap} = $V_{domestic} - S(0) V_{foreign} = \$784,016 - (1/125)(USD/¥)*¥99,000,254 = -7,986.17$.

(But isn't the value at initiation supposed to be zero? Yes, so one of the fixed-rate payments would be adjusted until equilibrium was attained. Which should be adjusted, and what should the rate be? We leave it up to you to answer -- it's easy.)

3. No one would do this. Fixed-fixed swaps are only done with cross-currencies. Why would someone agree to pay US 6% fixed to receive US 5%? The value of the swap must be zero at initiation in order to avoid disadvantaging either party.

4. The expected spot price six months from now is computed using spot-futures parity as $F_{t,T} = (S_t + s)e^{r(T-t)} = (\$24 + \$0.50)e^{0.05(0.5)} = \$25.12$. Since the quoted futures price is lower than the expected future spot price, the market is in *backwardation*. Prices for commodities such as these generally depend on supply and demand. Perhaps supply is short right now so that spot prices are driven up over what they would be normally, and perhaps other producers are expected to come online in the near future. Since the spot price is high today, there is incentive to put off purchases for the future and for any holders of paint to sell now. This seems to indicate a short-term squeeze -- Hildy is buying up so much black paint that it is now in short supply. Or, it may be expected that demand for black paint is high now but may be falling off sharply in the future -- perhaps it is speculated that Hildy will be leaving the show.

5. That depends. You could sell the paint short, collecting $24 now, and expecting that the price will fall as the future prices imply so that you can re-buy at the lower price later when it is time to deliver.

However, there is no guarantee that the spot prices implied by the futures prices will actually be realized. If you wanted to hedge your short sale, you would buy a futures contract locking in a price of $19 (agreeing to buy paint at this price), then you could make a profit of $5/gallon (less carrying costs) now. The counterparty that enters the other side agrees to deliver paint at $19/gallon. It can be assumed that he does not have it right now, or he would probably sell it at current spot. When it is time for delivery, the dynamics of the marketplace might cause the spot price to rise as any shorts rush to cover their positions.

6.   As economic growth slows, demand will slow. Less copper will be purchased. Copper producers will be operating at lower capacity and existing stores will not be consumed. The market may move toward contango (backwardation occurs when there are scarcity of resources). Volatility of copper prices occurs because of mismatches between supply and demand. At expiration of contracts, spot prices and futures prices converge. If economic growth slows enough, copper producers may reduce their supplies to such a degree that copper stores are completely consumed and the market will then be in backwardation. In this case, prices become volatile. In a full-carry market, there is a strong link between spot and futures prices $F_{t,T} = S_T e^{r(T-t)}$. This link is weakened as the market goes into backwardation, and can even be broken.

RISK
MANAGEMENT

The need for effective **risk management** has exploded over the past decade. Story after story of huge derivatives losses at companies such as Barings Bank, Gibson Greetings, Procter & Gamble, Showa Shell, Metallgesellschaft, Sumitomo, and Long Term Capital have illuminated the need for effective risk measurement, management and controls. Derivatives are not inherently dangerous. But the combination of potentially infinite exposure and the lack of internal controls can be devastating. Potential sources of risk include: market risk, business risk, event risk, credit risk, strategy risk, model risk, sovereign risk and foreign exchange rate risk. In earlier sections we saw how we use negatively correlated holdings to diversify away risk. So why do we need any further risk management techniques? Because, among other reasons, many risks aren't adequately understood or quantified, the unexpected catastrophic ("six sigma") event does happen, and many hedging vehicles are imperfect. If risk can't be completely hedged away, at the very least, exposure and risk sources should be quantified. This is the goal of **value at risk.**

When returns are reported, they should be risk-adjusted. If one trader earned a 10% return on a risky, highly-leveraged portfolio, while another trader earned 7% on a municipal bond portfolio, did the first trader actually perform better when risks are taken into account?

It is difficult to imagine any financial valuation that does not depend on the discounted present value of future expected cash flows. This is the heart of finance. But what should this discount factor be? We have used different definitions depending on what chapter of the book we were in. For example, in the equities section, we used the cost of equity capital; in the fixed income section, we used a series of forward rates matching the maturity of the cash flow being received. But the common theme in valuation of all financial instruments is that the discount rate used should capture and reflect all relevant sources of risk. Thus, we should capture default rate risk, interest rate risk, business risk, foreign exchange rate risk and so on, as appropriate to the problem at hand. Discussion of these sources of risk is the focus of this chapter.

Measuring Market Risk: Value at Risk

Market risk, which includes risks of changes in prices, interest rates and correlations, is the possibility that future cash flows will be different from expected cash flows. **Value at Risk (VaR)** is the economic loss that can be expected at a given confidence level under adverse market conditions. VaR can be calculated by using statistical properties of the normal distribution or through simulation. Monte Carlo analysis can be run in order to generate a distribution of possible payoffs and then quantifying the worst-case scenarios. VaR is fast becoming the accepted standard for reporting risk. Value at risk methods can be applied to all instruments. They are simply decomposed into "primitive" instruments (for example, a convertible bond would be decomposed into an equity instrument and a fixed income bond) and the VaR of each instrument calculated. The VaR of the portfolio is then constructed using the covariance matrix relating the primitive instruments. For many instruments, a linear aR is used, while for others, non-linear methods such as delta-gamma VaR is necessary.

Absolute risk is the value of risk quantified in dollar terms. **Relative risk** (sometimes referred to as **tracking error**) is loss measured against some benchmark, such as expected mean.

There are two factors contributing to any loss: the exposure and the adverse movement of the risk factor. Exposure is increased by leverage, which is one reason the derivatives losses have been so spectacular.

To measure value at risk, you first evaluate all possible risk exposures and choose a confidence level. Generally, 95%, 97.5% and 99% are all used. A time horizon is also chosen (for example, daily, every ten days, quarterly, and so on) over which you wish to quantify exposure.

Suppose you are managing a large cash fund of $15,000,000. Historically, the mean return has been 5% and the daily standard deviation 0.2%. Assuming that the returns follow a normal distribution, the cumulative probability distribution could be drawn as:

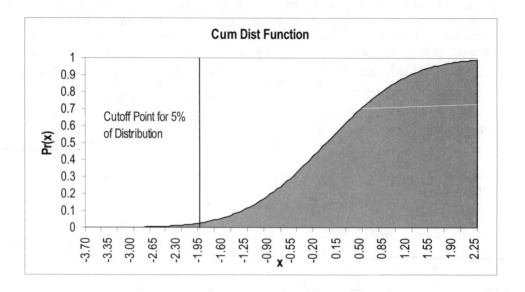

From the cumulative distribution function above, we find that 5% of the distribution lies to the left of $\alpha = -1.65$. A short table below summarizes these measures.

c	$1-c$	α
99%	1.00%	-2.326342
97.50%	2.50%	-1.959961
95%	5.00%	-1.644853
68.26%	31.74%	-0.474981
50%	50.00%	0

$0.0033 + 0.06$

If the mean is 5%, the cumulative distribution tells us that 50% of the time we expect a return lower than the mean, and the other 50% of the time we expect a return higher than the mean. With $\alpha = 95\%$, this means that 5 times in 100 we expect a return *lower* than $1.65*\sigma + \mu$, or 0.17%. The value at risk is the value within this left tail, which basically is just the answer to the question, "How much would we lose if a 2σ event occurs?" Value at risk can be calculated as a relative value to the mean, or in absolute dollar terms.

If V_0 is the value of the portfolio, the expected return is $(1+\mu)$ so the expected portfolio value would be $V_0(1+\mu)$. If the cutoff value at a confidence level of $1-c$ is $R_\alpha = \alpha*\sigma + \mu$ then the expected value of the portfolio under this scenario would be $V_0 (1+ R_\alpha)$ and the expected loss, $V_0 (1+ R_\alpha)-V_0(1+\mu) = V_0 (R_\alpha-\mu) = V_0 (\alpha*\sigma + \mu - \mu) = V_0\,\alpha*\sigma$.

For our example, at a 95% confidence level we would compute the expected value at risk as $15,000,000*-1.65*0.002 = \$49,500$.

The value at risk, then, provides the exposure in a single number. We have both the potential "worst case" loss, and the confidence level. Of course, VaR is not a guarantee, because extreme events (3σ events or greater) do happen. Even so, it is a first step. When used within a portfolio, VaR provides us with a common framework to identify and quantify risks of various instruments and positions.

VaR Over Longer Time Intervals

To extend the analysis out to a longer interval, just adjust s in the normal way – it scales as $\sqrt{t}$ so if we have daily volatility, to estimate annual volatility, $\sigma_{annual} = \sigma_{daily}\sqrt{t} \cong \sigma_{daily}\sqrt{250}$. Then VaR would be

$$VAR \cong V_0 \alpha \sigma \sqrt{t}$$

Types of risk

Directional risk is the exposure to direction changes in market variables. Some risk factors are asymmetric and depend on the direction of movement. Examples include duration for the exposure of bonds to interest rate risk, beta for exposure of equities to the market index, and delta for quantification of portfolio exposure to movements of the underlying.

Non-directional risk includes convexity, volatility and gamma as well as the residual or non-systematic risk in equity portfolios. So total risk will consist of both directional and non-directional terms.

For example, if you have sold a naked call, you are at risk if the price of the underlying increases. Your exposure in this case is potentially infinite. On the other hand, if the price of the underlying remains below the exercise price, there is no exposure. This type of risk depends on the strike price. The higher it is, the more the underlying can increase before there is a risk of loss. For CMOs, we saw that most of the tranches would be exposed to loss if interest rates increase (positive convexity) but that the value of the residual tranche will increase in a rising rate environment.

Credit risk is the risk of default on an obligation, such as a default on a bond, as well as the risk of ratings downgrades by agencies.

Counterparty risk is the risk that a counterparty in an OTC transaction will simply walk away from its obligation. Counterparty risk is a major concern in interest rate and currency swaps. If A is paying floating and B fixed, and rates increase dramatically, A may simply decide to default. B is at risk whenever it is in a net-gain position, since A will have incentive to not honor the obligation. Counterparty risk may be calculated on the basis of an average, maximum or potential exposure. For a bond holder, the counterparty risk is that the holder will not receive the par value of the bond (notional), so the maximum loss would be the principal plus last coupon assuming that all coupons were received to that point. Since notionals are not exchanged in an interest rate swap, the counterparty risk is much lower, typically 10-15% of notional. For a currency swap, counterparty risk is about 20-30% of notional.

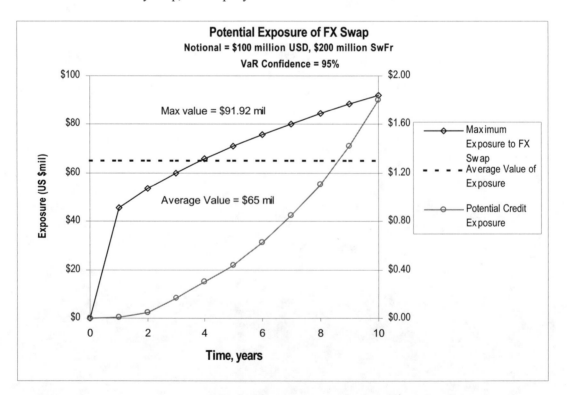

Event risk is the risk of corporate events such as mergers and acquisitions, credit downgrades, dividend reductions, leveraged buyout, lawsuits or other events with significant impact on the balance sheet. This would also include events such as war or collapse of the oil market.

Liquidity risk is the risk that instruments may not be readily liquidated. If a corporation faces a large margin call (think of the Barings example) and it does not have sufficient cash on hand, it will have to borrow quickly or liquidate holdings. If it is holding a large portfolio of CMOs or real estate, it may have to sell at a large discount since it won't have time for normal price-setting and due diligence to occur.

Model risk is the risk of using an inadequate or inappropriate model. There was a hedge fund trader named David Askin who lost millions for this reason. In CMOs, Askew had invested about $600 million, which was increased to $2 billion with his use of leverage. He marketed his fund as zero-risk and claimed zero correlation with any other instruments. Instead of using dealer prices, he used the prices returned from his proprietary model in attempt to identify undervalued securities. He ended up losing almost the entire value of the portfolio. He was sanctioned by the SEC and barred from the investment community.

Settlement risk, also known as **Herstatt risk**, refers to the risk that a settlement will not take place as anticipated. This type of risk has particular importance in foreign currency transactions, where there might be a significant lag between payment and subsequent delivery. The name Herstatt comes from the infamous 1974 case of the small German Bank, Bankhaus Herstatt, which was ordered into liquidation at the close of the German trading day, after the interbank trading system had closed. Several of Herstatt's counterparties had made payments prior to the liquidation, expecting to receive Deutschmark payments later in the day. It was only 10:30 a.m. New York time when the bank was liquidated, leaving creditors exposed – because, no matter what the underlying transaction (currency swaps, forward currency translations or DM purchases) was, creditors did not receive what they had paid for. For example, suppose a New York bank had an agreement with the Herstatt bank to enter into a currency swap. (Recall that notionals are exchanged in a currency swap.) Say the New York bank wired $10,000,000 USD to Germany at 10:30 am, expecting an offsetting amount to be returned in Deutschmarks. (Also recall that the value of any swap is zero at initiation.) By the time the money was wired, the German bank would have already closed down, thus there would be no possibility to get the counterbalancing notional. The Bankhaus Herstatt case was a major factor in today's practice of netting, where only net payments are exchanged.

Specific risk, or **nonsystematic risk**, is the risk due to strategy, key person, or price movements specific to the issuer. The total price movement should be the sum of the price movements attributable to the market factor, measured by the sensitivity to this factor β; and the issuer-sensitive price movement:

$$\Delta P_i = (\beta_i P_i)R_m + (\varepsilon_i P_i) = \text{market price risk} + \text{issuer-specific price risk}$$

Currency risk

This includes the risk of devaluation and currency volatility. It is linked to anticipated inflation and interest rates in the two countries through interest rate parity. Currency risk can be defined as the risk of adverse exchange rate movements. Multinational companies can be affected by both translation exposure and transaction exposure.

Transaction exposure is the exposure that results when commitments exist to transact future business in foreign currencies. If unhedged, exchange rate gains and losses may result. For example, if a Japanese company signs a contract to purchase $100,000,000 of real estate in New York when the exchange rate is ¥100/USD, the cost is anticipated as ¥10 billion. If the exchange rate changes over the year to ¥125/USD (the ¥ has depreciated against the dollar), the cost to the Japanese firm will be ¥12.5 bn, a 25% increase. Recall that the expected exchange rate may be calculated by EIRP (Expected Interest Rate Parity) as

$$E(F_0) = S_0 \left(\frac{1 + r_{dom}}{1 + r_f} \right)^t$$

where S_0 is the current exchange rate, domestic/foreign and $E(F_0)$ is the expected future exchange rate in the same units. Interest rate parity is expected to hold in the long run if globalization and free capital markets exist, but may not hold in the short term, so it may be possible to earn arbitrage profits in cases where discrepancies exist.

Translation exposure occurs when it is necessary to translate financial statements from one currency to the other, for example, when a domestic company has subsidiaries based in foreign countries that it wishes to consolidate with its own financial statements. Certain assets and liabilities may be translated at the current exchange rate (end of reporting period) while others are reported at historical cost. The assets and liabilities that are reported at current cost are subject to volatility if the exchange rate varies from accounting period to accounting period. This can be a problem for countries undergoing rapid inflation.

One famous example of currency risk came about when some Latin American countries including Mexico had exposure to the USD through floating rate debt. When U.S. rates increased sharply and unexpectedly, Mexico could not meet the payments and defaulted.

Fixed income risk

Interest rate risk

Interest rate risk can affect the value of fixed income instruments in several ways. First, there is the fact that fixed income securities are highly sensitive to changes in interest rates. This risk is measured to first-order approximation using duration, although the second order term of convexity should also be included. Recall that for instruments having positive convexity, as interest rates rise, bond prices decrease.

Then there is the problem of coupon reinvestment risk. When a par coupon bond is purchased, the yield is equal to the coupon and thus the bond is priced at par. If interest rates later fall, the coupons flowing from the bond will not be able to be invested at this rate, but will at a lower rate. The investor will not get the value they originally anticipated. Although the investor will receive par at maturity, the value of the bond is the value of all cash flows. And the stream of coupon interest, because it's earning a lower rate, will decrease.

As an example, let's calculate the return on a fixed income trading strategy. A portfolio manager is considering purchase of a 10-year, 5% coupon bond today for $100. This is a par bond so the yield to maturity must be 5%. He thinks interest rates will decline by 150 bp over the next three years, and plans to sell the bond at the end of three years and take his profit. What is his holding period return? He will finance the purchase of the bond with $100 borrowed at 4%.

The **holding period return** is composed of three components: coupon interest and interest on coupon interest; capital gain/(loss) on price appreciation/(depreciation) of the bond; and financing costs.

Coupon interest and interest on interest: Since the bond makes semiannual payments, he will receive coupon interest of $2.50 per $100 face every six months. There are six total periods in the anticipated three-year holding period, so he will receive $15.97, of which $15 is coupon interest and $0.97 is the interest on coupon interest.

Capital gains/(losses) on price appreciation/(depreciation): Since the current YTM when he buys the bond is 5%, if he assumes that rates will drop 1.5%, the bond at the end of the holding period will be a 7-year bond yielding 3.5% but still paying a coupon of 5%. The value of the bond will be $104.92.

Financing costs: A financing rate of 4% per year means the investor has to pay 2% per semiannual period, or $100(1.02^6-1) = 12.62.

Total Profit/Loss

Coupon income plus interest on coupon interest	$15.97
Proceeds from sale of bond at end of holding period	$104.92
Less: financing charges	($12.62)
Total proceeds at end of holding period	$108.27

Holding period return is that return r that grows the initial investment into the final value after six periods, or $100(1+r)^6 = 108.27, which gives $r = 1.3\%$/period, or 2.6%/year.

If the yield curve remained flat, what would the investor's profit be? The only thing that would change would be the proceeds from the sale of the bond at the end of the holding period; he would get par. The total proceeds would be $15.97 + $100 -$12.62 = $103.35, and the investor's annualized holding period return would be 1.1%.

If interest rates rose instead of falling as the investor expects, the profit could completely evaporate and the investor would be exposed to a loss. How do we calculate the value at risk? For this instrument, we can use a duration approach. VaR could be calculated on a straight duration basis as

VaR = Worst Expected Dollar Loss = Duration x Portfolio Value x Yield Volatility (Cut off Value)

For the 10-year coupon bond considered with YTM = 6%, the duration is 6.86 years. We could calculate historical volatility using fed data or download a RiskMetrics data set. Suppose we find the cut off value of yield volatility as the worst increase in one-month bonds at the 5% level to be 1%. Then, the VaR would be (6.86years)($100)0.01 = $6.86.

Real yield risk

The coupon rates and yields quoted are examples of nominal yields. Inflation can eat up these returns to the point where losses can actually be incurred. Real interest rates should be used to account for the effects of inflation. The real interest rate r_r is given as $(1 + r_r) \sim (1 + r_n)(1 + i)$.

Credit spread risk

Non-treasuries such as corporate bonds carry higher apparent yields than equivalent treasuries because of the additional risk of default. This spread is reflected in the bond price. If the spread between the corporate bond and treasury remains constant over the life of the bond, all is fine, but problems occur if an unexpected widening in the spread transpires. Most likely no one would try to trade the spread between a 10-year U.S. Treasury Bond and a 5-year bond, but people do commonly trade spreads between the U.S. Treasury Bill and Eurodollar Futures contracts. This is known as a TED spread, defined as the difference between the rate at which the T-bill is trading to 3-month LIBOR. Since the U.S. Treasury Bill and Eurodollar Futures Contracts have the same three-month maturity, people trade the spread between them. The spread can widen in times of international crisis. The spread exists because of a perceived difference in credit quality (though liquidity may also play a factor; it is difficult to separate the effect of liquidity from the total spread) between the U.S. government and high-quality European banks. If an international crisis erupts, investors might flee to U.S. securities ("the flight to quality"), widening the spreads.

A famous recent case was the case of Long Term Capital Management (LTCM). Long Term Capital Management had returns of over 40% for several years when suddenly it lost over 90% of its assets due to a combination of options, interest rate swaps and interest rate yield curve spreads. At that time, the assets under management consisted of almost five billion dollars, leveraged to $80 billion. The strategy used by LTCM was in purchasing what they saw as undervalued, "cheap" securities and selling overvalued, "expensive" securities. Suppose that historically the spread between domestic mortgage-backed securities (MBS) and US treasuries was 50 bp. If the spread widened so that the yield on the MBS was higher than the historical value, LTCM might try to buy MBS and short treasuries in expectation of the spreads reverting to mean levels at some future date. This is not really "hedging" since there is no guarantee that spread convergence will occur. They could expect that spreads might narrow under normal equilibrium conditions, but the duration of the unfavorable market conditions was long enough to wipe out 90% of the value of the hedge fund.

A famous recent case involved the company Long Term Capital Management (LTCM). Long Term Capital Management had returns of over 40% for several years when it suddenly lost over 90% of its assets (almost $5 billion dollars, leveraged to $80 billion) due to a combination of options, interest rate swaps and interest rate yield curve spreads. LTCM used a strategy of purchasing what they saw as undervalued, "cheap" securities and selling overvalued, "expensive" securities. Suppose that historical spreads between mortgage-backed securities and U.S. Treasuries were 50 bp. If the spreads widened so that the yield on the MBS was higher than the historical value, LTCM would have tried to buy MBS and short treasuries in expectation of the spreads reverting to mean levels at some future date. This is not really "hedging" since there is no guarantee that spread convergence will occur. Under "normal" equilibrium conditions, spreads might narrow, but the duration of the unusual market conditions was long enough to wipe out 90% of the value of LTCM's hedge fund.

Prepayment risk

Prepayment risk is particularly prevalent in mortgage-backed securities and collateralized mortgage obligations, and to a lesser extent in other asset-backed securities such as auto loans. The problem with prepayment is basically that it is unpredictable. Models can be built but, in the end, homeowners may not refinance in rational ways. There is also the problem of **burnout**. If interest rates are at 8% and then drop to 6%, homeowners who have never refinanced might have incentive to do so. If rates then rise and then drop back to 6%, there will not be as many refinancings: many of the homeowners who could refinance have already done so. This is called burnout. Also, as the mortgage pool ages, people will not refinance.

While automobile loans are much shorter in duration than home loans, refinancing tends not to be driven as much by interest rates because the term of the loan is much shorter than that for a home loan. There are other reasons driving refinancings, including buyers finding better rates (perhaps at credit unions) after car purchases using dealer credit, turning in the car for a newer model after one year, and destruction in a fire. These events are difficult to predict. As discussed in the fixed income chapter, prepayment risk impacts mortgage-backed securities in two ways. First, because prepayments flourish in a declining interest rate environment, accelerating the return of cash flows to investors can cause early repayment of principal, which must then be invested at lower interest rates. Second, prepayment events make the forecasting of the magnitude and timing of cash flows difficult. Since these cash flows are discounted at higher rates, the present value will be lower.

Default risk and credit ratings

The major ratings perform credit analysis studies on large bond issues. The prices of the bonds reflect the default risk of the bonds. Default risk is an important consideration for the investor in corporates and high yield bonds. Although bondholders are senior to equity shareholders in the capital structure, there have been several cases where, after liquidation, the bondholders received only pennies on the dollar. The default risk can be calculated using trees. First, the interest rate tree is computed from treasury bonds. Then the tree is calibrated to the price of the corporate bond to determine the default probability priced into the bond at each node.

Studies by the major ratings agencies show that the probabilities of default increase the lower the credit rating, and the risk of default across all ratings increases with time. The table below reproduces some sample historical default data from Moody's Investor Services.

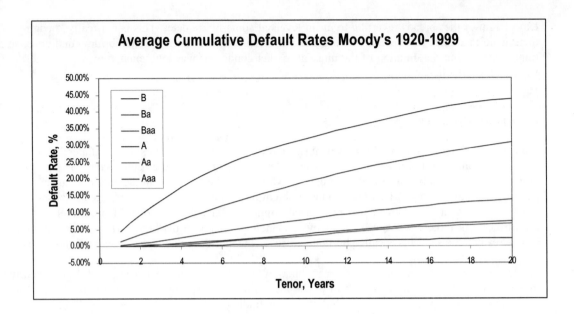

VAULT

Equity risk

Equity risk is highly important for investors because, whether one agrees with the CAPM or not, risk determines the expected return on a stock. Since equity shares are residual claims on assets of a corporation, evaluation of the risk involved in owning equity should include an analysis of the risks faced by the business. Most likely, the main risk factor affecting equity prices is volatility, although other factors such as foreign exchange rate risk, interest rate risk, liquidity risk and dividend assumption risk also affect price.

The higher the volatility, the higher the peaks and valleys of the stock price. These are average paths so

Stock Market Volatility The higher the volatility, the more extreme the price movements of the stock. Returning to the simplified Brownian motion model of stock price dynamics, we see that volatility directly affects the price of a stock, since $\frac{dS}{S} = \mu dt + \sigma dz$. The stock return is composed of a predictable expected return $\mu\, dt$ and a volatile, unpredictable component $\sigma\, dz$ that is driven by volatility. The chart below depicts the effect of volatility on the random walk of a stock. When $\sigma = 0$, the stock simply follows the path $\frac{dS}{S} = \mu dt$. This is shown by the heavy, linear line that runs between \$5 and \$7 in the figure below.

have been smoothed. But in the individual paths, some negative prices are seen that, of course, can only happen in models.

Because shareholders do not have liability, if the value of the company's equity becomes negative (value of assets lower than value of liabilities), they can simply walk away. Suppose a firm has \$100 of assets that were purchased with $50 of debt capital and $50 of equity. The debt holders are only entitled to $50, but if the firm's equity falls to $50, the debt holders will own the company. The equity shareholders have the option to repay the debt, regaining ownership of the company. Also, if the value of the company increases above $100, the increase accrues (in a residual fashion) to the equity holders. Thus equity shareholders are often thought of as holding call options with a strike price equal to the value of the liabilities.

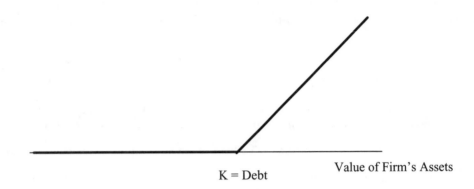

K = Debt   Value of Firm's Assets

Foreign exchange risk

Foreign exchange risk, which affects multinational companies, can shape the value of equity on the balance sheet as well as net income (which, of course, drives many critical financial ratios on which stocks are valued, including price/earnings). Foreign exchange risk consists of real economic exposure as well as accounting exposure, which may result in volatility of earnings.

Interest rate risk

Interest rate risk can affect the price of equity in several ways. First, the price of a stock is computed as the present value of discounted expected future earnings. The appropriate discount factor is the cost of equity capital. This rate is unobservable, but typically the corporate hurdle rate (the minimum required rate of return of the project as determined by management) is used. It should reflect borrowing costs to fund the project. If the assumed rate of borrowing costs used in the model is too low, the project return will be overstated and the company may end up investing in low-value projects, ultimately depressing the equity value. Another possible exposure is for companies trying to raise funds by going to the debt market. Suppose they have borrowed a significant amount of funds at short-term rates, or have entered into the floating leg of a swap. Then, a credit event occurs, or interest rates rise. They may find themselves in financial distress as they attempt to keep up with the heavy interest load. Since the total value of the

$$V = V_{CE} + V_D + V_P, \ WACC = \frac{V_{CE}}{V} r_{CE} + \frac{V_D}{V} r_D + \frac{V_P}{V} r_P, \ \text{where } WACC \text{ is the weighted Cost of Capital}$$

company is equal to the value of the debt plus the value of equity (plus preferred stock, if any),
used in discounting free cash flows to the firm, increasing the interest rate paid on debt rD will increase $WACC$, and thereby decrease the value of the firm.

Dividend assumption risk

When companies have positive earnings, they can either pay them out to the investor in the form of dividends, or retain them for investment in positive NPV projects to grow. Once a company can no longer find projects with returns at least equal the required return on equity capital, it is better off paying out the earnings in dividends. So, high growth companies should not pay dividends, while stable, mature companies should.

There are two ways that dividend assumptions create risk to the investor. First, there is the reinvestment rate risk. Dividends are paid in cash to investors and thus taxable at the highest rate. Second, recall that dividends form part of the expected return. In the simplest possible case, consider a mature, stable company. The expected return is given by

$$r = \frac{P_1 + DIV - P_0}{P_0} = \frac{P_0(1+g) + DIV - P_0}{P_0} = \frac{DIV}{P_0} + g$$

If the dividend is cut, the impact on the expected return is clear. Companies are reluctant to cut dividends because it sends a signal that poor earnings are expected. There have been cases (such as the Avon Corporation) where management cut dividends and the stock price was adversely affected. And rightly so. There are only two reasons a company would cut dividends. First, since they are paid out of free cash flow, the company might not have the funds to pay them. Second, they could cut them because they want to retain the cash flow for growth. Let's do a quick valuation to see the impact of a dividend cut on the price per share. Assume that the company is paying $1 and the dividend is expected to grow at 5% per year. The company runs pro-forma financial statements and anticipate that they will cut the dividend to 50 cents for years 3 through 6, after which it is assumed to resume growing at 5%. Assume that the required cost of capital for both cases is 10%.

Case 1 Value of company with no dividend cut. Using perpetuity model, $P = \dfrac{DIV(1+g)}{r_{CE} - g} = \dfrac{\$1(1+0.05)}{0.10 - 0.05}$

=$20.1.

Case 2 Forecast dividends at each year and discount to calculate price:

Year	Growth Rate	Dividend
1	5%	$1
2	5%	$1.05
3	0%	$0.50
4	0%	$0.50
5	0%	$0.50
6	0%	$0.50
7	5%	$0.525

$$P = \frac{DIV_1}{(1+r)} + \frac{DIV_2}{(1+r)^2} + \frac{DIV_3}{(1+r)^3} + \frac{DIV_4}{(1+r)^4} + \frac{DIV_5}{(1+r)^5} + \frac{DIV_6}{(1+r)^6} + \frac{DIV_6(1+g)}{(1+r)^7} =$$

$$\frac{\$1}{(1+0.1)} + \frac{\$1.05}{(1+0.1)^2} + \frac{\$0.50}{(1+0.1)^3} + \frac{\$0.50}{(1+0.1)^4} + \frac{\$0.50}{(1+0.1)^5} + \frac{\$0.50}{(1+0.1)^6} + \frac{\$0.50(1+0.05)}{(1+0.1)^7}$$

=$3.36. This is just a fraction of the price the company would have had, had they not cut the dividend.

Of course, it would be incomplete to conclude the section on equities without talking about the undisclosed risks that may be off-balance sheet, waiting like land mines to implode the stock. Enron was the target of intense media focus after its implosion, but other companies have followed. It's difficult to assess risks of these off-balance sheet transactions if they are either not fully disclosed or fully understood, but it is crucial. Equities also suffer risk of "guilt by association," when, for example, one tech stock plunges for company-specific reasons and the market may overreact, punishing companies in similar lines of business for no apparent reasons. For example, in the wake of the Sumitomo Copper debacle (discussed below), zinc prices also suffered.

Currency and Commodity Risk in the News

There are several risks inherent in dealing with currencies and commodities. These risks have been well documented in several huge derivatives debacles in the past decade. The Japanese company Kanematsu Corp. disclosed losses of $83 million caused by trading crude oil futures; Tokyo Securities lost almost $300 million trading U.S. treasury securities; Kashima Oil Company announced that it had incurred cumulative losses of $1.4 billion on foreign exchange contracts; and Showa Shell Sekiyu (an affiliate of Royal Dutch/Shell Group) disclosed losses of $1.54 billion on FX contracts. Currency and commodity risk go hand in hand. While commodities may be driven by supply and demand, international companies may have to use foreign currencies to transact in the desired commodities. According to a January 1999 article in *Derivatives Strategy* magazine, "Another problem affecting the U.S. metals business is the currency market. Many foreign traders are unwilling to buy and sell dollars in order to trade metals in the United States, because the dollar has fluctuated greatly against the yen and other currencies. While foreign traders may be right in their market hunches, they could lose all their gains in the dollar fluctuation." Let's consider a few of the most notorious cases in currency/commodity debacles of the past decade.

Showa Shell

This company was in the business of purchasing oil in dollars and reselling it domestically. Concerned about exchange rate risk, Showa Shell's traders began buying forward contracts to lock in exchange rates of ¥145/$. These contracts were rolled over as they matured, creating a form of "rolling hedge." Since Japanese accounting rules did not require marking to market, the losses incurred were able to remain hidden. By December of 1992, the dollar had weakened to ¥125/$. The total position size was $6.4 billion, so the loss was F = position size$(K - S)$ = $6.4 billion (¥125-¥145) = ¥128 billion or $1.024 billion.

Metallgesellschaft

This German oil company had a U.S. subsidiary, MG Refining and Marketing (MGRM), which had the idea of selling long term oil contracts to its customers. The plan was very successful as customers liked the idea of being able to lock in long-term oil prices. They ultimately sold contracts obligating them to provide 180 million barrels of oil over a 10-year maturity at locked-in prices, which far exceeded their production capacity, so they would have to purchase oil to make good on their contracts. To hedge against price increases, they wanted to buy long-term forward contracts, but the market for 10-year forwards did not exist. So they decided to buy short-term futures (three-month durations) and would roll them over at maturity.

There were at least two problems with this strategy. First, there is basis risk incurred by using short-term instruments to hedge long-term liabilities. When MGRM would call to roll over its hedges, traders reportedly "knew they were coming." This probably destroyed MGRM's chances of getting good prices. Second, the fact that futures were used as the hedging vehicle rather than forwards meant that the portfolio was marked-to-market daily. During 1993 spot oil prices dropped from $20 to $15 per barrel, exposing MGRM to a $1 billion margin call, which it was unable to hide from its parent company. New management was brought in and the positions liquidated, resulting in a loss of $1.3 billion. Once the dust settled, there was intense controversy during which academics debated whether MGRM was just a prudent hedger, whose losses were caused by management interference, or whether they were wild speculators. In theory, convergence of futures and spot prices must occur at contract expiration, so, some arguments go, had MGRM not been forced to liquidate, it would have made profits by selling to customers at the higher locked-in price while buying at the lower spot price.

Sumitomo Copper

In 1996 the Sumitomo Copper trading company disclosed a $1.8 billion loss that had accumulated over the prior 10-year period on unauthorized copper trades. Sumitomo's chief copper trader Yasuo Hamanaka was later fired. Hamanaka was referred to as "Mr. 5%" because the volume of his trades, 500,000 metric tons, accounted for five percent of annual worldwide volume of 10 million metric tons. It was reported that Hamanaka was able to hide his losses, at least in part, because he used the forwards markets rather than the futures markets for his long positions; recall that futures must be marked-to-market daily, which would possibly have alerted the company to the situation much sooner than was the case.

Because Sumitomo enjoyed a long history as a highly conservative company, Hamanaka was able to negotiate extended settlement dates with the counterparty, which relied on Sumitomo's perceived creditworthiness. At the time, there was intense competition between several competitors for control of the copper markets. Thus, Sumitomo's growing accumulation of copper was not really questioned by market observers, because it was assumed that Sumitomo was attempting to squeeze out competitors by cornering the market. The disclosure of Sumitomo's activity spawned a selling frenzy since it was anticipated that management would close out its position by selling all or most of the positions. Since Sumitomo had such a large position in copper, other market participants feared the drop in price of copper that would result from such a large quantity of copper being suddenly dumped on the market. This sudden increase in supply would drive the price down.

Currency and Commodity Volatility Risk Recall the futures-spot parity relation, $F_t = S_t e^{-(r-\delta)(T-t)}$ which can be used to price futures on stock indices, currencies, equities and commodities. In this equation, r represents the risk-free rate and, depending upon the application, δ represents the dividend yield, convenience yield or foreign currency interest rate. For commodities such as silver and gold, which involve storage costs, δ functions as a negative convenience yield.

If the price K has already been determined, such as in the MGRM contract, the formula becomes

$F_t = S_t e^{-\delta(T-t)} - Ke^{-r(T-t)}$. In order to assess the risk of this contract, take the total derivative with respect to all variables:

$$dF = \frac{\partial F}{\partial S} dS + \frac{\partial F}{\partial \delta} d\delta + \frac{\partial F}{\partial r} dr = e^{-\delta(T-t)}dS - S_t(T-t)e^{-\delta(T-t)} + K(T-t)e^{-r(T-t)}dr$$

So the risk of the forward/future comes from the individual sources of risk *(r, δ, S)* as well as from the co-movement of risk sources.

Liquidity and delivery risk

When physical delivery of an asset is specified, the parties to the contract are exposed to both liquidity and delivery risk. If a short is obligated to deliver, say, 1,000 bushels of #2 Yellow corn, they will have to go out into the market and buy it. If corn is being hoarded, or the weather has been bad so there is no corn to be had, or there are many other shorts trying to cover their positions, it may be difficult to obtain the corn for delivery. A famous case involving this situation occurred at the end of March 1996 on the July corn futures contract on the CBOT. There was a huge spike in spot prices at expiration driven by speculation of market squeezes by certain traders. To understand delivery risk, suppose you are a grain elevator trying to hedge against delivery of corn. The farmer bought a contract locking in a futures price and you have agreed to take delivery of the corn at that price. If the farmer can't deliver the corn, you are exposed because, probably, you have hedged your position by selling your expected corn to someone else. Many producers use rolling hedges termed **hedge to arrive (HTA)** contracts. This is where you agree to deliver your corn at a specified date at a specified price reference to some basis (such as March corn, for example), with the basis to be determined later. This introduces substantial risk.

According to a speech given by Joseph P. Dial, Commissioner of the CFTC (Commodities Futures Trading Commission) in August 1996, a hedge to arrive contract works like this: Suppose you are a farmer that will be selling corn in November 1995. You wish to hedge your risk, so in late spring or early summer you go to your elevator and enter into a futures contract to deliver your corn in December 1995 at $2.80/bushel. The elevator must roll his position forward to a short Dec 1995 futures as well. It is now November 1995. The spot price for corn has risen to $3.30/bushel. The farmer has three choices: he can close out of his futures position by delivering the corn to the elevator for the agreed upon $2.80/bushel (this is called "setting the basis"); he can do nothing, holding his corn until expiration of the contract, thus rolling the hedge forward another month; or he can sell his corn in the cash market now, and roll the futures position forward. Suppose he takes the last option. He puts the $3.30 in the bank and rolls his hedge forward to July 1996. The elevator has to also offset his hedge, so the actions by the farmer require him to roll his position forward as well. Suppose that the July 1996 futures price is $3.15/bushel. The farmer is hoping that corn prices will fall before his futures contract expires, so he can purchase corn at a lower price to sell to the elevator. However, the reverse happens. He watches the price spike to over $5.15/bushel at the end of March 1996. The elevator is now getting margin calls since he is short in a rising price environment. He doesn't even have an asset to pledge as collateral, because the farmer is not obliged to deliver his corn until July 1996. This caused severe financial distress to many elevators.

Hedging risk

The ideal hedging instrument is one that has perfect negative correlation with the underlying. Since such hedges don't exist, there will always be hedging risk. Hedging risk refers to the practice of hedging with an instrument that does not perfectly offset the underlying. An example would be using silver futures to hedge gold, or the 10-year U.S. Treasury bond to hedge a 10-year corporate bond -- but we don't even have to go that far.

There is significant risk involved when options are used to hedge individual equities. Recalling that the number of contracts required to hedge an equity position is given by

$$N_c = -HR \frac{NumberofSharesBeingHedged}{ContractSize}$$ where for a call or a put option, $HR = \frac{1}{\Delta}$ we see that in order to

hedge a long equity position with a call, since Δc is positive, we would have to sell N_c call contracts short:

$$N_c = -\frac{1}{\Delta} \frac{NumberofSharesBeingHedged}{ContractSize} .$$

For example, if a stock is selling at $90 and a three month call is available at a strike of $100 with a delta

of 0.329, in order to hedge 1,000 shares of the stock, we would need to sell short $N_c = -\frac{1}{0.329} \frac{1000}{100} = 30$

contracts. But delta of a call moves as the price of the underlying changes. If the price of the stock moves to $100, the delta becomes 0.563 and the number of contracts then required would be $N_c = -\frac{1}{0.563} \frac{1000}{100} = -17.76$. If the stock moves far enough in the money, say, to $120, the delta approaches 1. And in that case, only 10 contracts would be needed. A delta of 1 means that the prices of the option and underlying move together: a $1 change in the underlying results in a $1 change of the option. On the other hand, as the stock price moves further and further below the strike price, an increasing number of contracts would have to be sold short in order to maintain the hedge. In the limit, as the stock price approaches zero, delta would approach zero and the number of contracts required to maintain the hedge would approach infinity.

Puts can also be used as hedging contracts against adverse price movements, but in this case, the delta is negative, so puts would have to be purchased as a hedge against a long equity position. The delta of a put is -1 at the limit as the stock price approaches zero.

Futures and forwards would seem to be better hedging vehicles, but as they are not available for individual stocks, options must be used. The use of options as hedging vehicles is not a "set and forget" strategy. As the preceding has shown, the portfolio must be continually rebalanced as the price of the underlying changes in order to maintain a delta-neutral hedge.

Delta vs. delta-gamma

The delta of an option is used to quantify the change in value of a call or put with a unit change in the underlying. Since the delta of a long call is positive and that of a put is negative, we can quantify our total position delta as the sum of component deltas. Position delta = option delta x number of contracts x contract size.

As promised, we now return to our analysis of the Nick Leeson strategy. Recall that he sold about 35,000 naked calls and puts on the NIKKEI index at a time when the index was at about 19,000. Since the futures contract multiplier is 500 and the ¥/USD exchange rate at that time was approximately ¥100/$, this implies that for 35,000 contracts, the value would be about $35,000*500/100(F - S) = \$175,000(F - S)$. Leeson did not expect the market to move very much. Under such circumstances he would profit from the sale of the options because both would expire worthless. In fact, he had (before sinking Barings) made substantial profits on this very strategy. Leeson assumed he was perfectly hedged. Recall that the delta of the call option is $N(d_1)$ and the delta of a put option is $N(d_1) - 1$. Because the options had the same strike and maturity, the portfolio delta would be the sum of the individual deltas, or $2N(d_1) - 1$. The following graph depicts call and put deltas as a function of F. The strike is 19000.

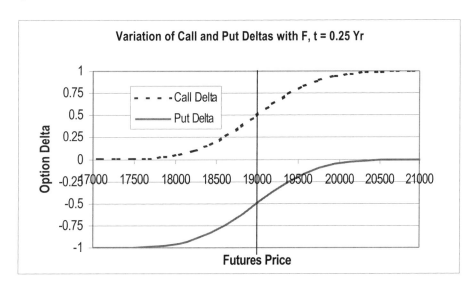

Plotting the sum of the call and put deltas, we see that, at the money, the portfolio delta is zero.

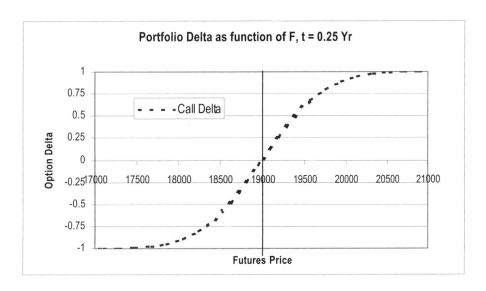

Leeson assumed that he was hedged because his portfolio had a delta of zero. However, far from the money, it can be seen that the delta is far from zero. The NIKKEI was at 17,000 when the portfolio was closed out. At this point, the change in value of the options would be $-\Delta\min((F - K),0)$ \$175,000 $= 0.506(-2,000)$175,000 = -177 million.

Recall that delta is a linear estimate of portfolio risk. This concept is very similar to the duration of a bond. If it is assumed that call value is a function of the underlying only (ignoring for the moment r and volatility), we can perform a Taylor Series expansion for the change in option value as:

$$dc = \frac{\partial c}{\partial S}\,dS + \frac{1}{2}\frac{\partial^2 c}{\partial S^2}\,dS^2 + \cdots = \Delta dS + \frac{1}{2}\Gamma dS^2 + \cdots$$

where Γ is the option gamma, defined as

$$\Gamma = \frac{e^{-D(T-t)}N(d_1)}{S\sigma\sqrt{T-t}} = \frac{\Delta_{call}}{S\sigma\sqrt{T-t}}$$

if dividends are ignored. Including gamma gives a much better price approximation, although gamma overestimates the price at both deep in and deep out of the money options.

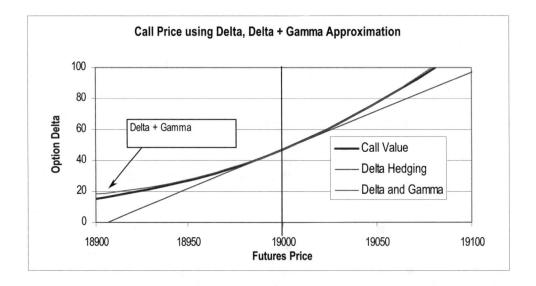

Leeson also lost money due to an improper hedge. He was short about \$16,600 million in Japanese Government bonds. Since there is a negative correlation between stocks and bonds, if he was long the NIKKEI index, he should have also been long the bonds so they could work as a hedge. Being short worsened the position.

Portfolio risk and correlations

We have already seen how to calculate the standard deviation s of a portfolio. To calculate the VaR of a portfolio, just calculate s of the portfolio, then multiply by desired a (say, 1.65 for a 95% confidence level) and multiply by the total exposure. Thus, $VaR_P = 1.65\sigma_P x$ where x is the total exposure. As an example, we follow Philip Jorion's analysis of the VaR of Nick Leeson's portfolio (from Jorion's book, *Value at Risk: The New Benchmark for Managing Financial Risk*, which we highly recommended if you are interested in this field).

Jorion identifies Leeson's portfolio as short $16,600 million in the 10-year Japanese Government bond and long $7,700 in the NIKKEI index. In order to compute the variance of the portfolio, we need the variance/covariance matrix of the instruments composing the portfolio. (A good source for such data is RiskMetrics Group, a risk management research company that offers, among other products, daily, monthly and annual data on many financial securities.) Then the total value of the portfolio is $7,700 - $16,600 = -$8,300.

Suppose that the variance of the 10-year JGB was 1.18%, the variance of the NIKKEI was 5.83 and the correlation coefficient between the 10-year JGB and the NIKKEI was -0.114. Then, the variance of the portfolio is just

$$\sigma^2_{P,JGB} = \sigma^2_{JGB}(-\$16,600)^2 + \rho_{JGB,NIKKEI}(\$7,700)(-\$16,000)\sigma_{JGB}\sigma_{NIKKEI}$$

$$\sigma^2_{P,NIKKEI} = \sigma^2_{NIKKEI}(\$7,700)^2 + \rho_{JGB,NIKKEI}(\$7,700)(-\$16,000)\sigma_{JGB}\sigma_{NIKKEI}$$

The first term gives the component due to the Japanese Government bond and the second, due to the NIKKEI. The variance of the portfolio is the sum of the component parts. Looking at the first term, the variance of the portfolio caused by the JGB should be equal to the variance caused by the JGB on its own and also to the part caused by the correlation of the NIKKEI index to the JGB. Then the variance due to the JGB = $-16,600^2(0.0118)^2 - 0.114(0.0118)(0.0583)(\$7,700)(-16,600) = (-16,600)(-2.311384 - 0.603874) = (-16,600)(-2.91) = \$48,306$.

For the NIKKEI, the contribution to the portfolio sensitivity is $(\$7,700)(-\$16,600(-0.114)(0.0118)(0.0583) + (\$7,700)(0.0583)^2) = (7,700)(1.30186 + 26.17) = (7,700) 27.47 = \$211,519$.

Thus, the total portfolio variance is $\$48,306 + \$211,519 = \$259,825 = \sigma_p^2$, so $\sigma = \$509.73$.

Now, the value at risk is $1.65\ \sigma = \$841.055$ million.

We can also calculate the incremental contributions to VaR of each security. Since the JGB contributes a total of $\$48,306 / \$259,825 = 18.59\%$ of the total variance, $0.1859(\$841.055) = \$156$ of the VaR is due to the short position in the Japanese Government Bond. The remaining 81.41%, or $684.7 million is due to the long position in the NIKKEI. So the mishedging using the bond added to the loss, but did not have nearly the impact of the long position in the NIKKEI.

Arbitrage

Risk arbitrage is the practice whereby arbitrageurs attempt to make profits through corporate control events such as corporate takeovers and mergers and acquisitions. A few of the more colorful and well-known risk arbitrageurs of the past were T. Boone Pickens and Ivan Boesky. **Riskless arbitrage** involves finding a situation where risk-free profits can be made, such as exploiting foreign exchange differences between countries. There is a big difference between these two types of arbitrage. Risk arbitrageurs often take very large risks in hopes of making large profits, while riskless arbitrageurs are taking no risk as their positions are completely hedged.

One situation that attracts arbitrageurs is when one company begins accumulating stock in another company in preparation for a takeover. The potential acquirer may mount a proxy battle or make a tender offer to the shareholders. A risk arb may buy up shares from the existing shareholders and hold on to them, hoping that another suitor will appear and bid the shares higher. As long as the expectation of profits exists, arbs will continue buying shares.

An example of a riskless arbitrage is the situation where the spot exchange rate between the Italian Lira (ITL) and the USD is 2,052.4380 ITL/USD in New York, the spot exchange rate between ITL and JPY is 16.4603 ITL/JPY in Rome, and the yen/dollar exchange rate is 128 ¥/USD in Tokyo. We can determine whether or not an arbitrage condition exists by assuming that the New York rate is "correct" and computing the cross-rate implied by the other countries (this is just an example for illustration. To really calculate this correctly, one would need the bid-ask spreads and would have to take care to use the correct side of the spreads). The implied cross-rate between the ITL and JPY is equal to (16.4603 ITL/JPY)(128 ¥/USD) = 2,106.918 ITL/USD. Since there is a variance between this rate and the rate quoted in New York, in absence of transactions costs, it is possible to make arbitrage profits.

For example, $1,000 could be converted into Lira in Tokyo to yield 2,106,918 ITL, which would then be converted in Rome at the rate of 1 USD per 2,052.4380 ITL for $1,026.54. There are many other examples of riskless arbitrage that can be constructed, but transactions costs and other market frictions render any real-life arbitrage opportunities untradeable, or short-lived.

Sample Questions and Answers

Questions

1. What would the VaR on Leeson's portfolio have been if he had been long, rather than short, the JGB?

2. A stock is selling at $90. A 3-month call with a strike price of $100 is selling for $3.104 with a delta of 0.329. How many call contracts are required to perform a hedge on 1,000 shares of this stock? Would they be bought or sold? What happens if the price of the stock falls to $70?

3. If the delta of the put is –0.671, answer the same questions as above.

4. What is the one-day VaR of a $10,000,000 portfolio with a daily standard deviation of 2% at a 95% confidence level? What is the annualized VaR?

5. You observe the following spot exchange rates: 0.4840 USD/DEM in New York, 3.3539 FRF/DEM in Frankfurt and 0.1444 USD/FRF in Paris. Is it possible to make arbitrage profits under this situation? If so, how much profit? Outline your strategy.

6. What is Herstatt risk?

7. I was just looking at Bloomberg and noticed that I can earn 3.872% on a one-year bond in the UK and can borrow at 2% here in the US. Can I make a risk-free profit by doing this?

8. Does this mean that the exchange rate in one year will be $1.52/GBP?

Answers

1.   The correlations don't change; only the -$16,600 in the calculations (it becomes positive). Redoing the calculations we find:

$$\sigma_{P,JGB}^2 = \sigma_{JGB}^2 (\$16,600)^2 + COV_{JGB,NIKKEI}(\$16,600)(\$7,700)$$

$$\sigma_{P,NIKKEI}^2 = \sigma_{NIKKEI}^2 (\$7,700)^2 + COV_{JGB,NIKKEI}(\$16,600)(\$7,700)$$

JGB = +$16,600(($16,000)(0.0118)^2 – 0. 114(0.0118)(0.0583)($7,700)) =$25,983.46

For the NIKKEI, the contribution to the portfolio sensitivity is
($7,700)(+$16,600(-0.114)(0.0118)(0.0583) + ($7,700) (0.0583)^2) = $191,495.88.

Thus, the total portfolio variance is $25,983.46+ $191,495.88 = $217,479.34 = σ_p^2, so σ =$466.35.

Now, the value at risk is 1.65 σ = $769.47 million. Still quite a lot, but the working bond hedge reduced the VaR by 9%.

2.   The number of contracts required to hedge is given by

$$N_c = -HR \frac{Number\ of\ Shares\ Being\ Hedged}{Contract\ Size} = -\frac{1}{\Delta} \frac{Number\ of\ Shares\ Being\ Hedged}{Contract\ Size} = \frac{1}{0.329} \frac{1,000}{100}$$

= - 30.4 contracts, would have to be sold short. If the price of the stock changes to $70, the delta would change to approximately 0.030 (the call is far out of the money so the delta of the call should approach zero). In this case we would need to rebalance the hedge so that 333 contracts are sold short.

3.   Here, the puts would be purchased because the delta of a put is negative. We need to buy $-1/-0.671*10 = 14.9$ puts. If the price of the stock falls to $70, the put is deep in the money and approaching one. We would only need 10 put contracts (one per one hundred shares of stock).

4.   VaR= \$10,000,000 * 1.65 * σ = \$10,000,000 * 1.65 * 0.02=\$330,000. To get the annualized VaR, just convert the standard deviation to an annualized value by multiplying by the square root of t. Assuming 250 trading days in a year, the annualized value would be $\$330,000*(250)^{0.5} = \$5,217,758$.

5.   With 0.4840 USD/DEM in New York, 3.3539 FRF/DEM in Frankfurt and 0.1444 USD/FRF in Paris, we assume (for simplicity, not actual fact) that the price is "right" in New York and calculate the cross rate implied by the other two countries. We find (3.3539 FRF/DEM)*(0.1444 USD/FRF) = 0.4843 USD/DEM to be the implied exchange rate, which does not equal the rate of 0.4840 USD/DEM quoted in New York. Thus a small profit may be possible of the amount (.4843 – 0.4840) USD/DEM = 0.0003 USD/DEM. Since the DEM is cheaper in New York, we would buy, say, 1,000,000 DEM paying $484,000 for them. We would convert to French francs in Frankfurt, receiving FRF 3,353,900, which we would then convert to USD in Paris, receiving $484,303.16. This yields a risk free profit of $303.16.

6.   An obscure question, but you never know. Herstatt risk is named after an infamous debacle involving a small German bank, Bankhaus Herstatt. At 3:30 pm on June 26, 1974, Herstatt's banking license was revoked and the firm was ordered into liquidation. The order cam during the business day in Germany, but after the close of Germany's Interbank payments system. Meanwhile, in New York, it was 10:30 a.m. And some of the bank's counterparties sent Herstatt Deutschmarks (DM), expecting to receive U.S. dollars in return. The DMs were caught in the Interbank payments system, and further outgoing payments to U.S. customers were prohibited. As a result, the counterparties were left exposed to the loss of their DM. Thus, Herstatt risk is a term used to describe this type of currency settlement risk, where one party pays out a currency but does not receive the currency it bought.

7.   Not necessarily. The reason for different interest rates across countries is primarily due to different expectations of inflation. High interest rates in the UK relative to the U.S. indicate that the British pound is expected to depreciate relative to the U.S. dollar. According to the theory of interest rate parity, high interest rates are offset by forward discounts and low interest rates are offset by forward premiums. For example, assume that the current exchange rate is 1.548 USD/GBP. I could take one dollar today and invest it at 2%. At the end of the year, I will have $1.02. I can convert this into pounds at the exchange rate that will prevail in one year to obtain pounds. Alternatively, I could convert my $1 right now into pounds, obtaining $1/($1.548/GBP) = 0.645995 GBP. I can invest this at the British rate of 3.872%, and at the end of the year I will have 0.645995 GBP(1.03872) = 0.671 GBP. This can be converted back at the exchange rate that will prevail in one year to yield dollars.

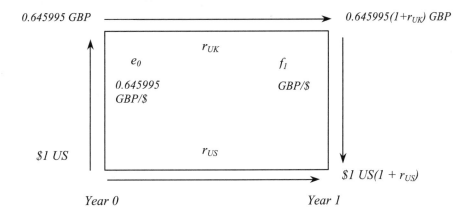

Whichever method you choose, the result must be the same. This means that the forward exchange rate f_1 must be such that the relationship $f_1(1+r_{US}) = e_0(1+r_{UK})$ or $f_1 = e_0 (1+r_{UK})/ (1+r_{US})$ must hold (where rates are in terms of GBP/USD). Then, this implies that f_1 = 0.645995 (1+0.03872)/ (1+0.02)= 0.657851 GBP/US or \$1.52 USD/GBP. It takes fewer dollars in one year to buy a british pound than it does now (\$1.52 as opposed to \$1.548) indicating that the currency is expected to depreciate relative to the US dollar.

If you try to lock into this today, you should find that the one year exchange rate is \$1.52/GBP. Otherwise, traders would arbitrage this all day long and the forward exchange rate would adjust until equilibrium is attained.

8. No, it is just the market's consensus of what the rate should be to prevent covered interest arbitrage as described above. In practice, exchange rates do not adjust precisely according to the theory of interest rate parity, and it is possible to make some profits.

APPENDIX

Finance Glossary

Accretive merger: A merger in which the acquiring company's earnings per share increase.

Balance Sheet: One of the four basic financial statements, the Balance Sheet presents the financial position of a company at a given point in time, including Assets, Liabilities, and Equity.

Beta: A value that represents the relative volatility of a given investment with respect to the market.

Bond price: The price the bondholder (the lender) pays the bond issuer (the borrower) to hold the bond (i.e., to have a claim on the cash flows documented on the bond).

Bond spreads: The difference between the yield of a corporate bond and a U.S. Treasury security of similar time to maturity.

Buy-side: The clients of investment banks (mutual funds, pension funds) that buy the stocks, bonds and securities sold by the investment banks. (The investment banks that sell these products to investors are known as the "sell-side.")

Callable bond: A bond that can be bought back by the issuer so that it is not committed to paying large coupon payments in the future.

Call option: An option that gives the holder the right to purchase an asset for a specified price on or before a specified expiration date.

Capital Asset Pricing Model (CAPM): A model used to calculate the discount rate of a company's cash flows.

Commercial bank: A bank that lends, rather than raises money. For example, if a company wants $30 million to open a new production plant, it can approach a commercial bank like Bank of America or Citibank for a loan. (Increasingly, commercial banks are also providing investment banking services to clients.)

Commercial paper: Short-term corporate debt, typically maturing in nine months or less.

Commodities: Assets (usually agricultural products or metals) that are generally interchangeable with one another and therefore share a common price. For example, corn, wheat, and rubber generally trade at one price on commodity markets worldwide.

Common stock: Also called common equity, common stock represents an ownership interest in a company. (As opposed to preferred stock, see below.) The vast majority of stock traded in the markets today is common, as common stock enables investors to vote on company matters. An individual with 51 percent or more of shares owned controls a company's decisions and can appoint anyone he/she wishes to the board of directors or to the management team.

Comparable transactions (comps): A method of valuing a company for a merger or acquisition that involves studying similar transactions.

Convertible preferred stock: A relatively uncommon type of equity issued by a company, convertible preferred stock is often issued when it cannot successfully sell either straight common stock or straight debt. Preferred stock pays a dividend, similar to how a bond pays coupon payments, but ultimately converts to common stock after a period of time. It is essentially a mix

of debt and equity, and most often used as a means for a risky company to obtain capital when neither debt nor equity works.

Capital market equilibrium: The principle that there should be equilibrium in the global interest rate markets.

Convertible bonds: Bonds that can be converted into a specified number of shares of stock.

Cost of Goods Sold: The direct costs of producing merchandise. Includes costs of labor, equipment, and materials to create the finished product, for example.

Coupon payments: The payments of interest that the bond issuer makes to the bondholder.

Credit ratings: The ratings given to bonds by credit agencies. These ratings indicate the risk of default.

Currency appreciation: When a currency's value is rising relative to other currencies.

Currency depreciation: When a currency's value is falling relative to other currencies.

Currency devaluation: When a currency weakens under fixed exchange rates.

Currency revaluation: When a currency strengthens under fixed exchange rates.

Default premium: The difference between the promised yields on a corporate bond and the yield on an otherwise identical government bond.

Default risk: The risk that the company issuing a bond may go bankrupt and "default" on its loans.

Derivatives: An asset whose value is derived from the price of another asset. Examples include call options, put options, futures, and interest-rate swaps.

Dilutive merger: A merger in which the acquiring company's earnings per share decrease.

Discount rate: A rate that measures the risk of an investment. It can be understood as the expected return from a project of a certain amount of risk.

Discounted Cash Flow analysis (DCF): A method of valuation that takes the net present value of the free cash flows of a company.

Dividend: A payment by a company to shareholders of its stock, usually as a way to distribute some or all of the profits to shareholders.

EBIAT: Earnings Before Interest After Taxes. Used to approximate earnings for the purposes of creating free cash flow for a discounted cash flow.

EBIT: Earnings Before Interest and Taxes

EBITDA: Earnings Before Interest, Taxes, Depreciation and Amortization

Enterprise Value: Levered value of the company, the Equity Value plus the market value of debt.

Equity: In short, stock. Equity means ownership in a company that is usually represented by stock.

The Fed: The Federal Reserve Board, which gently (or sometimes roughly), manages the country's economy by setting interest rates.

Fixed income: Bonds and other securities that earn a fixed rate of return. Bonds are typically issued by governments, corporations and municipalities.

Float: The number of shares available for trade in the market times the price. Generally speaking, the bigger the float, the greater the stock's liquidity.

Floating rate: An interest rate that is benchmarked to other rates (such as the rate paid on U.S. Treasuries), allowing the interest rate to change as market conditions change.

Forward contract: A contract that calls for future delivery of an asset at an agreed-upon price.

Forward exchange rate: The price of currencies at which they can be bought and sold for future delivery.

Forward rates (for bonds): The agreed-upon interest rates for a bond to be issued in the future.

Futures contract: A contract that calls for the delivery of an asset or its cash value at a specified delivery or maturity date for an agreed upon price. A future is a type of forward contract that is liquid, standardized, traded on an exchange, and whose prices are settled at the end of each trading day.

Glass-Steagall Act: Part of the legislation passed during the Depression (Glass-Steagall was passed in 1933) designed to help prevent future bank failure - the establishment of the F.D.I.C. was also part of this movement. The Glass-Steagall Act split America's investment banking (issuing and trading securities) operations from commercial banking (lending). For example, J.P. Morgan was forced to spin off its securities unit as Morgan Stanley. Since the late 1980s, the Federal Reserve has steadily weakened the act, allowing commercial banks such as NationsBank and Bank of America to buy investment banks like Montgomery Securities and Robertson Stephens.

Goodwill: An account that includes intangible assets a company may have, such as brand image.

Hedge: To balance a position in the market in order to reduce risk. Hedges work like insurance: a small position pays off large amounts with a slight move in the market.

High-yield bonds (a.k.a. junk bonds): Bonds with poor credit ratings that pay a relatively high rate of interest.

Holding Period Return: The income earned over a period as a percentage of the bond price at the start of the period.

Income Statement: One of the four basic financial statements, the Income Statement presents the results of operations of a business over a specified period of time, and is composed of Revenues, Expenses, and Net Income.

Initial Public Offering (IPO): The dream of every entrepreneur, the IPO is the first time a company issues stock to the public. "Going public" means more than raising money for the company: By agreeing to take on public shareholders, a company enters a whole world of required SEC filings and quarterly revenue and earnings reports, not to mention possible shareholder lawsuits.

Investment grade bonds: Bonds with high credit ratings that pay a relatively low rate of interest.

Leveraged Buyout (LBO): The buyout of a company with borrowed money, often using that company's own assets as collateral. LBOs were the order of the day in the heady 1980s, when successful LBO firms such as Kohlberg Kravis Roberts made a practice of buying up companies, restructuring them, and reselling them or taking them public at a significant profit. LBOs are now somewhat out of fashion.

Liquidity: The amount of a particular stock or bond available for trading in the market. For commonly traded securities, such as big cap stocks and U.S. government bonds, they are said to be highly liquid instruments. Small cap stocks and smaller fixed income issues often are called illiquid (as they are not actively traded) and suffer a liquidity discount, i.e., they trade at lower valuations to similar, but more liquid, securities.

The Long Bond: The 30-year U.S. Treasury bond. Treasury bonds are used as the starting point for pricing many other bonds, because Treasury bonds are assumed to have zero credit risk take into account factors such as inflation. For example, a company will issue a bond that trades "40 over Treasuries." The 40 refers to 40 basis points (100 basis points = 1 percentage point).

Market Cap(italization): The total value of a company in the stock market (total shares outstanding x price per share).

Money market securities: This term is generally used to represent the market for securities maturing within one year. These include short-term CDs, Repurchase Agreements, Commercial Paper (low-risk corporate issues), among others. These are low risk, short-term securities that have yields similar to Treasuries.

Mortgage-backed bonds: Bonds collateralized by a pool of mortgages. Interest and principal payments are based on the individual homeowners making their mortgage payments. The more diverse the pool of mortgages backing the bond, the less risky they are.

Multiples method: A method of valuing a company that involves taking a multiple of an indicator such as price-to-earnings, EBITDA, or revenues. Municipal bonds: Bonds issued by local and state governments, a.k.a., municipalities. Municipal bonds are structured as tax-free for the investor, which means investors in muni's earn interest payments without having to pay federal taxes. Sometimes investors are exempt from state and local taxes, too. Consequently, municipalities can pay lower interest rates on muni bonds than other bonds of similar risk.

Net present value (NPV): The present value of a series of cash flows generated by an investment, minus the initial investment. NPV is calculated because of the important concept that money today is worth more than the same money tomorrow.

Non-convertible preferred stock: Sometimes companies issue non-convertible preferred stock, which remains outstanding in perpetuity and trades like stocks. Utilities represent the best example of non-convertible preferred stock issuers.

Par value: The total amount a bond issuer will commit to pay back when the bond expires.

P/E ratio: The price to earnings ratio. This is the ratio of a company's stock price to its earnings-per-share. The higher the P/E ratio, the more "expensive" a stock is (and also the faster investors believe the company will grow). Stocks in fast-growing industries tend to have higher P/E ratios.

Pooling accounting: A type of accounting used in a stock swap merger. Pooling accounting does not account for Goodwill, and is preferable to purchase accounting.

Prime rate: The average rate U.S. banks charge to companies for loans. Purchase accounting: A type of accounting used in a merger with a considerable amount of cash. Purchase accounting takes Goodwill into account, and is less preferable than pooling accounting.

Put option: An option that gives the holder the right to sell an asset for a specified price on or before a specified expiration date.

Securities and Exchange Commission (SEC): A federal agency that, like the Glass-Steagall Act, was established as a result of the stock market crash of 1929 and the ensuing depression. The SEC monitors disclosure of financial information to stockholders, and protects against fraud. Publicly traded securities must first be approved by the SEC prior to trading.

Securitize: To convert an asset into a security that can then be sold to investors. Nearly any income-generating asset can be turned into a security. For example, a 20-year mortgage on a home can be packaged with other mortgages just like it, and shares in this pool of mortgages can then be sold to investors.

Selling, General & Administrative Expense (SG&A): Costs not directly involved in the production of revenues. SG&A is subtracted from Gross Profit to get EBIT.

Spot exchange rate: The price of currencies for immediate delivery. Statement of Cash Flows: One of the four basic financial statements, the Statement of Cash Flows presents a detailed summary of all of the cash inflows and outflows during a specified period.

Statement of Retained Earnings: One of the four basic financial statements, the Statement of Retained Earnings is a reconciliation of the Retained Earnings account. Information such as dividends or announced income is provided in the statement. The Statement of Retained Earnings provides information about what a company's management is doing with the company's earnings.

Stock: Ownership in a company.

Stock swap: A form of M&A activity in whereby the stock of one company is exchanged for the stock of another.

Strong currency: A currency whose value is rising relative to other currencies.

Swap: A type of derivative, a swap is an exchange of future cash flows. Popular swaps include foreign exchange swaps and interest rate swaps.

10K: An annual report filed by a public company with the Securities and Exchange Commission (SEC). Includes financial information, company information, risk factors, etc.

Tender offers: A method by which a hostile acquirer renders an offer to the shareholders of a company in an attempt to gather a controlling interest in the company. Generally, the potential acquirer will offer to buy stock from shareholders at a much higher value than the market value.

Treasury securities: Securities issued by the U.S. government. These are divided into Treasury bills (maturity of up to 2 years), Treasury notes (from 2 years to 10 years maturity), and Treasury bonds (10 years to 30 years). As they are government guaranteed, often treasuries are considered

risk-free. In fact, while U.S. Treasuries have no default risk, they do have interest rate risk; if rates increase, then the price of UST's will decrease.

Underwrite: The function performed by investment banks when they help companies issue securities to investors. Technically, the investment bank buys the securities from the company and immediately resells the securities to investors for a slightly higher price, making money on the spread.

Weak currency: A currency whose value is falling relative to other currencies.

Yield to call: The yield of a bond calculated up to the period when the bond is called (paid off by the bond issuer).

Yield: The annual return on investment. A high-yield bond, for example, pays a high rate of interest.

Yield to maturity: The measure of the average rate of return that will be earned on a bond if it is bought now and held to maturity.

Zero coupon bonds: A bond that offers no coupon or interest payments to the bondholder.

About the Author

Jennifer Voitle:

Jennifer has an MBA in Analytic Finance from the University of Chicago. She worked for several years in corporate finance and treasury risk management at one of the largest of the Fortune 500 companies, and as a Fixed Income Quantitative Analyst at a Wall Street asset management firm. Her web site address is www.TreasuryFinance.com.

Increase your T/NJ Ratio
(Time to New Job)

Use the Internet's most targeted job search tools for finance professionals.

Vault Finance Job Board

The most comprehensive and convenient job board for finance professionals. Target your search by area of finance, function, and experience level, and find the job openings that you want. No surfing required.

VaultMatch Resume Database

Vault takes match-making to the next level: post your resume and customize your search by area of finance, experience and more. We'll match job listings with your interests and criteria and e-mail them directly to your in-box.

VAULT
> the insider career network™

Increase your T/NJ Ratio
(Time to New Job)

Use the Internet's most targeted job search tools for finance professionals.

Vault Finance Job Board

The most comprehensive and convenient job board for finance professionals. Target your search by area of finance, function, and experience level, and find the job openings that you want. No surfing required.

VaultMatch Resume Database

Vault takes match-making to the next level: post your resume and customize your search by area of finance, experience and more. We'll match job listings with your interests and criteria and e-mail them directly to your in-box.

VAULT
> the insider career network™